# Evaluating
# Public Policy

# Evaluating Public Policy

Frank Fischer

*Rutgers University*

WADSWORTH

THOMSON LEARNING

Australia • Canada • Mexico • Singapore • Spain • United Kingdom • United States

Project Editor: Dorothy Anderson
Typesetter: E. T. Lowe
Printer: Capital City Press
Cover Painting: *West Side* by Mark Huddle

**Library of Congress Cataloging-in-Publication Data**

Fischer, Frank, 1942-
    Evaluating public policy / Frank Fischer.
      p.  cm.
    Includes bibliographical references and index.
    ISBN 0-8304-1278-6
    1. Policy sciences—Evaluation. I.  Title.
H97.F57  1995
320' .6—dc20                 94-43292
                                     CIP

Manufactured in the United States of America

10   9    8    7    6    5    4    3    2

 ™ The paper used in this book meets the
minimum requirements of American
National Standard for Information
Sciences—Permanence of Paper for
Printed Library Materials, ANSI
Z39.48-1984.

To the memory
of Hugh Tom Kirk

# Contents

# Preface

This book is an effort to contribute to one of the most important and long-standing discussions in modern social science, namely, the question of the relation of facts to values. In particular, how are the separate but interrelated tasks of empirical and normative inquiry to be dealt with in the field of policy analysis?

There is no shortage of literature devoted to the failure of the social sciences to adequately incorporate the normative dimensions of social and political life. Such writings tell the story of disciplines capable of collecting massive amounts of empirical data but lacking systematic methods for exploring the normative frameworks which give these data meaning. It is a problem documented by countless examples of social sciences's inability to deal with pressing normative social and political problems, especially during periods of rapid and turbulent change. Although empirical social science has held out the promise of scientific prediction, and thus the possibility of guiding social change, there are few significant examples of success. Much more typical has been the inability of social science to see what is coming. Indeed, there is no better or more important example than the most recent one: the failure of the social sciences to foresee the collapse of the Soviet Union and its empire. Given the enormous amount of time and resources devoted to both academic research and political surveillance of the former Soviet Union, the fact is more than a little astonishing. A history of such failures has raised basic questions about the normative relevance of the social sciences. Many have seen the need to rethink the nature of social science altogether.

This predicament is especially problematic for the field of policy analysis, a mode of inquiry designed to supply practical decision makers with useful information for political guidance. In the late 1960s, many social scientists offered policy analysis itself as a solution to the practical limitations of the traditional scientific orientations that have shaped the disciplines. During the late 1970s and 1980s, however, a spate of studies emerged showing this applied discipline itself to have very little direct payoff, at least as the term is commonly understood (e.g., effective solutions to pressing political and administrative problems). Although millions of dollars were being spent, there was little tangible evidence of useful outcomes. Given the meager benefits, as one writer noted, an economist would be hard pressed to explain the very large sums of money devoted to the policy analysis enterprise, virtually a small industry by the 1980s.

Many policy scholars expressed considerable concern about the apparent irrelevance of the discipline; some called for methodological renewal. The solution, according to writers such as Martin Rein, was to be found in a language capable of integrating empirical and normative concerns. Increasingly, policy-oriented scholars began to take an interest in normative inquiry. Unfortunately, much of the writing on this subject has been—and continues to be— at the level of critique. Few attempts have been made to move from theoretical critique to methodological reconstruction. The work presented here is advanced as such an effort.

This book is thus designed to fill a gap. It describes and illustrates an alternative logic of policy deliberation that places normative inquiry on an equal footing with empirical analysis. While the empirical approaches to policy analysis still have an important role to play in a reconstructed methodology, such inquiry is situated within the normative frameworks that give its empirical data meaning. In the process, the very thing we call empirical is seen to never be independent of the normative assumptions upon which it is founded. As the methodological framework makes clear, a comprehensive policy evaluation is constructed around ongoing interactions between normative and empirical discourses.

In the language of epistemology, the logic of policy deliberation seeks to contribute to a "postpositivist" approach. Although there is no firm agreement among postpositivists as to what the term precisely designates, postpositivism is used here to refer to an effort to provide a discursive framework capable of transcending the limits of the technical conception underlying much of empirical social science, especially as manifested in the field of policy analysis. Drawing on the epistemological concerns of practical discourse and informal logic, especially as advanced by writers such as Habermas, Toulmin, and Taylor, a discourse-oriented framework capable of incorporating both the rigor of empirical science and the classical traditions of normative theory is set out. The framework is designed to situate the dominant empirical conception of policy analysis within the structure of a more comprehensive theory of evaluation. Through the systematic interplay of four discourses, the method is structured to move inquiry from the most concrete concerns of empirical investigation up through the higher levels of abstract exploration of norms and values.

A fundamental goal of such a postpositive approach is to contribute to a transformational or emancipatory conception of social science (Habermas, 1973; Friedmann, 1987; Dryzek, 1990). Whereas the traditional goal of the social sciences has been to empirically discover and predict recurring regularities in the structures and processes of political behavior, the purpose of a transformational social science is to assist political actors in their own efforts to discursively understand the ways in which they can make and remake their social and political systems. Such a social science must clarify and theorize about the processes—both intellectual and material—through which political actors form, function within, dissolve, and restructure political worlds. To be sure, empirical research is important to such inquiry. But its importance lies in its ability to inform a larger normative deliberation, not in its empirical predictive powers per se. The task, as Dodd (1991: 277) has put it, is to help political actors "identify the processes of choice, experimentation, and struggle through which societies transform and conduct their politics over time, while being unable to predict specific political structures, policies, and behavioral patterns that will emerge." Rather than empirical prediction and social control, the fundamental goal is a discursive examination of "creative processes, dilemmas, and possibilities." It is with respect to this conception of politics that the logic of policy deliberation is put forward. It is advanced as a discursive framework for the organization and pursuit of a policy evaluation grounded in a transformational perspective.

The foundations of the methodological framework do not originate here. They first appeared in 1980 in my book *Politics, Values, and Public Policy: The Problem of Methodology*. Although the method remains fundamentally the same, numerous modifications and revisions designed to help clarify and elaborate the approach are added. In this respect, the overall objective of the book is to make the approach more accessible to scholars, students, and practitioners. As the method is intended for use in concrete cases, the reader will find only a limited epistemological discussion in the text itself. For those interested in such matters, the epilogue of the book, "Policy Deliberation in Postpositivist Perspective," offers an updated version of the theoretical foundations of the approach. The text is written in such a way that the methodological dimensions of the logic can be grasped without the need of the deeper theoretical discussion. For those with epistemological interests, the epilogue can be read in conjunction with the methodological chapters.

In addition to a more accessible presentation, each of the four discursive phases of the framework is illustrated with a contemporary case study. While this book is not a textbook per se, these cases are added to make it useful for classroom purposes, especially courses for upper-level undergraduates and graduate students. With regard to the cases themselves, it should be noted that they are intended only for heuristic purposes. They are not presented as definitive statements or analyses of particular problems, for example, Project Head Start, the Times Square redevelopment plan, disability policy, and environmental risk assessment. Rather, they seek only to bring out the main arguments that are relevant in each of the four discourses that constitute the logic of policy deliberation. Each case has been selected because of its special relevance to one of the discourses. They key conflict in the case is offered as an illustration of the nature of a specific type of problem and the discourse to which it gives rise. Where the author's discussion of the cases is seen to be problematic, the reader is merely invited to take these problems into consideration in the discussion itself. That is, the author's presentation of the cases can— and should—be used as part of the material for evaluation.

There are, of course, quite a few people who have offered assistance with the project as it has developed. I would like to thank those who took the time to read all or parts of the manuscript, as well as those who have more generally discussed aspects of the scheme with me. First and foremost, I have to thank Robert Hoppe for his careful reading of the manuscript, as well as his continual encouragement and support. Special thanks must also go to my former graduate student Margarita Jeliazkova. She read the entire manuscript, parts of it several times, and offered invaluable advice, both substantive and editorial. In addition, I extend my thanks to Alan Mandell, Susan Fainstein, Douglas Torgerson, Peter deLeon, Maarten Hajer, Peter Wagner, John Grin, Marion Nestle, Henk van de Graaf, Jeanette Hofmann, Michael Black, Nevin Cohen, Henk Verhoog, Rob Pranger, Gretschen Dyskstra, Denis Smith, Andreas Knie, and Pat Antoniello, and Vatche Gabrielian. Their comments proved to be most hopeful, and I remain indebted to all of them. Last, but not least, I wish to thank Dorothy Anderson of Nelson-Hall for making easier the otherwise tedious chore of editing the manuscript.

# 1     Public Policy Analysis as Practical Deliberation: Integrating Empirical and Normative Evaluation

Public policy analysis is now a major enterprise in the United States. Millions of dollars are spent each year on the evaluation of domestic and foreign policies—from welfare reform and environmental protection to international aid and military defense. Policy analysts conduct evaluations for a diverse set of groups: the executive office of the presidency, legislative committee staffs, cabinet agencies, political interest groups, policy think tanks, academic social scientists, and private consulting firms, among others. Whether one seeks to document the accomplishments of government or to criticize its failures, there is almost always a study available to help make the point. Policy evaluation has emerged as an important component of the policy-making process in American government.

Although this book is about the evaluation of public policy, it differs from other standard treatments of the subject. The typical approach tends to emphasize a "how to do it" or "cookbook" approach to evaluation (i.e., descriptions of the primary empirical methodologies and how to properly use them). This book casts the endeavor in a larger framework. Beyond evaluation of the empirical aspects of a public policy—principally the question of whether or not it accomplishes its stated purposes—this effort offers as well an analytic framework for assessing the value judgments that infuse policy decisions. Consider, for example, job training. Policy evaluation must not only determine the relative success of a specific program in helping people get into the work force, it must also consider whether the program itself reflects the kinds of things that society *ought* to be doing to help the unemployed. For example, is social assistance one of the obligations of an industrial society? Is it a mark of a just or good society? In short, does the policy facilitate accepted or desired goals and values? Toward this end, the book conceptualizes policy evaluation as a form of practical deliberation concerned with the full range of empirical and normative issues that bear on policy judgment.

In this chapter, the discussion begins with basic working definitions of public policy and policy evaluation. It then turns to a brief history of the political and intellectual roots of public policy analysis and the failure of the discipline or field to provide the promised payoffs. Next, in the context of specific political and methodological problems, the discussion examines the search for a more socially relevant approach to policy inquiry. It is to this search that the book as a whole hopes to contribute. The chapter concludes with an outline of an alternative logic of policy deliberation designed to return policy analysis to its original normative commitment.

## PUBLIC POLICY EVALUATION: BASIC DEFINITIONS

Policy evaluation is defined here as the activity of applied social science typically referred to as "policy analysis" or "policy science." (Box 1.1) The field according to William Dunn (1981), is an applied endeavor "which uses multiple methods of inquiry and argument to produce and transform policy-relevant information that may be utilized in political settings to resolve public problems." Designed to supply information about complex social and economic problems and to assess the processes through which their resolution is pursued, evaluations can focus on policy or program outcomes ("outcome" or "impact" evaluations), or on the processes by which a policy or program is formulated and implemented ("process" evaluations). Moreover, such evaluations can either focus on the outcomes *expected* to result from a policy (*ex ante* evaluation), or on the *actual* results from its introduction (*ex post* evaluation). As such, public policies can be evaluated at all phases of the policy-making process: in the identification and articulation of policy problems, in the formulation of alternative policy options, during the implementation of a particular policy choice, or at the termination of policy to determine its final impact. Ideally, policy evaluation provides politicians and citizens with an intelligent basis for discussing and judging conflicting ideas, proposals, and outcomes.

Public policy, the object of policy evaluation, is also difficult to define. Indeed, there is no standard definition of public policy.[1] For present purposes, public policy is identified as a political agreement on a course of action (or inaction) designed to resolve or mitigate problems on the political agenda—economic, social, environmental, and so on. Whether public policies are arrived at through political deliberation or formal vote, they involve a specification of ends (or goals) to be pursued and the means (or instruments) for achieving them.[2]

A public policy is constructed around a number of considerations (Dubnick and Bardes, 1983). Typically, we expect a public policy to supply a defin-

**BOX 1.1**

The task of defining policy analysis is problematic. In the literature one finds a certain semantic confusion associated with the terms "policy analysis," "policy science," and "policy evaluation." For this reason, it is important to be clear about usage. In this work, policy analysis and policy science are used interchangeably to refer to the applied discipline or field concerned with the evaluation of public policy. In referring to the work of the field's practitioners, we thus generally use the term "policy evaluation." The emphasis on the activity of evaluation, however, is not to be confused with the narrower methodological tasks of "evaluation research," concerned with "program evaluation." Evaluation research, in this respect, is understood to be only one of the methodologies of policy analysis. The term "policy evaluation" is employed here to refer more broadly to the evaluative tasks of the discipline as a whole. This broader concept, in the author's view, better lends itself to the more comprehensive conceptualization of the evaluation task that is presented here. The approach offered here is identified as the "logic of policy deliberation."

ition of the problem to be addressed (e.g., individual, environmental, political, economic, social, or moral). Stemming directly from problem definition, a second type of information should indicate the participants to be involved in the policy program and the ways the policy is to affect them (e.g., better job opportunities, escape from poverty, workplace safety, etc.). A third component of a policy should specify its intended effects on the society as a whole (e.g., increased economic growth, higher level of cultural life, or more harmonious race relations). Finally, the policy should include a declaration of the basic social and political values which it seeks to promote.

With regard to policy means (i.e., the ways of achieving policy ends), a public policy generally specifies the level of government that is to exercise control over the policy (federal, state, or city), as well as the principal sources of funding for the policy (taxes, user fees, or grants). The types of organizations that should implement the policy program (public, private, or nonprofit) are commonly indicated, along with the more specific administrative techniques to be utilized (rules, subsidies, or services). Moreover, there should be some indication of who is to be involved in the formulation and evaluation of a policy (the general public, clients, experts, or elected officials).

THE EMERGENCE OF THE FIELD

While the terminology of public policy is not new, the use of social science methods to evaluate public policies is a relatively recent phenomenon. Until the late 1950s, the systematic investigation of policy issues was carried out on a small scale and was only infrequently a formal part of the policy process. Since then, various intellectual developments have combined with political developments to give rise to the field of policy analysis, which in a very short period of time has become a major focus of the social sciences (deLeon, 1989). Although it is difficult to pinpoint a single stimulus behind the intellectual origins of the discipline, the publication of *The Policy Orientation* in 1951 by Harold Lasswell and Daniel Lerner is generally acknowledged to constitute the formal academic beginning of the policy research movement. The goal of the new endeavor was ambitious: it was to be nothing less than the "policy science of democracy," a discipline "directed toward the knowledge needed to improve the practice of democracy" (Lasswell, 1951). Toward this end, Lasswell envisioned the creation of a broadly interdisciplinary approach that would include a diverse range of scientific inputs, from anthropological research to the application of methods from the physical sciences, mathematics and statistics in particular. He further envisioned a discipline focused as much on the evaluation of the policymaking process as on the evaluation of their outcomes.

In spite of these lofty intellectual beginnings, policy evaluation today is more typically identified with the political and academic developments of the 1960s. In this respect, it is closely associated with President Lyndon Johnson's "Great Society" and the War on Poverty program. During the Johnson years, social-scientific policy research and evaluation were widely celebrated as the proper basis for decision making in public policy. As one leading policy writer put it, "research was touted as a determinant in and of itself of new policy directions, or at least as an input with a presumed special claim and higher standing than others in the policy-making process (Nathan, 1985).

Many of the key programs of the Great Society were in fact highly influenced, and in some cases directly developed, by policy analysts (deLeon, 1989). As the period progressed, studies were undertaken to measure the effectiveness of these expanding programs, as well as to assess the performance of the government bureaucracies that carried them out. Operating under the assumption that the decision-making process could be effectively rationalized— that is, rigorous analysis could produce information capable of improving the decisions of public organizations—President Johnson instructed federal departments and agencies to develop adequate staff for planning, analysis, and program development. Responsible to the top-level decision makers of the federal agencies, the new policy staffs were to contribute directly to the overall planning of the agencies' policy missions. The consequences of this executive mandate profoundly stimulated the emergence of policy analysis, both in terms of the development of new analytical techniques and the training of policy analysts to fulfill the new job requirements.

If the governmental interventions of the 1960s ushered formal policy evaluation into the public agencies, the 1970s witnessed an even more dramatic expansion of its analytical capacities. In significant part, the continuing surge was driven by Congressional legislative enactments that legally mandated program evaluations. Such requirements strengthened the need to upgrade and expand staffs at all levels of government. State and local evaluation staffs proliferated to keep up with the increased reporting requirements attached to federal intergovernmental grants-in-aid programs. Often the volume of evaluation activity required government agencies at all levels to seek assistance from private consulting firms, which, in turn, generated a lucrative evaluation industry in the private sector. Moreover, Congress itself became a major source of policy evaluation (Robinson and Wellborn, 1971). Not only did its independent agency for auditing and evaluation, the General Accounting Office, become recognized as the most sophisticated and reliable source of evaluation studies in the federal government, Congress also established the Congressional Budget Office and the Office of Technology Assessment.

Beyond these governmental initiatives, major universities developed policy research institutes designed both to supply research data and to train policy analysis personnel for the expanding job market. Graduate students from various disciplines, political science and economics in particular, flocked to policy research and new policy journals rapidly appeared to record progress in the field. In the process, the words *analysis* and *evaluation* literally became the rallying symbols of professional managers and experts concerned with governmental planning and performance.

With the emergence in 1980 of the Reagan presidency and its "mandate" to eliminate governmental programs, policy research appeared to fall upon hard times. But early in the decade, it became clear that conservatives themselves would be major consumers of policy evaluation. Although policy analysis had generally been identified as part of the Democratic Party's approach to policy formulation, particularly as manifested in the Great Society programs, conservatives recognized the necessity to develop and fund policy research suited to their own political needs. In sharp contrast to the use of policy analysis by liberal administrations to innovate new governmental programs, conservatives discovered that the *same* empirical-analytic tools could be employed to eliminate public programs, often the very ones policy analysis had helped to create (Fischer, 1987). Indeed, this recognition was basic to a dramatic expansion of conversative policy think tanks. Such institutions were designed to provide the Republican party with the kind of policy advice that the Brookings Institution (a major policy research center) was seen to have provided the Democrats in the 1960s. And in many ways the conservative think tanks have done the job more openly and assertively. Not only did the American Enterprise Institute for Public Policy Research and the Heritage Foundation, for example, regularly supply the media with conservative commentators on the pressing issues of the day, such institutions more generally came to be recognized as informally established actors of the policy-making process (Fischer, 1991a; 1993).

However dramatic the rise of this kind of policy work has been, the approach to policy evaluation practiced by both liberal and conservative policy institutions is very different from the type envisioned by its initial proponents. Since the 1960s, policy evaluation has staked out a much more limited perspective than the bold vision called for by Lasswell and his followers. Today its scope is largely confined to the task of evaluating the rather narrowly defined actual or expected empirical outcomes of given policy goals. Borrowing heavily from the methodologies of economics, particularly cost- benefit analysis, policy evaluation focuses primarily on the task of determining whether or not a particular action can be judged successful in terms of specific programmatic criteria. The criteria specified in the policy itself, explicitly or implicitly, are accepted as providing the legitimate, and often the only, grounds for deciding whether a program fulfills the policy goal.

But what happens when a someone says he or she doesn't believe in the program? Take again the example of job training. If a free-market conservative argues that government has no legitimate role in the training of workers for jobs in the private sector, no collection of statistics demonstrating the success of a government program will suffice to convince the person otherwise. Judgment of the program turns on a matter of principle and can only be further explored through the discussion of and deliberation about competing value orientations and ideologies (deLeon, 1989).

Unfortunately, policy evaluation has largely ruled such discussion beyond the bounds of its methods and practices. We are thus left with an elaborate set of methodologies for researching important but often relatively noncontroversial aspects of the problems plaguing society (Fischer, 1980). When questions about the appropriateness of policy goals or processes arise, as they frequently do in politically turbulent times, policy evaluation falls disturbingly silent. Missing is a form of policy evaluation that can not only assess the progress in achieving a particular goal, but the appropriateness of the goal itself.

The task of this book is to offer just that: an alternative methodology capable of integrating the *normative* evaluation of a policy's goals with the kind of *empirical* work already characteristic of policy evaluation. Before turning directly to this objective, however, it is important to situate it within the disciplinary discussion to which it belongs, namely the search for a more socially relevant methodology.

## THE QUESTION OF RELEVANCE

The failure to adequately confront the inherently normative side of policy evaluation has led numerous scholars to question the social relevance of the activity itself. As we illustrate in the next two chapters, many of the principal consumers of policy analysis during the 1970s—politicians and government administrators in particular—began to criticize policy analysis findings as being unusable, if not useless (Lindblom and Cohen, 1979). Examples seemed to abound. Why did Great Society policy analysts fail to anticipate the urban riots that followed the introduction of their own programs? Why were analysts unable to predict the failure of the Reagan administration's "supply-side" economic policies to stimulate productive business investments, not to mention the ensuing federal budgetary crisis? How could the United States spend $30 billion a year on foreign intelligence and fail through the 1980s to see the coming collapse of the former Soviet Union?

In fact, at the very time that the discipline was obtaining new status in terms of its institutional role in government, its practical achievements were more and more being called into question. As the head of one government agency put it, everybody was for policy analysis, but few had come to expect much from it (Schlesinger, 1969). It was a criticism that would continue to plague the discipline through the 1970s and 1980s (Caplan et al., 1975). Indeed, by the late 1980s Peter deLeon (1989) could sum up the issue this way: An economist "would be hard put to explain why policymakers are willing to spend significant resources for a commodity that they hardly use."

Doubts about the usefulness of the discipline led a growing number of scholars to speak of the need to rethink the methodological foundations of policy evaluation.[3] One of their primary responses was the introduction of the concept of "usable knowledge" as an empirical focus of study.[4] These scholars began to study the ways in which decision making and evaluation could be brought into a more fruitful relationship. Nobody doubted the modern decision maker's need for information; the questions were "What kind of information?" and "In what form?"

For some scholars, the task was to refine the process of advice giving. Rich (1979) argued that new ways of making the evaluator's empirical analysis more directly applicable to the concerns of decision makers had to be created. The problem was seen as a matter of more carefully integrating the decision maker's goals and objectives into the analyst's research design. In this respect, scientific methodology itself was not brought into question. The problem was largely seen as a matter of better coordination of the analytic and decision processes. As we shall see in the evaluation of the Head Start program

in chapter 3, the issue was often defined in terms of bringing the analytical effort to bear more directly on the needs and criteria of the program, rather than
the political interests of a particular administration.

Still another group of critics began to see the issue of policy evaluation's
usefulness in different terms. For these writers, the problem was not that policy evaluation was unusable, but rather that policy scholars had failed to properly grasp the function of its product. Whereas the traditional approach had
conceptualized the goal as plugging the analyst's empirical findings into the
decision process, these writers reconceptualized the task in terms of "deliberation" and "enlightenment" (Weiss, 1977). In this view, policy evaluation was
seen to play a less technical, more intellectual role. It wasn't so much that
evaluators should be expected to discover usable solutions to complex problems; the task was more appropriately understood as supplying information
and analytical perspectives that could assist decision makers—albeit more indirectly—in refining their reflection and deliberation about public problems.
From this point of view, the conceptualization of a problem was seen to be as
important as an innovative solution.

To be sure, an "enlightenment role" for policy analysis presents a less direct, more intangible role than that offered by the standard conception of the
empirical policy evaluation. But this scarcely makes such a role less important
or useful. Indeed, many have argued that it holds out new and exciting
prospects for policy inquiry. From this perspective, the question of the usabil-
ity of policy evaluation is largely a matter of designing better ways of utilizing
the enlightenment process. Policy evaluation, for example, might be more effectively redesigned as an informed debate among competing interests than as
scientific problem solving per se (Churchman, 1971). Although this enlightenment approach has often lacked methodological specificity, its basic line of argument has highlighted the normative character of policy evaluation.

While the enlightenment perspective has helped to draw attention to the
role of norms and values, it took another group to bring out the deeper set of
questions posed by these issues. Drawing on the works of political philosophers and others outside the policy analysis discipline per se, writers such as
Tribe (1972), Gunnell (1968), and Rein (1976) saw the problem of integrating
norms and values to involve more than rethinking the relationship between decision makers and policy analysts. Whether this relationship was viewed as a
matter of better analytic coordination or enlightenment, it pertained to the very
nature of knowledge itself. What troubled these "policy philosophers" was the
belief that policy evaluators were *misapplying* their sophisticated quantitative
methodologies to questions inherently grounded in normative concerns. The
dominant methodologies, it was argued, are incapable of addressing the underlying normative "value" issues upon which public policy questions turned
(Fischer, 1980; Fischer and Forester, 1987).

Most often this concern emerged around a debate about evaluation criteria, in particular the question of whether policies should be evaluated in terms of efficiency or equity. This debate, moreover, has proven to be anything but academic. Confronted with such deep-seated crises as enormous budget deficits, the decline of industrial manufacturing, the collapse of savings and loans, farm foreclosures, homeless people, transportation gridlocks, environmental degradation, and Acquired Immune Deficiency Syndrome (AIDS), America is often said to face a "crisis of values." The very solutions to these deeply entrenched problems often raise questions more about the configuration of social and political values underlying contemporary society than they do about technical matters regarding policy design and program implementation. Thus, as these policy-oriented theorists have argued, policy evaluation can be seen as addressing only part of the problem, if not missing it altogether (Fischer and Forester, 1987).

The political frustration underlying this search for usable knowledge was spread widely across the political spectrum. Those accepting the basic priorities of the established power structure have lamented the failure of the policy-oriented social sciences to provide the kinds of usable knowledge required for effective social guidance and control (Scott and Shore, 1979). In sharp contrast, those speaking for the interests of the poor and minorities have accused the same social scientists of political manipulation and ideological distortion (Friedmann, 1987). Indeed, by the 1980s the role of policy expertise had become highly politicized. (Some even spoke of a "new class" of intelligentsia that sought to replace traditional politicians with a cadre of technical experts.[5]) So disparaged had the technical or "technocratic" approach to policy analysis become that many began to openly identify it as an ideological tool disguised as science (Tribe, 1972). Forcefully advanced by conservative (Banfield, 1980) as well as liberal social scientists (Goodman, 1971), this critique exposed many of the discipline's overly narrow, technically oriented assumptions and, in the process, tended to throw the objective character of the whole enterprise into question. For many, policy analysts began to behave more like lawyers than scientists, merely advancing arguments that suited the needs of their clients.

The issue of social relevance was increasingly recognized to be a matter of how to bring facts and values together into a more systematic mode of analysis (Anderson, 1979; MacRae, 1976). Rein (1976), for example, contended that the future of a relevant policy science hinged on the methodological integration of empirical and normative judgments. Such an integration was, as the philosophically oriented policy scholars have made clear, easier to advocate than to supply. In short, the possibility of uniting the two types of knowledge rested upon an extremely complex and long- standing methodological question that continues to trouble philosophers: what is the proper understanding of the relation of facts to values, of empirical to normative inquiry? To raise the possibility of integrating facts and values was to invoke questions about the theory of knowledge underlying the policy analysis discipline per se. The search for relevance thus posed profoundly important questions about the "positivist" theory of knowledge and the technocratic approach it supports. We turn in the next section to a more detailed discussion of the positivist form of empirical policy analysis and the methodological critique of its theory and practices.

### POLICY EVALUATION: POSITIVISM AND VALUE NEUTRALITY

The contemporary empirical approach to policy evaluation is constructed on the foundations of the scientific method called "positivism."[6] (For clarification of the methodological terms employed in this discussion, see the glossary at the end of this book.) Positivism in the social sciences is built on concepts and methods borrowed from the positivist account of the natural and physical sciences; it represents a commitment to the development of "factual" knowledge about societal structures and processes.[7] In contrast to knowledge about specific times, places, or circumstances, positivist knowledge seeks to explain behavior across social and historical contexts, whether communities, societies, or cultures. Such knowledge is said to be "generalizable." In the positivist view, the ability to produce reliable empirical data that can be generally applied to a wide range of social contexts is basic to the possibility of solving societal problems.[8] For instance, if social scientists command a body of scientifically tested propositions about the concepts and variables related to political revolutions, they can utilize such data to help either contain or promote revolutions, whether in Latin America or Eastern Europe. For the positivist, however, the decision to contain or promote a revolution is a value question (concerned with what "ought" to be the case) that falls *beyond* the realm of empirical social science (concerned with what "is" the case). It is the pursuit of empirically based causal knowledge that qualifies social science as a "scientific" endeavor (Falco, 1973; Fay, 1976).

Positivist social science is most easily identified as the stuff of the research methodology textbook, including a focus on empirical research design, the measurement of outcomes, the use of sampling techniques and data gathering procedures, and the development of causal models with predictive power (Lin, 1976). In the field of policy analysis, positivism is manifested in a collection of empirical-analytic techniques: cost-benefit analysis, quasi-experimental research designs, multiple regression analyses, survey research, input-output studies, operations research, mathematical simulation models, and systems analysis (Putt and Springer, 1989; (Sylvia et al., 1991).

The use of such policy analysis techniques is typically identified with the "rational model" of policy decision making. The rational model can be formally outlined in five methodological steps: (1) Decision makers first empirically identify the existence of a problem; (2) They formulate the goals and objectives that would lead to an optimal solution; (3) They determine the relevant consequences and probabilities of alternative means to the solution; (4) They assign a value, that is, a numerical cost or benefit, to each consequence; (5) Finally, they combine the information about consequences, probabilities, and costs and benefits, and select the most effective and efficient alternative. Basic to this method has been an effort to sidestep the partisan goal and value conflicts generally associated with policy issues (Amy, 1987). Through its emphasis on the calculation of the efficiency and effectiveness of means to achieve goals, the method has largely reduced policy analysis to a strategy designed to serve a "technocratic" form of decision making. Policy analysis seeks to translate political and social issues into technically defined ends to be pursued through administrative ends. Vexing economic and social problems are interpreted as issues in need of improved management and program design; their solutions are to be found in the application of the technical decision approaches that have defined the policy sciences.

Technocratic policy analysis is thus a matter of uniformly applying empir-

---

### BOX 1.2
### The Technocratic World View

Positivist policy evaluation has been widely criticized as being both a product and agent of the "technocratic world view," a pattern of thought which emphasizes technical solutions to social and political problems. According to the technocratic view, the social world is composed of a "system" of component parts which can be abstracted from the social whole and independently analyzed to gain specialized knowledge about subsystems (in particular, knowledge about how these function in relation to the system as a whole). Society, in this view, is represented as a system of components (social as well as physical) that can be technically redesigned in ways that make it more efficient and controllable. The key to this rational mode of control is the increasing accumulation of specialized knowledge about each of the parts. Establishing such knowledge is a primary goal of the empirical social and policy sciences (Fischer, 1990).

By viewing society and its problems in technical terms, the technocratic world view frees them from their cultural, psychological, and linguistic contexts. Breaking the social traditions of "ordinary knowledge" and the recipes of "common sense" through the unique power of its abstract language, the positivist/technocratic mode of rational decision making strives to achieve a sense of political and moral neutrality by transcending cultural and historical experience (Berger and Luckmann, 1966). Expressed in the precise but abstract symbols of mathematics, the methodologies of positivistic research are designed to bypass partisan political interests. Their findings are said to be "value free."

ically based technical methodologies, such as cost-benefit analysis and risk assessment, to the technical aspects of all policy problems. The function of such a policy science has been likened to a modern fuel injection system in an automobile (Hofferbert, 1990:12). The fuel injector's function is to keep the car running smoothly by merely adjusting the mixture of inputs, external temperature, humidity, and vehicle operation; the mission of the policy scientist is the design of programmatic adjustments and regulatory mechanisms to guide the harmonious and efficient interaction of the societal system's social and political components.

Numerous writers have identified a subtle, apolitical form of authoritarianism in this technocratic strategy. In the policy science literature, this is often fairly explicitly reflected in a denigration of the political process, and democratic decision making in particular. Terms such as "pressures," "expedient adjustments," or "haphazard acts—unresponsive to a planned analysis of the needs of efficient decision design," are derogatorily employed to describe pluralistic decision making.[9] Such characterizations capture a belief in the su-

---

## BOX 1.3
## The Authority of the Expert

C. A. Bowers (1982) has captured the deference to policy expertise in a critique of educational policy analysis. As he explains, "reading programs, learning packages, and management systems...created by experts [are] imposed on schools and communities without regard for local and cultural differences." If the policy planner "has demonstrated through a process of measurement a degree of reliability and efficiency," those who oppose his or her recommendations can more or less be judged to act irrationally. Because of fundamental differences in the legitimacy and power of their respective languages—technical versus everyday language—the interaction between the educational planners and the other members of the local school community gives shape to an unequal communicative relationship, or what Habermas (1973) calls "systematically distorted communication." When the experts' technical knowledge "can be legitimated in terms of being rational, efficient, educated, progressive, modern and enlightened, what metaphors can members of other speech communities use to challenge them?"

Once we accept the idea that we can empirically calculate and administratively design "the right way" to accomplish our goals, there is little reason to engage in the exploration of other views and perspectives. The "rational" person is the one who agrees to submit to the properly derived technical and administrative knowledge of the scientific expert. The authority of the expert, from this perspective, ultimately takes precedence over the democratic exchange of opinions.

periority of scientific policy methods over political decision processes. If politics doesn't fit into the methodological scheme, then politics is the problem. Some argue that the political system itself must be changed to better accommodate policy analysis (Heineman et al., 1990).

Underlying the technocratic approach is a basic positivist principle that mandates a rigorous separation of facts and values, the principle of the "fact-value dichotomy" (Bernstein, 1976; Proctor, 1991). According to this principle, empirical research is to be conducted without reference to normative concepts or implications. The effort to do this, however, reflects one of the oldest methodological disputes in philosophy and the social sciences. Pointing to the inherently normative, value-laden character of social and political phenomena, political theorists and normatively oriented sociologists have long complained that the positivists' attempt to separate facts and values reflects a profound misunderstanding and distortion of the nature of the social world itself. Missing from positivism, its critics argue, is an adequate understanding of the inherent link between social action and social values (Box 1.4).

The critics of the fact-value dichotomy understand society in a very different way than do positivists. For these interpretive theorists, the social world is not to be understood as a mere set of physical objects to be measured; it is an "organized universe of meanings" that normatively construct the "social world" itself. Such meanings shape the very way ordinary people normatively experience and interpret the world in which they live. They shape as well the

---

## BOX 1.4
## The Critique of the Fact-Value Dichotomy

In most basic terms, the critique of the fact-value separation can be organized around four arguments:

1. The concept of value neutrality itself must be considered a value orientation, as it has clear implications and consequences for evaluation.
2. Insofar as every political action is purposeful, and thus is based on a point of view, the investigation of political phenomena is unavoidably based on a value orientation.
3. There is no language available for the study of political events that is inherently nonevaluative, as language is itself a construction of a social world.
4. The very process by which social scientists establish the concepts to be employed in their examinations of particular actions or events rests upon implicit value judgments.

Source: Fischer (1980), 37; Strauss (1959), 9–55.

**BOX 1.5**
**The Failure of Positivist Methodology:**
**The Case of Higher Education**

During the 1960s, positivist social scientists frequently proclaimed and even celebrated the role of the modern university in American society. The system of higher education in the U.S. was described as a significant and effective socializing agent that prepared America's youth for an adult role in the highly successful and much admired world of American capitalism.

Such conclusions were largely based on the immediately observable dimensions of the university system; namely, the fact that compared to other Western nations, large numbers of American students went through rationally constructed tiers of American higher education and entered the world of business and the professions. From external observations of the process, however, these same social scientists were unable to detect the growing resentment to the rigidities of the system that was building up inside the students and within the institutions themselves. That is, by concentrating on these external realities and observable processes from some remove (for example, through "objective" questionnaires of educational researchers and formal interviews of university counselors), social scientists were unable to uncover and come to understand the increasing dissatisfaction and social alienation that was beginning to infect the entire system.

To be sure, these same social scientists did claim to be aware of an assortment of radicals who existed on the fringes of campus life; but for them, these students were easily judged as "deviants" who posed no clear threat to the system as a whole. What the observers failed to see was that the "deviants" were only one manifestation of a set of dissatisfactions that were shared by a larger number of students. They were thus clearly caught off guard by the student uprisings on the elite campuses of the late 1960s, most particularly by the fact that an ostensibly unrepresentative minority could enlist the support of such actions with a large following from an otherwise content if not docile student population. Indeed, most of these social scientists had altogether failed to see that it was the presence of this large group of disaffected students that made the student revolt possible in the first place.

Educational experts had essentially become the prisoners of their own "objective" methods. By limiting their observations to the external behavior of the student population, they ignored the students' internal subjective goals and values—lived experiences—that more fundamentally shaped their attitudes and ultimately their protest behavior. These social scientists failed to grasp the link between subjective values and social action. They had constructed explanatory models of student behavior on what *they* interpreted the empirical data to mean (that is, on the goals that *they* had imputed to the students) rather than searching for and grappling with what the students themselves were thinking, feeling, and experiencing (Wallerstein and Starr, 1971; Searle, 1971).

very questions that social scientists choose to ask about society, not to mention the instruments they select to pursue their questions. The problem with positivist social scientists, as interpretive theorists explain it, is their failure to take these meanings adequately into account. Rather than drawing on these inherent meanings and points of view to help explain social behavior, positivists tend to construct explanatory models that implicitly *impute* assumptions and value judgments to the social actors. That is, instead of incorporating the social actors' own understandings of the social situation into their explanatory models, positivists tend themselves to attribute the motives and goals to the actors. The failure to properly understand the nature of social action on the actors' own terms can, as illustrated in Box 1.5, lead to serious explanatory failures.

Positivism fails to capture the fact that social action "has in itself a directness towards knowledge of the good," including the good life or society (Strauss, 1959). To explain adequately such social phenomena, according to positivism's critics, the investigator must get *inside* the situation and "understand" the meaning of the social phenomena from the actor's own goals, values, and point of view. As we make clear in Chapter 4, a growing number of social scientists have argued for the introduction of qualitative approaches better suited to investigate this dimension of social action. What is needed, as they see it, is a methodological framework more appropriately designed to bring together, rather than separate out, the most unique and essential aspect of human behavior, the intermixing of facts and values.

The point here is not that scientific social scientists altogether ignore the role of values. Rather the issue is their treatment of value discussions as inferior to scientific discourse, even as "irrational." According to the positivist view, human value judgments are essentially subjective responses to life conditions. (The son of an aristocratic family tends to accept the values and beliefs of the upper class while the son of the steel worker will generally adopt the values and beliefs of the labor movement.) As emotionally based judgments, a person's value choices are understood to be matters of faith, personal conviction, or taste; judging between such choices is ultimately based on criteria relative to the situation and interests of different people. Often referred to as "value relativism," such value judgments are held to be beyond the reach of rational scientific methodologies. They are deemed to be "unprovable" and are said to ultimately rest on irrational foundations.[10]

Thus values and value judgments, containing no verifiable "truth content," are to be relegated to the "intellectual limbo of personal preference" (Weldon, 1953). Social scientists should assume a "value-neutral" orientation and limit research to the investigation of empirical, or "factual," phenomena.[11] Even though there are various degrees of adherence to the "fact-value dichotomy," especially in the conduct of actual research, at the methodological level this approach remains a dominant principle in the social sciences (Box

---

**BOX 1.6**
**Value Neutrality in the Social Sciences**

Value neutrality in mainstream social science is generally traced to the writings of the German sociologist Max Weber (1949), particularly his essay on the relationship of social science to social policy.[12] As interpreted in modern social science, the doctrine of value neutrality charges that the advocacy or affirmation of value judgments in the data collection and analysis stages of the research process introduces subjective biases which contaminate or distort people's perceptions of the phenomenon under investigation. The study of political and social phenomena is thus best promoted by the suspension of value orientations. Although scientists have value orientations like everyone else, in their professional role they must endeavor to stand above these beliefs and commitments. This is especially important when it comes to interpreting the subjective value implications of their scientific research findings. Regardless of how objective and comprehensive their empirical results might be, scientists are in no special position to prescribe norms or value judgments based on their scientific findings.

In the final analysis, the scientists' judgments about what *should* be done (e.g., what course of action to follow), like those of laypersons, are seen to rest on irrational components. Norms and values establish a framework for the selection of ends and goals, but under the reign of the fact-value dichotomy such normative contents are beyond the legitimate sphere of scientific policy investigation.[13] As Barnes (1985) explains it, if an analyst is studying the effectiveness of military procurement expenditures, the focus should center on the cost-effectiveness of a particular weapon system in killing the enemy, while avoiding any value judgments about the right to possess the capacity to kill, or to kill particular groups of people (for example, civilians rather than armed soldiers).

---

1.6). To be judged as proper, research must at least officially pay its respects to the principle.

In practical terms, the outcome of this separate treatment of facts and values has given rise to a convenient division of labor between the scientific and political communities. Falling beyond the legitimate sphere of scientific policy investigation, questions of value constitute the agenda of the *political* process: the analyst, for example, focuses on the cost-effectiveness of a nuclear power plant, but leaves to the politicians the question of whether or not to build it. Because resolving such normative questions involves a contest of personal preferences in which reason plays a subordinate, if not minor, role, political criteria rather than scientific principles govern the determination of value disputes. Thus, the fact-value dichotomy identifies not only the appropriate focus for policy inquiry and the methods necessary for attaining "objective" knowledge, but the zone of demarcation between legitimate *scientific* authority and *political* involvement. The fact-value dichotomy, as such, provides the foundation for a clear-cut partition of scientific and political functions.[14] However, regardless of whatever clarity the fact-value dichotomy might seem to offer the division of labor, it rests on a fundamental misunderstanding of the nature of normative value discourse. Whereas in this view policy evaluation starts only after the relevant values have been authoritatively established, in reality such values are never given or fixed. They are themselves a function or outcome of the policy-making processes they are otherwise said to guide (Majone, 1989:24).

In the next and final section, we briefly introduce "practical deliberation" as an alternative approach to policy evaluation, the details of which are worked out in subsequent chapters. Offered to help bridge the fact-value dichotomy, this approach builds upon the earlier critiques of positivist social science, those of the "usable knowledge scholars," "the enlightment theorists," and the "policy philosophers." As a fourth model, practical deliberation seeks to offer and clarify a method for systematically integrating the "value-critical" questions of the theorists with the empirical concerns of the policy scientists.

### Integrating Facts and Values: the Logic of Practical Deliberation

What follows is a way to think anew about the task of policy evaluation. Transcending the narrow technocratic orientation of conventional policy evaluation, the methodological framework offered here seeks to overcome, if not resolve, the long-standing impasse between the advocates of empirical and normative analysis. It presents, in short, a deliberative scheme for simultaneously investigating empirical and normative policy judgments (Fischer, 1993). Designed to illustrate and clarify the nature of a full or comprehensive evaluation, practical deliberation offers a *multi*methodological approach to the evaluation of public policy problems (Grauhan and Strubelt, 1971). While the methodological foundations of the approach are reserved for the discussion in the epilogue of the book, it is useful to indicate briefly that the logic of practical discourse is in large measure the product of philosophers who have sought to confront directly the fact-value problem, in particular those identified as "ordinary language" philosophers concerned with the "informal logic" governing normative or "practical" discourse.

The theorists of practical discourse or deliberation have challenged the positivist contention that normative argumentation is irrational (Toulmin, 1958; Taylor, 1961; Habermas, 1973). For these writers, normative deliberation about goals and values is not inferior to scientific discourse; rather it is only different. The positivist's error arises from an attempt to judge normative discourse by an inappropriate set of criteria, namely those of scientific verification and validity. Only by misappropriately extending their scientific criteria into the realm of normative evaluation have positivists been able to proclaim the irrationality of discourse about values and norms. When examined in terms of its own inherent standards, those of an "informal" logic, normative evaluation is seen to be a rational exercise, even if less exacting than the scientific mode of reason per se.

The following approach thus outlines the framework of a practical or informal logic of policy deliberation (henceforth used synonymously with the "logic of policy evaluation"). It is designed to illuminate the basic discursive components of a full or complete evaluation, one which incorporates the full range of both the empirical and normative concerns that can be brought to bear on an evaluation. Structured around four interrelated discourses, the approach extends from concrete empirical questions pertinent to a particular situation up to the abstract normative issues concerning a way of life.

The first two discursive phases of the logic of policy deliberation, constituting the level of "first-order evaluation," consist of verification and validation. First-order evaluation focuses on the specific action setting of a policy initiative, probing both specific program outcomes and the situational (or circumstantial) context in which they occur. The second two discursive phases of the logic, or the level of "second-order evaluation," are vindication and social

---

## BOX 1.7
## The Logic of Policy Evaluation in Basic Outline:
## Levels, Discourses, and Questions

Level: First-order Evaluation
    Technical-Analytic Discourse: Program Verification (Outcomes)
        Organizing Question: Does the program empirically fulfill its stated objec-
            tive(s)?
    Contextual Discourse: Situational Validation (Objectives)
        Organizing Question: Is the program objective(s) relevant to the problem
            situation?
Level: Second-order Evaluation
    Systems Discourse: Societal Vindication (Goals)
        Organizing Question: Does the policy goal have instrumental or contribu-
            tive value for the society as a whole?
    Ideological Discourse: Social Choice (Values)
        Organizing Question: Do the fundamental ideals (or ideology) that orga-
            nize the accepted social order provide a basis for a legitimate resolution
            of conflicting judgments?

choice.[15] Here evaluation shifts to the larger social system of which the action context is a part; it focuses on the instrumental impact of the larger policy goals on the societal system as a whole, and an evaluation of the normative principles and values underlying this societal order. Each of these discourses has specific requirements that must be addressed in making a complete justification of a practical judgment. For a reason to be considered a "good reason" it must satisfy all four discursive phases of this methodological probe.

The logic of policy deliberation thus works on two fundamental levels, one concretely concerned with a program, its participants, and the specific problem situation to which the program is applied, and the other concerned with the more abstract level of the societal system within which the programmatic action takes place. A policy evaluation, in this sense, must always look in two directions, one micro, the other macro. For example, a policy to introduce a multicultural curriculum in a particular university should not only indicate specific course offerings, but should address as well the larger requirements of a pluralist society, such as the need for a set of common integrating values capable of holding the social system together.

In the interest of logical clarity, we begin the discussion with the first discursive phase and work our way through the fourth level of evaluative discourse. Such an ordering both facilitates a systematic presentation of the discourse of the logic, and helps to elucidate the critique of conventional policy analysis. The order of the presentation should not, however, overshadow the fact that policy evaluation can commence with problems emerging in any of the four discursive phases of inquiry. In practice, there is no inherent priority or necessity to commence with one phase over another. Choosing the place to begin is dictated by the practical aspects of the policy issue to be resolved. Although the presentation starts with the most empirical questions, in the real world of politics the process begins, as often as not, with ideological considerations, and works back to the empirical level of the program.

It is important to emphasize that this logic of policy deliberation organizes four interrelated *discourses* rather than a single methodological calculus per se. The goal is not to "plug in" answers to specific questions or to fulfill prespecified methodological requirements. It is to engage in an open and flexible exploration of the kinds of concerns raised in the various discursive phases of the probe. In this regard, the questions do not constitute a complete set of rules or fixed requirements that must be answered in any formal way. Rather, they are designed to orient evaluation to a particular set of concerns. Within the framework of discourse, the deliberation may follow its own course in the pursuit of understanding and consensus. Toward this tend, the questions serve as guidelines to orient a deliberative inquiry. The methodological orientations accompanying each phase are tools capable of supporting the deliberative process and need be brought into play only where deemed appropriate. For example, it is in no way mandatory to carry out a cost-benefit analysis in the verification of a program outcome. Cost-benefit analysis is understood to be a methodological technique that addresses empirical concerns of verification, but need only be used when deemed appropriate to the specific concerns at hand. There are, in this sense, no hard and fast rules that must be followed. Rather, the objective is to initiate and pursue reasoned dialogue and consensus at each of the four discursive phases of deliberation. Short of consensus, the goal is clarification and mutual understanding among the parties engaged in the deliberation.

### Technical-Analytic Discourse: Program Verification

Verification is the most familiar of the four discursive phases. It is addressed to the basic technical-analytic or methodological questions that have dominated the attention of empirical policy analysis. Concerned with the measurement of the efficiency of program outcomes, the methodologies typically used to pursue questions of verification are the established tools of conventional policy evaluation. Examined in detail in chapter 2, the basic questions of verification are:

Does the program empirically fulfill its stated objective(s)?

Does the empirical analysis uncover secondary or unanticipated effects that offset the program objectives?

Does the program fulfill the objectives more efficiently than alternative means available?

Here a typical verification might concern whether or not an educational reading program fulfills its goals as measured by test reading scores. As illustrated in chapter 3, program verification employs such methodologies as experimental research and cost-benefit analysis. The goal is to produce a quantitative assessment of the degree to which a program fulfills a particular objective (standard or rule) and a determination (in terms of a comparison of inputs and outputs) of how efficiently the objective is fulfilled (typically measured as a ratio of costs to benefits) compared to other possible means.

### Contextual Discourse: Situational Validation

From the empirical verification of outcomes, first-order policy evaluation leads to questions of validation. Validation focuses on whether or not the particular program objectives are relevant to the situation. For example, are educational reading scores the most important criteria for a particular group of students (rather than, say, more general learning-achievement-oriented criteria). Instead of measuring program objectives per se, validation examines the conceptualizations and assumptions underlying the problem situation which the program is designed to influence. Validation centers around the following questions:

> Is the program objective(s) relevant to the problem situation?
>
> Are there circumstances in the situation that require an exception to be made to the objective(s)?
>
> Are two or more criteria equally relevant to the problem situation?

Validation, illustrated in chapter 5, is an interpretive process of reasoning that takes place within the frameworks of the normative belief systems brought to bear on the problem situation. Validation draws in particular on qualitative methods, such as those developed for sociological and anthropological research.

### Systems Discourse: Societal Vindication

At this level, the logic of policy deliberation shifts from first- to second-order evaluation, that is, from the concrete situational context to the societal system as a whole. In vindication, the topic of chapters 6 and 7, the basic task is to show that a policy goal (from which specific program objectives were drawn) addresses a valuable function for the existing societal arrangements. Vindication is organized around the following questions:

> Does the policy goal have instrumental or contributive value for the society as a whole?
>
> Does the policy goal result in unanticipated problems with important societal consequences?
>
> Does a commitment to the policy goal lead to consequences (e.g., benefits and costs) that are judged to be equitably distributed?

Here evaluation might ask if a focus on educational programs geared to test scores tend to facilitate a class-oriented meritocratic social order (as opposed, say, to a society that fosters greater social equity and racial justice). As such, second-order vindication steps outside of the situational action context in which program criteria are applied and implemented in order to assess empirically the instrumental consequences of a policy goal in terms of the system as a whole. As we see in chapter 7, coming to grips with unanticipated consequences often involves testing the policy's underlying assumptions about a system's functions and values.

### Ideological Discourse: Social Choice

The fourth and final discursive phase of the logic of policy deliberation turns to ideological and value questions. Social choice seeks to establish and examine the selection of a critical basis for making rationally informed choices about societal systems and their respective ways of life. Explicated in chapters 8 and 9, social choice raises the following types of questions:

> Do the fundamental ideals (or ideology) that organize the accepted social order provide a basis for a legitimate resolution of conflicting judgments?

> If the social order is unable to resolve basic value conflicts, do other social orders equitably prescribe for the relevant interests and needs that the conflicts reflect?

> Do normative reflection and empirical evidence support the justification and adoption of an alternative ideology and the social order it prescribes?

Social choice involves the interpretive tasks of social and political critique, particularly as practiced in political theory and philosophy.[16] Most fundamental are the concepts of a "rational way of life" and the "good society." Based on the identification and organization of a specific configuration of values—such as equality, freedom, or community—models of the good society serve as a basis for the adoption of higher level evaluative criteria. Or, put more concretely, what kinds of social values should the educational curriculum be built upon and toward which end? Although the function of such discourse is to tease out the value implications of policy arguments, it involves more than mere value clarification. As we see in chapter 9, discourse is concerned as well with the ways in which it structures and restructures the world in which we live.

As a methodological framework, these four interrelated discourses contribute to an alternative conception of social science and policy evaluation. Moving beyond the traditional empirical orientation of the positivist, the scheme offered here attempts to facilitate a transformational or emancipatory social science (Habermas, 1973; Forester, 1989; Dryzek, 1990a). Whereas the goal of the positivist social sciences has been to discover and predict recurring empirical regulatories in the structures and processes of political behavior, the purpose of a transformational social science is to assist political actors in their own efforts to discursively understand the ways in which they can make and remake their political systems (Carroll, 1992). Such a social science seeks to clarify and theorize about the processes—both intellectual and material—through which political actors form, function within, dissolve, and restructure political worlds. To be sure, empirical research is important to such inquiry. But its importance lies in its ability to inform a larger and more encompassing normative deliberation, not in its empirical predictive powers per se. In this context, lawlike empirical relationships are important insofar as they can set off a process of reflection and discourse among those whom the laws are about (Habermas, 1971: 310). The task, as Dodd (1991: 277) has put it, is to help political actors "identify the processes of choice, experimentation, and struggle through which societies transform and conduct their politics over time, while being unable to predict specific political structures, policies, and behavioral patterns that will emerge." Rather than empirical prediction and social control, the fundamental goal of such a social science is to assist and facilitate a discursive exploration of creative social potentials, political dilemmas, and democratic possibilities (Fay, 1975; Friedmann, 1987). It is with this image of politics in mind that the logic of policy deliberation is put forward. It is advanced as a discursive framework for the organization and pursuit of a policy evaluation grounded in a transformational perspective.

## CONCLUSION

In this chapter, we have attempted to weave together a number of themes. We focused first on the emergence of the concept of policy science, including the emphasis on "the policy science of democracy." The discussion then turned to the actual development of policy analysis beginning in the 1960s. Here we examined the appearance of a very different kind of technocratic enterprise based on the empirical principles of positivism and narrowly geared to the analysis of efficient program performance. By the mid-1970s, as we saw, this technocratic practice was foundering on its own methodological difficulties, particularly as they related to the problem of values. Indeed, in the face of the social turmoil of the late 1960s and 1970s, a discipline limited to the analysis of empirical realities proved itself unable to address many of the pressing issues of the day. To the degree that the social problems of that period, what many would call "crises," rested fundamentally on conflicting social values, the failure to incorporate analytically this more fundamental dimension of social reality led many decision makers to dismiss the discipline of policy science as socially irrelevant. In search of a more "value-critical" methodological orientation, a number of scholars sought to confront directly the discipline's positivist orientation, in particular its problematic effort to separate facts and values. We examined, in this regard, three alternative orientations: the usable knowledge approach, emphasizing the coordination of analysis and decision making; the enlightenment model, stressing the deliberative process itself; and the critique of the policy philosophers, focusing on the deeper methodological implications of integrating facts and values.

Finally, in an effort to build on these contributions, the chapter concluded with an outline of a logic of policy deliberation designed to integrate systematically both empirical and normative evaluation. Presented as four separate but interrelated discourses, the proposed model provides a multimethodological alternative to the narrow empirical methodology that has dominated policy analysis.

In the following chapters, this model is explored. We seek to show how it works and to illustrate why it is important. Not only is each of the four discursive probes of the logic described in detail, each is demonstrated with a case study that emphasizes the dynamics of a discourse at the particular phase or level. For example, verification is illustrated with the long-standing debate about the empirical success of the Head Start program designed to help move poor and disadvantaged children into mainstream educational institutions. The policy debate derives from a discussion of the validity of a quasi-experimental research project that found the program to be a failure and was used politically to undercut Head Start's budgetary allocations. Validation is demonstrated with a case study of the Times Square redevelopment project. Here the debate turns on the question of what kind of social phenomenon Times Square is, and what kinds of evaluative criteria should be applied to the evaluation of its redevelopment. Vindication then focuses on the disability movement and shows how conflicts between the principles of rights and the fiscal requirements of the economic system can set off debate about the nature and functioning of the social system itself. Finally, the question of social choice is explored through clashing environmental policies about risky technologies derived from competing ideologies, those of contemporary techno-industrial enthusiasts who support the use of risk-benefit decision criteria, and those of the green persuasion who advance environmental democracy as the solution to risk.

### READINGS

Frank Fischer and John Forester, eds. 1987. *Confronting Values in Policy Analysis: The Politics of Criteria*. Newbury Park, CA: Sage.

Martin Rein. 1976. *Social Science and Public Policy*. New York: Penguin.

Peter deLeon. 1989. *Advice and Consent: The Development of the Policy Sciences*. New York: Russell Sage Foundation.

Davis B. Bobrow and John S. Dryzek. 1987. *Policy Analysis by Design*. Pittsburgh, PA: University of Pittsburgh Press.

William Dunn. 1990. *Public Policy Analysis: An Introduction*. Englewood Cliffs, NJ: Prentice-Hall.

M. E. Hawkesworth. 1988. *Theoretical Issues in Policy Analysis*. Albany: State University of New York Press.

# Part One
## PROGRAM VERIFICATION

# 2    Evaluating Program Outcomes: Empirical Logic and Methods

This chapter begins a more detailed presentation of the logic of policy deliberation. It takes up the discussion of verification, the discourse most typical to the field of policy analysis. Specifically, two principal methodologies used to verify program outcomes are considered—experimental program research and cost-benefit analysis (including two primary variants, cost-effectiveness analysis and risk-benefit analysis). An examination of the steps involved in the use of these methods, as well as their practical applications to policy problems, constitutes the focus of the first half of the chapter. The second half turns to the ways in which these particular methodologies have mistreated the larger range of normative issues pertinent to policy evaluation. The discussion seeks to underscore the normative limitations of verification and the need to include the other three discourses of the logic of policy deliberation in the evaluative process.

## EMPIRICAL VERIFICATION OF PROGRAM OUTCOMES

Verification focuses on the program *objectives* of a public policy. Because scientific evaluation requires a high degree of empirical specification to make quantitative measurements possible, program verification depends on rigorously defined criteria. For this reason, verification is concerned less with policy goals per se than with the program objectives derived from them. Empirical evaluation focuses on the predetermined objectives—quantifiable programmatic criteria—of policy goals. Whereas policies state relatively broad socially oriented goals, based on higher level ideals, programs are concerned with much more clearly defined and concretely specified objectives based on the general policy goals. For example, a liberal education is an

ideal, while schooling is a goal. School attendance would constitute a particular objective.

To be administered by a governmental agency a policy must be translated into a program. A program identifies and spells out specific objectives
deduced from the general goals.[1] For example, the interstate highway program
is a programmatic objective of national transportation policy (which would
also include mass transit, aviation, and so on). Thus, where policies seek to respond to a broad and often interrelated range of problems in the social system,
programs are directed at specific situations within that class of problems. As
such, a program establishes a means-ends relationship designed to forge "a
chain of causation" between the initial conditions of the problem and future
policy induced changes (Pressman and Wildavsky, 1984: xxiii).

In verification, as in the logic of policy deliberation, the central organizing questions are the following:

> Does the program empirically fulfill its stated objective(s)?
>
> Does the empirical analysis uncover secondary or unanticipated effects that
> offset the program objective(s)?
>
> Does the program fulfill the objective(s) more efficiently than alternative
> means available?

Most fundamentally, verification is based on the rules governing empirical inquiry in the social sciences. It measures whether a policy program does
or does not fulfill a specified criterion. In scientific terms, the crucial question
is whether a judgment can be shown to be correct through publicly demonstrable procedures. As a basic concept of science, publicly demonstrable procedures stress the ability of other observers to confirm such judgments through
the replication of the empirical tests and outcomes.

Scientific investigation encompasses a variety of methodological approaches, and thus a key consideration is always the question of which
methodology best fits the research question at hand. This is true for program
evaluation as well as scientific research more generally. The evaluation
methodology that best reflects the formal postulates of scientific investigation
is the experimental approach. As experimental evaluation is the most sophisticated scientific methodology of program verification, we turn to it first.

## EXPERIMENTAL PROGRAM RESEARCH

The methodology of experimental evaluation research con-
stitutes the ideal logic of rigorous scientific assessment.[2] Sometimes referred
to as "evaluation research" in the policy literature, experimental research rep-

resents the formal application of the scientific method to the social action context of public programs. Pioneered in large part by applied psychologists, especially those concerned with the evaluation of educational programs, experimental research focuses on the identification of the basic policy objectives, and the relevant consequences that result from following them. Often identified as "outcome" or "impact evaluation," such research emphasizes those aspects of the problem situation or target population that are to be changed by the program, the measurement of their state before the introduction of a program, and their measurement again after completion of the program. Specifically, the research involves four basic steps.

*Step 1:* Experimental research first requires the specification of one or more programmatic objectives as the criteria for analysis. For instance, a job training program with a goal of preparing unemployed people for new work careers might have instruction for jobs in word processing as one of its specific objectives. The objective of a sex education program in high schools might be to reduce teenage pregnancies. Or the objective of a new police program for deploying policy patrol cars might be an increase in the number of arrests on the streets. Ideally, such objectives are determined by the legislation that authorizes the program (Sylvia, Meier, and Gunn, 1991). In fact, however, enabling statutes are often rather broad and ambiguous, and the specific objectives may be set by program administrators rather than legislators.[3]

*Step 2:* Once one or more objectives have been identified, it is necessary to find or to develop quantitative indicators that appropriately measure them. For example, an empirical indicator of academic success for a skills enhancement program might be the percentage of students who obtain a C average or higher at the end of a reporting period. Depending on the program, indicators may be measured with standardized tests, survey questionnaires, close-ended interviews, or through the use of secondary sources (such as arrest records, complaint files, or per capita uses of a service). Ideally, an evaluator will measure several indicators before and after program implementation, either at one point in time (a cross-sectional design) or at different points in time (a longitudinal or time-series design). The choice of indicators, the extent of their application, and the duration of the research is governed by the purposes of the evaluation, the resources available to the evaluator, the time constraints on the completion of the research, and the nature of the program under examination.

*Step 3:* After the indicators have been selected, the next task is to determine the appropriate target population and the corresponding sample for the evaluation. The target population is defined in terms of the program under consideration; the sample is chosen to represent the population (Fitz-Gibbons et al., 1987). Ideally, the evaluator randomly divides the sample into two equivalent groups: the "experimental group" which receives the program benefits and the "control group"which does not. The control group exists to see what happens without the introduction of the program. Its purpose is to assure that the effectiveness of the program is measured rather than other extraneous variables.

*Step 4:* The final part of experimental research is to analyze the data collected after the experiment has been carried out. In the language of research methodology, a hypothesis is tested to determine whether the program, as an "independent variable," has an effect on various conditions and factors which are constituted as "dependent" variables. If a program is effective, the statistical presentation of experimental data should show a positive correlation between the program and the experimental group's responses, and a negligible or negative relationship between the program and the control group's responses. Statistical procedures are used to analyze the variance between the groups. Designed to detect substantive differences between control and experimental groups, such procedures result in a statement of the "level of statistical confidence" in the research findings.

## BOX 2.1
## Threats to Internal Validity in Experimental Research

**External Events.** Sometime events other than the experimental stimulus occur between the pretreatment and posttreatment examinations of a program. For example, if we were examining the effectiveness of an automobile safety inspection program, an evaluation might be biased by a crackdown on drunk driving that began during the implementation of the program. Thus, a decline in the traffic fatality rate could be due to the inspection program, the drunk driving campaign, or a combination of both. The research must take in account the effects of such extraneous factors.

**Maturation.** The passage of time may also affect subjects and create differences between experimental and control groups. For example, people may become tired, get hungry or become more mature during the course of an experiment. These changes may affect their reaction to a program or a test of a program and introduce an unanticipated effect on posttreatment scores.

**Testing Bias.** The standard experimental research design includes a measurement of the dependent variable before and after the experimental stimulus. However, the act of measuring the dependent variable prior to the experimental stimulus may itself affect the posttreatment scores of subjects, thus sensitizing the subjects to certain topics or issues.

**Instrument Bias.** Sometimes the instrument used to measure the dependent variable changes during the experiment so that the pretest and posttest measures are not made in the same way. For example, a research subject may

*External and Internal Validity*

The concepts of "external" and "internal" validity constitute the two primary criteria used to judge the acceptability of experimental findings. External validity refers to whether the findings of an experiment can be replicated in similar circumstances and generalized to a larger population. Replication is best measured when several experiments, conducted by different researchers in various places, arrive at the same results. The ability of an experiment to be generalized to larger populations is primarily determined by whether the subjects and setting for the analysis are representative of a larger population. For example, the ethnic composition, age, and density of the samples used in an experiment should be similar to the population about which the evaluator is making inferences.

Every bit as important for the reproducibility of an experiment is the minimization of threats to internal validity. The question of internal validity concerns the ways in which an experiment is designed and implemented. To

become tired and not respond to the posttest measurements as carefully as pretest ones. Or different persons with different biases may conduct the pretest and posttest. These changes in the dependent variable may be due to measurement changes, not the experimental stimulus.

**Selection Bias.** Sometimes a person is selected for participation in an experimental program because of some extreme or unusual characteristic, such as very high or low reading test scores. These scores may be temporary deviations—due to illness, fatigue or emotional upset—from what the person would normally measure. After subsequent retesting, the scores would be expected to return to normal and become less extreme, regardless of the impact of the person's participation in any special program. If this happens, improvements in scores may be attributed erroneously to the program.

**Nonequivalence.** Bias may also occur if experimental and control group subjects are not equivalent. If the groups are unequal, then differences between the groups at the end of an experiment cannot be attributed conclusively to the independent variable. Questions may also arise when a researcher does not control assignment of subjects to experimental groups or when subjects volunteer to participate in a program. Volunteers may differ significantly from nonvolunteers.

**Attrition.** In assigning subjects to experimental and control groups, a researcher hopes that the two groups will be equivalent. If subjects drop out of the experiment, experimental groups that were the same at the start may no longer be equivalent. Thus differential loss of participants from comparison groups may raise doubts about whether the changes and variation in the dependent variable are due to manipulation of the independent variable.

maximize the internal validity of an experiment, the researcher must focus on the explicitness of the definition of the research question or hypothesis, and the development of a research procedure that provides for early estimates of both immediate and long-range effects. He or she must also confront the ever-present concern that the study can become contaminated by social and technical factors extraneous to the experiment itself, the appropriateness of the people selected to participate, and the tests chosen to measure the experiment. These depend on the kinds of issues presented in Box 2.1.

### Ethical Issues

Experimental research often raises important ethical problems concerned with detrimental effects that may be suffered by those individuals and groups who serve as the subjects of the research, including the possibility of financial or material exploitation (Veatch, 1975). For example, should experimental subjects be withheld a service or benefit that would make them worse off as a result of having participated in the research project (Thompson and Gutmann, 1984)? Although the ethical issues surrounding experimental program research have long been recognized, only in more recent years have useful guidelines for determining whether or not an experiment produces unethical impacts begun to emerge. The most basic rule is simple and straightforward: wherever possible, it is essential to inform the experimental subjects of the costs and risks associated with the experiment, as well as to allow them to withdraw freely from the experiment if they so choose. Major universities now have "Human Subject Committees" that monitor all such research carried out by their faculty members. But, in the final analysis, it remains the evaluator's responsibility to recognize the potential detrimental effects of an experiment and to develop less "intrusive" methodological designs.

### Quasi-Experimental Evaluation

The validity of an experimental design is essentially a function of the evaluator's ability to control the research setting. In medicine and physics, for example, *controlled* experimental designs are typically employed in laboratories to facilitate the random assignment of subjects and to ensure that confounding variables are eliminated from the process. Even in natural settings, biologists seek to closely regulate all aspects of the research process, including the use of empirical indicators, the assignment of subjects, the duration of the treatment, and the application of pretest and posttest measures.

In the case of public program evaluation, it is rarely if ever possible for every aspect of an experiment to be carried out under completely controlled conditions. For example, it may be ethically, politically, or legally improper to

## BOX 2.2
## The Kansas City Patrol Experiment

One of the classic examples of a survey based quasi-experimental design is the Kansas City Patrol experiment conducted in the early 1970s by the Police Foundation, a nonprofit organization established by the Ford Foundation to study law enforcement practices. The purpose of the Kansas City experiment was to determine whether or not police patrols made a difference in the reduction of (1) crime rates, (2) police response times to crime, and (3) citizen perceptions of the police.

The basic design of the experiment was structured around the division of citywide levels of police protection. One area of the city was assigned two to three times the normal number of police patrol cars, another area had no patrol cars, and a third area was assigned the regular number of patrols; the third area represented the control group. The central hypothesis behind the experiment was the contention that crime would increase in an area with fewer patrols, decrease in an area with more patrols, and remain the same in an area where the patrol levels remained unchanged. Similarly, researchers hypothesized that an area with greater police presence would demonstrate both a better police response time to the report of crimes and show more positive attitudes among the citizens toward the police generally. A team of investigators conducted the research over a one-year period.

What made the project especially interesting was its unconventional findings. Contrary to the conventional wisdom, the survey outcomes showed that the number of patrols assigned to the designated areas by the Kansas City police force made little statistical difference in the amount of crime that occurred in the various areas. Moreover, the experiment showed no change at all in the amount of time it took the police to respond to the report of a crime, and it revealed only a marginal impact on the citizens' perceptions of the police themselves.

What could be made of the findings? This question proved to be the source of considerable debate. Many, especially those in the criminal justice community, argued that the findings of the experiment were not valid due to flaws in the research design. The basic criticism was that the research had not been conducted under truly controlled experimental circumstances. Thus the results could not be validly generalized to apply to other cities. A charge often leveled against large-scale experiments, the research design was seen to have suffered from a lack of external validity. For example, it was argued that the almost exclusive use of automobiles in the Kansas City police patrols is strikingly dissimilar to the use of foot and horse patrols in New York City. The fact that Kansas City is ethnically a relatively homogeneous city in comparison to many cities in the country also raised questions of external validity. Even the types of crimes committed in Kansas City (primarily home burglaries) are different from the crimes committed in, say, Boston (a city plagued by auto thefts). Such dif-

(*continued next page*)

**Box 2.2** (*continued*)

ferences raised significant problems for those who sought to generalize the results of the Kansas City experiment.

The evaluation was thwarted as well by problems of internal validity. It
was argued, for instance, that people's movements in and out of the city's experimental areas during the course of the study may have skewed the citizens'
perceptions of the presence of police. Moreover, the experiment may have been
contaminated by the fact that police cars in pursuit of criminals often traveled
through zones that were supposed to have no patrols. Similarly, the survey questionnaires used to measure attitudes toward the police may have been directed
toward those who are more likely to have positive perceptions of the police;
criminals, for example, typically did not complete such questionnaires. Such
problems were seen to have posed major threats to the internal validity of the
experimental design.

The Kansas City experiment, like most experiments, raised important ethical issues as well. One group, for instance, was far less concerned with the outcomes than with what they perceived to be unethical aspects of the experiment.
The police force, they argued, had no right to arbitrarily assign different levels of
police protection to different groups within the city. Indeed, the patrol experiment came to an end for this very reason. Once people learned that certain areas
of the city were without police protection, or at least police patrols, elected officials quickly realized that a major controversy would ensue if a killing took place
in the area with no police patrols. Not only were the evaluators legitimately criticized for not taking the issue into consideration, the project as a whole was ter-
minated shortly thereafter.

Source: Kelling et al. (1974).

create a control group by denying a service to people. Or it may be impractical
to use pretest measures for a program that is already in operation. When events
or circumstances prevent a truly controlled experiment, a *quasi-experimental*
design may be employed. The evaluator, in such cases, makes use of as many
"true" experimental elements as possible.

There are many different forms of quasi-experimental designs. Four are
particularly important. A "true control group, posttest only design" is used
when a pretest is not available or when it would take too much time (Fitz-Gibbon, Morris, and Lindheim, 1987). A "pretest-posttest, non-equivalent control
design" is employed when the researcher cannot randomly assign subjects to
the control group. A "single group time-series design" is undertaken when a
control group cannot be established, but the same measures can be applied to
one group of people or things several times before and several times after the
program's implementation. Finally, a "pretest-posttest design with no control

group" may be employed to examine obvious effects, but without the confidence that the program and not an outside variable has influenced the results.

Each of these quasi-experimental designs introduces a degree of uncertainty about the reliability and validity of the experimental findings. Typically, such designs are employed when an experiment is encumbered by cost considerations, client needs or expectations, measurement problems, or ethical issues.

## COST-BENEFIT ANALYSIS

Once an outcome of a program has been empirically established, evaluation can further measure it, as a "benefit", against the costs that were involved in achieving it. That is, the program inputs can be balanced against the program outputs. Typically this is the objective of a cost-benefit analysis. Whereas experimental research focuses on the calculation of program consequences, cost-benefit analysis assigns numerical costs and benefits to the inputs and outputs and calculates in monetary terms the most efficient of the alternative programs (Gramlich, 1990).

Cost-benefit analysis is used to verify the performance of programs according to their economic value. Based on the concept of technically rational decision making, the methodology uses monetary values as the standard of measurement. The basic objective is to determine whether an investment of funds in a program is economically advantageous. In more sophisticated analyses, the method is also used to identify the policy goal that benefits the largest number of people in the society as a whole.

The idea of cost-benefit analysis is conceptually simple. The analyst first identifies the monetary costs of the input factors needed to accomplish a particular program, then assigns monetary values to the estimated or actual outcomes associated with the programs, and finally calculates the efficiency of the program as a ratio of costs expended to benefits produced. An efficient program is one in which the benefits outweigh the costs; an inefficient program is one in which the costs outweigh the benefits. In using cost-benefit analysis to formulate public policy, the decision maker implicitly relies on a specific type of ethical decision rule based on the theory of "utilitarianism." Later in the chapter we examine this rule, often referred to as the "greatest good for the greatest number." For now, we outline the method of cost-benefit analysis in four steps.

*Step 1:* It is first necessary to define who pays for and benefits from a program. The payees and beneficiaries of a program may be a social group, neighborhood, city, state, or society as a whole. In most cases, this is determined by the type of policy under consideration. Typically, the beneficiaries of a policy are limited to those with some direct involvement in the program, for example, those who have completed a job training program. In contrast, however, the beneficiaries of an environmental policy designed to reduce global warming can encompass the population of the nation as a whole, if not numerous nations. To capture this larger conceptualization of cost-benefit analysis, a number of writers have begun to speak of "macro" cost-benefit analysis. Instead of examining benefits or costs of a program in relation to a specific set of individuals, groups, or government jurisdictions, macro cost-benefit analysis extends the measurement of costs and benefits to a whole set of criteria or preferences at the level of the social system as a whole (Schmid, 1989).

*Step 2:* After the target group has been identified, a monetary value must be placed on the inputs and outputs. In the majority of studies, costs are defined in budgetary terms, that is, actual outlays made by government. The two major categories of budgetary expenses are material costs (equipment, buildings, etc.) and administrative costs (salaries, health benefits, etc.). Besides these costs, there must be some determination of "opportunity costs," defined as the costs of doing something else with a resource. For example, in measuring the costs of a college education we would not only include direct expenditures on materials, but also the opportunity cost of the earnings that could have been gained had the student been working instead of studying.

Benefits are also measured in monetary terms. Some typical benefits include increased tax revenues, greater productivity, and additional jobs created. Besides these direct benefits, there must be a calculation of benefits that cannot be measured directly. Two classic examples are scenic beauty and human life. For these benefits, a "shadow price" must be determined. "Shadow pricing," as Dunn (1981: 259) puts it, "is a procedure for making subjective judgments about monetary value of benefits and costs when market prices are unreliable or unavailable." Shadow prices are usually derived by establishing the value of the benefits and costs in a similar context or by forecasting them over time. A simple measure of a human life might be an estimate of the amount of money a person would have earned if he or she had lived a full life expectancy.

*Step 3:* Most cost-benefit analyses have to "discount" costs and benefits over time. Equipment and buildings may lose value as they grow older, while other items may become more beneficial over time. To account for such occurrences, a discount rate is established. Discount rates are expressed as percentages or dollar amounts and are typically based on constant dollars. If the discount rate is set at $5, for example, a person who has been promised a benefit of $100 from a project next year can calculate that the $100 in today's value is worth only $95.24 a year later. There are several different sources for establishing a discount rate—market interest rates determined by banks or government agencies, corporate discount rates, and personal discount rates (Sylvia, Meier, and Gunn, 1991). The differences among these approaches is a subject of debate among economists.

*Step 4:* The final step in cost-benefit analysis is the calculation of a cost-benefit ratio. The cost-benefit ratio provides a single numeric value that summarizes the relationship between costs and benefits. Ratios of less than 1.0 mean that costs exceed benefits and ratios above 1.0 mean that benefits exceed costs. In a report, these ratios, along with the costs and benefits for different items, are normally presented in a summary table and discussed in a descriptive narrative.

A very important variant of cost-benefit analysis is "cost-effectiveness

---

## BOX 2.3
## Cost-Benefit Analysis: Measuring Distributional Impacts

Beyond monetarizing and measuring the inputs and outputs, attention in cost-benefit analysis should be given to the distribution of costs and benefits resulting from a public program.

For Benefits:
1. What is the purpose or objective of the public program or legislation, part of which is the question, Who should benefit?
2. Who actually benefits? What groups? It is sometimes not easy to identify beneficiary groups clearly.
3. How much are the total benefits of the program? Placing a value on the benefits of many programs is also not an easy analytical proposition.
4. What is the distribution of program benefits among beneficiaries?
5. What is the current distribution of incomes and assets or other relevant dimensions of welfare among (a) actual beneficiaries and (b) intended or potential beneficiaries?

For Costs:
6. Who should pay the program costs? Sometimes the nature of the program contains strong implications as to whom the burden should be given; at other times this is an almost unanswerable question.
7. Who actually does pay the cost of the program? Identification of the burdened groups should consider not only the tax structure, but direct price and income effects and the indirect effects of major factor and product substitution caused by the program.
8. What are the total program costs? Many times this includes, as it does in Question 7, economic and social costs not reflected in federal budget expenditures but market and non-market costs generated through the operation of the program itself....
9. How are program costs distributed among the burdened groups?
10. What is the current distribution of incomes and assets among (a) the actual burdened groups and (b) the intended potential burdened groups?

Source: J. T. Bonnen (1969).

analysis." In contrast to cost-benefit analysis, cost-effectiveness analysis does not place a dollar value on a program. Costs are measured instead against a specific level of output—lane-miles of snow removed, per capita garbage collected, number of students graduating, etc. In the typical cost-effectiveness analysis, a comparison of alternative courses of action is made in terms of their costs and their relative potential or capacity in attaining some objective (Quade, 1982). This form of analysis is useful when the purpose is to determine which of several alternatives best achieves a given objective and when it is difficult to place a monetary value on outcomes.

The principal way to perform a cost-effectiveness analysis is to calculate average costs relative to outcomes. To do so, it is necessary to calculate the normal costs of each alternative under consideration, to measure each alternative's effects, and then to judge the alternative that achieves the most effect for the least amount of money. For example, if a community were to examine the most cost-effective way to transport people to an airport, it might compare the average per capita costs of buses versus trains.

### Risk-Benefit Analysis

Another variant of this method is risk-benefit analysis. Essentially, risk-benefit analysis is "a type of cost-benefit analysis in which the negative consequences of a project or program are measured in terms of the types and magnitudes of risks to individuals or to communities instead of in monetary units" (Sylvia, Meier, and Gunn, 1991: 60). As in cost-benefit analysis, the methodological decision-making process is formally geared toward the final task of choosing the best policy alternative. Within the standard framework of risk-benefit analysis, perhaps more accurately described as "risk-cost-benefit" analysis, the basic objective is to choose the alternative that has the highest quantitative value for the total amount of expected benefits minus the total number and level of risks summed up over all of the affected members of the relevant community (Hiskes and Hiskes, 1986:180).

Risk-benefit analysis, a topic of chapter 9, was developed in response to the special decision-making problems that have emerged with techno-industrial society, particularly the array of technological and environmental hazards that have accompanied it. Because of the threats resulting from a growing number of health and environmental problems, from nuclear power and chemical wastes to air pollution and the greenhouse effect, the necessity of developing methods for empirically measuring the actual risks associated with such phenomena and for judging their acceptability has become increasingly apparent over the past two decades. Designed to confront this challenge, risk-benefit analysis not only emerged as a widely approved decision methodology, but was also formally adopted by the Environmental Protection Agency as the

basic decision criterion governing the development and evaluation of all regulations pertinent to the environment.

The methodology of risk-benefit analysis is fundamentally an integration of two methodologies: risk assessment and cost-benefit analysis. The first
method, risk assessment, is employed to evaluate risk resulting from both hazardous technologies and toxic health threats. Although the principles are the
same, the assessment procedures are applied somewhat differently, depending
upon whether the focus is on technology or health. Because the discussion in
chapter 9 refers to toxic emissions from hazardous waste incinerators, we direct our attention here to the methodology as it is applied to toxic exposure
(Covello, 1993).

The goal of risk assessment is to accurately predict the health implications of a hazard before or after it exists, and to establish valid safety standards
to protect the exposed population. The methodology typically specifies four
interrelated steps: (1) a process of hazard identification (e.g., Does a waste incinerator emit dioxins or heavy metals?); (2) an assessment of human exposure (e.g., Can the various routes of the toxin to the affected population be
traced and how much of it enters the human body?); (3) the modeling of the
dose responses (e.g., What is the empirical relationship of the exposures to the
chemical under investigation and the frequency of adverse impacts?); and (4)
a characterization of the overall risk (e.g., How does the data as a whole provide an overall evaluation of the toxic's implications for human health, most
commonly defined in terms of cancer?). In an effort to err on the conservative
side of safety, risk assessors most often use "worse case scenarios." The overall risk is generally expressed as the probable number of cancers per million
people are exposed to over the course of a standard life expectancy.

Basic to the process are questions concerning the ability of risk researchers to quantify accurately the particular risks, especially given a general
scarcity of empirical data about chemical effects, and the nature of the assumptions about exposure and responses that guide the assessment process.
With regard to quantification, the assessment of exposure is especially complicated. Here the evaluator typically attempts to construct a sophisticated statistical model based on simulations of the movement of the hazardous substance
(e.g., air, water, and animals), and estimates of human activities that would
create exposure to it, along with hypotheses about how the substances actually
get into the human body. In particular, disputes emerge over the extrapolation
of findings from high dose experimental settings to low dose real-world circumstances, over the applicability of animal tests to decisions about human
health, and over the comparability of short- and long-term exposures. (Others
raise ethical questions about the use of animals in testing.) Disputes also arise
over the question of which health outcomes the researcher should concentrate
on. Most commonly, risk assessors limit their focus to cancer and ignore other

detrimental effects to the human immunological, reproductive, and nervous systems.

The second phase of the risk-benefit analysis is the cost-benefit analysis (Crouch and Wilson, 1982). Here the goal is an explicit comparison between the benefits derived from a hazardous activity and the risks that are involved. The costs, however, are defined in terms of specific levels of risks rather than monetary value. The method thus involves calculating the benefits of a project (adjusted against regular costs, such as plant construction and maintenance costs), comparing the ratio of the risks to the benefits, and multiplying the resulting figure by the total number of people affected. For example, it might be discovered that a power generator located in a particular community would spew toxic chemicals into the air that would lead on average to one death for every million local residents per facility per year and would offer power for $0.11 per kilowatt hour of electricity. Another type of generator, it might be determined, would lead to an average of two deaths per million community members per facility per year, but would offer power for $0.08 per kilowatt hour of electricity. For the risk-benefit analyst, these two types of impacts— deaths per million and price per kilowatt hour—are said to be "objective categories," as their actual levels are taken to be empirical facts. (Hiskes and Hiskes, 1986: 177).

## THE NORMATIVE LIMITS OF VERIFICATION

The approach to policy evaluation presented in this book recognizes empirical verification of program objectives as a valuable and essential aspect of policy evaluation. What this approach does not accept is the presumption that empirical verification is the sum total of a rational policy evaluation. The problem arises not with the use of experimental designs or cost-benefit analysis to collect data about the results of a program, but rather with the positivist's efforts to construe these methods as the essence of rationality, if not social theory per se. In this concluding section, we attempt to highlight several of the more problematic normative limitations of the experimental method and cost-benefit analysis. Three types of issues are discussed: the presumed objectivity of empirical policy research; the application of research to social (action) contexts; and the ideological biases of positivist policy evaluation.

### Objectivity

At the most apparent level, the problems associated with a verification focused evaluation, whether a policy experiment or cost-benefit analysis, are seen to be merely technical in character. The task is to construct objectively appropriate indicators and recording devices that can be easily employed and justified. This conceptualization, however, rests on the mistaken assumption that the analyst can objectively identify goals or benefits, select indicators and samples, and quantify and measure program performance. In reality, each of these tasks entails normative judgments about what is important in public policy and what is unimportant for analysis.

Consider first the act of identifying the objectives and benefits that program verification is designed to assess. Two problems are evident. Rein and Weiss (1969) make explicit the first one. Evaluation, as they put it, "asks the extent to which predetermined goals are reached. But how will such goals as increased opportunity, a more responsive institutional system, and a richer cultural atmosphere show themselves? What operations can be chosen, in advance, to decide whether these goals have or have not been realized?" The development of social programs by political decision makers, unlike, say, the development of an electrical motor by an engineer, involves goals and objectives that are often so broad and ambiguous that it is virtually impossible to measure their impacts and benefits in any precise or rigorous way (Beardsley, 1980).

### Social Context

A second problem is political in nature. In the socio-political context of an evaluation study, which group is entitled to interpret and decide the meaning of a given policy goal and its criteria? Given the fact that a social context typically involves a host of conflicting assumptions, the question of what constitutes the appropriate goal itself, let alone its interpretation, will remain controversial and thus always subject to political debate, if not renegotiation. This fact hardly establishes the kind of "given" social reality essential to the successful use of positivist methods. How, for example, is an evaluation to be judged on the basis of its reproducibility when there is major disagreement on what to measure in the first place? Such decisions are grounded in political decisions, a fact which must remain at the forefront of our understanding of the evaluation process (as we shall make clear in the more extended discussion of situational validation).

Beyond the political identification of goals, the problem of social context penetrates into the research design itself. While research textbooks typically lay great stress on attending to the statistical variances encountered in different contexts, it is widely conceded that in practice, experiments and cost-benefit studies cannot be conducted systematically in many social contexts. Such evaluations are constrained by a multitude of potential problems: too few subjects, lack of access to records and data, unexpected changes in program procedures, unintended consequences, program dropouts, demands for quick feedback of information, and inadequate funds, among many others (Sechrest, 1985). There are, moreover, no standard operating procedures for experiments to determine appropriate sample sizes, methods assigning subjects to experimental groups, or for that matter, any other aspect of the process. (In the policy literature, these problems are typically discussed as threats to the internal and external validity of an experiment.) With many otherwise technical issues left either to the discretionary judgment of the analyst, or to the vagaries of the political process, objectivity becomes a dubious proposition. Indeed, the problems are often so numerous that many policy analysts themselves see the social context of public programs (especially in education, social welfare, criminal correction, health, job training, and community action) to be intrinsically inhospitable to rigorous empirical program evaluation (Weiss, 1972).

Even quantification is fraught with subjective considerations in policy research. Having more or less of something, for instance, does not tell us what is important. Is a hazardous waste plant that produces one thousand jobs really better than an ice cream shop that only produces 10 jobs? "Numbers in policy debates," as Stone (1988:146) put it, "cannot be understood without probing how they are produced by people; what makes people decide to count something and then find instances of it; how the measurers and measured are linked together; what incentives people have to make the numbers appear high or low; and what opportunities they have to behave strategically."

### Policy Science as Political Ideology

Beyond the problems of objectivity and social context, the tendency of policy analysis to distort conceptually the nature of the political process and the functions of public policy is even more troublesome. As we saw in chapter 1, this problem stems from the effort to "technocratically" extend the emphasis on technical (means-ends) rationality to the society as a whole. Rather than recognizing the social and contextual limitations of their techniques, policy scientists have often tended to blame the political system itself for their own analytical failures. A system which fails to conform to technical requirements is inevitably judged to be irrationally structured and in need of reform. One of the best contemporary examples is provided by cost-benefit analysis (Weimer and Vining, 1988; Bobrow and Dryzek, 1987).

To grasp cost-benefit analysis's tendency to distort the nature of public decisions, one must examine its assumptions, particularly those drawn from welfare economics. As typically practiced, cost-benefit analysis is employed "to replicate for the public sector the decisions that would be made if private markets worked satisfactorily" (Haveman and Weisbrod, 1975:171). Most important is its conceptualization of society as a set of marketlike exchange relationships between autonomous individuals. Society is assumed to be a collection of self-interested, rational decision makers with no collective community life per se. Such people interact with each other entirely for the purpose of maximizing individual well-being. Government in this formulation should do little more than serve as a benevolent mechanism for the allocation of costs and benefits among its individual citizens.

The main issue is the questionable relationship of this theoretical conceptualization to political reality. Invariably, one of the most fundamental questions concerns the reduction of policy problems to a matter of costs and benefits. Cost-benefit analysis depends entirely on the ability to assign monetary values to economic and societal factors. To be sure, the allocation of costs and benefits is a central consideration in the evaluation of public policy. But the more important question is whether or not *all* policy issues can be reduced to costs and benefits. There are some very valuable things upon which people feel uncomfortable and hesitant to place monetary value.

The standard examples of this problem include such questions as how one places a value on the cost of human life, or what is the value of a natural wonder such as Yosemite National Park? For cost-benefit analysts, such matters are merely resolved by assigning estimated dollar values to such noneconomic social values and comparing them with the dollar values of any other economic commodity. Indeed, analysts often argue that social values are merely private interests disguised in the language of the public interest or the common good. But for many social and political theorists, this practice of translating moral considerations into the units of economic self-interest is a misunderstanding of the nature of social and political values (Tribe, 1972). A good deal of political experience, moreover, shows that citizens often feel that some things are not to be compared. Many people, for instance, believe it to be immoral to trade off a certain number of lives against the benefits of nuclear power.

Another basic problem concerns the emphasis of cost-benefit analysis on market forces. Welfare economics overlooks the fact that governments are typically assigned tasks that are not well-organized by market forces in the first place (hence the private market failures). That is, government is assigned the job of taking care of problems that businesses themselves find unprofitable in a market setting. Thus, it is not so much a matter of establishing the market's shadow prices to reflect the true market value of a publicly provided commodity, but rather a problem of determining the value of an activity or commodity in just those policy areas which do not lend themselves well to the use of market values.

The emphasis on market arrangements in cost-benefit analysis also overstresses the importance of policy *outputs* in comparison to the political input processes through which policy itself is made. The formation of public policy, in this respect, is treated in terms of a rational calculus of unitary actors pursuing their own individual self-interest, rather than as a clash of interests between competing political groups. This distinction, in fact, is frequently reflected in the political troubles associated with the presentation of cost-benefit results. Quite commonly, participants in the policy process resist the use of "anonymous techniques" they see to be insensitive to their own political coalition-building activities. For them, at the heart of such conflicts is not so much the question of how a given set of preferences can most efficiently be carried out, but rather the inherently political debate over whose preferences should prevail (Wildavsky, 1967).

This emphasis on unitary actors is further manifested in an economic interpretation of the policy implementation process. Policies are implicitly conceived of as directives that are automatically carried out. In reality, implementation is such a highly uncertain political phenomenon that it is often a surprise that some programs ever get implemented at all (Pressman and Wildavsky, 1984). Thus, because the political struggles over how to implement a policy intervene between policy analysis and policy consequences, the latter often fail to live up to the evaluator's expectations. For positivist analysis this is only another indication of the irrationality of the policy process and the need to technically restructure or "rationalize" the policy-making process.

Indeed, in more recent years such institutional failures have led to the development of "public choice theory," a cost-benefit oriented approach to the organizational dimensions of policy formulation and implementation. Based on the same set of economic assumptions, public choice theory is a rigorously positivistic effort to establish marketlike rules for efficiently and effectively designing government organizations, setting political boundaries, and constructing bargaining mechanisms that best facilitate the implementation of the aggregated preferences of individuals pursuing their own self-interest. (Ostrom and Ostrom, 1971). The problem is that public choice theory treats government institutions as little more than institutional mechanisms for aggregation of individual preferences. In the process, democracy tends to be evaluated merely in terms of its ability to facilitate the expression of *self*-interest (Mitchell and Mitchell, 1986). Some public choice theorists have gone so far to suggest that we replace democratic institutions with a demand-revealing process (Tullock, 1979). In this approach, there is no place for the collective concept of a public interest. The well-established fact that the intrinsic properties of public policy making are themselves often very important to the affected citizens is simply disregarded. As Bobrow and Dryzek (1987:57) have summed it up, "a citizen is more than a consumer."

Finally, in cost-benefit analysis, there is the question of how to treat the most essential political problem, that of distribution. At best, cost-benefit analysis underplays the distribution of resources; at worst, it ignores it altogether. According to Bobrow and Dryzek (1987:37), "Much of the substance of politics and policy concerns who should get what, rather than how much of the good in question should be produced." In what some theorists judge to be a near fatal flaw, cost-benefit analysts have nonetheless sought to sidestep this issue by transforming it into a technical question of efficient arrangements designed to aggregate individual interests. According to such principles of optimality, the only distribution that can be justified is the one shown to be most efficient for the society as a whole.

The basic ideological problem, then, is the extension of economic reasoning and its criteria into the social and political realms governed by very different kinds of judgmental criteria and processes of reasoning. While it is one thing to tally up the costs and benefits of a program, it is altogether another to interpret the political process itself merely as an economic mechanism for organizing the allocation of inputs and outputs. What we get from cost-benefit analysis is essentially an apolitical interpretation of the political process, one which judges political decision making to be irrational and deficient. While shrouded in the garb of science, this interpretation in fact rests only on the ideological value assumptions of welfare economics. In short, cost-benefit analysts tend to impose a technocratic value system onto an inherently political process designed to do much more than allocate costs and benefits. Indeed, the most fundamental task of the political system is to determine *which* value system should be accepted and applied. From the perspective of the logic of policy deliberation, cost-benefit economics not only distorts the nature of societal level vindication—that is, the third discourse of policy deliberation—it also overlooks the fundamental normative concerns of social choice.

The purpose of this chapter has been twofold. First, the task has been to demonstrate the nature of the leading policy evaluation methodologies—experimental program research, cost-benefit analysis, and risk-benefit analysis—to make clear their contribution to the logic of policy deliberation. Second, the objective has been to illustrate the limitations of a policy analysis dominated by these methodologies. The result has been to reveal the discipline's theoretical misunderstanding of the nature of the political system; and, as we see in the next chapter, to shape evaluation reports often judged by many to be irrelevant to the pressing public issues of the times. It is to the task of correcting these failures that this work is devoted.

We turn next to an evaluation of the Head Start program. The chapter first provides a practical illustration of an quasi-experimental evaluation, and second, the way its normative limitations were probed in the public debate that accompanied the announcement of its findings. The case study concretely demonstrates the need for a more expanded conception of evaluation and establishes the basis for the further elaboration of situational validation, societal-level vindication, and social choice.

### READINGS

Alan D. Putt and J. Fred Springer. 1989. *Policy Research: Concepts, Methods, and Applications*. Englewood, Cliffs, NJ: Prentice-Hall.

David L. Weimer and Aidan R. Vining. 1988. *Policy Analysis*. Englewood Cliffs, NJ: Prentice-Hall.

Edward M. Gramlich. 1990. *A Guide to Benefit-Cost Analysis*. Englewood Cliffs, NJ: Prentice-Hall.

Deborah Stone. 1988. Policy Paradox and Political Reason. Glenview, IL: Scott Foresman.

Ronald D. Sylvia, Kenneth J. Meier, and Elizabeth M. Gunn. 1991. *Program Planning and Evaluation for the Public Manager*. Prospect Heights, IL: Waveland Press.

Richard I. Hofferbert. 1990. *The Reach and Grasp of Policy Analysis*. Tuscaloosa: University of Alabama Press.

Dennis J. Palumbo, ed. 1987. *The Politics of Program Evaluation*. Newbury Park, CA: Sage.

# 3 Debating the Head Start Program: The Westinghouse Reading Scores in Normative Perspective

The empirical verification of program objectives is, as seen in the two previous chapters, an essential component of the logic of policy deliberation. In this chapter we offer a concrete example of empirical verification, while at the same time demonstrating its limits. Specifically, the purpose is to show that empirical tests alone are an insufficient basis for judging a program to be good or bad. Toward this end, both the contributions and limitations of technical verification are illustrated in the context of a particular policy debate. The focus is on arguments that arose in response to the findings reported in the Westinghouse Learning Corporation's (1969) evaluation study of Project Head Start, a compensatory education program for preschool children from poor families. Much discussed and debated in both the public media and the literature of policy evaluation, the controversy that surrounded the Westinghouse study was instrumental in prompting the need to rethink the uses of policy evaluation. No policy discussion has better clarified the role of normative criteria in the evaluation process than that associated with Head Start and the Westinghouse study, a discussion which still continues today.

In the interests of such clarification, this chapter begins with a brief history of the Heat Start program and the theoretical assumptions upon which it was founded, principally the War on Poverty. Next we examine the experimental evaluation of the Head Start program and the range of criticisms that followed its public presentation. Finally, the chapter concludes with an illustration of how the logic advanced here can be used to organize and analyze the normative arguments that arose in the debate over the findings of the Westinghouse Corporation's experimental evaluation.

## HEAD START AND THE WAR ON POVERTY: THE BASIC POLICY ASSUMPTIONS

The Head Start program was a prototype of Lyndon B. Johnson's Great Society and its War on Poverty. In part a response to politically explosive conditions in the country's urban ghettos in the 1960s, the basic conviction motivating the development of the program was the idea that something had to be done about the problems of poverty, hunger, and malnutrition in America (Rodgers, 1979). Although the issue of poverty in America began to draw attention during the Kennedy years, it was the administration of President Johnson that took the lead in developing the vast outpouring of economic and social programs for the poor that came to constitute America's attack on poverty. One of the most significant features underlying the design of these programs was a reliance on social science theory and research.

Most fundamentally, the War on Poverty sought to transcend the widely held argument that the able-bodied poor are poor simply because they are uneducated and indolent—that is, their poverty is attributable to personal defects such as a lack of ability, initiative, or persistence. While many of the poor do in fact exhibit these traits, the Great Society policy planners did not locate the primary reason for their poverty in the poor themselves; rather they found it in the poor's relationship to the major economic and political institutions of the society. As President Johnson put it in a report to Congress in 1964, the poor live "in a world apart...isolated from the mainstream of American life and alienated from its values." Moreover, poverty was not to be understood as a *fundamental failure* of the economic and political institutions per se, as argued by the more radical critics of American society (Piven and Cloward, 1993; deHaven-Smith, 1988). With the exception of racial discrimination, which was interpreted as a sociocultural phenomenon resulting from unfortunate historical circumstances (rather than, for example, an inherent byproduct of private enterprise), poverty was not conceptualized as an institutionalized problem. Instead of defects attributable to either the poor or the dominant institutions, the working hypothesis located the problem in the separation between them (DeHaven-Smith, 1988).

The foundation for this explanation of poverty was a set of theoretical assumptions that combined ideas prominent during the 1950s in sociology, economics, and political science. Sociological theory provided the view that many of the poverty-causing traits of the able-bodied poor resulted from a political and economic isolation that offered few possibilities for achievement (Marris and Rein, 1967). The outcome of such isolation was the development of a set of deviant norms best described as a "culture of poverty" (Moynihan, 1968; Lewis, 1959). Often passed from one generation to the next, this culture of poverty was characterized by a short time horizon, a limited ability to defer material gratification, unemployment, slothfulness, and crime. What is more, the theory further predicted that because cultural changes occur more slowly than changes in socio-institutional structures, the culture of poverty would prove to be highly resistant to change.

From the disciplines of economics and political science came support for the argument that the poor's lack of opportunity is due to their situational circumstances rather than to basic defects in the political and economic systems. Economics contributed the thesis that much unemployment among the hard-core poor is due to a mismatch between labor force qualifications and independently evolving employment opportunities (Levitan, 1969; Lampman, 1965). In this view, the hardcore unemployed lacked jobs because of their inappropriate skills and poor work habits. In political science, the pluralist theory of groups supplied the idea that the political system responds only to organized interests, thus producing decisions that neglect the interests of the unorganized (Donovan, 1967; Graham, 1965). Lacking access to the political system, so it was hypothesized, the unorganized poor were unable to effectively register their demands.

Such assumptions were central to the design of the poverty program. Because the culture of poverty theory suggested that cash transfers to the poor would simply be absorbed into the poor's pathological life-style, the policy planners emphasized in-kind transfers (such as food stamps, rent supplements, health care, counseling services, job training programs, etc.) to ameliorate economic deprivation. Similarly, social action programs were designed to break up the poverty culture by removing program participants from their regular environment; such programs focused in particular on the young through projects like Head Start, as children were believed to be more malleable than adults. In short, the War on Poverty was not to be simply understood as a welfare program; more fundamentally it was a social action program.

The Johnson administration's antipoverty policy emerged as an array of statutes, programs, and rules designed to attack the culture of poverty. Taken together, they specifically addressed several major goals: (1) the provision of economic resources to the poor, ranging from income and in-kind transfers to business assistance programs; (2) the prevention of unfair barriers to employment and political participation through the active enforcement of economic employment laws and the expansion of voting rights; and (3) the development of programs to educate and socialize the poor in how best to gain entrance to both the workplace and the political system through skills training and compensatory educational programs. Project Head Start was conceived as the model compensatory education program.

## THE HEAD START PROGRAM

The specific ideas for the Head Start program originated in the early 1960s in the work of a presidential panel charged with creating programs that could increase the educational achievement and employment opportunities for the poor. Chaired by Dr. Robert Cooke, professor of pediatrics at Johns Hopkins University School of Medicine, the panel of educational and social work professionals targeted in particular the preschool population of the poor for assistance (Zigler, 1992). Drawing upon accepted social scientific assumptions about the nature and causes of poverty, including an empirical study which had found that over 50 percent of a person's intellectual and emotional development was established by the age of four, the panel recommended a comprehensive preschool program that would give children from poor families a "head start" in developing skills, nutritional habits, and social customs equivalent to what nondeprived children received from their families (Sagen, 1987). The assumption was that preschool intervention could contribute to the ultimate elimination of poverty by enabling children to get the most out of schooling, achieve academic excellence, acquire skills, and eventually obtain good jobs (Zigler and Valentine, 1979).

In 1964, Congressional supporters of the Johnson administration's antipoverty efforts introduced into the U.S. Congress the "Cooke Amendment," calling for the establishment of Project Head Start. Perceived as relatively safe in traditional political terms, the amendment passed easily through the legislative process with substantial bipartisan support; it formally became law in 1965. Set up as federally funded programs delivered in community centers throughout the country, Head Start was viewed as a reasonably inexpensive major social program with substantial potential for success. Moreover, the program had the personal and enthusiastic backing of President Johnson, as well as the support of prominent policy professionals, both inside and outside of government (Nathan, 1988).

Congress formally assigned administrative responsibility for the Head Start program to the U.S. Office of Economic Opportunity, the major antipoverty agency of the federal government. The stated objectives of the program included the following:

1. Improving the perceptual, conceptual, and verbal skills of disadvantaged children;
2. Developing cultural and educational curiosity;
3. Providing better medical and dental care to poor children;
4. Assisting in improving the self-discipline of disadvantaged children;
5. Enlarging a sense of personal dignity and self-worth.
6. Developing a socially responsible attitude toward the community and the larger society among preschool children and their parents.

Clearly, the basic Head Start program was intended to provide far more than preschool education. Following the Cooke panel's recommendation, it was also supposed to supply access to health care, adequate nutrition, social services for children, and training and career assistance for parents. The program sought to engage the parents of the children through participation in both the classroom and a variety of career development services. In short, Head Start was intended to be a comprehensive family-oriented service delivery system for the poor and their disadvantaged children.

Of all the Great Society programs, initial expectations for Head Start were perhaps the highest. Educational psychologists spoke in glowing terms of the anticipated outcomes (Some even seemed to believe that several years of educational neglect might be compensated for in the short space of several summer sessions). Such enthusiasm and excitement was in fact reflected in the early enrollment figures. As the program opened its doors in the summer of 1965, administrators expected to enroll about 100,000 children. In fact, over 500,000 children enrolled in 11,068 Head Start centers.

The excitement did not last long however. After three and a half years, negative reports began to appear. The first evaluation studies of the educational effects of the program failed to confirm the initial expectations. As Harrell Rodgers (1979:235) put it, "The studies showed that the...educational gains tended to be small, especially for children who had not participated in year-round programs." The most significant of these critical studies was commissioned by the federal government and conducted by the Westinghouse Learning Corporation of Ohio University, a policy research organization specializing in educational affairs. According to the Westinghouse evaluation, after three-and-a-half years of operation the program's educational effects had failed to achieve the initial expectations. Despite high enrollments, the experimental evaluation by the research corporation indicated that the program was not achieving two of its primary goals, namely the improvement of intellectual and emotional (psychological) development among preschool children. Next we look more closely at how this important verification-focused study was conducted.

EVALUATING HEAD START: A QUASI-EXPERIMENTAL
RESEARCH DESIGN

The Westinghouse Learning Corporation evaluation study, commissioned by the federal government shortly after the onset of Head Start, employed experimental research design. The evaluation sought to determine whether the educational progress of primary grade children who had been through a Head Start experience was improved relative to that of comparable children without Head Start experience. Specifically, the research followed the steps of an quasi-experimental research design (introduced in the previous chapter), but with several significant variations.

## Program Objectives

In the Westinghouse study, it was assumed that the primary objectives of Head Start were to improve the cognitive and emotional development of the children who participated in the program. Specifically, the criteria for analysis were measurable gains in the ability of the children to read and write (cognitive development) and to see themselves in a more positive manner (emotional development). Although the evaluators knew that Head Start had additional objectives related to improving children's health and nutrition, as well as changing parental attitudes and creating community changes, they chose to focus on intellectual and emotional factors. It is not clear why the evaluators did this; one speculation is that these were the aspects of the program that most easily lend themselves to empirical measurement.

## Empirical Indicators

The standardized test instruments commonly used in schools at the time were employed to measure the effectiveness of Head Start in educating poor, preschool children. Such intelligence tests required a student to answer a series of questions about various aspects of his or her existing knowledge and capacity to learn. One instrument, designed to measure both a student's willingness to learn and ability to read, focused on tests of word meaning, ability to comprehend phrases and sentences rather than individual words, recognition of lower-case letters of the alphabet, knowledge of numbers, visual perceptual skills, and motor control. A second test measured the ability of students to read words and paragraphs, spell, and perform mathematical exercises. And a third instrument measured auditory and visual reception, the ability to reproduce geometric figures, and the capacity to express oneself with gestures.[1]

A battery of tests assessed the effects of Head Start on the emotional or affective ability of children to interpret information about themselves and others. For example, one test involved the presentation of a pair of stick figures to a child with corresponding pairs of statements, one favorable and the other unfavorable (e.g., "The balloon-child is learning a lot in school," "The flag-child isn't learning very much"). For each item, the child was asked to indicate which was most like him or her. The number of favorable or unfavorable self-identifications were then used to establish a child's level of emotional development.[2]

Following good experimental practices, Westinghouse sought to apply all of the test instruments in an uniform manner. This was done in an effort both to maintain the internal validity of the experiment and to maximize the possibility of replicating it in similar circumstances at a future point in time, i.e., to establish its external validity. Westinghouse was particularly careful in the recruitment and selection of the field examiners (or "interviewers," as they were called) who administered the instruments. Once selected, the examiners were given extensive training in the procedural uses of the instruments, as well as instruction in the theory underlying their construction. Moreover, the examiners observed practical demonstrations of each instrument and participated in real and simulated testing exercises.

## Sampling

The units of analysis for the study were six geographic areas of the country served by 104 Head Start centers. Within each target area, all children who were eligible to attend Head Start from September 1966 to August 1967 were identified and classified into two subpopulations—those who had attended Head Start and those who had not. A random sample of children enrolled in Head Start was selected as the experimental group and a random sample of children who had not attended Head Start was assigned to the control group. Within the experimental group, the sample of children was further divided into those who had attended only a summer session and those who had experienced Head Start for a full year.

To minimize problems of equivalence and attrition, all of the children in the two groups had to live in the target areas and attend the same school during the specified time period. Thus, the study excluded any children who migrated from one target area to another, those who had changed schools, and those children who had moved from one Head Start center to another. Since the students in each of the groups were randomly selected, the researchers could not, however, ensure exact equivalence in terms of sex, race, and socioeconomic status.

The Westinghouse research group limited its measurements to a "posttest design." As such, the children were not tested prior to entering the program (a pretest design) or while participating in the program (a time-series design). According to the evaluators, the posttest design was necessitated by the decision to conduct the experiment after the students had already begun the program (Westinghouse Corp., 1969).

## Findings

The Westinghouse study found that: (1) summer Head Start programs were ineffective in producing lasting gains in cognitive or emotional development, (2) that full-year programs were ineffective in aiding emotional development and only marginally effective in producing lasting cognitive gains, and (3) that Head Start children were considerably below national norms on tests of language development and scholastic achievement. Arriving at these conclusions through statistical comparisons of the experimental and control groups for each of the utilized instruments, the evaluators further found that cognitive and affective scores were considerably lower for the Head Start students than for the students not enrolled in Head Start. This was true even when the results were considered within regions and among students with different socioeconomic backgrounds. Similar results were found in the other tests. Thus, when all of the information was aggregated and analyzed, it was concluded that Head Start was not effective.

### PUBLIC DEBATE: THE POLITICS OF AN EXPERIMENTAL EVALUATION

The findings of the Westinghouse evaluation were initially "leaked" to the *New York Times* and reported in a story that emphasized the one word no Head Start proponent wanted to hear—failure. Indeed, one Head Start administrator later referred to the *New York Times* article as the blackest day in the program's history (Zigler and Muenchow, 1992). In fact, the pessimistic media coverage and the eventual release of the formal report in 1969 gave rise to a public controversy that nearly led to the program's termination. Much of the reason had to do with President Richard Nixon, who used the evaluation as convenient ammunition for his assault on the War on Poverty. President Nixon had based his 1968 presidential campaign to a great extent on the "failures" of the War on Poverty, and once in office, he continued to stress the theme. Consequently, in his nationally televised 1969 economic opportunity message to the Congress, Nixon brought the negative reading scores in the report to the attention of the American public as a whole.[3] Proclaiming that the Head Start program was a "proven failure," he triggered an intense debate about the program that ricocheted through Congress, the executive branch, educational circles, and the communities of the poor. In particular, the outcry centered around three types of arguments.

One of the first arguments against the Westinghouse evaluation came from other social scientists. Mainly focusing on empirical considerations, they questioned whether the research organization had in fact validly demonstrated the failure of the program. Did the evidence really show that participation in Head Start had no long-term results? Many leading social scientists were skeptical (Williams and Evans, 1972; Smith and Bissell, 1970). Steeped in the empirical techniques of mainstream social science, they questioned whether the evaluators had used proper methodological procedures. Were the statistical samples properly chosen? Did the empirical instruments accurately measure reading achievement? Was the posttest research design inherently faulty? And so on.[4]

Even more important, at least for present purposes, was a second type of argument concerned with the program objectives measured in the Westinghouse evaluation. In emphasizing the measurement of cognitive scores, many educational experts, program administrators, and representatives of the poor argued that the evaluators had failed to understand the nature and purpose of the Head Start program. The legislation, for example, had posited improved reading scores as only one of the program's objectives. Equally important, they pointed out, was the provision of *socially relevant* experiences for ghetto children and the improvement of the health of the children.[5] Many sociologists and psychologists maintained that social experiences were critical for the transition from poverty to mainstream American life. Only through the assimilation of mainstream social values could these disadvantaged children successfully function in middle-class institutions. Thus, to judge the Head Start program a failure based on narrowly conceived empirical measurements of individual cognitive and emotional tests was a methodological error. Instead of merely amassing empirical data from such test scores, evaluators should as well develop subjectively relevant measures of social progress derived from firsthand experience with the disadvantaged community and its children.

A third type of argument raised larger ideological concerns that pertained to the development of attitudes toward the larger society itself (Gordon, 1972). Worried about the longer term social harmony of the society, those who advanced this view maintained that, regardless of outcomes or consequences (whether based on objective reading scores or on community-related standards), empirical measurement was an insufficient ground for judging Head Start a failure. In this view, Head Start had been designed to promote and facilitate a basic value that must extend to all citizens in a democratic system: the right to equal opportunity. Thus, the evaluation of such a program had to include its normative contribution to the equal opportunity principle, regardless of its secondary or indirect consequences for other dimensions of the social system. Compensatory programs such as Head Start were seen to be designed to nurture long-term harmony and stability in the social order and should be judged accordingly.

Because of the ideological foundations of this argument, in the pragmatic realm of public policy it was frequently advanced more through implicit assumptions than stated premises (Bowles and Gintis, 1976). The argument can, however, more or less be constructed as follows: Equal opportunity is one of the basic legitimating principles of liberalism. In this system, educational institutions (designed for social mobility through the principle of merit) are the primary vehicles for the realization of equal opportunity. Thus, in a society marked by growing social inequalities, educational programs for disadvantaged children are of critical importance, symbolic as well as instrumental. Without programs such as Head Start, explicitly designed to give material meaning to the opportunity principle, the social system is left vulnerable to what has been referred to as a "legitimation crisis" (Habermas, 1973). To avert the social and political turmoil that can result from a general collapse of belief systems, compensatory programs must ensure adequate socialization of disadvantaged children, the potentially problematic citizens of the future generation. At this level of analysis, cognitive scores are of secondary importance; the program's primary achievement is measured in terms of its basic contribution to social legitimacy. Indeed, one of the primary factors that confers this legitimacy is the very existence of the program.

The foregoing arguments—the criticisms of Westinghouse's empirical analysis, the questions about the social relevance of the program criteria employed in the evaluation, and the ideological commitment to equal opportunity—all shared a common political concern, namely, that the Westinghouse study would be used to eliminate the Head Start program. As one source explained, it was "feared that Congress or the Administration [would] seize upon the report's generally negative conclusion as an excuse to downgrade or discard the Head Start program" (Williams and Evans, 1972). These fears were in fact justified. While the Nixon administration was never able to eliminate the Head Start program entirely, the program budget was continually cut. According to Rodgers (1979: 235), the Westinghouse Report's "negative findings were basically accepted at face value and cost Head Start much of its support in Congress." During the 1970s, the program experienced significant cutbacks in terms of enrollments and budget allocation.

### THE HEAD START DEBATE AND THE LOGIC OF POLICY DELIBERATION

What does one make of these competing perspectives? On the surface of the matter, they would appear to have little in common with one another. Such arguments make it difficult for the trained observer, let alone the average editorial page reader, to form an intelligent opinion about Head Start. In fact, how to make sense of the situation became a prominent part of the public debate.

In the face of such confusion, it is not surprising that the issue began in social scientific circles to move away from the question of "Which methodological orientation is right?" to "What is the relationship among them?" In this respect, it was more and more recognized that empirical data based on "objective criteria" could no longer simply be offered as value-neutral evidence. Evaluators would have to acknowledge that criteria such as reading scores are drawn from particular belief systems and conceptions of social life. It was a concern that bore directly on the evaluation of the Head Start program.

In the remainder of this section, the way in which the logic of policy deliberation addresses this concern is illustrated. As seen in chapter 1, a critical-comprehensive logic of evaluation is concerned with more than just the verification of a program; it also sets forth the guidelines implicitly or explicitly followed in an attempt to engage the full range of empirical and normative questions that constitute a comprehensive evaluation. We show how the logic can be used to systematically organize and interpret both the empirical and normative arguments in the Head Start debate. What at first appears to be a disparate set of criticisms is with the assistance of logic seen only to be different components of a complete or comprehensive evaluation.

### Verification of Program Objectives

Here verification can be dealt with summarily, as the debate about the results of the empirical measurements of Head Start test scores has already been presented in some detail. The phase of evaluation most familiar to policy analysts, verification focuses on empirical-analytic observation, experimentation, measurement, and hypothesis testing. We easily recognize these concerns to be the ones that triggered the Head Start debate. The initial questions raised about the Westinghouse evaluation involved empirical methodology: was the control group adequate? Was sufficient attention paid to program variations? Was the sample random? The correspondence between technical verification in the logic of policy evaluation and the issue in the Head Start debate is direct and requires little further elaboration.

### Situational Validation of Program Objectives

As seen in the two previous chapters, the critique of the positivist conception of policy evaluation is largely derived from a failure to extend evaluation beyond the verification of program objectives. At the first-order level of discourse, little attention in policy evaluation has been paid to the normative assessment of a policy's program objectives and the situation to which they are applied. Validation seeks to correct this failure. It probes the validity of the situational definitions and assumptions upon which the program objectives have been constructed.

Pursuing the Head Start illustration beyond empirical verification, those who criticized the Westinghouse conclusions for failing to employ socially relevant criteria are easily recognized to be addressing the basic questions of validation. To counter the conclusion that Head Start had failed, minority leaders and academic researchers raised two types of criticisms. The first concerned the multiple goals of Head Start: the Head Start evaluation, critics argued, was too narrowly conceived. They questioned the validity of reading scores as the primary criterion for judging the overall success of a program designed to improve the life opportunities of socially deprived children. Head Start, they pointed out, was also designed to teach other types of socially relevant knowledge, such as self-discipline, personal health, and socially responsible attitudes toward the community. Such knowledge was as important to program success as cognitive skill levels; many in fact argued that it was even more important.

Basic to this discussion were "the facts of the situation." Most important was the issue of a "culture of poverty," the fundamental assumption upon which the Head Start program was designed. Those who criticized the Westinghouse findings were quick to point out the unique social circumstances of the program participants. Without denying the general importance of reading levels, the program's supporters argued that the basic objective was to help ghetto children—children born into the culture of poverty—gain the kinds of social experiences that would make it possible for them to function successfully in middle-class–oriented educational institutions. Without denying the general importance of cognitive skills, socially relevant experiences had to be the first priority. Lacking such social skills ghetto children were forever doomed to educational failure. Social culturation, in this respect, was an educational precondition. Cognitive skills, as long as they came at some point in the elementary educational process, could come somewhat later.

The presence or importance of such a culture—or subculture—is an empirical question open to investigation. However, few of the program's major critics constructed their arguments around this question, at least in situational terms. A major reason, no doubt, was a preponderance of evidence suggesting the validity of the concept (although, as we shall see in the next section, this would not hinder some from criticizing the implications of the poverty of culture at the level of systems vindication). Indeed, more central to this aspect of the debate were the numerous academic researchers who focused on the empirical and methodological issues raised by the unique characteristics of the Head Start learning situation.

Often drawing on the holistic techniques of anthropologists and interpretive sociologists, such researchers argued for—and typically sought to develop—experience-related criteria for the contextual and longitudinal measurement of cognitive skills. If the general purpose of the program was to provide children with both the cognitive and social skills necessary to function successfully in mainstream middle-class institutions, the evaluation of the program should follow the children's life situations from Head Start into those institutions. In short, the educational development of these children should be monitored contextually through a progression of institutional situations (Goodson and Hess, 1977).

These arguments turned out to be much more than partisan criticisms, as had often been suggested during the initial Head Start debate. Indeed, a decade later new research was to present a much more positive picture of Head Start, which educational experts have mostly attributed to the introduction of methodological improvements better designed to evaluate these institutional experiences, including longer time spans appropriate to the measurement of the program effects.

### Societal-Level Vindication of Policy Goals

The shift in evaluation from situational validation to systems-level vindication is a move from a first- to second-order evaluation. Here evaluation turns to the broader policy goals from which the program objectives were derived and examines their instrumental or contributive value for the larger social system as a whole.

Although the empirical complexity of the questions raised in vindication are often beyond the capabilities of existing social science methodologies to settle with any certainty, it is nonetheless possible to locate the concerns of this level of evaluation in policy debates. In the case of Head Start, the most salient issue at this level again turned around the culture of poverty, but this time with respect to its implications for societal institutions rather than program participants.

As already pointed out, few of Head Start's critics raised questions about the validity of the culture of poverty per se. More typically the critics of such compensatory programs took a different line of attack. In this respect, no one was more important than Edward Banfield, a prominent social scientist who helped to lead the intellectual assault on Great Society programs. Banfield's (1970) approach was to accept the culture of poverty thesis, but to shift the argument to the capacity of American social and political institutions to deal with it. For Banfield, the more fundamental concern was the severity of the problem posed by the culture of poverty, as documented by program supporters. The problem, as he saw it, was essentially beyond the reach of governmental programs such as Head Start. A primary source of governmental policy failures in this area, according to Banfield, was to be found in the unwillingness or inability of liberal reformers to address the deeper cultural differences that entrench urban poverty. Solutions effectively designed to penetrate the problem at this level would have to be massive in scope, both institutionally and financially. Anything short of a massive intervention in the system, Banfield argued, would amount to mere situational change, with only temporary ameliorative effects. However, in his view, intervention on such a scale was politically unacceptable to the power structure governing American economic and political institutions. For example, given the existing political structures and their policy decision rules—particularly interest-group politics and incremental policy-making—such intervention would not only be too costly, but it would also rest on ideological value beliefs outside of the American governmental system and its political culture. Banfield thus rejected liberal governmental antipoverty programs because they could not be vindicated by the dominant political value beliefs of the social system.[6] At this point, he rested his case. In the urban literature this view was identified as a "new realism" based on the "hard facts" of the political system.

To be sure, Banfield's position has been attacked from numerous liberal quarters. One such assault criticized his treatment of the existing political system as "frozen." Timothy Hennessey and Richard Feen (1974) attributed Banfield's treatment to his underlying political philosophy. Banfield, they argued, "rejects out of hand the possibility that the opinion makers' propensity to imagine a future may lead them to a view of the facts decidedly different from [his]—namely an alarming deterioration in the social and political climate in American cities which in turn impels the opinion makers to use considerable skill to design realistic programs to alleviate the problem (Hennessey and Feen, 1974).

This argument opens the way for a different line of discourse. Fundamental to the logic of policy evaluation advanced here is the possibility of an alternative vision of the political system and its underlying values. Evaluation would halt at vindication only if all parties agree on the answer to the question, "Do you accept this political way of life?" It is, indeed, on this point that Banfield's most truculent critics have launched their objections. This recognition of alternative visions of a political system moves the argument from vindication to the next and final phase of the evaluation process, social choice. At this stage in the Head Start debate evaluation shifts attention from the existing or "real" political system to the possibility of a more socially just—albeit ideal— political system, which public policy itself might help to bring about.

### Social Choice

Normative disparities between the dominant political beliefs of the extant societal system and the social implications of the culture of poverty for ghetto children thus triggered political debate about the societal system itself, leading to the political-ideological concerns of the fourth level of evaluation. During the period of the Head Start debate, political philosophers focused on a number of issues that bear directly on the evaluation of compensatory educational programs. Of particular importance were the principles of equal opportunity and the nature of an egalitarian society (Fishkin, 1983).

Those in the Head Start controversy who argued that evaluation must ultimately rest on ideological or philosophical principles were essentially arguing at the second-order level of political choice. Specifically, exchanges regarding the relative importance of reading scores and socially relevant standards had a second-order counterpart in a debate that focused on the nature of the good society. One group contended that the good society emerges from the long-term social benefits of a meritocratic system based on the values of individual competition and native skill (generally measured as IQ). Another group stressed the advantages of pursuing an egalitarian social order founded on the values of community and fraternity. While to many observers these arguments seemed to have little practical import for the immediate issues in the debate arising from the Westinghouse evaluation, on closer examination they were essentially the theoretical and ideological counterparts of the more practical concerns surrounding the project. In short, those advocating a meritocratic social order were presenting second-order philosophical reasons for emphasizing the importance of reading scores as the primary measure of progress. Those representing the egalitarian cause were offering a second-order justification for the first-order emphasis on socially relevant standards.

One of the most interesting studies that illustrates the nature of argumentation at the level of vindication was conducted by Samuel Bowles and Herbert Gintis. In *Schooling in Capitalist America*, Bowles and Gintis (1976) sought to show that the principle of equal opportunity cannot be realized through compensatory education programs in a capitalist social order. Addressing first the kinds of concerns confronted in vindication, they provided an impressive array of historical data to demonstrate that commitment to the equal opportunity principle has not led to greater equality in capitalist societies. The primary function of this principle is not, they asserted, social justice but rather the facilitation of social control. By blurring the class divisions that constitute the basic realities of the educational system, belief in the principle serves as a powerful stabilizing force in capitalist societies.

Where others, such as Banfield, reject genuine equal opportunity as an overly idealistic principle, Bowles and Gintis use it to call for alternative egalitarian institutions. Rather than rejecting the equal opportunity principle because it clashes with extant political and social values, they employ the principle as the basis for a critique of the real values of capitalism. For them equal opportunity can be achieved only by a radical change brought about by the adoption of socialist value principles. In short, they call for a new socialist political order.

The call for a new social order was not restricted to academic debates. Numerous leaders of the black community, especially of the more militant groups such as the Black Panthers, rejected outright the idea of integrating ghetto children into mainstream middle-class American institutions. Radically indicating what they saw to be the social injustices of the American system, they advocated a new way of life based on black culture and experience. In particular, they called for setting up their own Afro-American schools outside of the dominant system. Dedicated to the teaching of black history and culture, as well as the fostering of black role models for young black children, such schools would not only work to better improve the lot of American blacks, but do so on their own cultural terms as well. Although the idea would languish in its more radical formulations, it in no way disappeared from the political scene. Indeed, it has today very much experienced a revival with the emergence of the "multicultural" movement in the United States (Asante, 1987; Hughes, 1992).

In the actual debates over the Westinghouse evaluation, then, the critics are seen to be talking past one another. Each has chosen a specific dimension of the Head Start program as the crucial issue on which the debate should turn. As figure 3.1 makes clear, however, each of these orientations is only a part of a full assessment. Using the diagram introduced in chapter 1, the figure illustrates the way in which the four arguments are distributed across the logic of a comprehensive policy evaluation. The diagram helps to make clear the requirements of a critical-comprehensive policy evaluation: evaluators must not only present their empirical findings, but also the full range of assumptions on which their criteria (norms, standards, and values) are based. This provides the basis for a systematic critical debate that explores the full range of issues, from evidence to principles.

**Figure 3.1:** Head Start Arguments and Policy Deliberation

| Methodological Orientation | Levels of Deliberation | Political Issues |
|---|---|---|
| Ideological Critique | *Social Choice* Legitimation Crisis ↑ | Equal Opportunity versus Egalitarian Society |
| Social Systems Analysis | *Societal-Level Vindication* Institutional Barriers ↑ | Power Structure versus Poor |
| Qualitative Methods | *Situational Validation* Culture of Poverty ↑ | Reading Scores versus Socially Relevant Experiences |
| Experimental Research ⟶ | *Verification* Research Design and Measurements ⟶ | Conclusion: Head Start Has Failed versus Deficient Research Design |

## HEAD START TODAY: EMPIRICAL VERIFICATION RECONSIDERED

It is instructive to close with an update on the Head Start program. While for analytical purposes we have chosen to focus on an earlier episode in the history of Head Start, the methodological issues raised by the case in the early 1970s continued to live on in ways that only provide further insights into the interactive relationships between political judgment and social scientific policy evaluation. As we saw, in spite of the charges that the Westinghouse evaluation was not "scientific" enough, both the Nixon administration and many members of Congress used the findings to reduce the size and scope of the program. Retrenchment in Head Start continued in the Nixon administration and throughout the term of Gerald Ford. Interestingly enough, however, appropriations for Head Start under Carter began to grow again and enrollments increased. While one might be inclined to assume that a Democratic party president was simply restoring his party's programs, which no doubt is part of the story, there was another important wrinkle here—namely, that a new round of evaluation studies began to show the program to have positive outcomes. Although the new studies received much less fanfare than the Westinghouse study, further academic research in the 1970s began to show that participation in Head Start did in fact improve cognitive skills and affective development, as well as improve attitudes among children toward themselves and society. As an expert in the Office of Child Development explained, new evaluations offered "compelling evidence that early intervention works, [and] that the adverse impact of a poverty environment on children can be overcome by appropriate treatment" (Brown, 1977). In general, these new studies differed from the Westinghouse study in that before and after tests were performed and the effects of Head Start were examined for a longer period of time. The Carter administration wasted no time using these studies to restore the Head Start budget cuts of the Nixon and Ford administrations.

The new findings were largely the result of two major activities. As Head Start dangled by a budgetary thread throughout most of the 1970s, and was constantly forced to respond to repeated efforts to eliminate it altogether, the program underwent a significant administrative reorganization. In the early 1970s, responsibility for the program was moved from the Office of Economic Opportunity to the Office of Child Development in the Department of Health and Human Services. This department was later renamed the Agency for Children, Youth and Family Services. This signified a basic change in outlook for the program from a broad antipoverty focus to an emphasis on education and community service. Formally, the shift was made primarily to encourage the development of innovations that would make the program more effective, such as increasing the involvement of parents and offering service delivery options to local centers. Informally, the shift helped at the same time to remove the politically problematic stigma that plagued former Great Society antipoverty programs during the conservative years that followed.

A second activity was the instigation of research to reexamine the Head Start program. Research projects were undertaken not only by Head Start agencies, but also by child care advocates, policy research specialists, Congressional staff members, and university scholars.[7] In fact, almost a thousand studies were conducted by the mid-1980s, motivated by a wide variety of factors, such as the urgent need for comparative data, criticisms of the Westinghouse experiment, and the importance of the program to millions of young Americans.[8] Especially interesting is the fact that this research not only involved replicating and improving on Westinghouse's verification of Head Start's effectiveness, but it also included the use of alternative approaches and methodologies to improve the examination of Head Start's policy goals and assumptions. Especially important was the use of new experience-related teaching techniques and their socially based measurement criteria.[9] Moreover, the results achieved through longitudinal measurements were impressive. As Rodgers (1979:235) has summarized them, "the studies showed that Head Start is very successful in cutting down in the rate of school failure, in improving IQ scores and reading achievement, and in helping children gain self-confidence." They show that "the earlier and the more exposure children had to Head Start, the greater the gains they tended to make and maintain."

As a result of these positive findings, Head Start has enjoyed a major resurgence in public confidence. Both the Reagan and Bush administrations supported its continuation, and the Congress increased funding for the program. Indeed, by early 1992, the issue of Head Start would seem to have come full circle. In a television interview, Bush declared Head Start to be one of the "rare exceptions" of a government program that works, and that based on this proven experience, he would increase the funding for Head Start.[10]

Now widely acclaimed by members of both political parties in the U.S. Congress, the program was in fact federally budgeted in 1987 at over $1 billion dollars, a 100 percent increase over the amounts it received during the Johnson years. Most recently, the Clinton administration has proposed to further increase program funding to $9 billion over the next five years, a sum which is estimated to double the size of the program (Box 3.1). Buttressed by new scientific evidence, the present status of the program is now largely due to a conservative argument that education is a meaningful way for people to emerge from poverty. Education, according to conservative logic, helps the poor to "pull themselves up by their bootstraps." However, without the long-running methodological arguments, which led to the development of more sophisticated techniques for measuring program outcomes, the new evaluation studies—and hence the revitalization of Head Start—would never have come about.

---

**BOX 3.1**
## Head Start: The Clinton Administration

*Deja vu,* the Head Start program seems again to encounter criticisms about program verification. No longer is the question about whether the program works, but rather whether its effects are lasting. Critics of Clinton's new appropriations typically point to experimental studies of Head Start which now show that the program's "academic benefits tend to wear out after three years, with children who attend the program then performing no better than those who did not." Some conservative politicians in Congress "have seized on the criticisms to oppose Mr. Clinton's proposal and paint the President as a spend-happy liberal who is wasting taxpayer money" (DeParle, 1993: A17).

But these verification arguments are again countered by arguments of social relevance. Supporters of the program "contend that it also produces other benefits, like bringing improved health care to children and better social services to their families" and has to be judged accordingly, even if academic benefits wear off. Others argue that the weakening of the effects must be blamed on the poor quality of the elementary system into which the children matriculate, rather than Head Start itself.

Still other Clinton enthusiasts argue that his goals cannot altogether be judged by the numbers. "They believe that a nation in need of skilled workers can no longer afford to let a substantial number of its citizens fail, and there is enough research to support the view that government [Head Start] programs can make a difference." Even though scholars debate the statistics, argues Lisbeth Schorr, a lecturer at Harvard University, "as long as we know we're going in the right direction, we have to make the investment because the alternatives are so expensive—to both government and society."

---

The main purpose of this chapter has been to offer a case illustration of empirical verification in relation to the full range of normative arguments that constitute the concerns of validation, vindication, and social choice. In addition to demonstrating the limits of verification, the case study has shown how the logic of a more comprehensive evaluation can systematically sort out both empirical and normative concerns. While the Westinghouse research shows empirical inquiry to be an important part of a comprehensive evaluation, such inquiry is also seen to be only one component part of a larger inferential process. The four modes of evaluative discourse—verification, validation, vindication, and social choice—are all shown to be interrelated components of a comprehensive evaluation of the Head Start program. Each has its own types of data and internal logic, but none can stand entirely alone. As coexisting perspectives on the same sociopolitical reality, they are integral components of an expanded conceptualization of policy evaluation.

At this point, we can move on to the more detailed exploration of the normative phases of the logic of policy deliberation, although we do not altogether leave the Head Start case study behind. Head Start remains an overarching illustration that is used to help reintroduce and integrate each of the subsequent parts of the book. In Part Two we turn to situational validation. Chapter 4 takes up the validation of program objectives, emphasizing the role of qualitative research and interpretive methods. Chapter 5 illustrates this mode of inquiry with a case study of New York City's Times Square Redevelopment project.

## READINGS

Edward Zigler and Jeanette Valentine, eds. 1979. *Project Head Start*. New York: Free Press.

Valora Washington-Smith. 1987. *Project Head Start: Past, Present, and Future*. New York: Garland.

Westinghouse Learning Corp. 1969. *The Impact of Head Start: An Evaluation of the Effects of Head Start on Children's Cognitive and Affective Development*. Athens: Ohio University Press.

Richard Nathan. 1991. *Social Science in Government*. New York: Basic Books.

Oscar Lewis. 1959. *Five Families: Mexican Case Studies in the Culture of Poverty*. New York: Basic Books.

Sar A. Levitan. 1969. *The Great Society's Poor Law: A New Approach to Poverty*. Baltimore, MD: Johns Hopkins University Press.

Daniel P. Moynihan. 1968. *On Understanding Poverty*. New York: Basic Books.

## DISCUSSION QUESTIONS

1. How might the criticisms of the Westinghouse research be discussed in terms of the internal and external validity of the quasi-experimental design that was used to test Head Start children?
2. In what ways does the Westinghouse evaluation illustrate the technocratic tendencies associated with policy analysis?
3. What does the case say about the relationship of politics to social scientific research?
4. Discuss the relation of the normative assumptions underlying the Great Society more generally to the evaluation of the Head Start program more specifically.
5. How might cost-benefit analysis be brought to bear on the Head Start evaluation?
6. Classical philosophers such as Aristotle have argued that the final judgment of a course of action must ultimately depend on the good of society. What does this mean in terms of the evaluation of the Head Start program?

# Part Two
## SITUATIONAL VALIDATION

# 4   Evaluating Program Objectives: Multiple Criteria and Situational Relevance

The validation phase of policy evaluation is concerned with the *relevance* of the policy objectives employed in an evaluative judgment. Whereas verification attempts to show that a program fulfills or fails to fulfill an objective, validation asks whether the policy objectives are appropriate to the specific problem situation under investigation. To render such an assessment, evaluation turns from an emphasis on the empirical rigor of quantitative research to normative discourse and the interpretive methods of qualitative analysis. The goal of this chapter is to examine more closely the logic of the validation phase of policy deliberation and to introduce the kinds of methodological issues that it raises.

## THE BASIC QUESTIONS

Consider again the case of Head Start. In the previous chapter the issue was whether or not the claim that the Head Start program failed to fulfill specific cognitive objectives had been empirically verified. The Westinghouse evaluation stated that the objectives had not been fulfilled, but the methodological criticisms asserted that the program's performance had not been adequately measured to justify the judgment. At this point in the evaluation process, a judgment can be thought of as true or false in the conventional scientific/empirical sense of the term. But assume that we accept the outcome of the Westinghouse study (namely, that the students have failed to read at a specific level) and someone asks: "Why should reading be the objective criterion for judging the Head Start program a failure?" Indeed, various critics of the Westinghouse evaluation argued that the study was too narrowly focused on cognitive outcomes. More important than reading scores, it was argued, were the socially relevant experiences that the children receive. Providing so-

69

cially relevant experiences for ghetto children is a good reason for judging the Head Start curriculum "good" because the goal of education is to train such children for entrance into society. This question and such arguments shift the evaluation to validation.

As a normative process of reasoning, then, validation turns the focus of deliberation from program outcomes to the justification of the objectives—that is, criteria—which the outcomes measure. Situational validation centers around the following questions:

- Is the program objective(s) relevant to the problem situation?
- Are there circumstances in the situation that require an exception be made to the objective(s)?
- Are two or more objectives equally relevant to the problem situation?

In the language of methodology, this transition rests on the distinction between an "explanation" of the outcomes and an "understanding" of the situation in which they occur. Although validation draws heavily on empirical data pertaining to the specific situation, its fundamental judgments are based on the establishment of logical/interpretive relationships between the empirical situation and specific normative criteria. In verification, where the purpose is to render a valid judgment about empirical relationships among specified variables, normative standards and rules are imported into the empirical context as constraints. In validation, where the objective is to render an interpretive understanding of the meaning of the empirical relationships, facts are brought to the normative context of standards and rules. In verification, the key relationships between empirical data are causal; in validation, the essential connections are logical.

There are a number of social-analytical frameworks that help to explicate the relationship between verification and validation. Robert MacIver, for example, provided a useful conceptual framework for comprehending this shift from verification to validation. The transition centers around his concept of a two-level analysis. For MacIver, the study of politics is first empirical. Statistical analysis and related techniques are employed to determine whether and to what extent the events under investigation are empirically associated with other phenomena. All hypotheses must pass these tests before they can be considered at the next level. Once such relationships are established, they must be analyzed on a higher level to discover the meaning of the associations or correlations. In MacIver's (1942) words, "We must here assay the task of projecting ourselves by sympathetic reconstruction into the situation as it is assessed by others." This requires an examination of "the dispositions, avowals, confessions, justifications, and testimonies offered by agents, participants, or witnesses" giving their answers or interpretations about motivation and meaning.

The logic of this relationship can also be clearly grasped in Alfred Schutz's (1967) phenomenological approach to sociological analysis. In terms of Schutz's framework, verification is a test of "causal adequacy," while validation is an inquiry into the "adequacy of meaning." As a problem of understanding, the second level, concerned with meaning, entails a logical shift from causal explanation to the interpretation of the situation in which these causal relationships occur. One does not typically speak of testing such interpretive judgments, but rather of providing good reasons for or against (their) applications or validity in a particular context or set of circumstances (Gunnell, 1968: 187).

The interpretivist perspective in social science is grounded in the theories of social phenomenology, symbolic interactionism, and ethnomethodology. Whereas the empirical approach conceptualizes individuals as abstract behavioral objects for the testing of hypotheses about causal linkages, interpretive approaches treat individuals as subjective agents acting in social situations in pursuit of their goals and objectives (Fischer, 1980). For interpretive social science, social action is "rule-governed." The social scientist explores the ways in which social actions can be seen to fall under the applicable social rules that are available to the members of society. In this sense, an interpretation of a social or political decision can be likened to an explanation governed by social rules. The constitution of action is thus examined through the logical rules employed by the members of the social system trying to make sense of the interactions that surround or include them (Walsh, 1972: 30). We can turn at this point to a more detailed examination of each question.

## SOCIAL RELEVANCE

Is a program's objective relevant to the problem situation? The answer to this question requires bringing together a normative criterion and the facts of the situation. Indeed, the relationship of these two elements determines the nature and existence of a problem situation. A "problem," in this respect, is understood to exist when there is a gap between a normative standard and a perception of an existing or expected situation. In every "problem," as Hoppe and Peterse (1993) explain, two heterogenous elements are linked to each other: normative criteria (objectives, standards, rules, etc.) and empirical situations or conditions. As such, a "problem" is not a given fact, not something from the outside world; rather it is a social construct. Norms, principles, and values are valuations attributed by people to objects or relations. People either do or do not value a particular government objective; they attach more or less value to it. The importance of an objective is thus subjective (or inter-subjective).

The point applies as well to social situations, either existing or expected. Human perceptions of events and situations, as social psychology teaches, are determined by concepts and frameworks of our own construction. Reality, in short, is seen through colored lenses (a point which applies to scientific as well as everyday perceptions). That is, what we "see" is socially constructed from a particular point of view. In other words, the perceptions of existing and ex-pected situations are just as much a "social construct" as are the normative standards by which we judge those situations (Box 4.1).

We say, then, that a policy problem involves (1) a gap between a stan-dard and a situation, and (2) that neither the standard nor the situation, and hence the gap, is an objective datum exterior to ourselves (Hoppe and Peterse, 1993). On the contrary, both of these social constructs are based upon individ-ual or human social actions. We can, in this respect, only say that there are

---

## BOX 4.1
## The Logic of the Situation

A number of social scientists have evaluated the concept of the "logic of the situation" to a primary status in social science explanation. According to I.C. Jarvie (1972:4), the basic explanatory model of the social sciences is situational. He outlines the concept this way:

1. A man, for purposes of the social sciences, can be viewed as in pursuit of certain goals or aims, within a framework of natural, psychological, and eth-ical circumstances.
2. These circumstances constitute both means of achieving his aims and con-straints on that achievement.
3. A man's conscious or unconscious appraisal of how he can achieve aims within these circumstances can be called sorting out the logic of the situation he is in (or his situational logic).
4. [It is called] "logic" because he trie[s] to find out the best and most effective means, within the situation, to realize his aims. There is *no* suggestion that there exists some perfect scrutiny of the situation which yields a uniquely ef-fective move: most often several moves are indicated, although it is unlikely the actor will be emotionally or morally indifferent to them.
5. The actor's ideas are part of his situation in a complicated way. It is assumed that the situation, if objectively appraised, should favor certain means which are more effective than others and that the measure of rationality consists in the success in approaching such an objective appraisal.

standards which command more or less consensus; and that there are situations about which there are greater or lesser amounts of certain knowledge.

Given this understanding of a problematic situation, the relevance of a program objective can be established through both an appeal to the facts of the situation and the more general (or higher) goal from which the objective at issue has been reduced. The appeal to higher goals is essentially an exercise in logic. It entails a logical demonstration that the objective under investigation actually meets the requirements of the higher criterion. According to the principles of normative logic, it is said that the objective falls within the range or scope of the higher goal. In terms of the Head Start program, this involved an appeal to a criterion concerned with society, namely to ready children for entrance into society. The appeal could be satisfied by showing that the educational principle concerned with preparing children for entrance into society included in its range of application curricula that were designed around socially meaningful experiences.

With regard to the facts of the situation, the focus is on the empirical context from which the program variables are selected and measured. Generally descriptive in nature, the task of empirically exploring the relevance of the situation can best be discussed in the next section concerned with situational circumstances. Here it is enough to say that the evaluator must establish the facts to which the objective is purportedly addressed.

Finally, it should be noted that the discussion of the socially constructed nature of public problems is one of the basic issues in politics and policy.[1] Indeed, as writers such as Bachrach and Baratz (1963) have shown, the conflict over problem definition is one of the most crucial aspects of any political struggle. As definitions become fixed in the decision processes of political institutions, they serve to determine which factual propositions are admissible and which goals are acceptable.[2] From this standpoint, political conflict in public discourse is very often about incompatible definitions of particular problem situations (Schneider and Ingram, 1993; Gusfield, 1981). The point is quite relevant to policy evaluation. Much of the discussion of the failure of policy evaluation to produce "usable knowledge" has focused on its limited relevance to the situation as defined by the relevant stakeholders (Fischer, 1980; Dryzek, 1982).

## SITUATIONAL CIRCUMSTANCES

The second concern of validation focuses on identifying exceptions to a given situation. In such discourse, those who oppose a particular program objective might typically argue that "the objective is in general a good one, but not in this situation." The case for making an exception to an objective under specific circumstances must be based on evidence showing that it is better to permit an exception to the objective than to fulfill it. A circumstantial exception requires showing that the objective under judgment is applied to a situation in which it leads to secondary or unexpected consequences that offset—qualify, compromise, or perhaps even negate—the beneficial outcomes.[3] Such consequences can result from either conflict between competing criteria, specific empirical dimensions of the situation, or both.

Basic, then, to such a deduction is the empirical description and definition of the particular facts of the situation. In the case of the Head Start education program, for example, this concern was frequently invoked by many as the critical point in the public discussion and debate. Numerous leaders of the black and Hispanic communities, it will be recalled, raised criticisms about the propriety of imposing educational programs based on middle-class standards on the disadvantaged children of the lower classes. The test instruments utilized in the study, it was pointed out, were statistically standardized on middle-class children with social and educational experiences very different from less advantaged minority children. Therefore, the conclusion that no significant learning occurred could only be the result of the use of objectives with which lower-class children were less familiar. If measured in terms of objectives derived from the children's own cultural experiences, the program outcomes might well show substantial progress.[4] In fact, this later proved to be the case.

Underlying this line of argument was the concept of the culture of poverty. The question was whether or not the ghetto children enrolled in the Head Start program lived under social circumstances—broken families, lack of achievement motivation, slothfulness, etc.—that required an exception be made to the use of standardized educational tests. In short, the issue turned on the question of how to define the situation of the program participants.

The second question of validation, then, involves determining what constitutes a good reason for inferring conclusions entitled by particular circumstances. In practical terms, this involves assembling both the arguments for and against specific programmatic objectives and the empirical facts of the situation and subjecting them to the logical rules of reason. The most basic objective is to decide whether or not there is anything about the factual circumstances themselves which requires that an exception be made to the application or use of the criterion.

## CONFLICTING OBJECTIVES

The third question of validation directs attention to the problem of conflicting objectives. Objectives are in conflict with one another when an aspect of one that is judged to be bad is considered to be good by the other. To resolve such a conflict it is necessary to determine which of the objectives takes precedence, a process involving a logical appeal to higher-order criteria.

Whether one or another objective is better is established by ranking them according to a higher standard or goal. When one objective is determined to take precedence over the others, it can be said that the first one has a "higher" claim or establishes a "heavier obligation."[5] Furthermore, it is possible to have criteria beyond this criterion that can be appealed to for the validation of this third criterion itself.

The probe of conflicting objectives, it will be recalled, was a basic issue in the case of Head Start. Those who sought to justify socially relevant experiences over standardized knowledge and academic skills generally appealed to the principle of human equality; those who supported academic tests pointed to long-run societal benefits to be gained from the principle of advance through merit. At this point in the evaluation, however, it is most likely that the two discussants will have reached their highest standards and will no longer have criteria to which they can appeal. Further progress in the dialogue can be made only by shifting to vindication, the next level of evaluation.

In the instance of conflicting criteria, the evaluator's task is to explicate logically the objective that fulfills the appropriate requirement of a higher-level goal on which the conflicting parties agree. The policy evaluator must, in short, attempt to show that a particular claim is normatively acceptable to the higher goals or principles of the full range of relevant political interests or stakeholders.[6]

There is, of course, no guarantee that the evaluator can find a higher level goal or principle capable of forging such a consensus. In the search for agreement it may be the case that policy discourse has to be pursued to an even higher, more abstract level of criteria. But in validation the pursuit is not limitless. It is bound by the particular normative policy beliefs from which the program objectives and policy goals are drawn. If a disputant comes to a point at which no higher criterion can be found—that is, finds him- or herself arguing that he or she has no higher principle—the disputant has reached the highest value/goal principle in his or her normative political or policy belief system. At this point, there is no possibility of resolving a dispute at the level of validation. If the parties are committed to pursue the discourse further, they must move to the level of vindication. Vindication, involving a fundamental shift from first- to second-order evaluative discourse, requires that the disputants step outside of their normative situation and illustrate empirically the instrumental or contributive value of their highest level policy goals for the social system as a whole.

## SITUATIONAL VALIDATION AND QUALITATIVE RESEARCH

While validation, like the other four levels of evaluation, does not prescribe hard and fast methodological rules and criteria, it tends to draw on the interpretive frameworks of qualitative analysis. This results directly from the nature of the processes of problem identification and definition themselves. These processes, as we have seen, can only be understood as socially constructed phenomena. Both the normative standards brought to bear on an evaluation, as well as the understanding of the situation to which they are applied, are grounded in the subjective perspectives of the actors involved. For this reason, the concerns of validation are theoretically informed by the "phenomenological" approach to social research.

---

## BOX 4.2
## Social Science and Situational Analysis

Sir Karl Popper, the famous philosopher well-known for his studies of the scientific method, elevated the concept of situational analysis to major status in history and the social sciences. In particular, Popper sought to establish the objective character of situational analysis. Unlike those who have viewed the process of subjectively interpreting a situation (*Verstehen*) as a psychologically intuitive—sympathetic and emotional—reconstruction of an original experience, Popper conceived the process as a metatheoretical attempt to reconstruct an actor's reasoning. As he described it, "Being on a level different from the [actor's] reasoning, it does not re-enact it, but tries to produce an idealized and reasoned reconstruction of it" (Popper, 1972:188). *Verstehen,* as metatheory, thus addresses the decisive or essential aspects of the social actor's problem situation. To the degree that the social scientist is successful in grappling with this metaproblem, he or she understands the situation.

In Popper's (1976:102) words, the historian or social scientist "is not to re-enact the past experiences, but to marshal objective arguments for or against his conjectural situational analysis." Objective understanding of the situation essentially involves determining whether the social or political action was "objectively appropriate to the situation." Social actors are thus people with intentions or motives whose situations can be elucidated by reference to the objective intentions they pursue. Holding specific ideas, information, and goals, an actor must be characterized as attempting to achieve ends or purposes within the particular circumstances of a social situation, which establishes both potentials and limits. Such explanatory characterizations are rational, theoretical constructions. As Popper (1976:103) said, "They can possess considerable truth content and they can, in the strictly logical sense, be good approximations to the truth, and better than certain testable explanations." For the method of situational analysis, the logical approximation is an indispensable explanatory concept. The important point is that such explanatory approximations are capable of improvement through empirical criticism.

Phenomenological or interpretive social research is designed to get inside the social actor's situation and to understand the actor's own subjective interpretations of the situation (Box 4.2). Interpretive social science is concerned with the social actor's cognitive perception of reality; its task is to explicate empirically the actor's experientially based subjective framework which determines his or her problem definitions and the social actions based on them. Social actors interpret their experiences and observations, define the situations they are in, identify the problems they face, or make plans for actions by consulting their existing store of experience and knowledge. The orientation, as shown by Fischer (1980), corresponds closely to the questions of program relevance, circumstances of the situation, and the interplay of competing objectives based on multiple realities.

### Qualitative Methods

The qualitative methods of an interpretive approach typically entail a less structured form of analysis, relying heavily on direct observations, localized surveys, secondary documents, case studies, detailed descriptions, field notes, and in-depth personal interviews. Basic to the fields of applied anthropology, sociology, and psychology, such "naturalistic" methods have only more recently been employed in the study of public policy. During this time, however, some of qualitative research's staunchest enthusiasts have launched a frontal attack on the dominance of standard empirical methods in program evaluation. Advocates of "naturalistic research" such as Guba and Lincoln (1981; 1987) argue that even the empirical verification of program outcomes should be measured through qualitative methods, rather than experimental and quasi-experimental research methods.

In the discourse of policy validation, qualitative methods can be useful "tools" that help evaluators uncover the operative definitions of the situation, describe the ways in which policy goals and program objectives fall under the applicable social rules that are available to the members of society, and to understand the institutional support and opposition to the imposition of specific criteria (Schneider and Ingram, 1993). They provide verbal descriptions and explanations rather than quantitative measurement and statistical analysis. Specifically, such approaches require evaluators to seek information in "field settings" and to obtain the opinions of stakeholders involved with the public policy under consideration (Walsh, 1972: 30). It is assumed that the relevance of program objectives and policy goals can be interpreted from the description of circumstances provided by the comments and actions of stakeholders, as well as various types of secondary documents (Stewart, 1984). The task is to gain "empathetic" understanding based on the subjective experiences of stakeholders and to comprehend how perceptions and behaviors help to define public problems and lead to the support of particular policy positions.

Interpretative inquiry does not follow an exacting step-by-step format as is the case with experimentation and cost-benefit analysis. Instead, the process is greatly dependent on the abilities of an evaluator to condense large amounts of written information into a meaningful form, to observe special quirks of human behavior, and to ask significant questions.[7] The more fluid nature of the qualitative approach does not mean, however, that this research is nonsystematic. Indeed, it is crucial for the issues of validity and reliability to try to picture the empirical social world as it actually exists to those under investigation, rather than as the evaluator imagines it to be (Patton, 1987). In this regard, the evaluator has to work with stakeholders to design an evaluation that includes any and all data that will help shed light on important questions, given constraints of time and resources.

The work of Michael Patton (1975) has been especially important in opening the way to qualitative policy evaluation. For Patton, policy evaluation methodology must focus on "the *meaning* of human behavior, the context of social action...and the connection between subjective states and behavior." According to him, such an evaluation paradigm must rely on field techniques such as participant observation, in-depth interviewing, detailed descriptions, and qualitative field notes.[8] Where the scientific method focuses on the generalizable event, Patton's paradigm includes the unique situation or event. Where science stresses objectivity and reliability, he emphasizes subjectivity and validity. To further illustrate the nature of such subjective data collection, we conclude this section with some brief comments on the role of the case study, direct observation, and in-person interviews.

### Case Studies

The case study is most typically the structural form of a qualitative or interpretive investigation. Most fundamentally, it is a means by which a particular policy objective and the specific circumstances of its implementation can be examined and documented in fine detail, especially over time. Many policy evaluators trained in economics and statistics have rejected the case study method as failing to meet the rigorous tests of empirical methodologies. However, its ability to get inside of a situation and to grasp its dynamics on its own terms can evocatively facilitate understanding. Case studies have in fact contributed much to our knowledge about the processes of policy formulation and evaluation (Yin, 1984). Indeed, one writer asserts that "probably no evaluation methodology has greater strengths than the case study" (Starling, 1989).

The use of a case study to explore how a program affects a policy situation has more in common with the fictive arts and history than the natural or empirical social science. In a sense, the evaluator is telling a story about what has happened or will happen in a situation as a program develops from formulation through implementation. It is entirely appropriate, therefore, for an evaluator to enhance a case study with use of metaphors, analogies, symbolism (Stone, 1988). In examining a program, the evaluator draws on all sorts of information, including secondary data, interviews, observations, and the evaluator's own experience and approach to organizing ideas.

Case studies do not produce definitive answers. Rather, the goal of the case study is to provide a "fine-grained picture of the problem, capturing details and subtleties that slip through the net of the statistician" (Hexter, 1971). Thus such studies produce an enrichment of imagination that promotes a broad understanding of how policies affect society. In short, they help us to get inside the situation.

### Direct Observation

Observation is the most direct approach available for collecting information about social behavior in natural contexts. It may take a passive form in which the evaluator merely looks at occurrences and behaviors without any explicit personal involvement; it can also involve a more active role in which the evaluator becomes a participant in the social setting under observation. Whether passive or active participation is employed, the objective is to observe the incidence of certain types of events and behaviors during distinct periods of time in a real context. This might involve the observation of meetings, sidewalk activities, factory work, classroom participation, or contacts with government officials. To increase the reliability of observational evidence, it is common to have more than one evaluator making observations. It is also important for the evaluator to be trained to minimize bias in the information-gathering process.

Observation, for example, has been extensively employed as a way to evaluate the relevance of policies to ameliorate problems unique to urban settings. Participatory observation was the primary methodology used to describe urban problems, for instance, in both Herbert Gans' *The Urban Villagers* (1982) and William H Whyte's *City: Rediscovering the Center* (1988). The Whyte book is a good illustration of how observation can be used to assess the relevance of urban development policy goals (which we take up as an illustration in the next section). In one part of the study, Whyte and his research team observed how long and under what circumstances people stood and talked to each other on the street in New York City. He found that the longest encounters took place on the busiest street corners, and that these encounters seemed to subsequently generate more pedestrian traffic and friendly interactions, as well as the purchase of goods from street vendors and in nearby stores. From this and other similar data, Whyte concluded that a community is more likely to produce greater economic productivity (a typical goal of urban development) if it encourages pedestrian traffic rather than removing people from streets by putting them in overhead skyways (such as in Minneapolis) or in underground concourses (such as in Montreal or Houston).

### In-Person Interviews

Another important approach for collecting information about the logic of a policy situation and the applicability of particular program goals is an in-person interview. Interviewing is designed to tap the cognitive realities of those knowledgeable about the situation, in particular the "policy stakeholders." The purpose is to systematically explicate various definitions of problems and to identify the social and political frameworks which provide the rules and standards for actions (Putt and Springer, 1989).

The assumption is that those involved with a public policy, both collectively and individually, have unique "experiences" and "ideas" that lead them to focus on social situations in different ways, thereby reading (or accounting for) what is ostensibly the same situation differently. It is further assumed that a variety of policy perspectives exist in most areas, each refracted from the angle of its own subjectively experienced everyday world, each anchored in its own expectations, purposes, and motives. Interviews attempt to draw out these perspectives, to understand how people interpret their experiences and observations, define the situations they are in, identify the problems they face, and formulate plans for action.

In-person interviews may be either open-ended or close-ended. In an open-ended interview, the evaluator asks people about facts and opinions in a free-flowing, conversational manner that may differ in scope and content from one interview to another. This method is advantageous for discovering issues that might otherwise be missed by the evaluator's own frame of reference. In the close-ended interview the evaluator asks all stakeholders a standard list of questions to obtain a fixed set of responses. This permits a more reliable comparison of information gained from interviews with diverse stakeholders.

A major issue for evaluators is who to interview and how many interviews to conduct. While it might be useful to interview all people involved with a policy problem, in many instances this is impractical, too costly, and unnecessary for obtaining pertinent knowledge. It is more common to interview a sample of stakeholders and other interest groups who are as close as possible to the population in question. In a given policy area, an evaluator might seek to gain a variety of perspectives by interviewing program clients; managerial and street-level agency personnel; federal, state, or local policymakers; representatives of business groups; interest group leaders and members; and lobbyists. In some policy areas, it may also be appropriate to focus exclusively on a particular group of stakeholders. For example, Patton (1987:52) has suggested that if the purpose of a program is to reach lower socioeconomic groups, one may want to do an in-depth study of the needs, interests, and incentives of a small number of carefully selected poor families.

To validate program objectives, interviews seek to bring out the shared stories, images, and myths that are the substance of the discourse among stakeholders (Best, 1989; Gusfield, 1981). In this regard, in-person interviews are particularly useful for understanding the situational relevance of policy goals and program objectives. Questions might be asked about the importance of different policy problems, subjective experiences in the problem area, the level of involvement with existing programs, and beliefs about the appropriate way to resolve various problems.

Finally, qualitative research must confront the problem of bias. Evaluators, in short, must be careful not to unconsciously allow their own values and opinions to distort the analysis. They must guard against selectively examining only one goal while ignoring other competing goals. Second, the evaluator must not allow his or her own views to shape or be shaped by those being observed or interviewed. It is a common tendency for people in social settings, including researchers and the subjects of research, to mutually adapt to the opinions and beliefs of each other. Finally, for those evaluators working in bureaucracies, either public or private, there may be latent or direct pressures to skew analysis in such a way as to validate those goals and objectives that enhance organizational survival, if not growth and expansion.

Dealing with bias in evaluation is, to be sure, problematic. First, there is no such thing as a completely objective or "value-free" method in the social sciences, and second, no one can expect evaluators to divorce themselves altogether from their own subjective leanings. What, then, is the answer? Many ethicists argue that the most we can hope for is that researchers will recognize their own inclinations, the biases of their methodologies, the demands of their organizations, and the effects of these factors on their research. As Rosemarie Tong (1987:210) puts it: "To know the good may not be to do good, but it certainly takes a person some distance in the right direction."

By way of closing, this chapter has described the logic of situational validation and some of the methods that can be brought into play to help justify programmatic objectives. While clearly less exact in methodological terms than verification, validation is seen nonetheless to be every bit as essential to the justification of a policy judgment. As an illustration of the validation of policy goals and objectives, the next chapter examines the effort to validate program objectives of New York City's Times Square Redevelopment Project.

READINGS

Joel Best, ed. 1989. *Images of Issues: Typifying Contemporary Social Problems*. New York: Aldine De Gruyter.

Michael Quinn Patton. 1987. How to Use Qualitative Methods in Evaluation. Newbury Park, CA: Sage.

Egon Guba and Yvonna Lincoln. 1989. *Fourth Generation Evaluation*. Newbury Park, CA: Sage.

Robert K. Yin. 1984. *Case Study Research: Design and Methods*. Newbury Park, CA: Sage.

Paul Filmer et al. 1972. *New Directions in Sociological Theory*. Cambridge, MA: M.I.T. Press.

David Schuman. 1982. *Policy Analysis, Education, and Everyday Life: An Empirical Evaluation*. Lexington, MA: Health.

## 5    Contesting the Times Square Redevelopment Study: Problem Definition and the Politics of Criteria

In this chapter policy validation is illustrated with a case study concerned with the redevelopment of New York City's famous Times Square District. Focusing on the policy arguments that emerged with the appearance of a major redevelopment study, the emphasis is on the political struggle that ensued over the proposed use of specific commercial objectives to guide the redevelopment project. The conflicting views about the appropriateness of the criteria are presented to show the relevance of three kinds of questions that come into play in validation: Is the program objective relevant to the situation? Is there anything about the situation that suggests an exception be made to the objective? Are there conflicting objectives of equal importance? We introduce the case with a brief history of the Times Square area.

### THE TIMES SQUARE DISTRICT

Times Square is a square block district in the mid-Manhattan area of New York City (see figure 5.1). The district begins at Broadway on Forty-Second Street, crosses Seventh Avenue, and ends on Eighth Avenue. In the center island between Broadway and Seventh Avenue sits the One Times Square building, the former home of the New York Times. The building is known for the famous news ticker tape that wraps around its exterior and as the place where thousands gather on New Year's Eve to celebrate the incoming year. In the area on Forty-Second Street between Seventh and Eighth Avenues are various fast-food restaurants and several sexually oriented establishments, including theaters and peep shows. The area just east of Times Square primarily houses commercial and retail businesses. Much farther east is the Graduate Center of the City University of New York, and the New York Public Library. North of the Times Square District are the offices of the New York Times, fa-

83

**Figure 5.1:** Forty-Second Street Development Project: Project Area and Secondary Impact Areas

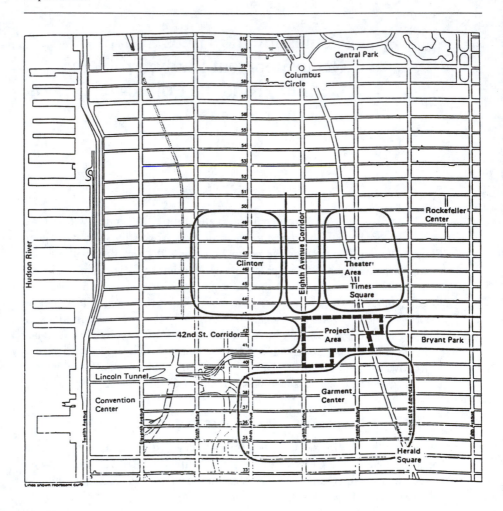

mous Broadway theaters, and movie houses that show major motion pictures. To the south are buildings housing the garment industry, a mix of businesses that design, produce, and show clothes for wholesale distribution. West of the Times Square District is the Port Authority Bus Terminal, small off-Broadway theaters, churches, and residential apartments. A major residential area, referred to as the Clinton District, is slightly northwest of Times Square; it is composed of mostly low- and middle-income residents.

In the late 1800s, Times Square was already a vital part of Manhattan's commercial and entertainment world. It was a major public transportation terminus, home to the carriage manufacturing industry, and the center for entertainment and culture. Between 1889 and 1920 the Forty-Second Street area contained thirteen theaters featuring live performances of the leading actors and actresses of the time. Constructed with elaborate edifices often resembling the classic opera houses of Europe, the theaters were also adjacent to many of the most fashionable hotels in the city, such as the Knickerbocker and the Astor. These hotels housed prestigious nightclubs, restaurants, and roof gardens. All of these entertainment activities were accessible to the city as a whole through an elaborate transportation system of subways, elevated trains, and trolleys. Unquestionably, the area represented the center of both high and popular culture in turn-of-the-century New York (Taylor, 1992).

The financial success of Times Square's legitimate theaters of the early 1900s was in no small part due to the unique combination of cabarets, restaurants, and nightclubs that surrounded them (New York Urban Development Corp., 1981). With the advent of Prohibition in the 1920s, however, many of these accessory enterprises were driven out of business. As a result, theater crowds diminished and many theaters were themselves forced to close. At the same time, new businesses oriented toward a different clientele began to compete for the available space. Taking advantage of the large flow of people through the area from early morning to late evening, due in particular to Forty-Second Street's twenty-four-hour transit system, an array of entertainment arcades, silent picture movie houses, and vaudeville and burlesque houses emerged on the scene (establishments which, unlike the traditional theaters, were not limited to one or two performances a day). By the Depression of the 1930s, Times Square was filled with high-turnover businesses that brought a "honky-tonk" atmosphere to the area (Friedman, 1986).

During and after World War II, the seamy side of Times Square was even further transformed into a neon bazaar of cheap goods and bawdy adventures. The dance halls and burlesque houses of the 1930s, after having given way to souvenir shops and shooting galleries, were converted to penny arcades and cheap auction houses. Moreover, as the rapid success of television in the 1950s led to the closing of neighborhood film theaters, the low-budget movie houses on Forty-Second Street began to feature sex, violence, and class "B" action films. Many of the remaining legitimate theaters moved to the blocks just north of Times Square, while those left behind were converted into twenty-four-hour movie houses featuring graphic sex and violence. Dance halls, cut-rate liquor shops, sidewalk barkers, and pornographic bookstores proliferated. Street crime became a serious problem, and the area was widely perceived as a "combat zone." This was especially so during the war, when U.S. Military Police waged a losing battle to keep order among the thousands of soldiers who flocked to Forty-Second Street in search of "girls and kicks" (Kornblum and Boggs, 1985:17; Kornblum, 1979).

By the late 1950s and early 1960s, Forty-Second Street was truly home to the unusual, the weird, and the outlandish. Prostitution ran rampant, bright neon lights flashed the titles of the latest pornographic movies, and grotesque characters lingered in the front of rundown buildings, often waiting for their next heroin "fix." Not only had the buildings in the area fallen into serious disrepair, the people themselves increasingly appeared to be in want of better times. The novelist Jack Kerouac coined the term "beatnik" to describe the men who shuffled around Times Square with their hands in their pockets "looking beat." Although city administrations continued to sponsor cleanup campaigns periodically, new construction was nonexistent and vacancy rates soared.

By the 1970s, Times Square's bright lights fully illuminated a dilapidated run-down area. But, curiously enough, even with the litter and debris—human as well as physical—Times Square remained *the* place for a large cross section of the City's population to gather in large numbers. It was, and still is, the most famous place for thousands of New Yorkers—along with a fascinated nation of television viewers—to toast the coming of each New Year. Indeed, the dropping of the ball from the Times Square Tower has come to symbolize an important part of the American experience—an event on a par with Macy's famous Thanksgiving Day parades, Wall Street ticker-tape parades, and other New York happenings.

Times Square continued both to deteriorate and to flourish in the late 1970s and early 1980s. On the one hand, tourists and thrill-seekers continued to flock to Forty-Second Street, and the existing entertainment and amusement parlors on the street flourished commercially. In 1981, these establishments included thirteen movie theaters between Seventh and Eighth avenues alone showing the latest hardcore pornographic films and violent action movies, as well as eighteen adult peepshows, a live sex show, a topless bar, and a massage parlor. If these factors can be positively judged as the flourishing side of Times Square, on the negative side urban blight and crime—particularly drug-related felonies—continued to rise significantly. The human reality of the situation was captured in this less than flattering portrait:

> At most times of the day and night commuters, theatergoers, and visitors are confronted by aggressive street hustlers, pimps and panhandlers, drug dealers

and addicts who threaten assault, loiter in subway entrances and obstruct pedestrian traffic. Passersby and tourists face filthy, litter-strewn, sleazy advertisements for sex-related businesses, posters advertising action movies, and window displays of knives and blackjacks. (New York Urban Development Corp., 1981: 15)

In the late 1970s and early 1980s powerful economic and political groups began to think seriously about what to do with the area. Although Times Square had clearly served many different functions, and had come to mean very different things to a large number of people, these reform groups saw the problem in rather narrow terms; they wanted to address the problems of crime and economic blight. In particular, they focused on commercial decline, a perspective thoroughly consistent with their own interests and beliefs. In the next section we examine the emergence of this commercial interpretation of Times Square's problems and the reform movement to which it gave rise.

### THE NEED TO DO SOMETHING: TIMES SQUARE AS A COMMERCIAL PROBLEM

Because of its worldwide notoriety, combined with the presence of the nearby Broadway theaters, Times Square attracts large amounts of money from the city's tourists. Nobody can visit New York without at least having a look at Times Square. The fear that the area might become too seedy and dangerous for tourists, as well as the fact that crime was already spreading to both the theater blocks and the Clinton residential area, gave rise to a serious commitment to clean up the area in the 1970s (Fainstein, 1987).

The first concrete proposal to change Times Square came in 1974 from the newly elected mayor, Edward I. Koch. Addressing many of the immediate problems of the area, Mayor Koch announced an "Action Plan" intended indirectly to foster a climate of economic renewal through increased public services in the area. The plan called for increased police patrols, added sanitation crews, more building inspections, and stricter zoning regulations (New York Urban Development Corp., 1981). Because of the arrival of New York City's major fiscal crisis in 1976, however, the plan never got off the ground. The impending bankruptcy of the city simply shifted attention to other pressing matters.

With the arrival of better times in the early 1980s, concern for Times Square moved again to the front burner of city politics. This time the issue was much more directly concentrated on the possibilities of reaping economic benefits from the area. Most important, pressures to capitalize on the commercial potential of the area came from an alignment of real estate developers, construction companies, and investors in search of profits. As the amount of space for building in Manhattan shrank, developers searched out new areas in the city to support the city's phenomenal rate of building construction. Because of the sheer amount of underutilized and cheap space, the Forty-Second Street area caught the attention of these groups. Times Square, in short, was ripe for commercial redevelopment. Many developers and the construction industry saw it as a virtual gold mine.

In addition to the direct pressures of the developers, other factors influenced the acceptance of a commercial interpretation of the problem. Of particular importance to urban planners, governmental officials, and academic research centers was the overall success of various commercially oriented urban renewal projects in numerous American cities during the 1960s and 1970s, including New York itself. Introduced mainly as a response to the urban crisis of the period, a variety of urban renewal projects had proven quite successful. In large part, they were motivated by a specific set of economically oriented policy beliefs: in particular, the belief that the business revitalization in urban centers would enhance through a "multiplier effect" the overall economy of the larger metropolitan area. Construction of new and appealing facilities were seen to add economic value to the local economy through the attraction of new businesses which, in turn, increased tax receipts. The basic assumption was that directing investment and employment to those areas of the city with poor economic performance would generate a wide range of benefits to the city as a whole.[1]

A third reason for this commercial conception of economic development had to do with the role of the powerful and experienced New York State redevelopment corporation, the Urban Development Corporation (UDC). A quasi-independent public authority designed to simultaneously operate like a government agency and like a private corporation, the UDC is governed by a board appointed from the business and professional communities. Formally, it is mandated to operate in the public interest, free from the stymieing effects of public pressure, political compromise, and bureaucratic red tape that typically thwart other development agencies. At the same time, however, UDC is structured to function as a self-supporting public business, which to its critics is a serious flaw in the corporation's mandate. Indeed, experience has often shown that the two requirements can constitute a contradictory set of goals which are quite difficult to fulfill simultaneously. Typically, the UDC has sought to bridge the tension between these two goals by proffering an economically oriented conception of the public interest. As a policy belief, the orientation is in significant part a product of the capitalist economic philosophy of its business-oriented board of directors and the practicalities that confront the corporation's managers in their efforts to operate as a self-supporting enterprise.

Economic redevelopment, moreover, is in fact what the UDC is best equipped to do. It brings powerful economic incentives and fiscal tools to the task of stimulating economic redevelopment. For example, it is permitted to issue tax-exempt municipal bonds, as well as receive Urban Development Action Grants (UDAG) from the federal government. In addition, it has the power of eminent domain [the power to condemn and take over privately owned property]; it is exempted from property taxation; it has the freedom to determine its own personnel policies, and the ability to establish subsidiary corporations structured to function like private sector organizations. Employing these powers, the corporation was successful in developing other areas within New York, such as the large housing complex built on Roosevelt Island in the East River. These advantages made UDC the logical choice for many of the supporters of the Times Square project (Brilliant, 1975). Large numbers of business and professional leaders saw it to represent the entrepreneurial force required to initiate and manage large-scale commercial redevelopment and urban renewal projects (Schumaker, Bolland, and Feiock, 1986).

With the support of New York Governor Mario Cuomo, Mayor Koch, and influential city business leaders, responsibility for improving Times Square was turned over to the UDC. This move signaled a major step in the effort to transform Times Square. Exercising its powers to condemn real property, to issue tax exempt and nontaxable bonds, to offer incentives to developers, and to override local zoning regulations, the UDC was to wage a full-scale attack on Times Square's problems (Brilliant, 1975).

## COMMERCIAL REDEVELOPMENT: THE PLAN AND ITS EVALUATION

Working with the city's planning agencies and private developers, the UDC designed a major plan that advanced large-scale commercial development as the primary goal of its economic redevelopment effort. Although the plan addressed a range of concerns, in particular preserving the Broadway theaters and renovating public facilities, commercial development was principally defined as the need to develop the area's potential for commercial office space. The plan was modified somewhat as it moved through a series of public discussions, but its basic contours remained intact in the final version. What follows is an outline of the fundamental aspects of the commercial redevelopment plan as it was presented to the public in 1981.

The first and most fundamental step of the plan was the formal declaration of Times Square as a "blighted area." Such designation empowered the UDC to purchase seventy parcels of land within the project area through its power of eminent domain. This was to be followed by the leasing of these parcels to private developers. Most important, the leasing arrangement required the private developers to design and construct the actual physical project. To encourage the interest and participation of the private sector, the developers were generously absolved from paying property taxes in the initial years of the project, provided with various forms of tax abatements, and exempted from city planning and zoning regulations (Bingham, 1985).

The plan ultimately assembled by the UDC and the participating developers represented a massive undertaking. The existing structures on the four corners of Times Square would be replaced with four major office buildings, totaling more than four million square feet. The heights of the buildings would be twenty-nine, thirty-seven, forty-nine, and fifty-six stories. On two of the corners of Eighth Avenue were to be constructed a 2.4-million-square-foot wholesale mart and a 550-room hotel. The large size of these commercial developments was required, according to the UDC, to generate extra funds for the revitalization of the theaters in the area, as well as to upgrade public facilities. Nine of the theaters on Forty-Second Street between Seventh and Eighth Avenues would be renovated and reconverted into legitimate theaters, and the Times Square subway station, still the major terminus in the area, would be completely overhauled. Finally, the plan called for large signs and bright neon lights to be placed on the new Time Square buildings to retain the flashy "entertainment" character of the area.

Commercial development, according to UDC planners, would mean more than new economic activity in the area. The stimulation of commercial activities would also mean an elimination of physical decay and social blight; the new buildings and the upgrading of the public facilities in the area, especially the subway station, would dramatically change the physical face of the area; the new influx of office workers in the area and the revitalization of the entertainment industry would bring a new class of people into the area; and more police protection made possible through new tax revenues would drive away the criminal element. Moreover, the restoration of the area as a whole would have a positive influence on the adjacent communities (Bingham, 1985).

Given the scope of the project and its potential impact on the community, the evaluation of the plan generated a significant public dispute. A wide variety of groups had their own ideas about what caused the problems plaguing Times Square, as well as what the proper objectives of the development should be. The primary vehicle that gave vent to this ensuing political struggle over policy goals and development criteria was the UDC's environmental impact study (EIS). We thus turn to EIS's evaluation of the Times Square Redevelopment Project and the political debate that it unleashed.

PROJECT EVALUATION: THE ENVIRONMENTAL IMPACT
STUDY

During the early 1980s the UDC undertook an Environmen-
tal Impact Study to examine the positive benefits and negative consequences
of its proposed plan. Mandated by various federal and state laws, EI studies are
typically required for all large-scale projects that threaten to disrupt environmental quality. An important evaluation methodology since the 1970s, the objective of an EIS is the prediction of future changes in environmental quality
due to the introduction of a major technology or development project, as well
as the valuation of these changes. In particular, an EIS is designed to provide
decision makers with guidance for making informed trade-offs among conflicting aspects of environmental quality, and other social objectives (Hyman
and Stiefel, 1988). In this respect, environmental quality is understood to encompass both the functional and aesthetic attributes of systems that sustain
and enrich human life.

In its EIS, UDC employed a wide range of methods to collect information about the problems in Times Square and to estimate the impacts of the
commercial redevelopment objective. Secondary statistical data was collected
on such things as building occupancies, floor space uses, vacant lands, zoning,
traffic volumes, building regulations, median rents, transportation uses, water
uses, employment, pollution, and criminal activities. In-person interviews
were also conducted to assess why pedestrians were in Times Square, to evaluate why people were willing to shop and work in the area, and to assess their
perceptions of crime in the area. Methods of participatory observation were
utilized to assess criminal activity and patterns of loitering in the area.

Upon completion of its research, the UDC developed a draft of the EIS
study. Emphasizing the advantages of the comprehensive plan to redevelop the
District commercially, the report was first presented to the public for comments in 1981. Between 1982 and 1984 the draft went through continual modifications, was litigated in the courts between 1985 and 1989, and was
scheduled for implementation during the 1990s. Throughout the period, the
UDC received direct comments on the plan from hundreds of individuals representing various interest groups and positions. In the final draft of the two-
volume EIS, titled *42nd Street Development Project: Final Environmental
Impact Statement,* the UDC included not only its environmental impact
methodology and findings, but also a categorization of the comments received
on the draft EIS, as well as its responses to them in the form of counterargu-
ments. In some cases, the comments and responses dealt with the process used
by UDC to develop and present the plan; in the majority of instances, the discussion concerned the use of different criteria to evaluate and justify the project. This reflected the political struggle over problem definition and the

selection of project objectives. The debate over objectives, as reflected in the environmental impact report, centered around three concerns: the appropriate *type* of commercial development, the need for social equity, and historic preservation. It focused in particular on the choice of which criterion should be applied to evaluate the redevelopment policy and why. That is, which criterion was most relevant to the Times Square situation.

### SITUATIONAL RELEVANCE: COMMERCIAL OFFICE SPACE AS PROJECT OBJECTIVE

The majority of the people who responded to the UDC's study agreed that commercial redevelopment was, in principle, an appropriate goal. Times Square was widely accepted to be a blighted area in the middle of one of the world's most thriving commercial centers; its resources were clearly underutilized. Most respondents agreed that commercial redevelopment should be measured in terms of the plan's ability to mobilize the area's slack resources for the benefit of the city economy as a whole. There was, however, far less agreement on whether UDC's programmatic objective of developing office space adequately fulfilled the goal of commercial redevelopment. For many, the objective of more office space conflicted with other important commercial considerations relevant to Times Square.

The most powerful economic and political interests in the city saw the problem in terms of the efficient functioning of the city's commercial marketplace. These included not only the UDC and the project's developers, but also Mayor Koch, Governor Cuomo, the city's planning agencies, and powerful civic groups. These people, and the groups they represented, portrayed commercial decline to be the fundamental source of Times Square's problems and advanced the criterion of market efficiency to justify support for the UDC emphasis on commercial office space.

From a market perspective, the redevelopment plan was said to meet the test of a good commercial development strategy (Regan, 1988). It eliminated the existing barriers to commercial office expansion, contained few negative externalities for the neighboring parts of the area, played to the strengths of the district's location, emphasized the creation of new jobs, and featured the role of the private sector. The direct and indirect benefits of office expansion would be substantial. The plan was predicted to add 16,500 jobs to the area during the construction period and 20,000 new permanent jobs when the construction was completed (Bingham, 1985). Moreover, the project was seen to reduce city expenditures significantly for police, sanitation, and other city services. By the end of the fifteen-year tax abatement, the developers would be expected to pay $116 million in new real estate taxes to the city (UDC, 1984). Finally, no public subsidy was involved since the developers would pay UDC for the land (up to a fixed limit) and incur all the construction costs (although this does not consider the forgiven taxes).

Most fundamentally, the UDC's conviction that the revitalization of office space in a blighted area such as Times Square would enhance the overall economy of a city was based on the economic concept of the "multiplier effect." The study drew on numerous urban economic analyses which have shown that new office construction and attractive facilities in blighted areas can create new jobs, encourage commuter spending, attract new business, and increase tax receipts (Levy, 1990). As Zimmerman (1989:11) summarized the basic conclusion drawn from this research, "guiding investment and employment to areas that have had low levels of economic activity provides benefits to society in excess of what would be obtained if the investment and employment were directed to areas that experience healthy economic growth." Government, in this view, has to serve as the stimulus for such economic redevelopment, as market forces cannot be expected to redevelop distressed areas alone, primarily because of high start-up costs. Therefore, the invisible hand of the market must be aided by tax abatements and incentives provided by state or local governments (UDC, 1984:10–92).

To support these arguments, the study made various estimates of space utilization, building vacancy rates, and property tax evaluations. Through the hidden hand of the market, it was argued, the UDC plan would generate higher tax receipts, add new jobs to the economy, and stimulate tourist spending. In short, everyone would be better off: commercial office development was thus in the public interest of the city.

This policy orientation was scarcely novel; it corresponded to the widely held urban development beliefs among public officials throughout the country during the 1970s and 1980s (Gratz, 1989). As empirical evidence of worthiness of such projects, economic redevelopment advocates pointed to the successes of various commercially oriented urban renewal projects in cities as diverse as Charleston, Savannah, Boston, New Haven, Phoenix, and San Diego. The study also cited evidence, although perhaps somewhat limited, that commercial economic development activities in central cities had begun to slow the pace of suburbanization and to halt the troublesome fragmentation of metropolitan areas (Harrison, 1974).

Given this experience in other parts of the country, the UDC judged its objectives to be relevant to the problems confronting Times Square, and stressed a number of important facts. First, the UDC found that Times Square, compared to the rest of the city, had an extensive amount of cheap, underutilized space. Figures compiled from the city's planning department largely told the story. For example, figures in 1981 showed the total zoning capacity of the area to be approximately 6.2 million square feet. Of this, only about 34 percent was actually occupied. During the same period, the city's assessed valuation totaled about $44.7 million for the entire two-and-one-half block area, including both land and buildings. This was less than the assessed value of a number of single midtown buildings; the Citicorp Center, for example, occupying less than a block, had an 1981 assessed value for the office building alone of $68.8 million.

The second major circumstance to be dealt with was crime. Police data showed that in 1979 an average of two serious felony crimes were reported each day on Forty-Second Street and that in one month alone during 1980 more than one hundred arrests were made for narcotic sales and possession. Such criminal activity, according to the UDC, was highly correlated with a third circumstance, namely, the unsavory types of establishments located in the area and the deteriorating conditions of the buildings that housed these businesses. Most of these businesses—pornographic theaters, sex shops, cheap entertainment arcades, and so on—were housed in structurally unsound, aesthetically unpleasing buildings constructed in the 1940s and 1950s. In the agency's view this seedy, rundown side of Forty-Second Street provided something of a natural environment for crime, prostitution, and drug addiction. Nothing, it was argued, would go further toward getting rid of this "social sleaze" than forcing out these businesses and tearing down the dilapidated structures that housed them. Indeed, this was the basic assumption underlying the UDC plan.

According to the UDC's analysis, these various factors interacted to create a chain of negative economic consequences. Because of a lack of commercial activity for a number of years, no new jobs had been created in the area. The character and condition of the buildings in the area prevented more respectable established businesses and new theaters from moving into the area; and the specter of crime caused shoppers and tourists to stay away from Times Square. All of this, moreover, placed an inordinate drain on the city's public services, especially the need to increase police patrols and visits by sanitation trucks. Under these conditions there seemed little prospect for change.

If physical reconstruction and employment growth were the answers to this downward spiral of Times Square, the restoration of the historic theaters, the reconstruction of a major wholesale mart, and the elimination of establishments that encouraged criminal behavior would dramatically enhance the business climate. By reviving the flow of respectable entertainment and commercial life in the area, as well as compelling the criminals to ply their trade elsewhere, Times Square would once again become "an attractive destination" for workers, shoppers, playgoers, and diners. What is more, the project was expected to reduce city expenditures for police, sanitation, and other city services in the area, and to provide extra revenues for the city coffers. After the end of the fifteen-year tax abatement, the developers were expected to pay millions in real estate taxes to the city (UDC, 1984).

To be sure, the UDC recognized that the project would present some negative externalities for the neighboring parts of the city. As the UDC conceded, during the construction phases of the project there would be vehicular and pedestrian disruptions, increased noise levels from demolition and jackhammering, and diminished air quality from fugitive dust and vehicle emissions. Moreover, the agency admitted that in the long term the amount of light and fresh air on the street would be reduced by the bulk and height of the new buildings, that many of the existing businesses in the area would be displaced, and that there would be a loss of parking spaces.

But compared to the advantages of the project, the UDC saw these disruptions as fairly minor inconveniences. The agency adamantly concluded that the "overall benefits of a coherent rational design for the area should far outweigh the detriments" (UDC, 1984:6–2). In the language of validation, the UDC argued that its commercial redevelopment objectives were wholly relevant to the situation at hand. Not only were they especially relevant to the strengths of the district's unique location, they confronted all of the major social problems of the area and added few long-term negative impacts.

## REJECTING COMMERCIAL REDEVELOPMENT: THE PRESERVATION ARGUMENTS

Not everyone was willing to consider commercial redevelopment as a valid goal. Some citizens' groups, in particular the Municipal Art Society and the New York Landmarks Conservancy, were highly critical of the plan and saw a more appropriate goal to be "the preservation of the character of Times Square." For them, the project fundamentally misunderstood the nature of Times Square and threatened to obliterate a "unique" part of New York City. It was necessary, such groups contended, to exempt an area like Times Square from the application of commercial criteria, especially high-rise office development. While such criteria are surely appropriate for the city in general, it was argued, an exception must be made for a district like Times Square. In other words, for the preservationists, the UDC's policy goal was irrelevant to the situation.

There were, in fact, two different types of arguments in favor of preserving the traditional character of Times Square. The most prominent preservation argument focused on aesthetic considerations. Numerous urban groups, civic associations, and academics believed that UDC's redevelopment project did not preserve the distinctive and historic "character" of the area, especially that of the Broadway theater district. For example, Brenden Gill, Chairman of the New York Landmarks Conservancy, asserted that the "dreary office space created by the project will adversely affect the Times Square area by destroying its character as a lively entrance to the theater district" (UDC, 1984:10–18).

Supported by a growing gentrification and the creation of historic landmarks, this view suggested that to remove the historic layer of a city is to destroy its very soul (Gratz, 1989).

While these historic preservationists tended to reflect the opinions of a culturally elite group of citizens, others advanced a very different version of the preservation argument. From a sociological perspective, they argued that Times Square represents "a kind of natural space" that urban centers must have for those "left out of" mainstream society. As evidence of the natural character of the phenomenon, they pointed to other historic districts such as the Tivoli Gardens in Copenhagen, the St. Pauli district in Hamburg, Kaiserstrasse in Frankfurt, Picadilly Circus in London, the Ginza in Tokyo, St. Mark's Square in Venice, and Red Square in Moscow (Kornblum and Boggs, 1985; McCloud, 1985). According to this sociological line of reasoning, placing large boxlike office buildings in Times Square would severely damage the area's urban ecology and foster greater social anomie among the less advantaged sectors of the society.

This second argument had its origins in the work of Lewis Mumford, William H. Whyte, and others who had insisted that urban life is more than going to and fro in a car and buying work attire on weekends in faceless shopping malls. Mumford (1970: 9), for instance, had argued in several books that the office complex mentality (reflected in the UDC's plan) results in an "assembly line existence, in which all human functions take place in an increasingly sterilized and uniform environment, cut off from every reality except that which serves the machine." From this perspective, the elimination of adventure, danger, and decay in Times Square would only serve to make life more homogeneous, grim, and dismal (Tierney, 1991).

Unlike the UDC's description of Times Square as a place of filth, perversion, and loitering, these sociological preservationists saw the area in more positive terms (Hiss, 1990). According to the UDC, people standing on street corners were loiterers; according to the preservationists, they were interesting characters. To the UDC, people were fleeing from Times Square; to the preservationists, people were fleeing to Times Square. Take, for example, the following anecdote from Friedman's *Tales of Times Square* (1986: 200):

> Where else can an eighteen-year-old A&P stockboy from the Bronx escape with his girl on Saturday night for twenty bucks? They hop a D train down to 42nd, all snazzy and dressed to kill. This is a heavy date, and the boy wants to impress. Charcoal greasy sirloins upstairs at Tad's, at $4.39 a side, including rubbery garlic bread, watery onions, and baked spud with melted lard! They stroll arm in arm down 42nd, their pick of fourteen movies before them, at $3.50 per ticket; the rest of the city charges $5. It might be cinema . . . kung fu *(Kill or Be Killed),* slice-em-up *(I Spit on Your Grave),* black exploitation reruns *(The Mack),* vio-

lent sexploitation *(Barbed Wired Girls)*, or first-run Hollywood *(Breakin' II: Electric Boogaloo)*.

Movied-out afterwards, at eleven-thirty they might pick from a dozen Playlands, where a photo-booth souvenir costs a buck for four poses. Finally, they take a neon suntan under the Godzilla-size Japanese ads, and . . . he embraces her closely for a $3 color Polaroid, on the advice of a cultured street photographer. Ah, ghetto romance.

The UDC was not altogether insensitive to the preservation arguments. Fundamentally, the corporation's planners insisted that the objectives of commercial enterprise and entertainment need not be incompatible. Such criteria could, in fact, be integrated to preserve much of the unique character of the Times Square district. As evidence, the UDC pointed to the fact that Times Square had always been a mixture of commercial and entertainment activities. For example, the UDC offered a number of historic examples: "One Times Square, the Paramount Building (1401 Broadway) and several others were all built during the theater district's heyday and have been occupied in office use continuously since then." Furthermore, in the 1970s "three large office buildings were constructed in the heart of Times Square, without detracting from the liveliness of the entertainment environment" (UDC, 1984:10–94). More concretely, in an effort to integrate commerce and the traditional character of Times Square, if not simply to placate its critics, the UDC established a requirement mandating that bright lights and large signs be placed on the sides of the new buildings.

Most important, however, the UDC continued to note that their surveys of tourists and residents of the area, as well as interviews with police officers, showed that the largest number of people preferred redevelopment over the existing blight. Although the UDC insisted it was sensitive to the preservation arguments, especially those of the advocates of historic preservation, its bottom line remained firm: The objective of commercial development established a "heavier obligation" than did the call for preservation.

The UDC's position, however, scarcely satisfied the true preservationists, historic or sociological. For them, the addition of bright lights would only add an artificial quality to the area, perhaps an "urban version of the American shopping mall." Neither economic progress nor majority opinion was seen as a valid reason for transforming Times Square. The problem for the preservationists, however, was more political than intellectual: they simply did not have enough political clout to compete successfully against the powerful commercial interests in the struggle to win public opinion.

## CONFLICTING OBJECTIVES: OFFICE SPACE VERSUS SOCIAL EQUITY

The greatest challenge to the UDC's commercial redevelopment plan came from groups who lived and worked in the area. These local stakeholders largely agreed with the UDC that the major problems facing Times Square were crime, blight, and the underutilization of space. Most of them also accepted the goal of commercial redevelopment. What they did not accept, however, was UDC's heavy emphasis on high-rise office space. As they saw it, redevelopment in this form was not relevant to their own particular interests. For the local stakeholders, large-scale office development was an objective relevant primarily to the large private developers. In their view, the big developers and commercial office businesses would receive the major advantages from the proposal, leaving the disruptive costs to the existing—typically smaller—businesses and the residential community surrounding Times Square. In other words, the developers would receive both the benefits of the tax abatements and the profits from the increased land values, while local stakeholders would pay most of the social costs. As such, the project was judged to be socially inequitable.

At the root of the concern was the doubt that the commercial development plan, at least as designed by the UDC, would in fact automatically take care of the range of social problems that plagued the area. Specifically, local stakeholders questioned the argument that problems such as crime, drugs, and prostitution were easily understood in economic terms, particularly unemployment. Greater attention, they argued, had to be paid to the particular social circumstances of Times Square.

There were five major groups that expressed concerns about an uneven distribution of the plan's benefits—the Clinton residential neighborhood bordering the western edge of Times Square, the Broadway theater community just north of the district, the garment industry, hotel owners, and government officials from other parts of the city and the state. Although they were originally mainly supportive of the effort to clean up Times Square, most of the leaders of these groups, especially those representing the residents of Clinton, became more and more opposed over time as the details of the project emerged.

For the Clinton residents there were two primary worries. One was residential gentrification. They worried that the new influx of office workers—particularly middle- and upper-income workers—would put major pressures on nearby housing markets, especially theirs. Not only would many of the older long-term residents of Clinton be driven out of the neighborhood by a combination of rising rents and the conversion of apartments into resident-owned cooperatives, rents would dramatically increase for those who were able to remain.

The second concern was that Times Square's crime and sex-related businesses would only shift to the neighboring residential areas and the theater district just above Forty-Second Street. The Clinton residents in particular argued that the expanding drug problem would fully overrun their community (Fainstein, 1987; 1994). In fact, increasing crime, prostitution, and drug trade in the 1970s had already reached into the Clinton district (UDC, 1984). For Clinton's opposition leaders, "cleaning up" Times Square had to be understood as a social issue, not an economic problem (UDC, 1984:10-118). Like the social preservationists, they too argued that Times Square's problems were incorrectly defined, but for them the answer was more social services. The solution to crime, loitering, and prostitution was neither office space nor cultural preservation. Rather it was more social services, police protection, and affordable housing.

The theater owners and the theatrical community also shared Clinton's worries about both crime and rising rents. But they added additional concerns of their own. For them, Broadway itself was to be considered something like Chinatown or Little Italy. Because of its integral contribution to the city's cultural environment, Broadway had to be protected and strengthened (Goldstein, 1985). Without some sort of cleanup, crime and drugs would continue to drive theatergoers away and hence lead to the closing of more and more theaters. But was commercial redevelopment alone the answer? Not as the theater owners saw the situation. Indeed, they feared that the large-scale commercial ventures planned by the UDC would only raise land values and shift criminal activity to the theater district, further contributing to the demise of legitimate theater in New York. Along with Clinton residents and other small businesses in the area, they argued that real estate values would increase to the point where leases would become unaffordable and the continued operation of the existing theaters in the area would be impractical. For instance, Jack Goldstein (1985:23), president of Save the Theaters (a group of theater owners and actors formed specifically to contest the plan), concluded that the "Broadway Theaters cannot survive this kind of massive overbuilding, as everyone from the three-card monte player in Times Square to the city planner knows."[2]

The garment industry, located on the streets south of Times Square, was worried as well about its economic plight. Industry leaders believed that the UDC redevelopment plan was unfair because of job displacements created by the large office buildings. Jay Mazur, General Secretary-Treasurer for the International Ladies Garment Workers' Union, argued that the new merchandise mart and commercial office towers would encourage more conversions in the garment district, cause rents to rise, push out existing showrooms, and consequently have a negative effect on the 150,000 garment manufacturing jobs in the area (UDC, 1984:10–17). The wholesale merchandise mart, he maintained, "will encourage harmful out-of-town and foreign competition with the New York garment industry." The eventual loss of jobs would "primarily affect minority and immigrant workers." The project, according to the union, should not be undertaken without the implementation of mitigating measures to help protect the garment center (UDC, 1984:10–17).

Another group of businesses—small, low-cost hotel and motel owners—also claimed economic hardship. Indeed, as they saw it, the project would altogether price them out of the area. The owners of these establishments believed the project to be unfair to their middle-income clients, tourists in particular, who depended on low-budget lodging. Some of the owners even went a step further, contesting the judgment to condemn the area as "blighted." For them, the decision to declare Times Square a blighted area—thus placing it under the UDC's power of eminent domain—hinged as much on the UDC's conception of viable economic activity as it did on the physical conditions of the area. In the view of these businesses, the issue was basically another chapter in losing the battle by small business to maintain a niche in an economy dominated by large corporations.

Yet another argument came from government officials in other parts of the state and city. Less concerned with whether Times Square was an economic or a social problem, they argued that it was unfair for a particular place in Manhattan to receive so much assistance from the State government. Greater problems were to be found elsewhere. Howard Strauss, vice-president of the Kings County Board of Trade, emphasized the inequity of the project in these words: "State resources should not be used to develop already overdeveloped Manhattan when outer boroughs need development and hundreds of businesses now located in solid buildings well away from the Forty-Second Street impact area will be dispossessed." The money, he argued, should be spent instead on other blighted neighborhoods. Echoing the garment industry, he further asserted that the "City needs projects such as factories which create employment, rather than marts which benefit foreign manufacturers and put New Yorkers out of work" (UDC, 1984:10–23).

Finally, there was the somewhat short-term but nonetheless compelling consideration concerning the social disruptions that the plan would bring. The local stakeholders believed they would be inordinately disrupted by the physical construction of the new buildings and the traffic gridlock it would create. Moreover, it was argued that the sheer amount of construction, the size of the buildings, and the increases in traffic would cause excessively high concentrations of carbon monoxide in the area. None of the groups were satisfied with the UDC's claims that the project would have a fairly harmless impact on air quality, or that whatever negative impacts that did occur would in any case last no longer than two or three years. For the stakeholders, even two years of noise and air pollution was too much for those who lived and worked in the area.

Thus, while often conceding inherent conflicts between the objectives of social equity and commercial redevelopment, at least when rigorously pursued, these groups judged social equity to be at least as relevant—and in some cases even more so—than the efficiency of commercial markets. In short, they called for "commercial redevelopment with social equity." Without a more favorable distribution of economic benefits and social burdens, the proposed plan was for them unacceptable. The answer was to be found in some form of mixed development.

## COUNTERARGUMENTS AND OUTCOMES

In almost every case, the UDC formally replied to the arguments of the local stakeholders by elaborating the economic rationale underlying their project objectives. The basic approach was to acknowledge the criticisms, but seek to offset them by arguing that the UDC's commercial redevelopment plan was on goals and objectives that reflected the long-run interests of the public as a whole. To those who altogether rejected the goal of commercial redevelopment, the UDC argued that its plan was based on "higher-level" goals. By following a course of commercial redevelopment, all other major problems would recede over time and eventually disappear. To those who accepted commercial redevelopment but questioned its emphasis on office space, the UDC argued that the benefits would rapidly spill over to other businesses and neighborhoods to offset the initial social inequities that would come with construction.

In reply to those who argued that the EIS had falsely defined the problem confronting Times Square, namely that the problems there were mainly social rather than economic, the UDC argued that the social problems could be more fundamentally traced to underlying economic causes, unemployment in particular. According to the UDC, socially oriented solutions such as putting more social workers or police in the area were only prophylactic measures that would in the long run waste scarce resources and leave the problem fundamentally intact. With regard to more police, the UDC put it this way: "While major police sweeps have been temporarily successful in reducing criminal activity in the project area, these have required extraordinary deployment of police personnel, over two hundred officers per day during these sweeps. And, when the contingent of police on Forty-Second Street returns to 'normal' so does criminal activity (UDC, 1984:10–118)."[3]

To the argument that the residents and businesses in the area would suffer from the project, the UDC maintained the contrary. Positive economic benefits would spread through market mechanisms to the adjacent neighborhoods.

The report put it this way: Retail businesses in the project area will be of a different type and serve a different market from Clinton neighborhood business; no significant competitive impact is therefore expected on such businesses. General upgrading of the Clinton neighborhood over the past several years, which can be expected to continue in the absence of the project, will influence the commercial character of the Clinton neighborhood and will lead to some turnover of business establishments in the community" (UDC, 1984:10–124).[4]

With regard to the garment industry, UDC officials admitted there would be increased competition from new retail businesses. But they also maintained that such competition would eventually improve the overall economic vitality of the area (UDC, 1984). Furthermore, they suggested that minority employment programs could be established within the development project to help offset unemployment in the garment industry. The UDC and the city, however, resisted an argument that direct financial compensation should be given to the garment industry to help offset the problems it would suffer due to the plan.

The UDC countered arguments from the theater district with an analysis designed to show that the project would actually increase the number of legitimate theaters in the area, as well as remove the rundown buildings in the district. Commercial revitalization of the area, the UDC maintained, also meant an increase in theater business (Fainstein, 1987; 1994). Although the UDC was willing to estimate the total number of jobs that would be created by the project, it was unwilling to predict the ultimate impact on theaters in the area. This was described as a matter of economics that uniquely hinged on the rather atypical market characteristics of the entertainment industry.

But here the issue would seem to be more complicated. It is not altogether clear that commercial redevelopment, defined as the expansion of large-scale office space, would in fact be the most advantageous approach to revitalization for the legitimate theater. Even though more office jobs in the area might well increase the number of people attending the theater, a closer look at the theater business shows it to be highly dependent upon a wide range of small businesses. Indeed, a successful theater district is built around a world of small specialty services required to put on a show: costume designers, hat makers, seamstresses, tailors, recording studios, casting agents, and the like. All are small businesses and have slowly but steadily been driven out of the area for lack of affordable space. The absence of such services—especially those capable of dealing with every sort of production emergency—has begun to become a serious problem for the theater community.[5]

To the charge by city and state officials that the project distributed benefits inequitably throughout the city, the UDC merely restated its initial contention that the project had economic benefits beyond the project area. As the UDC put it, "The State and City have decided that the completion of the 42nd Street project would contribute to the realization of objectives which are significant to the City as a whole. Potential developments in other areas of the City must be assessed on their own merits independently of this project" (UDC, 1984:10–24).

To be sure, the UDC recognized that there would be some negative spillovers for neighborhood communities. But this, the UDC argued, was simply in the nature of things. Economic progress always brought with it some unfortunate consequences which merely had to be accepted, at least in the short run. Over the long haul, the market would sort out many of these problems. Leading to the greater good of the society as a whole, economic growth was promoted as the higher-order goal under which criteria such as equity and preservation would eventually find their proper place.

While the opponents of Times Square spoke with many voices, and were thus unable to advance a fully developed alternative to the UDC plan, there were among their supporters urban planners and interest group leaders who outlined the contours of an alternative approach. As a direct challenge to the assertions of the UDC planners, namely that the only alternative to massive redevelopment was no development at all, the opposition pointed to the possibility of a "mixed-use" redevelopment model. The model was based on two primary counterexamples—the Battery Park City Development in lower Manhattan, and the blocks between Ninth and Tenth avenues just to the west of the project site (Emickie, 1991; Fainstein, 1987). In the case of the block just beyond the Times Square District, the area had in the 1970s quite successfully undergone a mixed-use redevelopment on a smaller scale. Undertaken during a period when the major developers had in fact written this area off as unattractive, the mixed-development approach itself involves the rehabilitation of abandoned commercial space. The results included a lively row of off-Broadway theaters and restaurants, as well as a major subsidized housing complex for those engaged in the performing arts, and the renovation of the famous landmark McGraw-Hill Building.

A similar strategy, opposition planners argued, could appropriately be developed for the Times Square District itself. Instead of exercising its power of eminent domain to tear down a vast number of buildings indiscriminately in order to make room for enormous new structures, urban planner Susan Fainstein argued that the UDC could have used eminent domain to eliminate only the most undesirable land uses and to facilitate the rehabilitation of many existing structures.[6] Tax abatements could have been used to entice the theater owners to renovate their buildings without the contributions of office developers. Spot demolition could have created the opportunity for some new construction, including the construction of a building with a mix of commercial and residential occupants. The block closest to the existing subsidized apartment complex could have been used for a mixed residential-commercial building, containing some low-income units, thus adding much sought residential space to Clinton, and further upgrading the area. Space for more small businesses would have eased the plight of the ancillary world of arts and crafts that serve theater production. Rather than the shopping mall approach that was seen to characterize the UDC plan, the idea would be to return to Times Square some of the diversity and charm that had characterized it in the early part of this century.

Contrary to the contentions of the UDC's planners, there were some interesting alternatives to consider, had the agency been so inclined. Because no influential political or administrative entity seriously entertained alternative development strategies, however, their virtues were never widely considered. The ultimate decision boiled down to a choice between the UDC plan or no project at all (Fainstein, 1987). According to many observers, the UDC believed that the project had to be big or it wouldn't work. Translated into political terms, this meant that a smaller, mixed-development approach would not generate the kinds of huge public and private investments needed to attract the large developers. In this respect, the UDC appeared to overlook anything that did not favor their primary clients—the big developers, the governor, and the majority of city officials.

Although the UDC's project design remained basically the same after the environmental impact study and the formal hearing that followed its public presentation, some concessions were obtained by the opponents of the project. The Clinton area, for example, was given $25 million in public revenues over five years for low-income housing and community development (Fainstein, 1987). The merchandise mart was changed to a computer mart to reduce competition with existing industries in the garment sector and elsewhere in the city. Finally, additional signs and neon lights were added to the facades of the buildings to preserve the "gaudy" character of Times Square. But beyond relatively minor adjustments, the emphasis on commercial redevelopment remained intact.

After the public discussion, many of the opposition groups moved their case to the courts. Over a five-year period, forty-five different lawsuits were filed to stop or to change the redevelopment project (Fox, 1989). Even though millions of dollars were spent by the litigants, including the UDC, no significant alterations were made in the design of the project (Fox, 1989).

### SITUATIONAL VALIDATION AND THE POLITICS OF EVALUATION

The UDC project objective, commercial redevelopment, was opposed on two grounds—its perceived failure to preserve the traditions of Times Square and its lack of social equity. With regard to the first objection, the UDC was unable to convince the preservationists. For these groups, the primary issue ultimately rests with a different conception of the city and the way of life associated with it, hinging on choices beyond the reach of program validation, per se. The preservation arguments, historical as well as sociological, are rooted more in the fourth discourse of the logic of policy deliberation, social choice (the topic of chapter 8).

The question of why the UDC ignored the possibility of a mixed approach to development, however, is less easy to explain. One of the simplest but most credible answers is politics. It seems fair to say that the UDC simply stood behind its commercial conception of economic redevelopment, knowing that this was supported by a majority of the city's business people and politicians. These included the governor of the state, a majority of the city officials involved with the project, and the agency's primary clients, the big developers. Furthermore, those advocating mixed development had nothing like the kind of political clout that would have been needed to compel such consideration.

Even beyond the immediate politics of the situation, the UDC's market-oriented approach to public policy was fully in tune with the dominant policy beliefs of the period. Not only did the approach rest on the primary policy assumptions of the dominant capitalist belief system in the United States, but pro-growth assumptions were never stronger than during the 1980s heyday of "Reaganomics." In this sense, at least politically, the UDC did not have to explain its policy assumptions. They were part of a capitalist value system little questioned by society as a whole. Right or wrong, growth and development were widely accepted as tantamount to the public interest.

But what if UDC had chosen to pursue its position on the intellectual merits of the issue? Having argued that commercial redevelopment bore the "heaviest obligation of the competing criteria," the corporation's only recourse here would have been to vindicate the growth-oriented policy goals from which its commercial redevelopment objectives were drawn. That is, had the UDC attempted to pursue the possibility of establishing a policy consensus with its opponents, it would have had to elaborate and debate its argument beyond validation to vindication. At this point, the UDC would have had to show that its policy goals and beliefs, especially its economic conception of the public interest, served the social system as a whole. First, and most obviously, it would have had to demonstrate that mega–office development would in fact better promote economic growth than smaller-scale commercial development, entertainment oriented development, or mixed residential development. But even more important for the opposition groups, the agency would have had to demonstrate that commercial redevelopment would rid the area of crime, drugs, and prostitution. Instead of merely resting its case on the assertion that commercial redevelopment would over time take care of all the other social problems in the area, the UDC would have had to demonstrate empirically the validity of the underlying policy assumption.

One compelling reason the UDC might have considered such a discourse is its centrality to the primary source of contention. The majority of
those opposed to the commercial redevelopment project, especially those who
supported the need for a more equitable mixed-development approach, have in
fact largely refused to accept the argument that the project was good for all of
the groups involved. Whether or not the UDC could have actually vindicated
its growth-oriented policy goal is not the main point of the chapter. Rather, it is
to show that the UDC's only possibility of consensually overcoming the opposition of those who considered commercial redevelopment inequitable was to
vindicate credibly its policy assumptions.

During the 1980s, the choice not to engage publicly in a discussion
about the validity of its policy assumptions may not have seemed so crucial to
the UDC, given the widespread political support for those assumptions. The
agency had both the administrative power and know-how needed to design
and implement the work, and a green light from the politicians and developers.
By the early 1990s, however, the situation looked somewhat different. Some
ten years after the decision to proceed with commercial redevelopment, the
project was clearly in trouble (Dunlap, 1992:25). Because of depressed real estate markets resulting from a lengthy economic slump in the city, coupled with
long delays due to nearly fifty lawsuits, many of the big developers began to
express doubts about proceeding with their commitments and sought continual
postponements. Indeed, by 1992 the state itself began to readjust its commitment. In August of that year the UDC decided to relinquish the developers
from their obligations to the plan. Redevelopment was not to be altogether dis-
continued; rather the state would accept a more modest proposal for revitalizing the area. While the agency has not formally canceled the construction of
the four major office buildings that defined the large-scale project, the buildings were indefinitely postponed into the future—perhaps for ten years, if
ever. Nobody actually knows how long it might take. As one observer put it,
"the millennium may come and go before market conditions permit development of the project's dormant sites." Some argue that the developers' commitment to the four large office towers is for all practical purposes dead; that the
new proposals will in the long run prove to be little more than a face-saving
device.

This new development has in fact reopened the public debate on the future of Times Square. To be sure, opponents of the project are pleased, if not
ecstatic. The decision has led opponents such as Manhattan Borough President
Ruth W. Messinger to argue that public officials "should use this postpone-
ment as an opportunity to reconsider the entire premise of the Times Square redevelopment plan" (Dunlap, Aug. 4, 1992:1). The most appropriate way to
begin such a reevaluation, according to Herbert Muschamp (1992:15) of the

New York Times, "would be to simply stop, look and listen to Times Square's own ideas about what it wants to be."

And that seems to be what the UDC has in mind, at least for the immediate future. Although the revised plan had not been fully formalized as this book goes to press, most of the talk was about recapturing the lure of Times Square as a center of popular culture and retail. In what can only be described as a turnaround, New York Times journalist David Dunlap (1992:1; 1993:B1) reported that officials now "believe that Times Square would profit most from its reincarnation as a jumble . . . of small buildings topped by big signs and filled with stores, restaurants, theaters, amusements and night spots—in other words, fitting a description that might have been written 50 years ago." Rebecca Robertson, president of the Forty-Second Street Development Project (a subsidiary corporation of the UDC), has explained the new arrangement as a "quid pro quo." The developers are released from their commitment to build Times Square Center, but "are required to bring Forty-Second Street back to life" (Dunlap, 1992, Aug. 3:1).

What might that look like? According to an official of the Forty-Second Street Development Project, the goal is now to play to the "natural potential of the area" (Dunlap, Aug. 4, 1992:1; 1993:H33). Based on a new survey that shows "a tremendous unexploited potential for tourism," a market now described as "underserved," the UDC subsidiary points to the need for "restaurants, jazz and supper clubs, snack bars, tourist-information office, souvenir shops, music and book stores, newsstands and theaters where multimedia 'spectaculars' geared to tourists might be presented." Already, important opposition groups have pledged their support.

What happened to the argument about large-scale commercial development? Although no one is officially saying it, the quick retreat to low-scale, mixed development now seems to be tacitly accepted as a realistic and fully suitable alternative, in the long run as well as immediately. If that is in fact the recognition underlying this reversal, one can only wonder how much money and effort might have been spared had the UDC been more willing from the outset to listen to the project's critics. Time should tell.

## READINGS

William Robert Taylor. 1992. *Inventing Times Square: Commerce and Culture at the Crossroads*. New York: Russell Sage.

Ken Bloom. 1991. *An Encyclopedic Guide to the History of People and Places*. New York: Facts on File.

Tony Hiss. 1990. *The Experience of Place*. New York: Knopf.

Josh Alan Friedman. 1986. *Tales of Times Square*. New York: Delcorte.

New York State Urban Development Corp. 1984. 42nd Street Development Project: Final Environmental Impact Statement. Vols. 1 and 2.

Eleanor L. Brilliant. 1975. *The Urban Development Corporation*. Lexington, MA: Lexington Books.

## DISCUSSION QUESTIONS

1. Examine the evidence offered by UDC for its adherence to commercial redevelopment. Is commercial redevelopment the key to solving the other problems plaguing Times Square? Discuss.

2. In what ways might the UDC's environmental impact study have been redesigned to address—if not avoid—the kinds of opposition that the project was ultimately to face?

3. How would you go about interviewing people in the Times Square area to determine the appropriate definition of the problem? What kinds of questions would you ask? What would you not ask?

4. It has been said that "social constructions have an especially important role in understanding current policy [problems] because these constructions are instrumental in determining the policy agenda and the actual design of policy itself. The symbols and images evoked by social constructions of target populations become embedded in public policy and carried as messages that citizens absorb as they experience public policy in their everyday lives (Schneider and Ingram, 1993:2). Discuss this point in the context of Times Square and its target population.

5. The text states that "the preservation arguments, historical as well as sociological, are rooted more in the fourth discourse of the logic of policy deliberation." Explain.

# Part Three
## SOCIETAL-LEVEL VINDICATION

# 6   Evaluating Policy Goals: Normative Assumptions and Societal Consequences

The failure to resolve policy arguments in verification and validation can shift evaluative discourse to the question of vindication. In vindication, evaluation turns its focus from the concrete situational context to the societal system as a whole. The basic task is to show that a policy goal is or is not compatible with or instrumental to the existing societal arrangements. To elucidate policy vindication, the chapter is divided into three parts: a discussion of the concepts of system and systems assumptions; an examination of the empirical tasks of vindication; and the uses of social systems theory.

Vindication, as we saw in chapter 1, is organized around the following questions:

> Does the policy goal have instrumental or contributive value for the society as a whole?
>
> Does the policy goal (and its normative assumptions) result in unanticipated problems with important societal consequences?
>
> Does a commitment to the policy goal lead to consequences (e.g., benefits and costs) that are judged to be equitably distributed?

In terms of the logic of evaluation, vindication constitutes a fundamental shift from first- to second-order evaluative discourse. Whereas first-order evaluative discourse focuses on empirical and normative judgments made in the "local" or "situational" contexts in which policy criteria—programmatic objectives and goals—are applied and implemented, second-order vindication steps outside of this action context and tests the policy goal against its systems-oriented beliefs and assumptions. That is, vindication, as second-order discourse, turns to an evaluation of the instrumental consequences of a policy goal and its normative assumptions for the extant social system as a whole. In the language of politics and policy evaluation, goals and assumptions are examined for their contribution to the larger common good, public interest, or general social welfare of the society, shorthand normative standards for the social order as a whole.

The attempt to vindicate a policy goal is thus an effort to examine its normative implications and consequences for systemswide performance. Specifically, does a policy goal instrumentally facilitate the institutional practices and values of the larger social system? For instance, did the policy goal of the Great Society's War on Poverty (explicated in chapter 4) rest upon a valid understanding of the systematic aspects of the poverty problem? Was the goal well-designed to guide the War on Poverty toward the long-term eradication of poverty in America? Did the goal and its assumptions help to prescribe programmatic strategies and instruments capable of effectively moving poor people into American society in a way that can be judged as socially just? Did they, in other words, seek to redress instrumentally the poverty problem within the legitimate political and economic parameters of American society? Or, as the "Reagan Revolution" proclaimed some twenty years later, did the antipoverty goal and its assumptions about American society represent a fundamental perversion of all that Americans hold dear?

Lance deHaven-Smith captured the basic thrust of this analytical shift to the level of the social system when he wrote that policy analysts must at a point replace "their methodological microscope with a theoretical macroscope" so that they may "concentrate on the relationship between public policy and the overall political-economic system" (1988:49). Transposed into the logic of evaluation, this shift from micro to macro analysis refers to the shift from first- to second-order evaluative discourse. Similarly, Charles Lindblom (1977) argues that policy analysis must transcend its traditional emphasis on program participants and examine as well a policy's impact on the larger political-economic system. Recognizing that a program's impacts extend far beyond the groups intended to benefit, Lindblom sees a policy's ability to alter society's political-economic mechanisms as its ability to reshape fundamentally the scope and nature of public problems. The discussion in this chapter is concerned with the theoretical questions and methodological issues that this systems-level evaluation poses for the policy inquiry.

## SYSTEMS-LEVEL POLICY ASSUMPTIONS

At the level of policy vindication, the societal *system* is the normative frame of reference. A societal system, in this respect, can be broadly understood as an interdependent set of political, economic, and cultural relationships. The concept of the "system" is used here to refer to a set of arrangements principally structured by the state and the economy and governed by power and money (Habermas, 1973). As opposed to the face-to-face relations of the community or the social situation, in which people directly confront and talk to other members of the social group, the "system world" is a set of indirect relationships, mediated in society by the marketplace and the media.

Vindication most commonly proceeds with a given conception of the normative institutional goals and values of the societal system. These systems' goals and values are generally held constant. At issue is how policy goals and means function to facilitate, realize, or support these larger societal goals and values. Thus, fundamental to judging the success of a goal's impact on the larger system is a proper understanding, practical as well as theoretical, of the system itself. For a policy goal to achieve its intended system-level consequences it must be based on an accurate understanding of the structures, functions, and processes of the society as a whole. In this respect, the policy's basic normative assumptions about the workings of the societal institutions can, and often do, become sources of contention (Hofmann, 1993). In such circumstances, policy vindication must avail itself of the broader empirical findings of political and sociological research.[1]

Of special importance at this level of analysis are the political-economic mechanisms for achieving the extant society's basic core goals and values, for example, wealth, freedom, power, knowledge, beauty, and so on (Lindblom, 1977). Basic to these political-economic mechanisms is typically a set of political beliefs and a corresponding "policy framework" that specify fundamental political orientations and policy strategies for realizing the system's normative axioms (deHaven-Smith, 1988). These policy beliefs include the following types of normative considerations (Sabatier, 1987:667):

- The proper scope of market versus governmental activity.

- The proper distribution of power and authority among various levels of government.

- The identification of social and political groups whose welfare is considered to be most important.

- The positions on substantive policy conflicts, such as economic development versus environmental protection.

- The basic choices concerning policy means, such as inducements, persuasion, and coercion.

- The desirability of political participation by various segments of the social system: elite versus public participation; experts versus elected officials.

- The perceived ability of society to solve the various substantive problems, for example, technological optimism versus pessimism.

In the United States the concept of a political or policy framework can best be illustrated with the New Deal's "corporate welfare" state, which dominated American politics from the mid-1930s until the early 1970s, when it began to unravel under the conservative challenge that led to the election of Ronald Reagan. Resting on an integrated set of assumptions about the relation of the federal government to economic and social systems, the welfare state provided a system based on two fundamental postulates: the federal government would regulate the factors of supply and demand to help insure a profitable environment for corporate enterprise, and (2), the government would provide a social "safety net" for the unemployed or less fortunate who fell through the corporate economic framework. Whereas the first premise established a government-business partnership to facilitate economic growth in an increasingly technological society, the second worked to supply the system with political support and social legitimacy.

During the decades in which New Deal policy assumptions dominated American politics, each major new government initiative was more or less integrated into the policy framework. The Great Society's War on Poverty is an example par excellence. It was heralded by the Johnson administration as an effort to complete the New Deal project. As we saw in chapter 4, Great Society programs were expected to work because they rested on the assumptions of the liberal policy framework about the working of American political and economic institutions. A decade later, however, questions about the correctness of these assumptions paved the way for Ronald Reagan's triumphant election in 1980. Two basic arguments were advanced against the War on Poverty, both of which illustrate argumentation at the level of vindication.

One argument, it will be recalled, pointed to what conservatives saw to be the unintended consequences of the War on Poverty. For writers such as Murray (1984), the policy goal actually worked to exacerbate rather than ameliorate the problems of the poor. Indeed, beyond the policy's failure to eliminate unemployment, its assumptions were seen to be responsible for perpetuating a host of other social pathologies as well, such as crime, drug addiction, broken families, and prostitution. The second argument maintained that the culture of poverty was essentially beyond the reach of governmental policy capabilities. A prime source of the government's policy failure, according to neoconservative theorists, was the unwillingness or inability of the liberal-reform tradition to address these deeper cultural dimensions of poverty. If self-perpetuating cultural factors dysfunctional to the overall way of life are at the root of the malaise, effective solutions must confront the cultural barriers that stand between the poor and mainstream society. Such solutions would have to be massive in scope. Anything short of total intervention would amount to mere situational changes with only temporary ameliorative effects. Massive intervention, as Banfield (1970) argued, is politically unacceptable to the political system. Given the existing political structures and processes, especially interest group politics and incremental decision making, such policy intervention would not only be too costly, it would also rest on values outside of the dominant American political culture.

Finally, one might note that vestiges of these arguments reemerged after the Los Angeles riots in 1992. One of the first responses of the George Bush administration was to blame ghetto conditions in south-central Los Angeles on the misbegotten programs of the Great Society. Rather than pointing to specific failures of these programs, the complaint was against the more general ideas behind the Great Society policies—for example, the belief that government should redistribute tax monies from the affluent to the poor. Or, as one commentator put it, the notion that poor people should get something they don't deserve. The argument, however, received little credence, given the intervening twenty years of Republican administrations. A second, and even more important response, was the Bush administration's effort to limit the solutions to those compatible with the priorities of the capitalist system, for example, home-ownership for the poor, and urban enterprise zones. While there is nothing wrong with such goals, the more important question remains open—do these economic goals actually get at the root of such deeply entrenched social deprivations? Critics argue that the administration was merely a prisoner of its adherence to a particular set of normative assumptions about the social system, which themselves are seen to be at the root of the problem.

## EVALUATING SYSTEMS CONSEQUENCES: EMPIRICAL METHODS

Vindication, then, is an empirically oriented "pragmatic test" of normative assumptions which requires the formal assistance of sociological and political inquiry. Such research has contributed much to the evaluation of public policies, although its contributions to policy *science* over the past thirty years have largely been secondary and indirect (Bobrow and Dryzek, 1987). Whereas the early founders of the policy-sciences movement saw socio-political analysis to be very much a part of their project (Lerner and Lasswell, 1951), contemporary policy scientists have for the most part considered such research to fall beyond the bounds of policy evaluation per se (i.e., an emphasis on efficiency and effectiveness) and have thus neglected its relevance to their own concerns. Much of what is fundamentally important to a *critical* evaluation of public policy, however, concerns policy's normative impact on the larger social and institutional structures and processes that constitute a society (Stone, 1988).

Given the nature of the questions addressed at this level of evaluation, the full vindication of a policy goal often requires the passage of time. While the more immediate benefits of a program to its participants can usually be established in a fairly reasonable period of time after the onset of the program, it typically takes much longer for the consequences of policy goals to show themselves in the larger societal system. For example, it may require decades for a policy-induced culture of poverty to fully reveal itself.

Although the longer time perspective needed to fully settle questions at the level of vindication significantly contributes to the complexity of the evaluation, the logic of vindication is itself fairly straightforward. As an instrumental orientation, vindication involves first the identification of the goals, values, and practices of the institutional arrangements of the social system which the policy is designed to influence, facilitate, or change. Second, it involves an empirical assessment of the policy's desired impact on these normative processes. The comparison in the evaluation involves the adoption and testing of other actual or possible policy goals and assumptions that may or may not have instrumental or contributive value for the same social system. The basic task is to develop hypotheses about the wider societal impacts that would be expected to result from the policy goals and assumptions, and to test them to see if the predicted impacts occur.

In the field of policy studies, such investigation is largely identical with the "theory-testing model of policy research" (deHaven-Smith, 1988; Campbell and Stanley, 1963; Ridley, 1977; and Nathan, 1986). As deHaven-Smith (1988:12) explains it, "the theory-testing model of policy research involves explicating policymakers' assumptions about the problems they are trying to solve, developing hypotheses about the . . . impacts that would be expected on the basis of these assumptions, and then conducting research to see if the predicted impacts occur."[2] For some, the objective of such research is the development of "policy theory" (Albinski, 1986). Policy theory would constitute a body of knowledge concerning predictable relationships between societal outcomes and empirically tested problem- and system-oriented assumptions.[3]

As a pragmatic test of the instrumental or contributive value of a policy's goal and assumptions for a social system as a whole, then, vindication poses sophisticated empirical questions that require the assistance of social-scientific knowledge and techniques. But what kinds of knowledge and techniques? At this level of evaluation it is more difficult to identify the useful methodologies than in verification and validation. The problem results in large part from the complexity of the empirical task. Rather than relying on a particular set of methodologies, the policy researcher must eclectically draw on a range of approaches that can contribute to a vindication argument. The actual selection of methods can only be determined by the nature of the policy problem. Indeed, the attempt to vindicate different policy assumptions—economic, social, or political—will invariably require different points of view with their own modes of reasoning. An assumption concerning economic growth will engage a different set of theoretical concepts and methodological orientations than one which stresses the fundamental importance of social equality.

Given the general complexity of this question, such investigation can be expected to draw on or employ a wide range of empirical data collection methodologies, from mass opinion surveys, large-scale cross-sectional analyses, cost-benefit data, systems simulations, interviews, case studies, to more or less controlled social experiments. Such data collection, moreover, would employ a host of inferential statistical techniques to organize and make sense of the data, including interval-level multivariate statistics.

The complexity of such research can be briefly illustrated through a line of research related to the culture of poverty and the Head Start program. In the case of the Head Start program, it will be recalled, a crucial argument was whether or not the development of socially relevant attitudes must be accepted as a primary goal of the Project Head Start. Because of the culture of poverty, such children are assumed to be unable later in life to participate in the dominant achievement-oriented cultural system of American society. Project Head Start is thus an educational program designed to inculcate "ghetto" children with achievement-oriented value systems needed to enter and succeed in the American mainstream.

The question is, What kinds of evidence might be brought to bear on the systems assumption underlying Head Start's primary policy goal—that achievement-oriented values will move these children into the mainstream of society? For purposes of illustration, one possibility is to draw on the substantial body of evidence devoted to measuring and predicting the instrumental contribution of achievement-oriented values to industrial societies. Here, for example, one could turn to the work of David McClelland (1961). Utilizing a wide range of historical data, experimental evidence, case studies, national surveys, and cross-cultural perspectives, McClelland has managed to isolate the basic social and psychological factors—motives and values—that characterize the value-belief systems of the entrepreneurial classes, as well as to identify the socializing practices that instill and nurture these values. His research demonstrates a high correlation between the presence of entrepreneurial groups with achievement-oriented value systems in a given society and the pace of industrial growth. Specifically, it shows that countries with significant or growing numbers of groups with such value systems industrialize more rapidly than those societies without such groups. In the language of vindication, McClelland's work empirically establishes instrumental and contributive connections between achievement-oriented value systems and the advance of industrial socioeconomic systems. It suggests that governments interested in pulling the hard-core poor up out of poverty at the same time that they foster economic growth should be advised to target the beliefs, values, and child-raising practices of ghetto families.

The accumulation of social-science findings about the instrumental aspects of various behaviors has facilitated the development of a number of theoretical frameworks that help address the kinds of evaluative questions posed in vindication. In the following sections we present the two theoretical orientations that most clearly correspond to the instrumental logic of vindication. One is drawn from sociology and political science and concerns the analysis of the relation of individual and group actions to societal structures and processes. The other is taken from economics and policy science and focuses on the measurement of systemwide costs and benefits.

## SOCIAL-SYSTEMS THEORY AND THE LOGIC OF VINDICATION

The theoretical model that most clearly corresponds to the instrumental logic of vindication is functional systems theory. The functional approach to social systems, as Bobrow and Dryzek (1987: 68) put it, "explains individual and collective behavior through reference to its instrumental value in the harmony of social totality." In vindication we are judging the instrumental value of a policy goal and its systemic assumptions in terms of their contribution to the smooth functioning of the existing social system as a whole. Vindication is an attempt to measure the consequences of accepting and adhering to a policy prescription within the larger social system which it is designed to regulate or facilitate.

The social-systems orientation, in its various forms, has been among the leading theoretical paradigms in the social sciences. Focusing on the functional structures and processes that constitute and govern complex social systems, the approach offers a way of analytically modeling and empirically measuring the relations between systems goals and their subsystem criteria. It calls attention to the nature of complex interdependencies, examining the specific processes by which such relationships develop and unfold. One of the ways that functional relationships are measured is in terms of normative subsystem inputs to larger system outputs.

To explore the empirical connections between the behavioral assumptions of subsystems and their functional consequences, systems-oriented social scientists have modeled the interrelationships among organized and recurrent sets of institutional norms and their linkages to larger societal goals and interests (Gross and Springer, 1970). Societal subsystems such as economy, government, education, and family can be mapped out as networks of institutional norms, assumptions, and values. Empirical relationships between normative inputs and empirical outputs constitute data for the potential development of causal theories that relate action-oriented behaviors to system responses. Although rigorous causal connections between systems theory, normative orientations, and policy formulation are at present beyond the empirical capabilities of social and political research (and likely to remain so due to the overwhelming complexity of the task), the mapping of the logic of these interrelationships is important for systems-level evaluations.

One of the main contributions of the functional systems perspective has been to make clear that systems have "latent" as well as "manifest" functions. As systems research demonstrates, the stated purpose of a function or goal may not be the real or most important function of the goal for the system as a whole (Merton, 1957). For example, research on welfare programs shows that while the stated policy purpose is to help welfare recipients maintain a minimum standard of living, an important, and often contradictory, purpose is to restructure capitalist labor markets in accordance with the dictates of supply and demand (Piven and Cloward, 1993). Such theory can help us to understand why social problems such as poverty, despite endless reform rhetoric, are never eradicated. Whereas poverty is dysfunctional to poor people, it can be quite functional to other groups in the societal system: If some people are to eat in expensive restaurants, other people must wash the dishes for comparatively low wages (Gans, 1968:106).

In the competition among theoretical paradigms that typically characterizes the social sciences, social-systems theory and functionalism have to some extent fallen from favor. Although a dominant paradigm through much of the 1970s, social-systems theory was in the latter 1970s and 1980s widely criticized as resting on conservative biases. But the criticism need not be altogether problematic. Primarily it pertains to a theoretical error, namely the elevation of a heuristic framework to social theory per se. The mistake results from confusing a set of methodological categories with a natural (or lawlike) description of an extant social reality. Systems theory, in short, failed to recognize and acknowledge the socially determined nature of a set of social categories that change over time through political struggle and normative discourse. Social-systems theory has thus been widely criticized as a conservative ideology masquerading as scientific theory. As a methodological heuristic, however, there is in fact nothing that prohibits using the functional systems model for the exploration of radical as well as conservative social questions (Gans, 1968:118–20). Moreover, as a method at the level of vindication, systems logic constitutes a useful component of the logic of evaluation (Fischer, 1980). The methodological task is merely to limit the systems perspective to its appropriate place in the larger framework of a comprehensive evaluation.

## SYSTEMS THEORY AND SOCIETAL WELFARE: MACRO COSTS AND BENEFITS

A second version of systems theory is geared to the measurement and analysis of the economic optimality and effectiveness of policy impacts on the larger social structures of society. Often identified as the "systems approach," economists and policy scientists have developed a systems-based model for the analysis of optimal economic relationships (Churchman, 1968; Optner, 1973). Emerging after World War II as an amalgam of operations research and welfare economics, the economist's systems approach reached its peak of influence in the Department of Defense under Robert Mac-Namara during the Vietnam war years. As the underlying analytical logic of a governmental policy-planning technique called the "Planning-Programming-Budgeting System," it came in fact to be identified as the quintessential policy-science methodology in much of the 1970s (Fischer, 1990).

Efficiency-oriented systems theory, like the socio-functional systems perspective, is essentially an analytical model for empirically examining the instrumental relationships between a system's parts—or subsystems—and the system as a whole. Typically couched in sophisticated scientific and mathematical terminologies, the systems approach is designed as an empirical-analytical explanatory model for the analysis of the instrumental relationships that interconnect the normative structures and processes of complex organizational systems. It examines empirical and normative processes through which complex relationships rationally develop and unfold.

A key contribution of this variant of the systems approach is its ability to show that in complex systems the outcomes of specific policy goals are often not as straightforward as they might at first appear. A classic illustration is provided by the systems modeling of Jay Forrester (1971). Forrester has demonstrated that the normative assumptions underlying urban and economic policies can often lead to unintended—or "counterintuitive"—consequences quite different from those anticipated by policy planners. A public policy, according to Forrester, has to be understood as the component parts of a complex social system. When designed in isolation from larger societal processes, a program will often function counterproductively. The problem is that in complex social systems the linkages between causes and outcomes are generally difficult to establish.

Thus, Forrester's work suggests that evaluation cannot simply be a question of determining whether or not a program's objectives have been met. Program success itself, according to Forrester's systems model, may only cause unanticipated counterproductive consequences for system performance as a whole. Since unanticipated consequences may not appear immediately, this also means that the appropriate time period for an evaluation must be substantially longer than generally assumed, perhaps one or even two decades (see Box 6.1).

The specific policy criterion brought to bear on the analysis is "systems optimality" (Optner, 1973). Analytical techniques such as computer simulations, decision analysis, and cost-benefit analysis are utilized to analyze the optimal mix of systems inputs designed to maximize some desirable amount

## BOX 6.1
## Forrester's Systems Models

Through computer modeling, Forrester shows "that social systems are 'multiloop nonlinear feedback systems'"; that is, there are many channels (loops) through which a result in the system can affect a cause in the system (feedback). As a result, a differentiation between causes and results is not possible. Also, the patterns of causation are nonlinear: a given increment in a causative variable will produce different amounts of effect on a second variable, depending on the initial level of both variables. Relationships between variables must therefore be expressed as complex curves, not as simple straight lines. . . .

For example, Forrester's computer models show four urban programs to be useless or counterproductive: the creation of jobs by busing the unemployed to the suburbs or by government as the employer of last resort; training programs to increase the skills of the lowest-income groups; financial aid to a depressed city, as by federal subsidy; and construction of low-cost housing. With regard to the latter, the model indicates that the fundamental problem is an excess of low-income housing in the central city; the moment conditions improve, population rises until the standard of living falls again. The solution is one opposite to that which is intuitively appealing. Instead of increasing the amount of low-income housing in the city, decrease it and increase income-producing land uses in the central city.

Not only is the construction of low-income housing in the central city counterproductive, but so are highway construction loans for suburban housing, since they help the middle class leave the city. While Forrester's solution might seem unfeeling toward the poor, one must remember that the financial disaster that has repeatedly confronted New York City is, in part, a result of its humane welfare policies. The city's short residency requirements and higher welfare subsidies attract a disproportionate share of welfare families. The problem can be solved only by a national welfare policy or partial municipal insolvency that forces New York to decrease welfare allowances to or below those of surrounding areas. . . .

Some programs have counterproductive consequences that pose difficult value conflicts for the evaluator. . . . Critics of Forrester's approach point out that computer modeling is highly dependent on the assumptions underlying the model, many of which concern important properties of society about which there is no consensus. . . . A safer approach might be to use modeling for the purpose of stimulating thought about problems, not for reaching firm conclusions about how a program will work.

Source: William R. Meyers (1981), 23–25.

and quality of output. Whereas the socio-functional approach to systems analysis presented in the previous section emphasizes in significant part the internal operations of a social system, the economic approach generally treats the "innards" of the system as a given. That is, the way in which the internal system operates on the inputs to transform them into outputs are not the primary concern. For the economic perspective, the output itself—both as benefit and unanticipated consequences—is of primary interest.

Concerned with the optimal allocation of resources, the systems approach often conceptualizes subsystems as "investment centers" governed by the effective flow of information, material, and financial resources. The proper flow of resources is seen to vary from system to system, depending on economic and organizational circumstances. Each focuses attention on goal realization. Subsystem processes are analyzed in terms of their instrumental contributions to optimal outcomes (Churchman, 1968). Of particular importance to this conceptualization is a systems-level cost-benefit analysis (Bozeman, 1979:308–29).

As already seen, cost-benefit analysis is one of the primary techniques for assessing criteria in program evaluation, i.e. technical verification. There is nothing to preclude, however, the extension of the logic of cost-benefit analysis to the evaluation of system-level inputs and outputs as well. This is, in fact, what the economist's theory of welfare economics has been structured to accomplish. Although in chapter 2 we criticized welfare economics for its ideological tendency to confuse its analytical framework with a natural understanding of social reality itself, its emphasis on cost-benefit analysis can have important uses at the systems level of vindication, where the focus is on the functional relationships that bind together the existing system. This is especially the case in a capitalist society.

The systems approach, then, offers a form of "macro" cost-benefit analysis (Schmid, 1989). While this constitutes a much more complicated, and thus much less empirically precise kind of calculation, the logic of the technique remains the same. It is mainly a matter of empirically drawing in a wider range of systemwide opportunity costs and benefits. In fact, as we shall see in the next chapter, this is just how the Reagan administration advanced cost-benefit analysis as a major decision tool to challenge the Great Society programs, the primary targets of the Reagan policy "revolution" (Noble, 1987).

In the language of the economist, the task of macro cost-benefit analysis is to include a wider range of "externalities" typically ignored by the more micro-oriented project analyses. Externalities are defined as costs that extend beyond the boundaries of a specific program or project and are not borne by investors or producers directly involved in the activity but rather by members of society. Consider the example of burning coal to produce energy. The result is an externality—air pollution. The air we breathe belongs to no one in particular, but to the society as a whole. Whereas traditional "micro" cost-benefit analysis—concerned mainly with the amount of energy obtained from a given amount of coal—would not typically include in the cost-benefit equation the costs of cleaning up the air or the health costs of living with pollution, a macro evaluation would extend the boundaries of the analysis to include these otherwise hidden social costs imposed on the society as a whole.

Once the boundaries of the evaluation are established, a welfare-oriented macro cost-benefit analysis offers a simple utilitarian decision rule: the best policy or course of action is the one that bestows benefits on some individuals or groups but leads to losses for none. Defined as the "Pareto optimal," this policy decision criterion is based on the construction of a "social welfare" function, a formula for aggregating net benefits (utilities) accruing to individuals in the society as a whole (Mueller, 1979:178–83). A social welfare or "utility" function is an instrumental ordering of social preferences designed to realize this optimal arrangement (Stokely and Zeckhauser, 1978:257–86).

Although it has been theoretically demonstrated that no such optimal utility function is in fact empirically possible in a complex social system, a number of rules designed to approximate the "Pareto optimal" have been developed, the "Kaldor-Hicks criterion" being the most important. According to this rule, the best policy course is the one which makes possible for those who potentially gain from the policy to compensate the potential losers and still retain a net benefit (Gramlich, 1990). All the analyst needs to do for each policy alternative under consideration is to sum up the program costs and the systemwide benefits. If the ratio of benefits to costs sufficiently exceeds unity enough to permit fulfillment of the Kaldor-Hicks principle, then the action is more desirable than the status quo. Much less clear, however, is the question of what would compel the beneficiaries to compensate the losers.

The critical theoretical question in such an analysis is where to draw the boundary lines of the evaluation. That is, how many externalities should be included? In an economically oriented systems perspective, where the boundaries of the extant society are typically taken as given, cost-benefit analysts typically derive rules for making judgments about both the boundaries of the analytical system and the distribution of costs and benefits from past experience in the policy process, particularly from tax and economic transfer policies. At the level of vindication in the logic of evaluation this procedure is acceptable, as here the system is taken as given. This is not, however, to overshadow the fundamentally political nature of questions concerning how a society distributes both its resources and social responsibilities. Such decisions, of course, are always open to renegotiation as the system, largely through political struggles, comes to be defined in new ways. Indeed, Werner Ulrich (1983) has developed an approach called "critical systems heuristics" which is designed to build into the analysis the normative justification of the boundaries themselves. But this issue pushes us into the fourth discourse of evaluation, social choice.

At this point, we can conclude our discussion of the analytical aspects of vindication and turn to a more practical illustration of the kind of policy argumentation that occurs at this level of evaluation. For this purpose, we examine the development of disability policy and the struggle in the 1970s and 1980s over the question of the impact of disability policy goals on mainstream American society as a whole.

### READINGS

Lance deHaven-Smith. 1988. *Philosophical Critiques of Policy Analysis: Lindblom, Habermas, and the Great Society.* Gainesville: Univ. of Florida Press.

A. Alan Schmid. 1989. *Benefit-Cost Analysis: A Political Economy Approach.* Boulder, CO: Westview.

C. West Churchman. 1968. *The Systems Approach.* New York: Dell.

Jay Forrester. 1971. *Urban Dynamics.* Cambridge, MA: Wright-Allen.

Charles E. Lindblom. 1977. *Politics and Markets.* New York: Basic Books.

Frances Fox Piven and Richard A. Cloward. 1993. *Regulating the Poor: The Functions of Public Welfare.* New York: Vintage Books.

Robert K. Merton. 1957. *Social Theory and Social Structure.* New York: Free Press.

# 7  Reassessing Disability Policy Goals: Equal Rights versus Societal Costs

Argumentation and evaluation at the level of vindication became prominent features of policy debates in the 1970s and 1980s. The reason had much to do with the fact that during this period the American political economy increasingly faced fundamental troubles, if not serious crisis. In response, political discourse shifted to issues concerning how to get the system back on course. Many people came to question the basic policy goals and assumptions that had been pursued by the government; for them public policy seemed to be causing the societal crisis, rather than solving it (Wildavsky, 1979:82). Policy debates, in this respect, shifted away from first-order questions concerned with program impacts on policy participants to the larger second-order questions concerning the implications of a policy's goals and assumptions for the social system as a whole.

Among the numerous policy illustrations that could be cited, none better exemplifies the nature of this second-order policy discourse than the case of disability policy. The following discussion thus employs the disability policy debates of the 1970s and 1980s to demonstrate a shift away from the more pragmatic first-order considerations associated with disability policy—such as program efficiency and situational circumstances—to questions concerning the effects of the policy's goals and assumptions on the larger society. Proceeding in three parts, the chapter begins with the historical origins of disability policy, emphasizing its place in the policy framework of the modern American welfare state and its professional-managerial approach to policy development and administration. Second, the discussion turns to the rise of the disability protest movement in the 1970s and its challenge to the economic and social dependencies that professionalization often meant for the disabled. Such dependencies are traced to a number of interrelated normative assumptions basic to professional disability policy. In the final section, the discussion

examines the ways in which the disability movement's alternative policy orientation clashed with the conservative politics of the 1980s. Whereas the
movement's challenge largely focused on the social dependencies resulting
from established professional-managerial goals, the conservative political
challenge was directed toward the larger normative implications of the proposed remedy for the society as a whole. Although conservatives have accepted the most basic premise of the disability movement—namely that the
social dependencies created by welfare state bureaucracies should be eliminated—they by and large have opposed the goals of the disability rights movement on the grounds that they impose inordinate economic and social costs on
the rest of society.

## THE SOCIAL SYSTEM AS WELFARE STATE: THE RISE OF DISABILITY POLICY

Fundamental to vindication is the turn from situational circumstances to the level of the system as a whole. The discussion, for this reason, first locates disability policy within the framework of the American
welfare state, the basic organizing concept of the sociopolitical system. The
welfare state, as the social policy framework of the modern corporate-liberal
state, supplies the norms and principles which have shaped disability policy
for much of the latter half of this century.

It has long been a basic function of government in the United States to
help people who experience blindness, deafness, mobility impairments, and
other physical or mental disabilities. To a great extent, America's efforts to
serve persons with disabilities has been forged by a combination of war and in-
dustrialization. After each of the nation's major wars, a large number of disabled veterans have needed care and assistance. At the same time, the
phenomenal growth in America's industrial production has led to more and
more on-the-job accidents and thus disabled workers in need of help. Over
time, then, various public programs have been established especially for the
disabled population, including various forms of financial compensation, re-
training and rehabilitation, special schools, and institutionalization (e.g., group
homes and mental hospitals).

Prior to the 1930s, the programs and services that existed for people with
disabilities were not based on any well-defined national policy. In some states,
disabled people received public pensions to help them buy housing and other
necessities, while in other states they and their families were left to fend for
themselves. A person with a mobility impairment could go through a rather
elaborate vocational rehabilitation program in Georgia, but not in neighboring
Tennessee. And even at the federal level, financial compensation and voca-

tional rehabilitation services were unevenly provided to war veterans, injured factory workers, and the elderly.

Beginning in the 1930s, this "hodgepodge" of policies and programs was remodeled by Franklin D. Roosevelt's New Deal. Indeed, basic to the New Deal was the introduction of a coordinated set of national social-welfare programs for disadvantaged groups, the result of which came later to be identified as the "American Welfare State" (Berkowitz and Quaid, 1992). The programmatic orientation of the New Deal was twofold: the regulation of the corporate economy to ensure economic growth and the provision of a "social net" for the less fortunate who fell outside of the corporate economic framework, particularly those who slipped through the system through no fault of their own (Rochefort, 1986). Disabled persons, particularly those disabled in American wars or on the job, were just such a group.

The two basic programs devised to meet the New Deal's social commitments were social security and vocational rehabilitation. The social net provided by the Social Security Act of 1935 was carefully designed to meet public demands within the framework of popular beliefs and constitutional understandings. Though bitterly opposed by some, the Social Security Act sailed through Congress and was signed into law by President Roosevelt in 1935. Fundamentally, it introduced two kinds of programs: (1) an insurance program for the unemployed and elderly based on workers' contributions, and (2) an assistance program for those with disabilities and their dependent children. The federal government used its taxing power to provide the funds, but all of the programs (except for old-age insurance) were administered by the states. Everybody, rich or poor, was eligible for the insurance programs. Only the poor, as measured by an income means test, were eligible for the assistance programs.

The major social-welfare programs today include Old Age, Survivors, and Disability Insurance, Medicare, unemployment insurance, Aid to Families with Dependent Children, Supplemental Security Income, food stamps, and Medicaid. While all of these offer assistance to disabled persons, three are of particular importance. Old Age, Survivors, and Disability Insurance provide monthly payments to retired or disabled persons and to surviving members of their families. Medicare pays for part of the cost of hospital care for retired or disabled persons covered by Social Security. And the Supplemental Security Income program supplies cash payments to aged, blind, or disabled people whose income is below a certain amount (Percy, 1989).

While financial assistance provided through the social security program (and state-based workers' compensation programs) was—and still is—an important element of disability policy, vocational rehabilitation became the focal point of the policy orientation. The federal vocational rehabilitation program, signed into law in 1921, emphasized medical treatment, occupational therapy, counseling, and intensive job training to give disabled people the skills to become functioning members of society. Based on the emerging field of "rehabilitation science," the program promised to remove the impediments to a productive life caused by a physical impairment. One of the more prominent rehabilitation enthusiasts of the period was President Roosevelt, who had used a wheelchair most of his adult life (Miller, 1983).

To supply the emerging rehabilitation profession with an appropriate standing within the social service oriented bureaucracies of the welfare state, rehabilitation programs were placed within the educational bureaucracy of the federal government and tied to its goals and values, principally training. In 1943 the federal government created within the Department of Health, Education, and Welfare the Rehabilitation Services Administration to manage rehabilitation policy. The functions of the agency were to oversee the operation of state rehabilitation programs and to establish national priorities for disability policy. The agency worked closely with the National Rehabilitation Association established two years later. Organized to facilitate the sharing of ideas and information in the rehabilitation field, the Association established standards for the training and certification of rehabilitation counselors, which in turn became agency policy (Sales and Harcleroad, 1986).

## THE PROFESSIONAL-MANAGERIAL APPROACH: POLICY GOALS AND ASSUMPTIONS

As the focus in vindication is on the relation of policy goals to the larger societal system, it is important to clarify the nature of the disability policy goals and assumptions that evolved with the welfare system. Toward this end, we examine the "professional-managerial approach" to disability policy development and administration.

The welfare state's disability bureaucracy and its professional theories of rehabilitation expanded greatly after World War II, the Korean conflict, and the Vietnam war. All significantly increased the number of people in need of disability payments and rehabilitation. Consequently, the demand for services precipitated an even greater expansion of the fiscal and administrative apparatus, resulting in the increasing domination of disability programs by federal and state rehabilitation bureaucracies. These officials were guided by two interrelated policy goals: (1) the timely dispensation of disability insurance program monies to disabled persons, and (2) the provision of vocational training for those who could benefit from the skills of professional rehabilitation counselors. By all measures, these goals came to dominate disability policy. They became the core objectives of the professional-managerial approach.

Basic to the achievement of these goals was a policy orientation developed around specific professional beliefs and managerial practices. In most general terms the framework can be characterized in terms of its definition of the disability problem, its conceptualization of the government's responsibility for the disabled, a set of basic policy goals, an approach to policy implementation, and its methods of program evaluation. The policy framework is summarized as follows:

- *Problem Definition*. Disability is fundamentally defined as a medical problem. Disabled people, in this respect, can be divided into two problem categories. One group is composed of those with severe disabilities whose primary problem is to take care of themselves. The second group includes those with less severe disabilities whose major problem is unemployment. The overwhelming majority of disabled people are in the latter category; in varying degrees they suffer "functional limitations." Moving them into the work force is dependent on successful compensation of these limitations.
- *Government Responsibility*. The responsibility of government is limited, whenever possible, to getting the disabled into the work force. The market system is seen as the basic mechanism for allocating resources and life chances. The problem is ultimately believed to rest with the individual, rather than the market. The individual must adjust to the existing society and its market arrangements; the disability problem is thus "individualized." Disability policy, as part of the welfare state, is designed to support and supplement the capitalist market system, not to impede it.
- *Policy Goals*. The basic goals are financial support, rehabilitation, employment counseling, and job placement. Employment provides people with disabilities with dignity and enables them to control their own lives. Once employed, the disabled contribute to the productivity of the nation and reduce the government's need to provide support.
- *Policy Implementation*. Public agencies, staffed with disability specialists and professional program administrators, provide care and rehabilitation through institutional residences (mental hospitals and group homes), as well as compensation through programs that supply a monthly income to people with disabilities to cover living expenses. Such services are believed to be best administered through local and state agencies, while overall policy coordination is seen to be best supplied through centralized federal agencies.
- *Policy Evaluation*. Given the nature of program goals—goals defined in terms of helping people with disabilities obtain employment within the established parameters of the American economy—professional disability experts have sought to justify the program at the level of verification. Toward this end, cost-benefit analysis has served as the primary methodological technique for disability policy evaluation.

The desire to professionalize disability workers permeated the program from its beginnings. As W. R. Tippet stated in an address before the National Civilian Rehabilitation Conference of 1925, "Effective placement is not an amateur job" (cited in Sullivan and Snortum: 1926: 268). Successful rehabilitation required a professional atmosphere. Disability specialists, it was argued, cannot work "in a dirty, noisy office where the men stand at a desk with a line of applicants trailing off behind them." Effective rehabilitation demanded an attractive office, "very much like the office of the better type of physician" (Sullivan and Snortum: 1926:272–73).

In view of this professional thrust, federal officials began to contemplate the creation of special rehabilitation fellowships and training courses. By the 1940s, it was common to hear the argument that "better-trained counselors would be more professional, and they would bring credit to the program by dealing more responsibly and effectively with the problems of the handicapped" (Berkowitz, 1987:171). In 1950, the Federal Security Administrator appointed a leading figure in the rehabilitation field to rejuvenate the program through a more distinctively professional approach, and by 1954, program officials had managed to convince the Eisenhower administration to sponsor major new legislation that would put rehabilitation on a more professional basis.[1] As Berkowitz (1987:171) put it, "the legislation initiated new types of federal grants to establish professional training programs in universities, to subsidize research on rehabilitation methods, and to enable counselors to attend the new programs at public expense." By 1965, the program had grown dramatically.[2]

Basic to the model guiding the development of these programs was the image of the "better type of physician." The result was the establishment of a highly refined rehabilitation paradigm based on a systematic set of "scientifically" rational treatment modalities and a professional model of disability treatment and services. The latter was directly adapted from the medical profession's model of the professional-client relationship. The professional disability expert, by virtue of his or her specialized training, was understood to have knowledge that disabled persons need. Rehabilitation experts were presumed to follow technically prescribed rules in the application and delivery of their knowledge and services to the limits of their competence, to respect the confidences granted to them by their clients, and not to misuse for their own benefit the special powers given to them within the boundaries of the relationship. In return, clients were expected to accept the profession's authority in specific areas of technical expertise, and to submit to the professional's ministrations. The professional disability specialist-client relationship thus established a clear-cut hierarchy between the superior and subordinate.

With regard to treatment, the scientific paradigm identified a basic set of strategies to be delivered through the professional-client relationship. These included treatment modalities for a set of narrowly defined physical impairments and occupational problems confronting disabled persons, a set of appropriate methods for occupational therapy and psychological social work, a job counseling employment approach to reentry into society, and the use of professional policy administrators to oversee and deliver rehabilitation payments and services. The acceptable parameters governing these practices were prescribed and monitored by professional organizations such as the National Accreditation Council for Agencies Serving the Blind and Visually Handicapped and the National Association of Vocational Rehabilitation Administrators (Sales and Harcleroad, 1986).

The focus on the patients' employment possibilities, the primary goal of the *nonmedical* phases of rehabilitation, was spelled out as the work of the occupational therapists and social workers housed in the professional service bureaucracies. For these specialists, unemployment among the disabled was seen to result from the restricted range of occupational opportunities available to the disabled because of bodily deficiencies (Hahn, 1987). This "functional-limitations" view, as it came to be called, took the environment of the disabled person as a given and focused on the individual's *defect* in relation to the environment (Hahn, 1987). As long as the environment was seen to consist of a set of stable economic and social roles, the inability of the individual to live up to the requirements of these roles was largely owed to his or her handicap. The goal was to tailor a remediation strategy that could bring the individual into line with the social and economic environment. The emphasis was on "regulating and conditioning behavior through such methods as itemized rules of conduct and prohibitions, monitoring systems, the long-term use of institutions, and specific behavior change mechanisms" (Rochefort, 1986:22).

The professional rehabilitation counselor thus became the key to program implementation. Equipped with a postgraduate education and federal funding, the counselor functioned as a job developer, personal advisor, administrative supervisor, budget analyst, correspondent, record keeper, program evaluator, consultant, and public relations expert. He or she opened client cases, determined eligibility, selected the right mix of services, and placed clients in jobs. In accordance with the professional-client hierarchy, rehabilitation counselors worked to control every aspect of a client's life—from personal dress, to where a person lives, to the types of occupations a person should choose (Johnson, 1986). The counselor's success in carrying out these responsibilities was seen to depend upon his or her "professional abilities coupled with planning, coordinating and managing skills" (Wright, 1980:53).

### Professional Evaluation: Program Costs and Benefits

The tasks of oversight and evaluation of the professionalized rehabilitation process became the responsibility of policy management experts who, consistent with standard managerial practices, followed the norms and standards of efficiency. In this respect, professional-managerial evaluations have largely side-stepped the questions of vindication. Having defined disability policy goals in terms of helping disabled people obtain employment in the economy—and thus having mainly accepted the priorities and requirements of the American economy on its own terms—they have sought to justify the program at the level of verification. Specifically, the focus has been on calculating the number of rehabilitated clients that have obtained jobs, the number of social benefits produced by those rehabilitated, and the amount of money saved when disabled compensation and social security recipients entered the workforce. Cost-benefit analysis has served as the primary methodological technique for disability policy evaluation.

To the credit of the professional-managerial approach, most cost-benefit evaluations of rehabilitation programs were quite successful in technically verifying the success of rehabilitation programs. For example, an early study concluded that the vocational rehabilitation program cost the government almost nothing. The 1948 annual evaluation of vocational rehabilitation indicated that an individual who worked 85 percent of the time could be expected to return in federal income taxes approximately ten dollars for every dollar the federal government expended on the person's rehabilitation (Berkowitz, 1987). Although there were difficulties with the calculation of the estimates (such as overstating the level of earnings), the 10 to 1 ratio was replicated for several years by rehabilitation administrators to justify their work (Berkowitz, 1987:164). In 1955, for instance, federal administrators told Congress a $39 million investment in rehabilitation would eventually yield $390 million in revenues.

In the 1950s and 1960s, however, the emphasis on cost-benefit analysis did generate a number of unanticipated administrative abuses that later were to plague the program. Basically, the cost-benefit orientation began to push rehabilitation administrators to get as many people as possible successfully placed in employment. Administrators consistently contended that money was wasted when people received services but did not obtain jobs. And the more money that was wasted, so the argument went, the lower the returns on the program and the less favorable the outcomes of the cost-benefit analysis (Berkowitz, 1987:166–67). The result was an administrative abuse described as "creaming."

Creaming was thus a way to improve the cost-benefit ratios of the disability programs through the development of easy employment opportunities (Oberman, 1965). Sheltered workshops, for instance, were created to provide immediate openings for rehabilitated clients. Limits were also placed on the entry into the rehabilitation process of severely disabled clients with low potentials for employment. They were largely left to long-term care facilities paid for by the social security system and other compensation programs.

Abuses aside, the cost-benefit arguments successfully paid off for vocational rehabilitation in the 1960s and early 1970s. Given the favorable ratios, vocational rehabilitation was regularly praised as a program worthy of both continuation and replication. Not only was it adopted as a hallmark of President Johnson's Great Society, it was also replicated in prisons, ghettos, and other areas where dehabilitating social problems existed. Total expenditures for vocational rehabilitation and related programs increased from approximately $80 million in 1960 to over $730 million in 1973. Clearly, both legislators and administrators were convinced that vocational rehabilitation was an investment with a high yield.

## CHALLENGING PROFESSIONAL ASSUMPTIONS: DISABILITY AS A SOCIAL PROBLEM

If vindication is a debate about the instrumental value of policy goals and assumptions, nothing better demonstrates the nature of such debate than the arguments advanced by the disability groups that were to challenge the professional-managerial policy framework. To illustrate this point, the discussion begins with the early rumblings of discontent.

Even as the rehabilitation community was receiving more funds and working with greater numbers of disabled people, voices of dissent began to be heard in the 1960s. While the disabled community by and large accepted the formal statement of disability policy goals—especially the emphasis on employment goals—a growing number of disabled people were beginning to complain that disability policy was in practice failing to adequately serve the needs of its recipients. It wasn't so much that those with disabilities failed to get jobs; rather it was a question of what kinds of jobs and how they got them. The critics, in this regard, argued that the professionals' overly narrow medical conceptualization of disability failed to adequately identify the nature of the problem and that the programs and services derived from this framework were not serving the best interests of disability clients. Indeed, by the middle 1970s, these complaints were to rise to the level of a major policy challenge.

In terms of the logic of evaluation, the policy challenge first emerged at the level of policy validation. Basically the reformers were arguing that disability professionals had failed to identify and deal with the *social* nature of the situation confronting the disabled community. The medical definition of the problem and its treatment modalities, particularly the emphasis on physical impairments and the medically oriented professional-client relationship that governed both disability treatment and service delivery, were seen to support a kind of second-class citizenship for the disabled in both the workplace and the society at large. Practices such as requiring applicants to the disability insurance program to obtain the certification of a medical doctor, or requiring clients to wear artificial limbs in order to look like able-bodied persons, were believed to perpetuate the image of the disabled person as an inferior being and thus worked in numerous ways to legitimate the barriers that already segregated the handicapped from the rest of society. Professional practices of this sort, disability movement leaders argued, implied that disability meant "biological inferiority" and led people to perceive the disabled as less intelligent, less able to make the right decisions, and therefore less able to control their own lives.

Disability groups were in many ways following the lead of other welfare state recipients who had begun to challenge the social dependencies created by established institutional practices (Piven, and Cloward, 1993; 1977). Focusing on the authority of those who made the basic decisions and rules about how they were to live their lives, many of those with disabilities began to feel themselves the victims of a destructive "culture of dependency" that bound them to the welfare state and its professionals. By the latter half of the 1970s, the "invidious paternalism" of rehabilitation administrators and counselors had in fact become the organizing slogan of an increasingly aggressive grassroots advocacy movement among the disabled (Hahn, 1987:572). Kenneth Jernigan (1979:26), director of the 50,000-member National Federation of the Blind, expressed the growing sentiment among disabled people when he described the National Accreditation Council for Agencies Serving the Blind and Visually Handicapped as symbolic of "everything odious and repulsive in our long and painful tradition—custodialism by government and private social agencies, ward status, vested interests, intimidation, exclusion, and second class citizenship."

Not only did professional practices encourage the larger society to view those with disabilities as inferior, they also led disabled people to see themselves in the same light. Believing themselves to be unable to function fully in mainstream society, a large majority of disabled people resigned themselves to long-term reliance on the disability professionals and their institutions. They learned, in fact, to accept the repressive forms of second-class citizenship promoted by these institutional practices. This, for the leaders of the disability movement, was the ultimate tragedy. The solution was to be found in a turn to "empowerment," "self-help," and "independence." These were to become the rallying calls of the movement in the late 1970s and 1980s.

As a direct challenge to the second-class citizenship of the disabled community, the ideology of empowerment gave shape to a much more radical approach toward rehabilitation. Most fundamentally, the empowerment argument turned the disability problem upside down and asserted that it was as much the society as the disabled person that needed adjustment. Based on a more expansive social definition of disability, empowerment specifically sought to replace the assumptions of the professional's functional-limitations model of the disabled individual with the tenets of an environmental-limitations model emphasizing the need to change society. In the movement's view, the problems facing the disabled community were "a function of the social arrangements of the community or society," not the disabled individual per se (Ryan, 1981:72).

The institutional embodiment of this emphasis on empowerment and self-help was the independent living center (ILC). Advanced as the major programmatic alternative, ILCs initially emerged on the campus of the University of California at Berkeley in the 1960s, where handicapped students had set up an independent off-campus living arrangement. Influenced by the civil rights and antiwar struggles of the late 1960s, the Berkeley effort was to become a source of inspiration and model for the movement in the 1970s and 1980s. ILCs, as the movement leaders argued, were the direct product of the experience of the disabled in *their own struggles* to help themselves; they represented their experience "of trying to survive away from the institution." It was, moreover, an argument that drew substantial support from the social-psychological literature on empowerment (Gottlieb and Farquharson, 1985).

In bold contrast to the professional view, then, this minority perspective took the societal environment itself to be the object of disability policy decisions. Public policy, it was argued, should not just help individuals to cope with the existing environment; it should also combat prejudice and discrimination and, in doing so, alter the established societal arrangements. The policy mechanism for effectuating such change, it was argued, was civil rights for the disabled. As Hahn (1987:552) put it, the "extension of civil rights" should be the "primary means of resolving the problems of disabled citizens."

With this civil rights argument, the disability groups began to emerge as a full-fledged movement. In the process, it elevated the disability challenge to the level of vindication. Beyond the challenge to the professional's medical definition of the disability problem, the call for civil rights turned the focus of the movement directly on the social system itself. According to movement leaders, the disabled had to be seen as nothing less than a minority group struggling to achieve full citizenship in American society. Arguing that political equality was not to be understood as a function of physical impairment (Liachowitz, 1988), the leaders demanded that the public fully accept persons with disabilities as first-class members of society. They agitated for new disability rights free of the kinds of traditional legislative and bureaucratic compromises that had long characterized disability policy.

In sum, the disability movement first argued that the treatment and employment goals of disability policy had to be restructured around a fully *social* definition of the disability problem and a broad commitment to the principles of empowerment and self-help (manifested in such institutions as the ILCs). Only in this way could such goals instrumentally contribute to fulfilling both the personal and societal potentials of disabled people. Second, the movement asserted that the way to bring this about was to endow the disabled with the equal rights of citizenship accorded to all others in a society built upon the ideals of individual initiative and self-reliance. It was this latter contention, concerned with the relation of the disabled to the rest of the citizenry as a whole, that advanced argumentation to the level of vindication.

### AMENDING THE ACT: THE POLITICS OF UNANTICIPATED CONSEQUENCES

Beyond questions concerning the instrumentality of policy goals and assumptions, the second question of vindication concerns whether or not the goals and assumptions lead to unanticipated—especially undesirable—consequences for the societal system as a whole. In the present context, the concern is clearly illustrated by the unexpected outcomes that followed the successes of the protest groups, especially the 1973 reform of the country's disability law.

The success of the disability groups was the result of a confluence of forces. Most important, at the beginning of the 1970s the dissatisfaction with the professional-managerial approach became intertwined with the emerging conservative political backlash against the social welfare state, the immediate manifestation of which was fiscal crisis. Under political attack from all sides, social welfare expenditures declined. With specific regard to vocational rehabilitation programs, the number of rehabilitations that agencies recorded, as well as the number of applications for the programs, began to drop significantly.

Rehabilitation thus confronted the troubles that affected nearly all social welfare programs. As the optimism of the 1960s gave way to the realism and pessimism of the mid-1970s, the Great Society approach to welfare was often charged with "throwing money" at problems without considering other fundamental institutional and social barriers blocking the advancement of the poor in American society. At the same time, the failure of the economy to match its earlier growth rates curtailed the number of jobs available and put substantial pressure on the federal budget. As the disadvantaged turned to social welfare programs for help, they increasingly found that the federal government had neither the kinds of resources needed to help them into the labor market nor the belief that it could afford to support a growing welfare establishment and still make good on other obligations placing heavy claims on diminishing federal funds, particularly military defense and other relatively protected entitlement programs such as social security. Vocational rehabilitation, a program lacking the open-ended budgetary status of an entitlement, was far more vulnerable to fiscal constrictions than were other disability programs such as workers' compensation and disability insurance.

As rehabilitation professionals became increasingly embroiled in financial battles, questions were also raised about various goals and practices associated with the rehabilitation process itself. Among the more specific complaints to come to the fore was the increasingly dominant practice of "creaming." Although creaming had generated bigger and bigger budget allocations, and was thus condoned by many program administrators, it increasingly led to a troublesome neglect of the seriously handicapped, many of whom began to complain vociferously to their congressional representatives. Worried about rising budget deficits, politicians latched on to the issue. Why, they asked, should the rehabilitation program devote a lion's share of its money to helping people who with a little effort would most likely find jobs on their own? That is, people who did not in any case require the services of very expensive professional training programs. Indeed, against the background of this apparent perversion of program goals, the pleas for independence by the disabled began to catch the ears of reform-minded legislators. What could be better, in fact, than releasing those with disabilities from their dependence on a self-serving bureaucratic apparatus? At this point, fiscal concern and the struggle for independence seemed to forge an alliance of political convenience.

Dwindling amounts of money and fewer applicants for rehabilitation training led to an extensive debate in both professional and legislative circles about the directions disability policy should take. The arguments ranged from phasing out rehabilitation counseling to rethinking disability goals altogether. It was in this context that Congress took up the task of reauthorizing the vocational rehabilitation program in the early 1970s.

The congressional bill that initially emerged focused on three major changes in the law. First, it sought to extricate the program from its association with the welfare system by relocating it in a newly created Rehabilitation Services Administration. Second, in response to the lobbying efforts of the disability movement, the legislation authorized the funding of independent living centers. And third, it mandated that priority be given to the severely handicapped, rather than to the mildly impaired or the culturally disadvantaged. For the first time, the law stressed that "additional emphasis should be placed on the vocational rehabilitation of the severely disabled, rather than those individuals who can readily be placed in employment." With this language, Congress and the supporters of the program hoped to redirect the drift in the 1960s toward serving people "handicapped in the social sense" to the "physically or mentally" disabled. In this respect, the new approach was radical in its emphasis on those with serious physical handicaps. More important than focusing on employment possibilities was the goal of "mainstreaming" severely disabled people out of the institutions and into the community.

The bill, however, had trouble getting White House approval. President Nixon refused to accept the independent living concept. In what constituted a surprising break with a long-standing practice—namely that a president would never interfere with "do-good" legislation—Nixon vetoed the bill twice. In his view, the ILCs smacked of the "false promises" of the 1960s. Such social concerns, he argued, diverted the program from its vocational objectives and "seriously jeopardize[d]" its fundamental goals. What is more, such diversions were believed to be just the sort of things that made it difficult to keep the federal budget in balance. Removing independent living from the bill was ultimately the price that had to be paid to gain Nixon's support.

### Disability Client Participation

The debate about independent living had nonetheless opened up the issue in ways that fundamentally changed the relationship between those with disabilities and vocational rehabilitation counselors. After 1973, even without the ILCs, the clients of the rehabilitation program demanded a greater role in the decisions pertaining to the services available. The clients increasingly dropped their roles as passive recipients of the services and began to act more like the program's *customers*. As Berkowitz (1987:180) put it, the handicapped now came to the program to "look at the samples that the counselors have to offer" and then decided "which of the program's services they [would] consume." This was, to be sure, a fundamental challenge to the traditional professional conception of rehabilitation. As analogies between rehabilitation and medicine gave way, counselors were no longer to practice what had come to be called the "clinical model" of rehabilitation (Woods et al., 1983). As Tubbins explained, the counselor no longer "dominated" the client; rather he or she consulted the handicapped person, and together they developed a course of action (Cited in Berkowitz, 1987:180).

Because people with disabilities have largely been excluded from the legislative and administrative processes concerned with policy and program development, they have had very little opportunity to think about and actively engage in the reform of disability programs. The new law included several steps to rectify this shortcoming. To effectuate and ensure the handicapped individual's right and "opportunity to participate in the decision-making," the law mandated the use of an individualized rehabilitation plan. This plan, to be formally worked out and signed by both the counselor and the client, was to serve as the consumer's warranty. Moreover, the law also initiated client-assistance programs that established ombudsmen in the rehabilitation agencies to protect the rights of the consumer. Although begun as discretionary projects, these client-assistance programs were later to become mandatory. A state without a client-assistance program found itself in the position of forfeiting its right to federal rehabilitation funds. What is more, these programs were required to be independent of the vocational rehabilitation program itself. To staff their client-assistance projects, many states turned to the advocacy groups that had emerged to protect the rights of the disabled. In this manner, the client-assistance programs became a source of legal advice available to a disgruntled client interested in pursuing his or her grievance through the courts. Indeed, the individual rehabilitation plans took on the status of legal documents explicitly spelling out claims that could be enforced in a court of law.

The elimination of the counselor's total discretion over the client, along with the introduction of client-assistance programs, constituted an altogether new approach to the delivery of rehabilitation services. Although many rehabilitation officials publicly praised the written plans, the new procedures exposed many of the conflicts between the handicapped and their professional counselors. While, to be sure, some of the recorded complaints were of the type to be expected in a large bureaucracy, others penetrated deeper and tapped long-hidden animosities between the counselors and the clients. In particular, the complaints brought to the fore a host of social judgments that the counselors had heretofore made in the name of their best "professional" opinion. To illustrate the point, Berkowitz cites the case of a client with cerebral palsy who, after having made his way through college, wanted to earn a Master's degree in philosophy (and possibly even a doctorate in the hopes of teaching). Should the rehabilitation agency become an advocate for this person, even though there are few openings for philosophy professors, and a person with cerebral palsy might find it difficult to lecture? Or, does a person with cerebral palsy have the same right to pursue a career as a philosophy professor as an able-bodied person, regardless of job opportunities?

As such a case makes clear, the conflicts between the handicapped community and the vocational rehabilitation program can be quite difficult, both pragmatically and morally. Counselors value their professional autonomy, while the handicapped community increasingly sees itself possessing inherent rights. As a result, the counselors and the handicapped have often found themselves disagreeing over where the limitations of the handicapped end and the failures of society begin.

## Section 504

The Amendments to the 1973 Rehabilitation Act also fundamentally changed the basic emphasis of disability policy on rehabilitation, replacing it with the goal of handicapped rights. Every bit as important as the aforementioned changes in the rehabilitation process was the seemingly innocuous inclusion of a single sentence in the 1973 Amendments. The sentence, in Section 504 of the 1973 Act, stated that:

No otherwise qualified handicapped individual in the United States shall, solely by the reason of his handicap, be excluded from participation in, be denied benefits of, or be subject to discrimination under any program or activity of Federal assistance. (U.S. Dept. of Education, Office of Special Education and Rehabilitation Services, 1988)

Section 504 was drawn directly from the language of the Civil Rights Act of 1964 and the story behind its inclusion in the Rehabilitation Act defies conventional political science theory. Lawmaking, according to the traditional textbook, occurs in response to interest group pressures. But in the case of Section 504 there were neither special efforts on the part of handicapped groups to promote the inclusion or wording of the provision, nor any particular interest concerning it in the House or Senate. Instead, this provision—which was to become the most controversial feature of the Act as a whole—was simply inserted into the bill by its Congressional sponsors with little discussion in Congress. It was largely included as a kind of afterthought, a gesture to the great civil rights and equal opportunity struggles of the 1960s. Other groups had fought to win these rights and, so the argument went, there was no reason not to include them in a bill designed to give greater protection to the disabled. Section 504, in short, was included without consideration of its political ramifications. No one seemed to recognize that it would provide the "political opportunity structure" (Kitschelt, 1989) capable of opening the way for major initiatives on the part of grass-roots protest movements, efforts which would extend the discussion of disability policy well beyond the disability community itself. It was to bring into the mainstream of policy politics the protest movement which had up to that point only managed to become a force within the disability community itself.

This otherwise obscure provision, as Berkowitz (1987:211) put it, "pulled the handicapped together in the 1970s." Acquiring "an almost religious aura within the handicapped community," it virtually "baptized" the movement's leaders. By providing legal recourse for disabled persons suffering from various forms of discrimination (employment, housing, transportation, or educational discrimination, etc.), Section 504 gave political birth to a host of advocacy coalitions, public interest associations, and legal defense centers designed to protect and advance the rights of disabled people. These in turn gave impetus to a wide range of advisory committees, information centers, and research institutes at the state and federal levels designed to promote the social acceptance of persons with disabilities and to counsel policymakers on various policy reforms. Seeking to discredit the traditional approach to rehabilitation, these groups worked to make equality and social acceptance meaningful goals within disability policy. Backed by an increasingly powerful grass-roots protest movement, they took their case to the media and the streets, state legislatures and the courts, and to the White House (Scotch, 1984). An immediate result was the quick passage of federal legislation establishing ILCs. Signed into law by President Carter, the law officially ended the complete dominance of policy administration by rehabilitation professionals.

While disability groups had not been behind the inclusion of Section 504 itself, they did not miss a chance when it came to lobbying the administrative agencies involved in writing the specific regulations. The primary goal was to ensure that the regulations were spelled out legally as basic human rights without regard to other considerations, especially the calculation of costs and benefits. In particular, this meant keeping the traditional rehabilitation administrators and the Office of Management and Budget out of the process. As one lawyer for the disabled put it, the fear was that "OMB would give too much weight to economic considerations which have a very small place in a program designed to vindicate basic human and legal rights" (Berkowitz, 1987: 213). In the end, the Office of Civil Rights of the Department of Health, Education, and Welfare received the assignment. Interpreted as a victory by disability groups, this ensured that in the formulation of regulations Section 504 was regarded as a civil rights clause. As civil rights lawyers of the Office explained it, the clause concerned basic rights that transcended costs.

These new regulations moved the handicapped movement into the mainstream of the minority rights movement, taking its place alongside of blacks and women. Learning from the leaders of the earlier civil rights movement, legal advocacy agencies used the new regulations to press their demands in the courts, the consequences of which were a flood of cases challenging federal agencies and their contractors to employ the disabled. Moreover, in response to continuing grass roots pressures, the new legal provisions were further amplified and extended in countless ways throughout the federal and state governments. By the late 1970s, there were forty different federal programs with over $60 billion in expenditures for the handicapped (National Council on the Handicapped, 1986). Among them were important but controversial programs such as the Education for All Handicapped Children Act in 1975, which required the states, as a precondition for receiving federal aid, to provide a free and appropriate education for all handicapped children.

Even if cost was not a mandated consideration, by the time these regulations had attracted public attention, it had become clear that their implementation was costing significant amounts of money. The most controversial and expensive of the regulations, at both the federal and state levels, were those that mandated handicapped access to buses and other forms of public transportation; the modification of building ramps, washrooms, doors, aisles, and elevators in public buildings; the reconstruction of university classrooms and dormitories to make them wheelchair accessible; the setting aside of convenient parking for the disabled at work and elsewhere; and the provision of special assistance to handicapped employees, including readers for blind workers, sign language interpreters, and talking calculators. By the time the full picture began to emerge, substantial political opposition was beginning to form against the regulations, as well as the policy beliefs of the disability movement more generally.

## CONSERVATIVE BACKLASH: DO DISABILITY RIGHTS JUSTIFY THE COSTS?

In this final section, we show that while the disability movement made significant gains against the established professional-managerial theory, it began at the same time to encounter political difficulties from another direction. Whereas the challenge to the assumptions of the professional-managerial approach largely focused on the efficacy of the social dependency resulting from established practices—that is, do these practices produce desirable long-term results for disabled persons—the political challenge to the disability movement focused on the larger normative implications of the proposed remedy for the rest of the society.

Rather than from the professionals in the rehabilitation community, the political challenge in the 1980s came from conservative politicians and journalists. Essentially, it appeared as part of the larger and more general conservative critique of liberal American society. Conservatives opposed the disability movement's efforts to advance its alternative policy goal in the name of long-established themes of equality, rights, and democratic participation in American politics. Basic to this conservative critique were the perceived failures of the social welfare system generally. Prominent among the conservative themes was the charge that both income maintenance and civil rights programs were "disabling" America itself (Morgan, 1986:7). Where, the conservatives asked, did the rights of various minority groups end and the rights of society begin? How, in short, could these rights-based beliefs be vindicated against the functional requirements of the larger society?

Fundamentally, the conservative argument rested on two prongs: one concerning discrimination and the other costs. With regard to discrimination, conservatives believed that affirmative action, the basic civil rights goal of the liberal movement of the 1960s and 1970s, was an inappropriate remedy for attaining equality in the society, whether it be in the workplace, schools, housing, transportation, and so on. As one opponent of affirmative action put it, "the belief that discrimination can be administered to the body politic in judicious doses in order to create nondiscrimination is akin to the medical wisdom of curing an alcoholic with whiskey. Discrimination is addictive. Its uses cannot be precisely controlled" (Todorovich, 1975:37). In this view, efforts to eliminate discrimination against the handicapped and other groups through preferential hiring could only create a perverse form of "reverse discrimination" (Greenawalt, 1983; Gross, 1977).

Although complaints of reverse discrimination were common in many quarters of the society, the argument was difficult to advance in connection with the handicapped. For fear of appearing cruel and heartless, those who opposed the new disability regulations often found it awkward to directly challenge the disability rights movement. Consequently, the growing political backlash against the disabled community tended to emerge more as a part of the economic assault on the welfare state. The central question was, how can American society afford to pay for these welfare programs and social regulations?

Basic to the cost argument was a simple slogan: "There are no more free lunches." Energy shortages and rising governmental deficits were pointed to as evidence of an era of scarce resources. Government, conservatives argued, could in the future only afford to do those things that maximize the net satisfaction of the society as a whole. Rights-based policies, they argued, tended to involve more benefits for a small group of individuals than for the larger society. In short, the costs were too great given the limited benefits.

The examples typically cited were not without persuasive force. For instance, equal rights provisions meant that universities had to determine if their classes, laboratories, and other facilities were accessible to the handicapped. Frequently cited as a case in point, George Washington University spent $2.5 million of its own money on modifications designed to bring their facilities into compliance. But for what, many asked? According to a survey by the *New York Times,* no more than 30,000 handicapped people were expected to be in college at any one time. In light of such statistics, the newspaper—like increasing numbers of public and private sector administrators around the country—questioned the need to make every university accessible.

The controversy in higher education was minor compared to the storm generated in the transportation industry, where the economic implications of the Department of Transportation's regulations became the source of a strident debate. In New York City, the chairman of the Metropolitan Transit Authority announced that a state law requiring subways to be accessible to the handicapped and therefore equipped with elevators imposed $100 million in extra expenditures on the city. "Spending the money to make the New York subways . . . accessible to the handicapped," said the chairman, "would mean less money to improve the security and comfort of the subways. Millions would suffer, and only a few would gain." As evidence, opponents pointed to the costly elevators installed in the Washington, D.C., subway system. They carried a daily average of only twenty-nine handicapped riders. The San Francisco system, also serving Berkeley (a center of the handicapped movement), transported only about eighty wheelchair riders daily.

The issue of making buses accessible to the handicapped was perhaps even more controversial. Not only did installing wheelchair ramps prove to be very expensive, it also generated heated disagreements over the appropriate design. Both the American Public Transit Association and General Motors opposed the idea of requiring ramps for all public transit systems. They criticized in particular the use of a specially constructed bus with wheelchair ramps designed by the Department of Transportation at a cost of $27 million. While handicapped activists strongly supported the proposed bus, a vice-president of the American Public Transit Association stated that "the imposition of any such program would imply the use of scarce federal resources . . . for what we believe is a non-solution in the first place." This, he argued, bordered on the ridiculous. Countering such arguments, leaders of the handicapped movement believed that the resistance to putting ramps on buses merely illustrated the prejudice against them. They pointed out, for example, that it cost twice as much to put air conditioning in a bus as it did to install a ramp. Yet no public outcry arose over the cost of air-conditioning buses.

Underlying the conservatives' position was the assumption that "major positive strides in U.S. economic and social development came from the workings of the free market, not regulation, planning, or any other type of government program or assistance" (Vedlitz, 1988:13). Such writers asserted that market competition is the most efficient and equitable mechanism for allocating goods and services in society. Accordingly, conservatives considered most government actions necessarily ineffective and typically more harmful than helpful. Basic to the presidency of Ronald Reagan, these policy assumptions were literally to redefine the terms of American political discourse in the 1980s. Indeed, their impact is still very much a part of American politics in the 1990s.

### REAGAN AND THE POLITICS OF VINDICATION

The Reagan administration and its conservative followers interpreted the 1980 election as nothing less than a public mandate to dismantle the social welfare state as a whole, save a program here or there. The basic targets were just those sorts of programs that the disability movement had struggled to win: social welfare entitlements, government regulation, and affirmative action. With no shortage of support from conservative think tanks, administration officials persistently argued that every public policy must pass a basic test: Did it make America better?

How was that to be determined? The Reagan administration's answer was to mandate a macro-oriented cost-benefit analysis for every regulatory rule, both old and new (Tolchin and Tolchin, 1985). In short, no new rule was to be proffered without consideration of its costs and benefits for the society as a whole.[3] Any regulatory rule that could be shown to cost a great deal of money to implement and/or involved sweeping interference in the operations of a private sector business or industry (particularly through voluminous paperwork and reporting) was a prime target for reform, frequently defined as elimination.

Against these requirements, Section 504 was almost a caricature of the kinds of policies the administration sought to eliminate. Reagan administration conservatives—joined to some extent by disgruntled vocational rehabilitation professionals—challenged the very premises of the disability rights movement. Where, they asked, did the rights of the handicapped end and the costs to society begin?

The challenge was not without success. Providing numerous concrete examples which gave credence to the conservative argument, the administration managed in a very short period of time to tap a latent but rather sizable antipathy against the disability regulations. News stories abounded on the rigidity, absurdity, and costliness of government regulation in general, and Section 504 was often singled out as a prime example of such administrative perversity. One of the most widely reported stories concerned the small town of Rudd, Iowa. A small farming community of less than five hundred people, Rudd was informed by a regional office of HEW's Office of Civil Rights that the town's public library would have to be made wheelchair accessible, despite the fact that none of the inhabitants used a wheelchair. The required ramp, according to the townspeople, cost $6,500 to build and was for no one but the bureaucrats. The result of such instances was a growing political backlash.

During the early years of the Reagan administration, the leaders of the handicapped rights movement recognized their vulnerability and formed coalitions with other civil rights groups. Indeed, they "spent most of their time during the 1980s trying to prevent the Reagan administration from dismantling the regulations" (Rasky, 1989:5). In the view of the movement leaders, victory was largely defined in terms of merely maintaining the status quo.

Most important were the efforts of the Disability Rights Defense and Education Fund, which established a Washington office in 1981 in an effort to protect the hard won disability benefits. Indicative of a new political sophistication on the part of the movement generally, the Defense Fund astutely developed a political strategy based on the argument that the movement's goals and those of the Reagan administration were not as dissimilar as they might first appear. Both saw big government as a hindrance to individual initiatives; both were "antibureaucratic" and denounced "paternalistic" government; and both approved of public welfare for only the truly needy. In short, both claimed to place a higher value on individual independence than government assistance. Whereas leaders of the disability movement had spoken in the past of disability entitlements and inherent rights, they now stressed independence.

And the strategy worked. After an initial decision to take action against the Section 504 regulations, the Reagan administration's Task Force for Regulatory Relief, the principal group established to determine the macro costs and benefits of government regulations, decided not to press for changes. In the end, the task force and its director, Vice-President George Bush, fearing the charge of heartless hypocrisy, decided instead to sing the praises of the handicapped. Indeed, Bush emerged as something of a political supporter of disability rights (perhaps influenced, as has been suggested, by the fact that members of his family have suffered impairments). One member of Bush's Task Force summed up the group's position this way: the administration and the handicapped community wanted the same thing—"to turn as many of the disabled as possible into taxpaying citizens." According to another, the point the handicapped community was making was basic to sound Republican principles. Rather than giving a man a fish, the goal was to teach him to catch his own. No self-respecting Republican could fault that.

In short, the movement had restructured its political discourse in a way that made it difficult for the conservative administration to oppose it publicly. Coupled with a massive letter writing campaign to protest the deregulation of Section 504, the strategy succeeded. What is more, as Berkowitz (1987:223) points out, the administration had "gained new respect for the handicapped as a potential interest group." As a concrete response, the administration elevated the National Council on the Handicapped to the status of an independent federal agency.

Initially established in 1978 as an advisory council in the Department of Education, the Council was charged with the task of reviewing all laws, programs, and policies of the federal government affecting disabled individuals and making such recommendations as deemed necessary to the president, the Congress, the secretary of the Department of Education, the commissioner of the Rehabilitation Services Administration, and the director of the National Institute of Handicapped Research. In particular, the Council was statutorily directed to submit to the president and the Congress in 1986 a report analyzing federal programs and presenting legislative recommendations to enhance the productivity and quality of life of Americans with disabilities.

The final report of the Council, *Toward Independence,* was in many ways a forerunner of things to come. Although at the time many wrote it off as a symbolic gesture, in the name of independence the report laid out a very progressive civil-rights orientation which further fueled the disability movement. As these efforts to advance the rights of the disabled garnered political support, they laid the groundwork for new and even more progressive legislation. Among the significant indicators of success was the fact that by 1988 George Bush, as a presidential candidate, endorsed legislation to further extend civil-rights protections to the disabled. Late in that year, as testament to the strength of the movement, the first version of a new bill passed the Senate.

## THE AMERICANS WITH DISABILITIES ACT OF 1990

As a far-ranging extension of the 1972 law, the 1990 act virtually ensured that the cost controversy will remain a major public issue. Formally, the act was passed in large part as a Congressional effort to clarify legal dilemmas and other entanglements the earlier law had not foreseen (Rasky, 1989). By the late 1980s, the demand for clarification was rife and the new law was drafted as a kind of rewrite of the 1973 law. Most fundamentally, its goal was to inform the administration of what the earlier provisions were now to mean, especially Section 504, and offered new guidelines for enforcement. The outcome was a very progressive bill that further extended the evolving civil-rights approach, although it specified the possibility of exemptions for businesses that would experience undue hardships caused by compliance (Holmes, 1990; Kolata, 1991).

The most important new provision in the law was its extension of the civil-rights provisions to the private sector. According to the provisions of the act, virtually every type of commercial establishment is to be made accessible to the handicapped (Holmes, 1991a; Holmes, 1991b). Newly constructed buildings are required to install ramps, elevators, and the like, while existing businesses must make such changes if they can be accomplished without undue expense or hardship (Andrews, 1991; Dugger, 1991). Lifts are required on new buses and telephone companies have to make phone service available to the hearing impaired. The rules are to be phased in over four years.

Altogether the legislation affects some 3.9 million business establishments and 666,000 employers. Although the law's supporters maintain that billions of tax dollars a year are likely to be saved in federal aid to disabled people who would rather be working, its opponents maintain that it will cost millions of business establishments and employers an untold amount of money. Because of the four-year phase-in period, it is a question that cannot at present be addressed with any certainty. What can be said, however, is that the business community is preparing for what it considers a potential disaster. In particular, many industries and businesses are planning to appeal to the undue hardship clause of the Act and the shape of the struggle, according to legal experts, will depend on how the clause is to be interpreted (Weaver, 1991a). One thing is certain: The business community is already gearing up for the battle.[4]

How, one might ask, could such legislation pass in a supposedly conservative cost-conscious age? The question is indeed interesting. Several forces were at work: the political sophistication and strength of the handicapped; the widespread recognition that the disabled community is among the deserving minorities and that opposing them, at least in public, often appears heartless (thus, very few are willing to publicly go on record as opposing them); and the fact that the legislation was only accepted after Congress included the undue hardship clauses—a clear concession to business and industry. To ensure White House acceptance of the bill congressional sponsors had to agree to eliminate provisions that would have required violators to pay punitive and compensatory damages in addition to significant fines. In the end, the sponsors agreed to a compromise: drop the damages provisions and keep the bill's wide scope. As Senator Kennedy put it at the time, "It's worth the trade-off because the concept was so important. This legislation will go down as one of the most important accomplishments in the history of the Congress" (Smith, 1989). But many conservatives see it differently. Without stiff penalties, coupled with the exemption clauses, the historic nature of the accomplishment will only be later determined as an outcome of the court struggles that ensue. Indeed, some argue that the provisions were so watered down as to render symbolic an otherwise profoundly important civil-rights victory.

### VINDICATION AND BEYOND

We have thus seen that the disability rights movement, having successfully challenged the professional-managerial approach for failing to integrate the disabled into mainstream society adequately, was later confronted by political conservatives. While conservatives have been sympathetic to the argument that the welfare state creates dependencies on its own bureaucratic service institutions, as well as the idea that people should help themselves, they have largely withdrawn their support for such arguments when linked to the advance of equal rights. Although the Reagan and Bush administrations were willing to compromise in the case of the disability movement for reasons of political expediency, the underlying conservative critique not only remains but in fact has continued to gain adherents: namely, the assertion that rights cannot be considered altogether independently of costs. The case for equal rights—and thus the rights movement behind it as well—is seen to be simply out of sync with the functional requisites and priorities of the established societal framework.

In many ways the conservatives win this argument. Without taking sides, it is easy to identify liberal capitalist democracy's need to balance the interests of the capitalist productive system with those of the political system. This, in fact, has been a central political-economic issue throughout American history. Although most people tend to think of the "American system" as a unified integration of capitalism and democracy, in point of fact the merger of these two systems has in part been built upon a tension between them. The two systems are constructed around separate normative logics that are at times necessarily in conflict with one another (Offe, 1984). Whereas capitalism is organized around the principles of cost efficiency and the pursuit of profits, democracy is governed by the principles of political rights and the struggle for equality. While the profit system generates socioeconomic inequalities as a normal part of its efficient operations, the political system strives to increase equality among all citizens (Box 7.1). As organized under liberal corporate capitalism, the result at times is an inevitable tension between capitalist efficiency and political equality, the outcome of which emerges as a *trade-off* between efficiency and equality (Okun, 1975). If we take the existing system of liberal corporate capitalism as a *given,* as the conservatives do, the advance of rights has to be influenced by considerations of efficiency and cost.

Against this perspective, what can we make of the disability rights movement's call for equal rights? One plausible answer is this: equal rights is to be understood as strategic rather than wrong or misguided. In this view, the

---

## BOX 7.1
## Political Equality versus Economic Efficiency

Kermit Gordon (1975:vii) succinctly captured the tensions between equity and efficiency in these words:

> Contemporary American Society is, in a sense, a split-level structure. Its political and social institutions provide universally distributed rights and privileges that proclaim the equality of all. But its economic institutions rely on market-determined incomes that generate substantial disparities among citizens in living standards and material welfare. The differentials in income are meant to serve as incentives—rewards and penalties—to promote efficiencies in the use of resources and to generate a great and growing national output.
>
> The resulting mixture of equal rights and unequal incomes creates tensions between the political principles of democracy and the economic principles of capitalism. Money is used by some big winners of market rewards in an effort to acquire extra helpings of those rights that are supposed to be equally distributed. For some of them, it obtains head starts that make opportunities unequal. For some who incur penalties in the marketplace, the result is a degree of deprivation that conflicts with the democratic values of human dignity and mutual respect. Yet some economic policies designed to reduce the scope and magnitude of inequality weaken incentives to produce and otherwise impair economic efficiency. At many points along the way, society confronts choices that offer somewhat more efficiency at the expense of equality. In the idiom of the economist, a trade-off emerges between equality and efficiency.

insistence that rights be considered independently of costs is fundamentally a political strategy to confront the basic tension between cost efficiency and social equality running through liberal capitalist democracy. Indeed, throughout American history the conflicts between efficiency and equity have remained problematic and the struggle for democracy can be understood as the effort of one group after another to secure greater rights and protections in the context of this larger set of political-economic priorities. Like the black and women's movements, the disability rights movement can be seen as only one of the latest to enter this continuing struggle (Barber, 1991).

In an important sense, however, the arguments advanced by these movements do not altogether squarely or directly address the concerns of vindication, at least when strictly understood in terms of existing societal institutions (Weaver, 1991). While rights movements generally tend to frame their challenges in terms of the concerns of vindication, the challenges themselves are driven by commitments that relate to social choice. This, in fact, is facilitated by the conflict between the principles of capitalism and democracy. The Constitution calls for equal recognition of all citizens; the rights movements simply stand on these principles and call for their full realization. Strategically ignoring the concerns of capitalism, the disabled community demands their rights in the American democracy. But America is also a capitalist society and nowhere is it made clear in any fundamental way which of these two systems, capitalism or democracy, takes precedence over the other (Cohen and Rogers, 1983). Indeed, this remains a major issue for ongoing ideological struggle and there can be little doubt that the implementation of the Disability Act of 1990 will only heighten these ideological tensions. As these tensions sharpen, the evaluation of disability policy will move more and more to the fourth and final component of evaluation, social choice.

### READINGS

Edward D. Berkowitz. 1987. *Disabled Policy: America's Programs for the Handicapped.* Cambridge: Cambridge University Press.

Claire H. Liachowitz. 1988. *Disability Policy as a Social Construct: Legislative Roots.* Philadelphia: University of Pennsylvania Press.

National Council on the Handicapped. 1986. *Toward Independence: An Assessment of Federal Laws and Programs Affecting Persons (With Legislative Recommendations). A Report to the President.* Washington, DC: National Academy Press.

William G. Emener, Richard S. Luck, and Stanley J. Smits, eds. 1986. *Rehabilitation Administration and Supervision.* Baltimore, MD: University Park Press.

Richard K. Scotch. 1984. *From Good Will to Civil Rights: Transforming Federal Disability Policy.* Philadelphia, PA: Temple University Press.

Stephen L. Percy. 1989. *Disability, Civil Rights, and Public Policy.* Tuscaloosa: University of Alabama Press.

Sara D. Watson and David Pfeiffer, eds. 1993, 1994. "Symposium on Disability Policy." *Policy Studies Journal,* 21 and 22 (1 and 4): 718–800 and 109–175.

## DISCUSSION QUESTIONS

1. In chapter 6 it was stated that vindication must often be conducted over a decade or more. In what ways do the issues of disability policy illustrate this contention?

2. The chapter provides a succinct picture of the professional-managerial disability policy framework and outlines the disability movement's challenge to it. Although the disability movement has not formalized its alternative approach in such detail, how might you reconstruct its goals and practices?

3. Examine the case for disability rights. To what degree, if at all, do you think it is appropriate to balance these concerns against the larger costs to society?

4. In the 1950s, professional disability managers used cost-benefit analysis to support the expansion of disability programs. How is it that conservatives in the 1980s could use cost-benefit arguments to challenge these same programs?

5. Beyond arguments about costs and benefits, what other types of evidence might be offered to determine the priority of equal rights over cost efficiency, or vice versa?

6. Discuss the disability movement's strategy of appealing to the established values of the American political system. Do you agree or disagree with the arguments advanced by movement leaders?

# Part Four
## SOCIAL CHOICE

# 8    Evaluating Ideological Commitments: Public Policy, Social Values, and the Good Society

In this chapter, we examine the nature of argumentation in the fourth and final phase of a comprehensive evaluation, social choice. The discussion first presents the questions of social choice as it is concerned with ideology and values; it then establishes social choice's basic methodological relation to social critique and political philosophy. Finally, the chapter indicates the ways in which fundamental questions of ideology and political philosophy have entered policy debates in the past two decades, as well as methodological discussions in policy analysis.

## SOCIAL CHOICE AND POLITICAL IDEOLOGY

Whereas social scientists tend to enter the logic of evaluation through the technical discourse of verification, at least formally speaking, political philosophers and ideologists typically start with social choice and deductively work backward toward verification.[1] The organizing questions of social choice are the following:

- Do the fundamental ideals (or the ideology) that organize the accepted societal order provide a basis for a legitimate and equitable resolution of conflicting judgments?
- If the social order is unable to resolve basic value conflicts, do other social orders equitably prescribe for the relevant interests and needs that the conflicts reflect?
- Do normative reflection and empirical evidence support the adoption of an alternative ideology and the social order it prescribes?

In this chapter the primary purpose is to illustrate the ways in which such theoretical concerns bear directly on the task of policy evaluation. Be-

155

cause this is a question around which there is some disagreement in policy analysis circles—some say that ideology has nothing to do with policy evaluation, while others say that policy analysis should ultimately serve to test ideologies—we shall first offer an explanation of social choice on its own theoretical terms. Moreover, the answer to the question of how much policy analysts should concern themselves with ideological commitments depends very much on how we understand the task and define the job.

In its fullest sense, social choice is about what kind of society we should like to live in. Reflecting the classical issues of political philosophy, social choice pertains to the effort to establish a reasoned basis for the selection of the principles—"ideological" principles—that should govern the development and maintenance of the good society or way of life. In the Head Start case we introduced a policy conflict between those who advocated an egalitarian society devoted to the value of social equality and those who advanced a more meritocratic conception of society based on achievement, particularly as measured by schooling and the acquisition of knowledge. Such questions, as that discussion made clear, are generally the formal subject of social and political theory.

Politics, in this respect, is understood as the "conflict over the search for the good life and the means of achieving it" (McCoy and Playford, 1967). Most basically, the activities of politics are about how we live together. The study of politics—political science—has thus emerged as the discipline designed not only to examine empirically the political structures and operations of power that govern our common life, but also to normatively evaluate the progress of the search for the "good society." Because of this emphasis on the good life, Aristotle defined political science as "master science."[2]

We turn at this point to a clarification of basic concepts, in particular ideology, value principles, and the good society.

## IDEOLOGICAL PRINCIPLES

The task of clarifying the concept of an "ideology" invariably encounters difficulties (Sartori, 1969). One problem is that which is associated with any highly abstract concept—the attempt to specify the concept's components is fraught with ambiguities, both semantic and substantive. Whole books have been written to clarify and give precision to the term *ideology* (McLellan, 1986; Geuss, 1981). The history of these efforts reveals the concept to be used to designate two very different kinds of thought systems. One refers positively to an ideal thought system and its vision of the "good society." In particular, we tend to identify this conception of ideology with the high-minded views of philosophers and social theorists. The other refers more negatively to the less-than-ideal beliefs of self-interested politicians, interest groups, and political pundits. To have only one word to denote these two very different connotations is, to be sure, unfortunate. For present purposes, the term *ideology* is used to refer to the concept of an ideal world view. The narrower political perspective is taken to be a rhetorical appeal to such ideals designed to obfuscate the pursuit of self-interest.

Beyond basic definitional considerations, there still remains conceptual confusion surrounding attempts to define more precisely the structural content of an ideology. For present purposes, following Dolbeare and Dolbeare (1976), we conceptualize an ideology as an ideal thought system composed of three distinct components. First, although not necessarily in order of formulation, is a world view that provides a set of broadly conceived beliefs about how a society's political and economic systems function, why they operate in specific ways, and who benefits from them both politically and economically. Second, an ideology includes a set of fundamental social and political values believed to be the most legitimate and desirable for the society as a whole, as well as the high-level policy-oriented goals that move society in the approved direction. And third, it contains a conception of how social change occurs in the society, along with a specification of the political tactics and methods accepted as appropriate for dealing with this political reality.

Ideologies are thus understood here as integrated systems of beliefs, values, and methods for realizing or changing the world. With regard to beliefs, the basic question concerns a person's or group's cognitive grasp of the surrounding world: What is the nature of the social order? "Is it egalitarian, or is it stratified so that some have more of the things that are valued (status, wealth, and the like) in the society?" Did the social system in a society "evolve because of inherent differences in the talents or capabilities of men, or is it the result of some other factors?" (Dolbeare and Dolbeare, 1976:5).

Important aspects of world views are amenable to scientific inquiry, although the validity of a world view cannot be established by empirical data alone. We can, for example, investigate the degree to which corporate capitalism generates—directly or indirectly—a "culture of poverty" which blocks the entrance of poor people into mainstream American society. We can empirically examine the degree to which the patterns of wealth and power in American society distort the redevelopment of the nation's cities. We can research the ways in which disabled persons are discriminated against in various aspects of social and economic life. And so on. Such empirical descriptions can be investigated and confirmed with varying degrees of accuracy. Different people, of course, assign different interpretations to the various findings. Some, for instance, show a great deal of concern for the problem of inequality, while others underplay it as an anticipated consequence of inherent differences among individuals or as a social condition that is slowly but surely changing for the better. Dolbeare and Dolbeare (1976: 6) explain this interpretive process this way:

Looking at the same facts, some see problems, while others see progress. These differences may be due not to disagreement about the facts, but to their meaning in the context of other facts. Our understanding of the nature and significance of the facts themselves reflects assumptions or outright guesses to go on. In all cases, all our perceptions (assumptions *and* facts) must be correlated in some coherent, interpretive way before they can have full significance for us.

Ideologies thus help people identify the larger significance they can find in the empirical facts—for example, what sorts of causal relationships the facts have to one another, or how facts must be supplemented and supported by normative assumptions. In short, how they all "add up" to a meaningful interpretation of reality. The question is thus not whether people's beliefs are true or false; rather, it is simply a matter of recognizing that behavior is based on people's beliefs, regardless of their validity.

Values and high-level goals, the second component of this conceptualization of an ideology, designate its fundamental normative commitments. The "first principles" of an ideology—that is, its basic commitments—make possible a coherent relationship between its view of the world and its aspirations and priorities. Anchored to fundamental values—liberty, equality, and justice—each ideology sets out different value rankings, preferring some values to others, particularly when conflicts arise among them. For example, equality can be defined in legal and procedural terms (i.e., the right to vote), or it can be understood in terms of the concrete socio-economic factors that structure social reality. Equality, moreover, can be in the forefront of political discourse, but in practice accorded little status (Dolbeare and Dolbeare, 1976:7).

One of the important tasks of political philosophy is to identify the meanings assigned to competing values. In the political world there is generally a good deal of ambiguity attached to such meanings. This often has to do with the fact that politicians find it advantageous intentionally to leave the meanings vague, permitting different groups to read into them what they want. The ambiguity of meanings is often the very thing that makes possible political compromise between groups with conflicting views.

The high level goal orientations drawn from fundamental values can be understood as reflecting the ideology's "perceptions of the *distance* between the conditions of the society today (as understood in its world view) and the values to which it subscribes" (Dolbeare and Dolbeare, 1976:7). Goals, as we saw in the preceding chapters, are the vehicles for moving concrete action in the direction of broadly understood social and political values. They seek to realize the conditions, institutions, and practices that make possible the realization of these values. Indeed, this is the connection that moves evaluative discourse from policy vindication to social choice (and vice versa).

The third component of an ideology concerns the desired process of so-

# BOX 8.1
# Ideological Change and Social Learning

People holding differing ideological commitments can—and often do—have a great deal of trouble agreeing with one another. As for ideologists themselves, they most typically occupy their time trying to demonstrate the superior interpretive capabilities of their own ideological orientations, i.e., how their belief systems best organize the available data, assimilate new societal experiences, and explain critical political events. Persuaded by their own arguments, ideologists rarely undergo political conversions.

Why then engage in such ideological argumentation? Or stated differently, who constitutes the audience for these competing arguments? In significant part, the answer is the larger group of people who hold positions somewhere between the two (or more) competing ideologies. The fact that such ideologies—at least in the real world of argumentation—are often fuzzier than their formal presentations would suggest makes it both possible and meaningful to debate and evaluate competing ideological arguments. Most typically, it is the possibility of influencing these overlapping consensuses that make such dialogue possible.

Occasionally, to be sure, ideologies simply lose their argumentative force. One need only witness the recent collapse of communist ideology in Eastern Europe. Moreover, it is possible to identify a political dynamic fairly typical to such processes. Most commonly there is an accumulation of problematic evidence that is not easily integrated into the ideology, coupled with some decisive events that publicly reveal or underscore the weaknesses of the ideology's basic premises. In the case of Soviet communism, for example, the systematic inability of the bureaucratic leadership to come to terms with and reverse the country's decaying economic position, accompanied by the rise of Gorbachev to political power and the emergence of political protest movements, is a clear-cut illustration of the process.

In theoretical terms such change can be understood as a process of societal learning. Habermas's (1973) theory of political crisis is especially instructive in this respect. Fundamentally, Habermas puts forward a model of history that links the evolution of economic and political organization to the emergence and development of specialized forms of ideological discourse. Social systems, he argues, evolve through a series of ideological "principles of organization" that govern economic production and politically institutionalize discourses on particular topics. Shifts from one ideological principle to another typically occur through a protracted process of political crisis. Invariably characterized by social turmoil, false starts, and regressions, such processes can be reconstructed as a three-stage development. First, the social system begins encountering problems that cannot be solved by society's existing mechanisms for social learning and systems adaptation. Although the ruling elites struggle to grapple

*(continued on next page)*

**Box 8.1** *(continued)*

with these problems, their discourses often ironically and unintendedly work to further reveal the system's limitations. Second, new social classes or political groups emerge with a political discourse based on a new set of ideological principles that penetrate and push beneath the communicative limitations of the prevailing ideologies and their reasoning processes. Third, as systematic problems mount, the more advanced principles of these classes gradually begin to drive out and dominate their ideological predecessors.[3] In the course of such transformations, suppressed learning processes are released that are capable of dealing with the crises confronting the social system. In terms of the logic of policy deliberation, such a transformation from one set of ideological principles to another would constitute a shift from the level of the system to social choice and an alternative societal construction.

cial change and the political tactics of bringing it about. For instance, a world view may offer a particular dynamic of change based on a small number of historical determinants. Fundamental change may be desired but its advocates may find they must await the arrival of the conditions that make it possible. "In other words," as Dolbeare and Dolbeare (1976:7) put it, "the process by which change is to be sought is not controlled by the scope of change; it depends also on the ideology's world view definition of present circumstances and power distribution within the society."

Tactical methods for a given ideology, of course, will generally vary over time with changing circumstances. Most commonly, these are developed to suit the demands of a specific phase of a long-term process of historical change, as interpreted by the ideology. A classical question here concerns the use of reform versus revolutionary tactics, including the use of physical violence. Very few ideologies have an unswerving commitment to the use of violence. Although most generally identified with revolutionary tactics, reform oriented as well as revolutionary ideologies may advance violence in particular situations. As well, either may decide that circumstances necessitate peaceful means. To confront the complexity as well as the uncertainty of social and political reality, then, an ideology typically subscribes to an assortment of political tactics and approaches to change (Dolbeare and Dolbeare, 1976).

ORDERING IDEALS: IDEOLOGY AND POLITICAL PHILOSOPHY

The fundamental goal of social choice is to substitute reason for arbitrary personal preference or self-interest in the choice of a way of life and its ideology. Basic to the test of reason is the first question of social choice: Do the social order's fundamental ideals provide a basis for a legitimate and equitable resolution of conflicting judgments?

In the real world of politics, as already noted, we take an ideology to be a mixture of social beliefs and political interests. People mix their own perceptions, formal learning, and experiences of reality with an interpretation of their own preferences and needs. For this reason, a real-world ideology almost invariably has self-serving dimensions. In order to advance their own social and material gain, people, to a greater or lesser extent, "rationalize" their beliefs. This is the conception of ideology that is most common in an everyday understanding of the term.

A first task of normative evaluation at the level of ideology is an attempt to identify an ideology's self-serving dogma. Toward this end, ideologies are examined and refined against empirical evidence and rigorous normative scrutiny. Such rigorous reasoning about ideologies is generally identified as a task of political philosophy. Although typically listed among the subfields of political science, political philosophy is in practice a highly interdisciplinary field that draws as well on philosophy, legal jurisprudence, social theory, and economic thought. As the consummate normative exercise, the development of alternative visions of the good society is the traditional task of political philosophy (Box 8.2). Concerned with what *ought* to be done, political philosophy is an interpretive and creative endeavor interested in existing realities only insofar as they assist in understanding and in constructing ideal models.

Political philosophy's ability to transcend the everyday reality of the political system gives it a special "diagnostic" character (Spragens, 1976). For this reason, political philosophy has tended to flourish in times of political crisis. In periods of severe social and political disorder, it can be a practical tool for exposing the problematic assumptions and normative contradictions that underlie the social turmoil.[4] William Scott and David Hart (1973), for example, have illustrated the way in which the contemporary crisis of modern bureaucratic society can be recast as the neglect of contemporary moral discourse. In their view, the complex social and economic problems confronting American institutions are most fundamentally manifestations of the value systems of the administrative elites who direct them. Subscribing to an "administrative metaphysic" founded on instrumental and technocratic conceptions of knowledge and reason, these elites base their decisions and behavior on unarticulated, unexamined normative premises. Requiring more than better administrative management, such problems ultimately yield only to moral discourse. As questions for "metaphysical speculation," they involve a vision of our moral nature and the normative criteria required to judge human actions.

The basic analytical or diagnostic tool for pursuing the paradigmatic assumptions and values that lie beneath everyday belief systems is the ideal

## BOX 8.2
## Political Philosophy: Wisdom and Vision

Like interpretive social science (discussed in Chapter 4), political philosophy calls attention to the unique normative character of the social world and the special epistemological requirements attendant to it. Although the discipline suffered a steady demise under the aegis of the positivist philosophy that dominated science during most of this century, including the positivist "behavioral revolution" in the social sciences, political philosophers began to reassert themselves forcefully in the 1960s (Bernstein, 1976; Bobrow and Dryzek, 1987: 101–16). Basic to its resurgence was the controversy over the ethical neutrality of social science and the separation of facts and values (Gunnell, 1968; Hawkesworth, 1988).

For political philosophers such as Wolin (1969), the social malaise of the present age can only be understood by turning to the normative questions and methods of the "epic theorists" of the past. Only through a return to the classical questions can the modern social sciences reunite theory with practice and thus fact with value. Traditional political theory was built on the recognition that political action rests fundamentally on the value judgments of political participants. To separate out values in the study of politics is to perpetuate a fundamental distortion of reality. For the political philosopher, action is inherently guided by the actor's thoughts about what is good and what is bad. As Strauss (1959:10) explained, political action "has in itself a directedness towards knowledge of the good: of the good life, or the good society." Even the most practical political action, therefore, is based on an evaluation or value judgment. Action and judgment are inherently linked. In this respect, political-philosophic interpretation parallels the approach of phenomenological social science (chapter 4); phenomenology itself first emerged as a field of philosophy.

But political philosophers seek to penetrate beyond the everyday normative beliefs of the social actors. For them, the task is to get at the more basic "truths" that underlie everyday beliefs. By limiting the focus to an actor's own account of his or her behavior, the social scientist is seen destined to fall "victim to every deception and self-deception of the people one is studying" (Strauss, 1959). By empirically focusing on the social actor's opinions and judgments, the social scientist formulates an analysis that is trapped in the conceptual framework of the actor's own society and historical setting. The result is social and historical relativity. To escape the pitfalls of relativity, theorists must make value judgments of their own about the subject matter. This attempt to penetrate and explicate the underlying everyday assumptions and judgments of what ought to be done in politics gives the questions and methods of political philosophy their special relevance.

The task of the political philosopher does not end with the explication of self-interested assumptions and judgments. Following in the tradition of the epic theorists, philosophers can seek as well to provide arguments for the choice

---

**Box 8.2** *(continued)*

of one theory over another. Beyond the positivistic "methodism" of the social sciences, in Wolin's (1969) view, political philosophers should find the basis for such judgments in "political wisdom" derived from "tacit" political knowledge and "vision." Rather than being judged against the kind of empirically rigorous standards sought by empirical social science, such vision or imagination depends on extrascientific resources for its richness. Its sources are more explicitly identified as "the stock of ideas which an intellectually curious and broadly educated person accumulates and which come to govern his intuitions, feelings, and perception." Seldom are such factors specifically acknowledged in the formal theory of social and political science, even though such tacit ideas provide the inspiration for its creation. "Lying beyond the boundaries of circumscribed methods, technique, and official definition of the discipline, they can be summarized as cultural resources and itemized as metaphysics, faith, historical sensibility, or more broadly as tacit knowledge" (Wolin, 1969).

---

model of society. Employing intuition, insight, and imagination, the political philosopher's primary task is to construct an ideal model of society that provides evaluative standards and principles against which empirical reality can be judged. The justification of such ideal constructions—for example, Plato's *Republic,* Hobbes's *Leviathan,* or Marx's communist society, along with their respective moral principles—is established if they pass the test of generalization or universalization. A generalizable moral principle is one that has been freed of logical inconsistencies and self-contradictions. It is the principle that can be demonstrated to hold in all cases, not allowing for exceptions.[5]

The philosopher's objective is to show what will happen if a society adopts a particular value system or set of beliefs. The question is not unlike the one asked in vindication; the difference is that here it refers to an ideal society rather than an existing regime (deHaven-Smith 1988). As in vindication, scientific information can be brought to bear directly on the question, but in social choice such data can be only a part of a larger exploration that also includes interpretive methods such as social imagination, political intuition, and moral speculation. Through the imaginative creation of alternative sociopolitical systems, the philosopher attempts to highlight the effects resulting from a surplus of one value (or value system) or the implications of the decline of another. Such a society is constructed as a logical system designed to demonstrate, given basic premises, that particular values can be marshaled to support one conception over another, although scientific "proof" is beyond reach. As the ideal model is necessarily speculative, evidence is generally available only through insightful extrapolation and analogy from existing systems.

---

**BOX 8.3**
**Human Nature: The Ultimate Criterion**

In general terms, a political philosopher constructs a model of a rational way of life by identifying political values (such as equality, freedom or community) that are adopted as the ultimate goals of all subsequent political undertakings. Each philosopher attempts to make a case for one set of values over another. One may argue that security is the highest value, while an equally intelligent and perceptive colleague may just as earnestly consider insecurity the thing for which to strive. Voegelin (1952) has advocated the construction of conceptual or paradigmatic representations of the good society to serve as frameworks for the evaluation of existing regimes. Recognizing the role of such reconstructions in public policy studies, Sjoberg (1975) has suggested that policy evaluation should include a form of "countersystem analysis" based on the dialectical approach to reasoning. "A countersystem is a negation of and logical alternative to the existing model" which provides the policy evaluator with a "means of transcending the inherent tension between the advantaged and disadvantaged in a society."

The ultimate reference points in social choice are human nature and the needs derived from it. As an anthropologically grounded referent, human nature serves as the basis for the construction of alternative models of the ideal person. Plato's "philosopher-king," situated at the pinnacle of the ideal Republic, provides an excellent illustration of such a theoretical exercise, as does Marx's concept of a productive, self-fulfilled man or woman.

---

The turn to ideal models in political science and sociology appeared most explicitly in the 1970s and 1980s in an ongoing debate over the relationship between utilitarian principles (particularly as manifested in such analytical methodologies as cost-benefit analysis) and the place of political rights in public policy discourse. This, it will be recalled, is the problem we examined in the preceding chapter on disability policy. At just this level of evaluation the case for disability rights (as against society's ability to pay) would ultimately have to be settled. Given the importance of the conflict between rights and utility, a brief outline of the philosophical nature of the debate surrounding them is illustrative.

### CONFLICTING PRINCIPLES: UTILITY VERSUS RIGHTS

If, as the second organizing question of social choice asks, the social order is unable to resolve basic value conflicts, do other social orders equitably prescribe for the relevant interests and needs that the conflicts reflect? Do social orders organized around competing principles lead to a more harmonious way of life? The contemporary debate in political philosophy that most clearly illustrates the nature of such argumentation is that between utilitarian and rights-based theorists. It is a debate that in fact bears directly on the issues and concerns of policy evaluation (Bobrow and Dryzek, 1987:108).

The utilitarian heritage in political philosophy reaches back to the late eighteenth-century philosophy of Jeremy Bentham, who argued that public affairs should be guided by the principle of "the greatest good for the greatest number." Classical utilitarianism's "felicific calculus" of pleasure and pain finds its most direct contemporary manifestation in welfare economics. By interpreting felt pleasures and pains as "revealed preferences," monetarized in terms of costs and benefits, welfare economics establishes a basis for the interpersonal comparison of utility preferences, and thus supplies a foundation for developing decision-making rules geared to the greatest good for the largest number of people. The approach, as already noted, has become a primary— indeed, in numerous quarters *the* primary—orientation in policy evaluation.

Many contemporary political philosophers, by contrast, prefer to work in the tradition of Immanuel Kant, the eighteenth-century German philosopher. In fact, the revival of political philosophy has in significant part been identified with a Kantian rights-based challenge to the utilitarian approaches that have dominated the social sciences in the twentieth century, especially economics. For Kantians, actions are to be evaluated in terms of their *intrinsic* qualities. As French (1983:29) explains it, "if the moral rightness of actions is not subordinate to the production of good consequences, that moral rightness is not determined merely by a consideration of the happiness of an individual or the general population." Following Kant, "the moral rightness or wrongness of an act is established by judging it against a formal criterion called the 'categorical imperative.'"[6] From this perspective, the determination of the rightness or wrongness of an action requires one "to know more about it than merely its 'cash value' for the general population" (French, 1983:29). The Kantian tradition, as French (1983:29) puts it, "identifies human beings as rational animals and points out that a key characteristic of rationality is that the basic principles by which it is identified are universal." For instance, "the laws of logic, such as the law that forbids self-contradiction, do not hold only at some times, in some places; they hold universally." Thus, as Kant believed, morality "can be no less rational, so its principles also must be made universal."

In politics and public policy the generalization principle is often operationalized as the "public interest."[7] As Bobrow and Dryzek (1987:109) explain, in policy argumentation this tradition involves "commending, protection, promotion, respect for, and facilitation of action upon the moral rights of individuals." During the 1970s, rights-based theories moved to the center of a renewed debate through Rawls's book *A Theory of Justice* (Oxford,

1971). The book not only revived general interest in the classic problem of political philosophy, it also became a heated source of controversy in public policy circles as well (Bloom, 1975).

---

# BOX 8.4
# Do Trees Have Intrinsic Rights?

One of the most interesting contemporary conflicts between utilitarian and rights-based theorists concerns the effort on the part of environmentalists to expand the moral community. Many environmentalists argue that natural objects such as animals, plants, trees, and rivers should have intrinsic value and should accordingly be granted rights. Beatley (1989:14) captures the argument this way:

> A major criticism of the Western view of nature is that it is so strongly anthropocentric—viewing . . . natural objects as contingent upon the utility that they have for man. This view leads writers such as Tribe (1974) to be highly critical of the trend toward replacing nature with artificial substitutes, such as the installation of plastic trees along the median strip of a Los Angeles highway. Much of contemporary environmental literature and thought has emphasized an expansion of the moral community to include obligations to these components of the natural system, particularly other forms of sentient life, and the development of arguments that they possess intrinsic values and rights irrespective of their utility and value to man. This non-anthropocentric view of nature poses difficult questions. How far should this broadened moral community extend (does it include insects as well as whales)? And . . . how do we resolve situations where their interests clash with humans?

Utilitarian writers view such arguments as the height of intellectual folly. To the criticism that the utilitarian or market ethic is highly anthropocentric, utilitarians argue that the only consideration in environmental policy should be the long-run benefit to mankind. Baxter (1986:215) argues the point in these words:

> My criteria are oriented to people, not penguins. Damage to penguins, or sugar pines, or geological marvels is, without more, simply irrelevant. One must go further by my criteria, and say penguins are important because people enjoy seeing them walk about rocks; and furthermore, the well-being of people would be less impaired by halting use of DDT than by giving up penguins. In short, my observations about environmental problems will be people-oriented, as are my criteria. I have no interest in preserving penguins for their own sake.

Essentially, Rawls was concerned with determining which type of social order a rational person would choose to adopt under ideal circumstances and the reasons that would be given for obeying its rules. To uncover the nature of such an order, he established a fundamental situation called the "original position." Free of distracting circumstances, the original position is a methodological device to assist social actors in making rational choices about basic values. Like the "state of nature" advanced by Rousseau or Hobbes, the device permits social actors to establish a hypothetical social contract with their fellow men and women. The result is a civil order that guarantees certain basic rights which each person agrees to accept and support. The participation in the formation of the contractual agreement itself is the source of the actor's motivation to accept the duties and rights of the ideal order and to further them as the legitimate base of a good society.

One of the controversial aspects of Rawls's work is his logical rejection of the principle of utility—the greatest good for the greatest number—as the fundamental basis for the ideal social order. Although Rawls and his followers do not altogether reject the utilitarian principle, his logical system is designed to prove that it is not the ideal rule which would be chosen as the basic organizing principle under the rational conditions of the original position. His purpose is to show that "utility," the dominant moral rule accepted in western capitalistic societies, provides insufficient basis for reconciling public and private interests in a just manner. In Rawls's conception of the good society, the utilitarian principle must be subordinated to a rights-based principle of justice.

From the original position, Rawls establishes his first principle of justice: "Each person is to have an equal right to the most extensive total system of basic liberties compatible with a similar system of liberty for all" (Rawls, 1971:302). These rights are a product of the consent of rational individuals established behind a "veil of ignorance" which, for purposes of deliberation, blinds them to any knowledge or information about what their own actual standing in society is likely to be, that is, they do not know if they will end up among the more privileged or the less fortunate in the society. In a similar manner, Rawls sets out a second principle which holds that any social inequalities are to be "to the greatest expected benefit of the least advantaged" and subject to "conditions of fair opportunity."

To put it modestly, rights-based principles like those advanced by Rawls set off a virulent controversy between liberals and conservatives in leading intellectual circles in the U.S. Given the emphasis of policy evaluation on utilitarian theory, such writings had a significant impact on the study of public policy as well. Their influence can be found in both the theoretical discussions in the policy literature and in substantive public policy debates in areas such as disability policy, affirmative action, economic opportunity, and environmental protection, as well as in methodological discussions. Many writers troubled by the discipline's "lack of social relevance" have cited Rawls principles of social justice as a foundation for a new policy science (Hart, 1974; Henry, 1975; Gastil, 1977; Tribe, 1972).

The point here is not whether Rawls's theory actually establishes such a foundation, but rather that his work has moved certain policy questions to the discourse of social choice. Indeed, other writers have taken strong exception to Rawls's arguments. Particularly important has been the criticism of the concept of the original position, especially the idea that people could come to agreement on universal principles through such an abstract exercise. Some economists, for instance, have contended that actors in the original position would in fact adopt the principle of utilitarianism, rather than Rawls's principle of social justice (Harsanyi, 1975). Marxists, among others, have questioned the social rationality of the original position itself (Miller, 1976). For them, the abstract, ahistorical nature of Rawls's thought experiment robs participants of the kinds of prior knowledge of historical relations, particular social contexts, and affective considerations required to specify concrete principles (Benhabib, 1982).

Rawls's work has also come under attack by "postmodern" theorists who argue that the construction of universal principles and standards is no longer possible, if it ever was. For these writers, there are no longer any ideological "master discourses" available for the interpretation of society, such as liberalism or Marxism. The inability to construct such "grand narratives" is said to be tantamount to the end of "foundational thought," that is, reason as a series of rules of thought that any fully rational person might adopt to establish universal principles, such as Rawls's original position and the veil of ignorance. Postmodern thought, according to its theorists, is bound to narrative discourses about the world that are admittedly partial. The crucial dimension of such discourse is the inherent link between knowledge and interest, the latter being understood as a "vantage point" from which reality is interpreted. Postmodernist theory thus shifts the object of knowledge from social action to language. Political agents are now situated in a discursive rather than a social field of action (Ross, 1988).

Others accept the turn to language and discourse, but not the degree of normative relativity emphasized by much of postmodern theory. They, too, criticize the attempt to establish universal or absolute social principles, but also reject the idea that such a conclusion renders normative reason hopelessly relative. For them, normative reason can be rescued by reanchoring it to procedural principles rather than substantive conclusions. That is, preferred normative principles can be rationally assessed in terms of the processes and practices—both intellectual and material—through which they are selected. This approach is commonly referred to as "discourse ethics." Insofar as the logic presented here generally adheres to this orientation, we return to it in chapter 10, concerned with the larger political and methodological implications of the logic of policy deliberation.

## PROBING ALTERNATIVE IDEOLOGIES

Finally, we come to the question of alternative ideologies and the social orders they prescribe. This issue concerns the kinds of empirical evidence and normative reflection that can be brought to bear on such judgments. It is an issue that must involve an interplay between the disciplines of political philosophy and policy analysis.

As conventionally understood, the methodological activities of political philosophy have not been considered a part of policy analysis. More broadly conceptualized, however, policy evaluation cannot sustain such a separation (Anderson, 1979). Through exploration of the normative foundations of policy research and deliberation, political philosophers can supply policy evaluation with decision criteria, assumptions, and models based on alternative political and social systems (Fischer, 1990:240–63). In fact, during the past two decades, political philosophers have in just such ways become increasingly engaged in policy-related studies. One sign is the growing number of political philosophers (often identified as "applied ethicists") employed in academic policy analysis programs. Another is found in the policy literature, reflected in significant part in the renewed interest in social justice and rights (see, for example, the *Journal of Political Philosophy and Public Affairs)*. Articulating this new policy orientation in political philosophy, William Brandon (1984) has gone so far as to suggest that public policy analysis can be understood as "the continuation of moral philosophy by other means."

Filtered into policy science in the 1970s, these philosophical concerns were increasingly brought to bear on theoretical and methodological reconstruction. For instance, writers such as Grauhan and Strubelt (1971), taking a position highly influenced by the German Frankfurt School, proposed an evaluative scheme for rational policy choices built on human emancipation and the principle of "self-enhancement." Derived from empirical analysis of basic human needs, such a principle is set in an historical framework designed to elucidate the potential of a social system at any given time. Such knowledge would open options or alternative visions of human self-realization. According to Grauhan and Strubelt, policy scientists should transcend their instrumental relationship to policymakers by assuming the larger role of "policy critic" (Box 8.5).

Even more concretely, throughout the 1980s there was a slow but fairly steady stream of efforts to come to grips methodologically with the deeper value assumptions underlying public policy and its evaluation (Fischer, 1980;

---

**BOX 8.5
Political Philosophy as Critical Theory**

If the job of the political theorist is to provide arguments for the choice of one theory over another, the work of the Frankfurt School in Germany, in particular that of Jürgen Habermas, represents one of the most penetrating achievements in the contemporary effort to rejuvenate political philosophy (Jay, 1973). Anchored to the dialectical tradition of Hegel and Marx, the Frankfurt School has attempted to recover and defend the critical impulse that must underlie an adequate political theory. Drawing on Marx's understanding of the use of "critique," as well as the work of Horkheimer and Adorno, Habermas has advanced critique as the practical interest in the quality and fate of political life. He has sought to move beyond the phenomenological interpretation of the social life-world and to posit critical theory as a genuine force for the self-awareness of the social order (Habermas, 1973). Designed to further human emancipation, a critical political theory transcends a merely negative stance toward existing social conditions. Seeking to present basic societal contradictions as more than an expression of an historical situation, the critical theorist shows how the contradiction is itself a force within the situation capable of stimulating change. The undertaking is described by some as one of the most important theoretical and epistemological efforts in modern times (Bernstein, 1976).

---

Hawkesworth, 1988). One of the influential approaches that helps to clarify the relation of policy analysis to social choice is that of Paris and Reynolds (1983). For these writers, the reform of policy analysis must ultimately be grounded in ideological argumentation. Insofar as no argument in the world of politics or policymaking can ever be conclusively correct or incorrect, all policy analysis must thus be seen as fundamentally rooted in ideological choice.

What then should be the proper goal of policy inquiry with regard to ideological discourse? According to Paris and Reynolds (1983: 207), it can be nothing less than "the construction of rational ideologies." For them, the most basic "function of empirical policy inquiry is to test ideology, not policies." Rather than testing hypotheses or developing policy evaluations and prescriptions per se, the ultimate goal of policy inquiry is to enhance the rationality of particular ideologies.

Understood as an encompassing world view with metaphysical, empirical, and normative components, "rational ideology" is seen to be characterized "by coherence, congruence and cogency" (Paris and Reynolds, 1983: 207). Coherence refers to the internal consistency and full articulation of the value judgments and action principles of an ideology. Congruence is the degree to which an ideology's empirical component is consistent with empirical evidence. Cogency refers to its capacity to provide good reasons (or warrants) for proposed policy claims and actions. No "rational ideology" can be judged "correct," as these three desiderata can be met only imperfectly. By contrast, an irrational ideology is seen to be pure dogma, as its metaphysical core allows for no falsifying instances.

Clearly, the adjective "rational" implies that some ideologies are to be preferred to others. Although ideologies resist explicit comparison (as they are selective in the empirical evidence they allow), the criterion of congruence implies the possibility of empirically grounded comparisons. To facilitate such comparisons, Paris and Reynolds (1983: 210) call for a "common body of basic data" against which ideologies can be tested. Here they tend to overlook the fact that ideologies often lead to different understandings of the facts themselves.

Beyond the methodological issues of policy analysis per se, Paris and Reynolds see in such policy debate the model of an alternative society. For them, the good society must be constructed as the "undogmatic, liberal polity" in which pluralistic compromises sustained by argumentation must replace the naked exercise of power. Referred to as a "polity of rational ideologies" the good society is a pluralistic system purged of dogma (Paris and Reynolds, 1983: 202–71).

Still missing in this approach is a clear sense of the standards for both testing and comparing ideologies. What, for example, does it actually mean to say that we bring empirical evidence to bear on competing ideologies? Some have sought to develop a concept of "frame analysis" to further refine the kind of testing that occurs at this level of evaluation. For Bobrow and Dryzek (1987) this involves explicit use of the technical "frames of reference" that constitute the theoretical orientations of policy evaluation. As they see it, standards for the testing of competing ideologies can be elaborated and refined by bringing the theoretical frames employed by policy evaluation to bear on the analytical assignment—for example, welfare economics, public choice theory, information theory, social structure theory, and so on. As conceptual lenses for interpreting social and political reality, such frames are "composed of theoretical orientations, methodological rules of evidence and inference, as well as a set of guidelines for identifying concepts, events, and trends worthy of attention." They provide principles for interpretation, explanation, prediction, and evaluation.

Another important effort to come to grips with this deeper level of assumptions that underlies and shapes our conception and identification of policy problems is Rein and Schön's (1993) attempt to explicate the real-world political and cognitive processes that govern the framing of policy arguments. Instead of focusing on the established analytical frames of policy analysis, Rein and Schön turn more directly to the raw material of policy arguments as

advanced in actual political controversy. In language very similar to that of
Bobrow and Dryzek, Rein and Schön describe framing as "a way of selecting,
organizing, interpreting and making sense of a complex reality so as to provide
guideposts for knowing, analyzing, persuading, and acting." A frame is a point
of view or "perspective from which an amorphous, ill-defined problematic situation can be made sense of and acted upon." Frequently constructed around
"generative metaphors" of world views, problem-setting stories and narratives
"link causal accounts of policy problems to particular proposals for action."
Rein and Schön focus in particular on the stories and narratives that people tell
when explaining a proposed policy scenario or outcome. They are especially
interested in how both policy analysts and lay citizens employ frames in the
problem-setting stages of their deliberations. "Frame-critical policy analysts,"
they write, "would uncover the multiple, conflicting frames involved in a
given policy dispute." Such analysts "would inquire into the sources of conflicting frames in the histories, roles, institutional contexts, and interests of the
participants." They would investigate "the ambiguities and inconsistencies
contained in conflicting frames and the consequences to which their use may
lead" (Rein and Schön, 1993:162).

## IDEOLOGY AND THE PRACTICE OF
## POLICY EVALUATION

The point here is not to argue that policy analysts must be-
come political philosophers per se. Rather, it is to show the ways in which policy analysis is already set in the context of ideological questions and that
policy analysts must at minimum be acknowledged consumers of the products
of political-philosophical analysis. Although the policy evaluator need not be a
direct participant in the tasks of ideological critique, such work must be
brought to bear when making a comprehensive evaluation.

The essential point is that the ideological context within which policy
evaluators carry out their work has a critical influence on their processes of analytical judgment. Indeed, at times it can be the major determinate of their conclusions and recommendations. This consideration raises two fundamental
points: one concerns political bias, the other bears on the nature of policy knowledge itself. With regard to bias, the issue is relatively straightforward. To avoid
interpreting a social phenomenon falsely, policy evaluators have to be aware of
the basic normative assumptions that they themselves bring to the tasks of judgment. This point we have dealt with in chapter 2.

With regard to the nature of knowledge, policy analysts must be cog-
nizant of the ways in which decision makers frequently fall back on political
ideologies to bridge gaps in the availability of reliable knowledge. As we have
already seen, ideologies offer pictures of how different socioeconomic sys-

tems and their political orders are believed to operate, why they work the ways they do, whether or not they are good, and what strategies to take if they are not. As evaluative frameworks, ideologies simplify the task of choice by offering decision rules that indicate which criteria take precedence in political judgments. Such rules generally reflect enough reality to serve specific needs and interests but stop far short of truth validity (Fischer, 1980: 193).

For policy decisions to be made in a particular political situation, there must first exist some fundamental political agreements. Such agreements serve as mediating principles under which conflicting elements of ideological belief systems can, at least potentially, be organized. The possibility of systematically organizing conflicting elements under a higher principle establishes a potential basis for normative consensus in policy deliberation. Without such a possibility, the use of policy evaluation is unlikely to facilitate consensual decision making, although it can serve to clarify fundamental normative differences.

In policy deliberation generally, the presence of fundamental ideological agreements functions to greatly simplify the evaluation process. As a loosely organized set of intersecting substantive generalizations and formal principles, ideological agreements allow policymakers to remove certain beliefs or alternatives from the realm of consideration (say, corporate profit margins under a socialist system). It permits the assumptions of particular arguments to be treated as facts, permitting decision makers and analysts to evade the overwhelming empirical task that assessing these assumptions often requires.

Writers such as Lindblom (1968: 23) have argued that even when such assumptions are mistaken, they can nonetheless be useful in guiding an evaluation toward policy decisions. For instance, a commitment to a market system may be based on false assumptions about the nature of an economy, but it can still be employed successfully as a standard in analyzing and formulating policies designed to combat the growth of monopolies. Lindblom contends that in such cases all that need be asked of policy evaluation is that it leads from unquestioned assumptions to a policy that secures agreement. On other occasions, however, political ideology is too far removed from the facts to be helpful in policy deliberations. In these instances, it may produce policies that are politically acceptable but fail to work. For example, the budget-balancing policies during the Great Depression of the 1930s, based on appropriate ideological standards, lengthened rather than shortened the depression (Lindblom, 1968: 23). Policy scientists, therefore, must at minimum include the values and norms of ideological systems within the purview of their activities. Even though not directly concerned with the development of ideological systems, they are necessarily consumers of such products. Ideological belief systems provide basic data for policy evaluation.

As practical tools employed in the everyday world, ideologies shift the emphasis from the philosopher's search for primary ideals to a more practical focus on the mixture or patterns of ideals that govern the decision making processes. Such a shift offers evaluators and policymakers a more manageable realm of workable consensus and agreement that avoids some of the more sticky epistemological questions that confront the justification of a primary ideal. In this respect, it is important to recognize that fundamental conflicts do not arise in every practical situation. Moreover, there is much greater consensus on the general configuration of ideals than there is on the relative merits of one particular ideal over another. For instance, widespread agreement exists on the general primacy of ideals such as economic progress, the reduction of human suffering, the protection of human life, political freedom, and social reciprocity. Such values emerge as fundamental agreements that command more respect than lesser values such as money making or winning political elections. It is, of course, possible to identify policymakers in dictatorial regimes who do not respect human life or decision makers in pluralist countries who accept the value of social reciprocity but make exceptions in the case of blacks and other minorities. In fact, at times the violation of an ideal may be sanctioned by official policy, such as the taking of human life during war. Nonetheless, there is enough agreement among theorists to expound a framework of ideals to serve as a guide for probing policy decisions (Fischer, 1980:190–214; Leys, 1962).

Having examined the concept of an ideology and its component parts, the methodological relationship of political philosophy to the concerns of social choice, as well as the practical import of such issues for policy evaluation, we can at this point turn to a concrete case study of an ideological conflict that bears directly on the evaluation of a public policy. We examine the clash of contemporary technocratic and environmental ideologies in the evaluation of toxic health risks.

## READINGS

Thomas E. McCollough. 1991. *The Moral Imagination and Public Life: Raising the Ethical Question.* Chatham, NJ: Chatham House.

David McLellan. 1986. *Ideology.* St. Paul: University of Minnesota Press.

David C. Paris and James Reynolds. 1983. *The Logic of Policy Inquiry.* New York: Longman.

Edward B. Portis and Michael B. Levy, eds. 1988. *Handbook of Political Theory and Policy Science.* New York: Greenwood Press.

Daniel Callahan and Bruce Jennings, eds. 1983. *Ethics, the Social Sciences, and Policy Analysis.* New York: Plenum.

Richard J. Bernstein. 1976. *The Restructuring of Social and Political Theory.* New York: Harcourt Brace Jovanovich.

# 9    Environmental Policy and Risk-Benefit Analysis: The Green Critique of Technocratic Ideology

During the relatively short period of two decades, environmental policy has emerged as one of the major political issues of our time (Paehlke, 1989). Indeed, as the 1992 Earth Summit in Rio made clear, environmental crisis has become the most pressing political question for the twenty-first century. Reaching far beyond the kinds of technical and political problems that typically define policy issues, environmental crisis portends a much more profound and enduring set of questions about the nature of our very way of life. Take, for instance, the issue of the greenhouse effect and global warming. Such problems raise serious questions about the United States's ability to continue its current levels of industrial production indefinitely, and thus the country's ability to sustain the affluent way of life taken for granted by most Americans. These questions now have a place among the most challenging political problems confronting techno-industrial society. Raising basic social and political value questions fundamental to the American way of life, political and policy debates about the environment are grounded in deep-seated ideological conflicts about both the nature of American society and the consequences of its current directions. We focus in particular on the conflict as it has emerged in the political clash between the "technocratic" and "green" ideologies now locked into a struggle over the contemporary interpretation of American values and the nature of the Good Society (Box 9.1).

The environmental condition is familiar enough to require little detailed clarification. Reports of environmental damage appear daily in the newspapers—for example, overconsumption of the earth's energy resources, the diminishing ozone layer in the atmosphere, growing health threats associated with toxic wastes, the contamination of rivers and oceans, the discovery of pesticides in the food chain, the dangers of nuclear radiation, the worsening of air pollution in many parts of the country, wider recognition of the extent of the hazardous waste problem and its implication for health, the destruction of

## BOX 9.1
## Defining "Green"

In recent years, the term "green" has been appropriated—and misappropriated—for numerous purposes. Although it has its origins in a radical environmentally oriented social movement, it has been adopted by a variety of different groups advancing varying political strategies, from radical to reformist. Even more problematic, the term is today not only misappropriated by governments attempting to promote their environmental policies, it is frequently used by businesses seeking to market products. For this reason, we need to be specific about our usage of the term. By "green" we mean those political activists and writers who see the institutions of contemporary corporate-bureaucratic society to be the fundamental source of an impending environmental crisis and who advance a political program for fundamental social and economic change. "Dark green" political thought and the social movement it has spawned represents a profound challenge to the economic, political, and social consensus—i.e. a techno-industrial world view—that has come to dominate the twentieth century (Dobson, 1990). We single out this group, as its critique most sharply illustrates the nature of ideological critique and the search for a way of life based on an alternative social order (e.g., Porritt, 1984; Capra and Spretnak,, 1984; Dobson, 1990).

the tropical rain forests and other habitats which harbor biodiversity, escalating population growth, and so on (Kennedy, 1993). Scarcely a day goes by that doesn't bring reports of new threats, at times real disasters—for example, the Love Canal toxic waste site in New York State that led to the complete disruption of a community and its social fabric, the near meltdown of a nuclear power plant at Three Mile Island that frightened the entire nation, the Bhopal toxic chemical leak that killed twenty-six hundred people and injured many more, the devastating nuclear catastrophe at the Chernobyl nuclear power station in the former Soviet Union, to mention only a few of the most well-known examples. As a result of such accidents, we have come to recognize technological risk to the environment as a basic feature of contemporary society. Some argue that if we are to survive the long-run consequences of such environmental degradation, changes have to begin with the current generation.[1]

### TECHNOLOGY AND ENVIRONMENTAL RISK: THE SAFEST OR RISKIEST OF TIMES?

Basic to the environmental problem is the role of technology. A great majority of environmental issues are, in one way or another, the byproducts of techno-industrial advance (Box 9.2). The chemical industry, for example, creates the toxic waste problem; the nation's nuclear power plants—the advanced technology par excellence—pose dangerous radiation threats; air pollution is in largest part a byproduct of the ubiquitous automobile, and so on. One can virtually assume that behind every environmental problem stands a technological issue (as cause, solution, or both). Thus, the environmental problem is increasingly associated with technological risk.

Although the advance of technological development has brought with it much of what we accept as good in modern society, the environmental movement and its sympathizers have increasingly questioned the country's unswerving devotion to techno-industrial progress. Fundamental to the movement has been a growing recognition that advanced technologies and the technocratic world view have brought with them many dangers. Indeed, in various quarters of society there is now substantial distrust of modern techno-industrial progress (National Research Council 1989, 54–71). In the face of growing reports about environmental damage and human health risks, the society has come to recognize that one of the costs of technological advance has been a dramatic increase in risk, or at least the awareness of risk (Slovic et al., 1980; National Research Council, 1989).

Such events have given both credibility and political influence to the environmental movement, which emerged in the 1970s as a response to these and other related events (Douglas and Wildavsky, 1982). The result has been a much greater awareness of the impacts of modern technologies on the environment, coupled with a questioning of our blind acceptance of technological progress. Indeed, the more radical groups in the environmental movement have raised basic questions about our very way of life. Proponents of the social ecological or green philosophy see the solution in a return to smaller, less hierarchial technological systems, with a much greater role for people (Porritt, 1984).

Today the issue of environmental and technological risk is divided politically into two deeply entrenched and ideologically opposed camps: those who see us living in "the safest of times," and those who see us in "the riskiest of times" (National Research Council, 1989). The first of these two perspectives, largely the techno-industrial view proffered by industrial and political leaders, takes life expectancy to be the best overall measure of risk to health and safety, points to substantial increases in this measure, and shows that these increases are parallel over time with the growing use of risky chemicals and dangerous technologies. In fact, they argue that many of the contemporary hazards have decreased overall risk by replacing more dangerous ones. People are seen to become more and more worried about less significant risks.

By contrast, the number of people who believe we live in the riskiest of times has increased dramatically over the past two decades. For these people,

# BOX 9.2
# Techno-Industrial Society and Technocratic Ideology

Historically, capitalism has been responsible for harnessing the forces of science and technology to generate industrial progress, but in the latter half of this century the relationship has actually begun to reverse itself. So important has advanced scientific and technological development become to modern economic advance that it is now itself increasingly the driving force of capitalistic markets. The evolution of these processes, moreover, has given rise to a particular societal formation associated with large concentrations of economic and political power. Its primary features include the central importance of science and technology for economic growth, large-scale technological complexity, a high degree of organizational interdependence, increasingly centralized forms of economic and political decision making, greater reliance on technical expertise, and rapid rates of economic and technological change.

Accompanying these techno-industrial processes has been a dominant technocratic ideology and a set of functional roles—or "technostructure"—designed to plan and steer the formation in accordance with the principles of the belief system (Galbraith, 1967). Shaped by the technological and organizational forces of the system, these principles are identified with a commitment to technological progress, the technically rational appraisal of means to achieve given goals, efficient organizational practices, managerial authority and control, the application of productive technologies that produce the most for the least amount of effort, and by a sense of *optimism* and *faith* in the ability of humankind to understand and control physical, biological and social processes for the benefit of present and future generations, or what O'Riordan (1981) calls "technocentricism." Thus, the application of technical knowledge to improve the condition of humankind is accepted as the fundamental and laudable objective.

Such applications of technical knowledge, however, largely occur in the absence of commonly accepted yardsticks for evaluating their contributions. Indeed, as we saw in Chapter 1, technological charges proceed without direct recourse to the kinds of normative discussions generally taken to be essential to the establishment of such standards. Two kinds of answers are offered to justify this disinterest in standards. The first is found in the objective principles of science itself. The scientifically informed decision methodologies seen to guide such technical applications are said to produce objective outcomes that are largely "value neutral" in their implications. Questions concerning the normative desirability of the outcomes are held to fall beyond the realm of rational analysis and thus outside the jurisdiction of science per se (Fischer, 1990).

The second has to do with the implicit normative commitments that technical experts bring to the job. While their methodologies might operate to generate empirically objective alternatives, they are applied to systems that have their own technical and organizational imperatives, in particular the growth and

> **Box 9.2** *(continued)*
>
> stability of techno-industrial society itself. As products of this system, tech-nocrats tend to define efficiency and effectiveness in terms of outcomes that functionally sustain this highly complex and interdependent system. In this sense, the system itself identifies the problems to be solved. The role of moral and political discourse is rendered more and more superfluous, as it often pro-poses ideas and solutions that are simply outside the realm of immediate possi-bilities and thus seen as idealistic.

particularly those of the green persuasion, the world is on the brink of ecolog-ical disaster. Modern technology is seen constantly to generate new threats to the earth's life-support systems and thus in turn to the stability of social sys-tems. Especially important to this argument is the synergistic effect of these problems. It is not just the appearance of new problems, but the emergence of so many at the same time, for example, toxic wastes, the ozone hole, the green-house effect, nuclear radiation, polluted air and water, the loss of diversity, nu-clear radiation, and so on. Even though people are seldom exposed to one risk in isolation of the others, there exists little empirical information on the inter-active effects of these dangers. For such reasons, those who see a dramatic in-crease in risks call for tighter control over technology, including the abandonment of some technologies considered to be particularly risky (such as nuclear power and genetic engineering), and the need for the development and introduction of more environmentally benign technologies.

This latter view, in fact, is objectively manifested in a very important contemporary political phenomenon, the so-called "NIMBY" phenomenon (Not In My Back Yard). In face of the risks associated with such industries as nuclear power, chemical manufacturing, and hazardous waste management, more and more environmentally concerned groups have begun to block the sit-ing of these facilities in their own communities.[2] This politics of NIMBY has become a serious threat to the future of such hazard-prone industries (Maz-manian and Morell, 1992; 1993).

Such worries about the riskiness of advanced technological society, cou-pled with the political gridlock often created by NIMBY, have elevated the "search for safety" to the top of the political agenda (Wildavsky, 1988). In-deed, the quest for safety has emerged as one of the paramount political issues of our time, both as a major public concern and a leading topic in intellectual discourse. In Germany, for example, it has led sociologist Ulrich Beck (1993) to define the contemporary postindustrial society as the "Risk Society."[3] Whether or not advanced industrial society is adequately characterized as a "risk society" is an important question that must remain the subject of debate.

Nonetheless the very nature of the polemic indicates the degree to which technological risk and its implications have emerged as fundamental societal concerns. For the proponents of large-scale technological progress, corporate and governmental leaders in particular, this central importance of risk and safety has meant much greater attention to the problem of NIMBY and the regulation of technological risks. The response has largely been technocratic in character. Before examining it in some detail, we first illustrate NIMBY and the problem of risk in the context of the particular problem of hazardous waste.

## HAZARDOUS WASTE AND THE PROBLEM OF NIMBY

During the 1970s and 1980s news reports of oil spills, nuclear disaster at Chernobyl, near disaster at Three Mile Island, pesticides in the food chain, and DDT damage to wildlife frightened people around the world (Piller, 1991). The result has been a widespread distrust of industry and a collective fear of all chemical processing facilities. As the public has become increasingly aware of the extent to which chemicals have now polluted the environment, the result has been a new anxiety often described as "chemophobia." Polls show that citizens are more concerned about the presence of toxic wastes than any other environmental problem, although the Environmental Protection Agency maintains that such waste is not the most severe threat. Problems such as the ozone hole and the greenhouse effect are scientifically judged to be much riskier. The public is said to be irrational.

Nowhere has this concern about the "irrationality" of the public been more prominent than in the political conflicts associated with the siting of hazardous waste treatment facilities. Such facilities are required to process the large number of industrial and commercial chemical waste products that possess such characteristics as toxicity, reactivity, corrosivity, or ignitability. Since the 1970s, Americans have become more aware of and concerned about the growing amounts and types of such hazardous wastes generated by industry and government, especially the military. A study conducted by the Congressional Budget Office, for example, concluded "that approximately 266 million metric tons of hazardous waste are generated in the United States annually, which amounts to more than one ton per person residing in the country" (Davis, 1993:4).

The production of hazardous industrial byproducts is not a new phenomenon. Rather the problem is found in the dramatic increase of such byproducts since the end of World War II, 50 percent of which are directly attributable to the chemical products industry. The largest share of this increase has resulted from petroleum-based chemical products such as pesticides, plastics, synthetic fabrics, paints, solvents, and wood preservatives. Other important sources of

hazardous waste include the petroleum, paper, and fabricated metals industries, and food.

A statistical profile of such wastes can inform policymakers about the
"who," "where," and "how much" of such waste production, but it conveys little about the actual risks to public health or environmental quality associated
with such materials. And it is just this question that has been the source of the
problem. Despite concerted attempts to assure the public of the safety of sophisticated treatment facilities, community groups have by and large been unwilling to accept such assurances. This has been the case particularly with
hazardous materials incineration. Although many argue that incineration offers
the least risky long-term alternative for disposing of such wastes, the process
has encountered fierce community opposition. No community wants to be the
site of an incinerator or a landfill.

The clearest manifestation of this anxiety is the NIMBY phenomenon.
Much discussed in both the academic and popular presses, NIMBYism is now
blamed as a major stumbling block for solving a growing number of environmental problems. As one leading journal put it: "Once the public went along
with everything: now it opposes everything." In Piller's (1991) words,
"Whether the matter is health, peace of mind, or protection of property values,
few Americans (activists or not) care to live beside chemical waste dumps, air-
ports, petrochemical refineries, nuclear power plants, or other standard features of modern industrial society."[4] Nowhere has the problem been more
chronic than in the case of the siting of hazardous waste treatment facilities.

Activists opposed to hazardous waste treatment facilities are quite varied in their strategies and objectives. Basic to their efforts, however, are a
number of common characteristics: "Nearly all begin with the frustrated rage
and fear of people who perceive themselves as victims and who see their quality of life threatened" (Piller 1991:12). Highly focused on protecting their
home environments, NIMBY activists have wasted little time in becoming
skilled at petition drives, political lobbying, street confrontations, and legal
proceedings (Box 9.3).

If frustrated rage and anxiety are the most general characteristics that
unite these groups, the most specific is their defiance of experts and technocrats as the ultimate arbiters of technological risk and change. The zeal of
NIMBY groups often, in this regard, takes on an aura of "proselytic self-right-
eousness." In fact, some have likened NIMBY activists to other moral and religious movements that have gained large followings by advancing what can
be described as "a spiritual critique of medical or scientific teachings and practices." Piller (1991:12) puts it this way: "Although the link between NIMBY
groups and right-wing religious movements are otherwise tenuous, they share
irreverence for official versions of reality offered by scientists and technocrats." Indeed, it can be ironically argued that NIMBYism "is partly a reac-

# BOX 9.3
## Love Canal

In 1977 the tragedy of Love Canal startled the American public into an awareness of the devastating consequences of the mismanagement of our hazardous wastes and toxic materials. Thirty-five years earlier . . . Hooker Chemical and Plastics Corporation began burying more than 20,000 tons of chemical waste in an abandoned waterway ironically named for its former owner, William Love.

In 1953 the landfill was covered with topsoil and the property sold to the Niagara Falls (New York) Board of Education for a token of one dollar. Later the school district parceled out lots to developers. Homebuilding in the neighborhood moved at a rapid pace throughout the 1950s, prompting the school district to build an elementary school and playing field on its remaining parcel.

By the conventional rules of that day, this procedure was a common occurrence in thousands of locations across the nation: Fill a pit or ravine with industrial or household garbage, cover it, level it, and build on it, because towns and cities were pushing ever outward amid the burgeoning prosperity of the post-World War II American industrial boom and suburban expansion.

The toxics time bomb exploded when the Niagara River overflowed its banks and flooded the buried canal a quarter mile away. Flood waters pushed the contaminated groundwater into the basements of residents. What had been suspected all along by a few could no longer be ignored by the many. Over two hundred dangerous chemical compounds were eventually identified in that waste pile, including benzene, trichloroethylene, and most potent of all, dioxin.

President Carter stepped in to declare Love Canal an emergency disaster area, with all the attendant federal governmental activities that that status brought, including the evaluation of 1,004 households and a $30 million government buyout for those living closest to the old canal dump. By the end of a decade, $150 million had been spent on the cleanup effort.

After having for years resisted all local calls for action, New York state placed a clay cap over the canal's most severely contaminated 16 acres, eventually extending the cover to more than 40 surrounding acres. The title of a 1978 report by the New York commissioner of health said it all: Love Canal: Public Health Time Bomb.

Biochemist Dr. Beverly Paigan's study of some 900 children from this area counted seizures, learning problems, eye and skin irritations, incontinence, and severe abdominal pains and found these problems much more prevalent among the children of Love Canal than those from nearby neighborhoods. . . .

The media were quick to take up the cause, playing on the fear of widespread chemical poisoning that had been creeping slowly into the gradually awakening American psyche. The tragedy of Love Canal was symptomatic, *Newsweek* said in 1978, of America's "Faustian" bargain: The products and byproducts of industrial efforts to improve consumer's standards of living are

---

**Box 9.3** *(continued)*

threatening those same people with disease and death. . . .

Clearly, Love Canal was a tragedy of significant human and environmental proportions. However, it was not the first such event; nor would it be the last or even the most dramatic revelation of toxics contamination from the largely forgotten landfills and industrial sites scattered across the American landscape. Yet this case remains outstanding in almost everyone's mind.

Source: Mazmanian and Morell (1992), 3–4.

---

tion to the effects of quasi-religious faith in science that emerged in this country following the second World War." It expresses a contemporary end to the technological optimism that has long defined the "American Century."

Community resistance to the siting of risky facilities can now only be described as a "full-scale public malady," a kind of malignant social "syndrome" (Portney 1991:10–11). Writers speak of "policy gridlock" and "policy stalemate." In the case of hazardous waste treatment facilities, for example,` sitings have come to a halt during the past decade. A primary response to this dilemma has been risk-benefit analysis. Governmental and industrial leaders have sought to assuage the anxieties of NIMBY groups by offering scientific evidence about the levels of risk involved in incineration to support their claims about the safety of such facilities.

### RISK-BENEFIT ANALYSIS AS TECHNOCRATIC SOLUTION

The future of many new technologies today is believed to depend upon the ability of regulatory institutions to assuage public fears about technological risks more generally. Accepting the challenge, the primary response of techno-industrial leaders has been an attempt to shift the political discourse to the search for "acceptable risk." (Wynne, 1987; Schwarz and Thompson 1990: 103–20). Toward this end, supporters of the modern techno-industrial complex argue that risk must be seen as a mixed phenomenon, always producing opportunities as well as dangers. Most often, they argue, the debate revolves only around potential dangers, all too frequently centering on high impact accidents with low probabilities, such as nuclear meltdowns or runaway genetic mutations. Risk taking, in contrast, must be seen as necessary for successful technological change and economic growth, as well as the overall resilience and health of modern society.[5]

The basic strategy of industrial and scientific leaders has been to focus the risk debate on quantifiable technical factors, established through the utilitarian methodology of risk-benefit analysis (described in chapter 2). The approach is grounded in the view that technological dangers have been grossly exaggerated (particularly by the "Luddites" in the environmental movement said to harbor a vested political interest in exploiting the public's fears). The result, it is argued, is a high degree of ignorance in the general public about technological risks. The layperson, so the oft cited argument goes, worries about living next to a hazardous waste incinerator, but thinks nothing of smoking cigarettes, which are said to be statistically much more dangerous to his or her health (Starr, 1969; Lopes, 1987). Because this uncontrolled expansion of "irrational" beliefs is quite threatening to technological progress, often specifically manifested in the issue of financial investment, managerial elites have seen the need to counter this antitechnology trend.

The answer is to supply the public with more objective (technical) information about the levels of risks themselves. That is, the "irrationality" of contemporary political arguments must be countered with rationally demonstrable scientific data. The solution is to provide more information—standardized scientific information—to offset the irrationalities plaguing uninformed thinkers, that is, the proverbial "man on the street." Supplying this information became the empirical task of risk-benefit analysis and its adjunct methodology "risk communication," designed to innovate better ways of effectively disseminating the results of risk-benefit analyses to the public (National Research Council, 1989).

Risk-benefit analysis has proven to be no small consideration. In 1984 the Environmental Protection Agency officially endorsed risk analysis and management as the primary framework for EPA decision making. By 1987, a major agency document flatly declared that the fundamental mission of the agency was to reduce risk. As Andrews (1990) explains, by the end of the 1980s "the vocabulary of risk" had literally become "the primary language of environmental policy analysis and management" at EPA. Formal risk-benefit analysis, in fact, came to constitute the basic test that each environmental policy decision must withstand.[6]

Despite the enthusiasm of its proponents, however, the turn to technological risk-benefit analysis has scarcely proven to be a success. Although the technique has produced a mountain of quantitative data, it has largely failed to reassure the public (Wynne, 1987). Indeed, in many ways it has only worsened public fears and anxieties, a point on which environmental activists have managed to politically capitalize. The use of technically based methods of risk analysis, according to the environmental critics, represents little more than an example of the technocrat's inability or unwillingness to comprehend the underlying sociopolitical nature of the environmental crisis. While there are a number of variations to this argument, including a deep-seated critique of techno-industrial society itself (taken up later in the chapter), in the next section we shall only sketch the  argument most central to the environmentalists' rejection of risk-benefit analysis per se, namely the argument that the technical framing of risk fundamentally distorts the socio-institutional nature of the environmental problem.

## THE GREEN CRITIQUE: RISK-BENEFIT ANALYSIS AS IDEOLOGY

The green response to risk-benefit analysis is essentially an illustration of the contention advanced in chapter 8—that policy evaluation at times takes the form of political philosophy by other means. According to the green policy analyst, risk-benefit analysis's troubles are rooted in the normative assumptions of a technocratic world view that is itself the fundamental problem. The green policy analyst cum policy philosopher, in this respect, outlines a number of interrelated lines of argument against the use of the methodology. Here we selectively present several of those which best illustrate the nature of a critique at this level of policy evaluation, social choice.

Most basically, greens charge risk-benefit analysts—wittingly or unwittingly—with introducing a way of understanding and treating technology that implicitly biases risk decision processes in favor of the dominant techno-industrial system and its values (Gutin, 1991). Through tacit assumptions that support the industrial status quo, the methodology mitigates or undercuts the very kinds of discourse about environmental problems that greens seek to inject. Some, in fact, see risk-benefit analysis to be a strategy designed to do just that, namely to deflect the environmental movement's ability to rally political support against hazardous risks.

Consider, for example, the argument advanced by Langdon Winner, a leading critic of risk-benefit analysis. Winner argues that the methodology's analytical emphasis on risk functions to shift inquiry away from traditional concepts such as "danger" and "hazard" to a more subtle and sophisticated exploration of statistical probabilities. What otherwise appears to be a fairly obvious link between technological causes and dangerous effects—for instance, the relationship between hazardous chemicals and cancer—tends to be transformed into a question fraught with scientific uncertainties. Whereas a hazard is easily recognized as a danger to health and safety—and thus reasonable people readily agree that something should be done about it—the conceptual transformation of a hazard into a question of risk works to soften the threat. By introducing a utilitarian calculus of risks and benefits—that is, by asking people to balance the threat of risk against the relative benefits that society more generally might derive from a techno-industrial process—the question of whether or not something should be done about the hazard becomes less clear. In fact, it might be decided that the benefit derived from learning to live with the danger outweighs a decision to take remedial action (Winner, 1986).[7] For those like Winner who believe in the right to a safe environment, such compromises are unacceptable. Any attempt to qualify such a right must be uncompromisingly rejected. NIMBY groups, among others, should just say no.

Equally deceptive, according to the greens, is risk-benefit analysis's subtle emphasis on expert decision making. Once the parties to an environmental decision agree to shift deliberations about technological hazards to the study, weighing, and comparing of the costs and benefits associated with different levels of risk, they enter into a realm of enormous uncertainties over which there is little chance of a relatively simple, straightforward consensus. Not only are the common sense assumptions upon which the concern for hazards and dangers normally rely abruptly suspended, any confidence people might have had in their own ability to deal with such hazards vanishes in favor of excruciatingly detailed inquiries. Furthermore, because the exact nature of this (technological) cause and (environmental) effect relationship is very difficult to "prove" in the scientific sense of the term, the question of risk always remains open to interpretation. That is to say, the interpretation remains open to the judgments of those who purport to have expertise in the matter.

The consequence of this reliance on experts is thus an intellectual barrier to popular participation. Beyond merely underplaying certain kinds of interests and values, the methodology functions in a way that impedes the very participatory processes that make the advancement of community interests and values possible. In the place of public discourse about what ought to be done, the decision process is de facto increasingly dominated by the opinions of experts. Experts, rather than the citizens themselves, decide whether or not people will live next to a hazardous waste site. This too has been described as a deliberate technocratic strategy to limit the public's role in issues basic to the advance of techno-industrial society.

Against these considerations, the risk debate is one that many environmental groups can easily lose by the very act of entering (Winner, 1986). From the outset, those who might wish to propose limits upon any particular industrial or technological application are placed at a disadvantage. By accepting risk as a legitimate concept, environmentalists are not only forced to judge the harmful technological practices that trouble them in terms of the standards of societal benefits with which the applications might be associated, the standards themselves rest as well on techno-industrial value assumptions that environmentalists might otherwise wish to reflect upon, if not flatly reject. In this regard, as Winner puts it, environmentalists "who enter the risk debate will resemble . . . the greenhorn . . . enticed into a poker game in which the cards are stacked against him."

The alternative, according to the greens, is to deny the legitimacy of risk and risk-benefit analysis's utilitarian language altogether in environmental discourse. To circumvent the often mystifying effects of such language, greens counsel a retreat to more direct and emotive concepts such as danger, hazard, or peril. Ordinary citizens, they point out, have had a very long history of orienting themselves to dangers and have little trouble participating in decisions about the technological hazards that encroach directly upon their own lives. Even more important, the greens insist on a wider discussion of the value and acceptability of the standards of benefit against which risks are measured. Beyond the procedural biases of the risk-benefit methodology—the balancing of risks against benefits and the turn to expert opinions—greens seek to engage the public in a broader discourse about the meaning of *progress* itself. Such a discussion raises basic questions about the techno-industrial society; it brings the technocratic worldview into question.

While experts present their judgments as value-neutral scientific findings, greens contend that risk-benefit analysis's emphasis on potential benefits rests in reality on basic value assumptions of a techno-industrial society. They point in particular to its commitment to the quantitative expansion of material production, higher levels of consumption, and a largely uncritical acceptance of new technological innovations (understood to be the basic engines driving production and consumption).[8] Indeed, the enthusiasts of the techno-industrial way of life underscore the fact that every area of modern life has been profoundly shaped by technological innovations—basic living standards, industrial production, medicine, agriculture, transportation, education, housing, furniture, and clothing—in short, just about everything we commonly take to be good in everyday life.

## CRITIQUE OF TECHNO-INDUSTRIAL PROGRESS

For many greens, this claim about technology and progress is the source of major contention. Quite to the contrary, they see the techno-industrial concept of progress to be anything but an unqualified force of the "good society." Technocratic assumptions, they argue, have led to a materialist conception of the good life that is not only wasteful but ultimately alienating in human terms. It is an "overconsumptive" society in which people increasingly attach more importance to unnecessary possessions than to their neighbors; it is a "throwaway" society in which people are increasingly threatened by their own garbage; it is a society that all too casually toys with dangerous technological processes, from nuclear power to genetic bioengineering (Porritt, 1984). According to the greens, this concept of progress rests on an antiquated—if not misbegotten—assumption about nature and natural resources.

In the techno-industrial concept of progress nature has its roots in the thought of the eighteenth-century Enlightenment. Nature, in this view, is fundamentally an object to be tamed and controlled by science and technology. Rather than something with its own intrinsic value, a natural resource

exists solely for expropriation by humankind; it is simply a raw material for
the techno-industrial machine (Leiss, 1974). The primary manifestations of
this assumption are evident—two hundred years of techno-industrial development in the West and an unprecedented level of wealth and living standards. But now the limits begin to become clear. As the ever greater quest
for material progress propels forward, the continual exploitation of the
earth's natural resources begins to take its toll. The industrial wear and tear
on the earth's resources, as greens are quick to argue, starts to reveal the
limits of contemporary techno-industrial practices. The "crisis ahead," is
thus portrayed as an extension of a process long in the making. Rather than
a matter of better policy per se, as green theorists contend, the environmental problem is lodged in the very mode of reason that underlies the development of techno-industrial society. At issue is nothing less than an historical
challenge to the techno-industrial worldview and its positivist mode of reason that have dominated the last two or three hundred years of Western society. The green critique of risk-benefit analysis can only be adequately
understood in the context of this larger critique of the technocratic worldview.

In another sense, however, the problem is more than just a way of thinking per se. What makes such change so difficult is that the positivist mode of
thinking is deeply embedded in the design of our societal institutions and practice, in particular bureaucratic government and the corporate marketplace. On
the one hand, to be sure, this institutional dimension of the problem holds out
some optimistic possibilities. Our institutions are our own creations, so we can
eliminate practices such as risk-benefit analysis. On the other, such changes
prove much more complicated than they first appear; they involve uprooting
assumptions basic to our very way of life. As one aspect of a way of life generally proves to be interrelated with other aspects of the same way of life, such
change proves to be no simple task.

To capture this institutional dimension of the environmental crisis,
greens often appeal to Hardin's (1968) metaphor of the "Tragedy of the Commons." In Hardin's metaphor the earth is analogized to a pasture (commons)
open to all, a place where the herdsman seeks to maximize his own gain by
keeping as many cattle on it as he can. As long as man and beast are kept
below the carrying capacity of the commons, such behavior is rewarded, the
tragedy lies in the herdsman's inability to recognize the physical limits of the
commons. Because nobody in particular bears the costs of the commons,
everybody overconsumes what is held in common and shepherds only what is
theirs. In the process, they fail to see the self-defeating nature of such behavior. When the carrying capacity of the commons is exceeded, the commons
collapses, and the conditions that sustain production are destroyed. "Ruin," as
Hardin warns, "is the destination toward which all men rush, each pursuing his

own best interest in a society that believes in the freedom of the commons."
Ultimately, "freedom in the commons brings ruin to all."

Green political theorists bring the analogy of the commons to bear directly on the structural tensions than now define the American political economy. Essentially it reflects the long-standing political conflict between short-term selfishness (largely defined as the individual pursuit of material gain) and enlightened long-term community interests (defined in terms of the public interest and social values). Indeed, some have traced the idea of the freedom of the commons back to the American Constitution, particularly the ideas about private property, individual liberties, and limited government basic to the document. Drawing on the eighteenth-century theories of John Locke and Adam Smith, the Founding Fathers understood government to originate from a contract agreed to by autonomous individuals in pursuit of liberty and happiness. The pursuit of individual happiness, increasingly interpreted in terms of free enterprise, became identified with the pursuit of material progress for which there was no natural limits. Taken together, these principles provided the most basic foundations of the American liberal tradition.[9]

The success of the Founders' experiment in liberal government was thus highly dependent on an infinite availability of the natural resources necessary for such pursuits. The contemporary discovery of the earth's "carrying capacity"—or limits to nature's "commons"—would appear to jeopardize the continuous success of the American experiment. In ecological terms, the rampantness of aggressive individualism and its short-term outlook is seen to be a course destined for disaster. "If," as Leeson (1979: 305) puts it, "American political ideology and institutions have been successful in encouraging the pursuit of happiness through material acquisitions, they appear incapable of imposing limits which are required to forestall ecological disaster." This capacity to impose limits in turn leads to the argument that popular government must give way to authoritarianism. If this proves to be the case, such authoritarianism can only be judged to reflect "the crisis to which modern political philosophy and liberalism have led."

In many important respects, greens see this potential for an increase in authoritarianism as an extension of troublesome techno-industrial patterns already present in the society (Bookchin, 1982). During the twentieth century, the very technological systems introduced to drive industrial development brought new political and economic institutional processes that have increasingly run counter to traditional American values. Indeed, greens see techno-industrial society itself to be responsible for the perversion of basic American values. The development of advanced technological systems have in systematic ways led to greater accumulation of power in smaller and smaller numbers of decision centers, constituting a growing threat to democratic processes. Because of the increasing scope of technological requirements, as well as their extensive "social externalities" (or "spillovers") into other areas of modern life—the risks to human health and safety being a primary case in point—the costs of large-scale technologies introduce immense demands that dramatically constrict the room for democratic politics and policymaking. This, in turn, works to limit the range of alternative policy goals and options.

Basic to the authoritarian tendencies of advanced technological society is the technocratic emphasis on experts and expertise. For technocratic theorists, greens point out, technical expertise is the essential commodity of an advanced industrial system. The sheer complexity of the system is seen to necessitate the dominant role of experts. Whereas greens are critical of what they see to be modern society's blind emphasis on technology, the technocratic answer to technological problems is more technical decision making. Scientific techniques of problem solving and decision making are said not only to hold the answer to the efficient operation of the system, but to the larger problems of confronting technological society as well, including risk. Political issues, in this view, can best be dealt with by transforming them into technically defined ends that can be pursued through administrative means (Stanley, 1978).

Nothing is more irrational to technocratic theories than the disjointed, incremental forms of decision making (typically described as "muddling through") that result from a democratic commitment to public bargaining and compromise (Sternberg, 1989). In the world as it exists, so technocrats maintain, democratic decision making is often impractical and outmoded.[10] Democratic decision processes, they argue, should be sharply restricted in a complex technological society. To put it pointedly, technocrats are prone to seeing politics as a *problem* rather than a *solution*.[11] Such arguments, greens stress, reflect a highly antidemocratic, elitist ideology of governance. Indeed, for some technocrats the ideology is the rationale for the ascent of a new technical elite trained to guide our political and economic system (Bell, 1973; Brzezinski, 1976).

Greens take a sharp view of the technocratic world view in virtually all of its aspects. But what do greens offer as an alternative? Can they offer a cogent program for societal reconstruction? Although it is common for the opponents of the greens to reject their criticism as misguided utopian rhetoric, the ecological critique of American institutions is scarcely the unprincipled attack that techno-industrial leaders often portray it to be.[12] Whether accepted or not, the critique represents one of the most thoroughgoing challenges to the American system, as well as a fascinating attempt to delineate an alternative set of institutions and goals.

What is more, greens offer a concrete alternative to risk-benefit analysis. Rather than locating the answer in an antidemocratic, technocratic decision methodology, they find it in more democracy. Indeed, greens advance a vigor-

# BOX 9.4
# Ecological versus Techno-Industrial Values

| *Techno-Industrialism* | *Green Ecology* |
|---|---|
| *1. Basic Values* | |
| Aggressive individualism | A cooperative communitarian society |
| Pursuit of material goods | Emphasis on spiritual and nonmaterial values |
| Rationality and technocratic knowledge | Intuition and understanding |
| Patriarchical values/hierarchical structure | Postpatriarchical feminist values/decentralization |
| Unquestioning acceptance of technology | Discriminating development and use of technology |
| *2. The Environment* | |
| Domination over nature | Harmony with nature |
| Environment managed as a resource | Resources regarded as strictly limited |
| High energy consumption/ nuclear power | Low energy consumption/ renewable energy sources |
| *3. The Economy* | |
| Economic growth and demand stimulation | Sustainability, quality of life, simplicity |
| Free market economy needs | Low production for local needs |
| High income differentials | Low income differentials |
| Production for exchange | Production for use |
| Capital intensive production | Labor intensive production |
| *4. Political Organization* | |
| Centralization/economics of scale | Decentralization/human scale |
| Representative democracy | Participatory democracy |

Source: Adapted from Porritt (1984), 216–17.

ous case for the institution of an "environmental democracy" grounded in social justice and human dignity. We turn to these ideas in the next section of the chapter.

## BEYOND CRITIQUE: THE GREEN WORLDVIEW AND ENVIRONMENTAL DEMOCRACY

Green ideology sets out a fundamentally different program from that of techno-industrial ideology. Where the latter emphasizes domination over nature and resource management, greens call for harmony with nature and a limited use of resources. Where techno-industrialists see the need for economic growth and demand stimulation, greens call for sustainability and quality of life. Where techno-industrialists rely on centralized administration and rational decision making, greens stress communal decentralization and participatory democracy. As Box 9.4 makes clear, greens would literally turn the technocratic world upside down.

From where do the greens draw their inspiration? For many, nature itself is the source of normative renewal. In their view, ecological values must supply the underpinnings of economic and political values (Commoner, 1972). While there are various conceptualizations of what this might mean in specific economic and social terms, in its more critical interpretations the transformation leaves few of American liberalism's basic values untouched. Most fundamentally, community interests and social interdependence have to be given priority over individualistic economic and social competition, especially as reflected in American capitalism; social and economic equality must supplant political and bureaucratic hierarchy; ecological wisdom must supersede technological knowledge (Goodin, 1992).

What kinds of social and political principles do such greens derive from nature? (See Box 9.5.) The most basic lesson is drawn from the concept of interdependence (Dobson, 1990). Human survival, like survival in the natural world, is seen to depend on an interlocking system of independent objects (both sentient and nonsentient). No part of the natural world is independent and therefore no part can lay claim to "superiority." There is a sense, then, that every relationship—from an ecological point of view—is a symbiotic relationship. In short, humans must learn to reconceptualize themselves as interdependent parts of the natural world, rather than as superior creatures out to conquer it, the view that has dominated modernity.

The view of the world as an interlocking system of interdependent objects generates a sense of equality, as each unit is held to be necessary for the viability of every other unit. Insofar as no part of the natural world can be independent, no part can lay claim to "superiority." Humankind, in this respect, has no basis for assuming the privileged position to which it has elevated it-

---

## BOX 9.5
## Nature and Environmental Values

One of the most interesting efforts to found an alternative green value system, at least for purposes of illustration, are those greens who attempt to derive normative principles directly from the principles of nature herself (Dobson, 1990). Indeed, the natural world is taken to be a model for the human world; many ecological prescriptions are derived from a particular view of how nature "is." Moreover, from the ecological perspective, nature is over time by and large "pacific, tranquil, lush—and green," rather than "red in tooth and claw."

The idea that the natural world provides a model for human society is derived from the belief that nature speaks with the wisdom born of long experience and that attendance to her lessons guarantees the best of possible outcomes. The contrast between the "puny . . . knowledge of modern science" and the tools it produces, and "the rich vein of wisdom" generated by forebears with an ear to the ground is taken to be evident. Thus, many green ecologists argue that we must learn to live *with,* rather than *against,* the natural world, and that this has profound implications for the ways in which we must restructure society, particularly at the community level. At the same time, appreciation of the natural world's longevity can help to move us away from the forms of human anthropocentricism which ecologists see to be fundamentally linked to individual competitiveness and the human potential for ecological destructiveness. Social ecology introduces an important element of humanity and compassion into our understanding of our place on earth. A view with roots in nineteenth century transcendental thought, greater attention to nature's own morality is believed to foster more sympathetic and responsive human beings with a new spiritual—and some would say "feministic"—awareness of their own potentials, obligations to others, and responsibilities to the life-supporting processes of their natural surroundings.

---

self. This premise is seen to be based on a directly observable principle of equality.[13]

In addition to equality, interdependence also points to the role of diversity. It is an ecological axiom that stability in an ecosystem is a function of the diversity in that system. In social and political terms, this translates into toleration of peculiarity and generosity with respect to a diversity of opinions. It gives rise to a strong conviction that the "healthy society" is one in which a range of opinions is not only tolerated but celebrated, in that this range provides for a repository of ideas and forms of behavior from which to draw when confronted with political and social problems. Environmental values are believed to fare best in processes built on the free discourse among equals

## BOX 9.6
## Green Tactics: Politics versus Life-Styles

According to green ideology, then, drastic action is required to save us from the impending plight portended by the environmental crisis. As Porritt and Winner (1988) put it: The most radical goal of the movement must be "nothing less than a nonviolent revolution to overthrow our whole polluting, plundering and materialistic industrial society and in its place, to create a new economic and social order which will allow human beings to live in harmony with the planet."

While the green critique has made substantial strides during the past two decades, the question of tactics has often been divisive. Both the scope of the problem and the distance between ecological solutions and present realities constitute an "immense gap . . . between the green-thinking dreamers and the political reality" (Schwarz and Schwarz, 1987: 253). While the question of appropriate tactics remains a source of serious debate among greens, it is possible to outline two primary orientations: one dealing with pragmatic political strategies, typically defined in electoral terms; the other more ideological, concerned with social consciousness, institutional transformation, and life-styles (The Green Program, 1991).

Electoral tactics are now widely identified with the Green parties that have sprung up around the world, especially in Europe. The primary efforts of the advocates of party strategies are devoted to political debate over issues, influencing legislative processes through electoral contests, the development of policy, and the shaping of policy implementation. The principal assumption underlying such activities is that liberal democratic decision-making processes are sufficiently open to allow the Green agenda to be carried out through them. Although the question of whether or not Green parties can be sufficiently powerful to bring about the sustainable society is a subject of much debate among ecologists, it is nonetheless the case that Green parties in many countries have gained influence, the most significant example being the Green party in Germany (Capra and Spretnak, 1985).

For more radical members of the Green movement, working through existing political institutions is inadequate (Bookchin, 1982; Roszak, 1978). Political institutions, they argue, are always tainted by precisely those strategies and practices that the Green movement seeks to replace. An important example is the way in which the principles of democracy have come to be embodied and practiced in Western political institutions. Although they function in the name of democratic participation, they have come to represent the formal abandonment of extensive and regular citizen involvement. Participatory politics, as greens see it, requires a radical restructuring (if not abolition) of present institutions.

Outside of the electoral arena, efforts focus on bringing about fundamental changes in social consciousness and life-styles. Sustainable living, greens argue, must be preceded by sustainable thinking. Such changes in consciousness

> **Box 9.6** *(continued)*
>
> are believed to lead to behavioral and life-style changes at both the levels of the individual and the community (Porritt, 1984: 194–211). Individual life-style changes center around patterns of behavior in daily life. Typical examples of individual change include becoming more conscientious about the things one buys (i.e., choosing recyclable bottles over plastic containers), the things one eats (muesli instead of bacon), where one invests one's money (solar energy companies rather than nuclear power utilities), the means of transportation one uses (bicycles instead of cars), and so on. Moreover, in the form of consumer campaigns, such actions are often aligned with Green party activities.
>
> But other greens see the individual approach to be in and of itself insufficient. While they agree that significant political change can only occur after people begin to think differently, they maintain that such changes in consciousness must be supported by institutional changes. Basic to tactics must be the building of the autonomous decentralized communities considered essential to a sustainable society. Designed to foster self-help, local responsibility, and political participation, the community strategy constitutes the foundation for a more complete and systematic set of ecological institutions and practices. Built upon an alternative set of ecological norms and values, they can show—to the extent that they in fact are demonstrated to work—that it is possible to live differently, both sustainably and democratically (Bahro, 1986: 29).

(Dryzek, 1987: 200–215). For such greens, this becomes the foundation of a radically participatory form of society—a kind of "grassroots environmental democracy"—in which discussion and consensus are sought across the widest range of political and social issues (Goodin, 1992: 113–68).

The link between diversity and participation, particularly in conjunction with the principle of interdependence, is the cornerstone of the green movement's decentralist, communitarian politics. Following the premise that "small is beautiful," social and political institutions should ideally be linked through a decentralized system of self-sustaining communities. (Schumacher, 1976; Bahro, 1986; Bookchin, 1982). The reasons typically given for the decentralized structure of an ecologically sound society include the argument that decentralized communities do not lend themselves to large-scale techno-industrial expansions, that they supply the political foundations for a participatory system of community decision making necessary to facilitate an authentic consensus on ecological issues, and that they are seen to better correspond with human nature than the alienating structures of the big city. Linked together through a system of natural "bioregions," decentralized communities "provide the site(s) on which personal relationships become fulfilling, and where people learn to live 'in place' (according to, and not against, their environment)" (Dobson, 1990: 123).

GREEN IDEOLOGY: FROM THEORY TO PRACTICE

But how does this green alternative bear directly on the more practical questions of public policy? In this final section, we shall offer a brief example to illustrate how an ideological difference can indeed sometimes be a major—perhaps even decisive—factor in a policy dispute. For this purpose, we return to the issue of hazardous waste policy.

At the outset, we saw that the technocratic solution to the hazardous waste problem was to supply increased technical information about the risks posed by such wastes. The methodology of risk-benefit analysis has been employed to get around what is seen to be the ordinary citizen's inability to deal rationally with complex technical problems. The method, it was argued, has explicitly sought to circumvent democratic political processes in an effort to avoid citizen participation. But what is the green alternative? For many radical environmentalists, the answer is democracy itself; they call for "environmental democracy" (Thornton, 1991; Paehlke, 1990; Kann, 1986).

Here greens draw on the experiences of community oriented environmental movements in North America, whose theoreticians and activities have emphasized small, decentralized communities. Basic to their environmental struggles has been "the right of the public to participate in—even collectively determine—decisions about technology." A basic goal of the environmental democracy movement should be to render obsolete the "expert" status of government and industry's scientists in order to "make every citizen conversant at all levels of the environmental debate" (Thornton, 1991: 15).

For most mainstream economic and political leaders—particularly those of technocratic persuasion—such language is merely ideology. But recent experience has begun to suggest that there is more to the argument than first meets the eye. According to greens, two types of evidence now seem to support—at least provisionally—the environmentalists' emphasis on democracy. One concerns the nature of the community decision process; the other concerns the emergence of new environmental projects that illustrate the importance of democracy.

The first has to do with the failure of risk assessment strategy to allay fears about technological and toxic hazards. A small but growing body of research into the question of why communities have so adamantly rejected the advice of the risk experts now offers quite a different perspective. Whereas risk experts have portrayed the public as incapable of digesting technical findings, and thus is left to fall back on irrational fears, environmentally oriented writers such as Plough and Krimsky (1987) make clear that such a conclusion rests on a limited understanding of the nature of the community decision-making process. In their work, they distinguish between two different types of rationality that guide risk assessment, a scientifically based "technical" conception of rationality and a community based "cultural" rationality.

"Technical rationality," according to Plough and Krimsky, is a mind-set that puts its faith in empirical evidence and the scientific method, appeals to experts for justifying policy decisions, values logical consistency and universality of findings, and judges nonquantifiable impacts to be irrelevant to political decision making. "Cultural rationality," in contrast, tends to emphasize (or at least give equal weight to) the opinions of traditional and peer groups over those of experts, focuses on personal and familiar experiences rather than depersonalized calculations, holds unanticipated consequences to be fully relevant to near-term decision making, and trusts process rather than evidence. That is, decisions are judged as much by the processes through which they are reached as by the outcomes, as in the case of technical rationality. Beyond probability and risk-benefit ratios, then, public risk perception is shaped by the circumstances under which the risk is identified and publicized, the place of the individual in his or her community, and the social values of the community as a whole.

While laypersons tend to be culturally rational in their own decision-making processes, few people think or act exclusively in one mode or the other. Such modes typically change with circumstances. This has been demonstrated with a simple test. Experts were asked to imagine themselves in situations in which they were not in control of the existing circumstances and to think of themselves as fathers rather than as engineers and businessmen. In such situations, the experts were themselves found to abandon the technical rational model of decision making for the culturally rational model of the citizen. The conclusion here is clear: cultural rationality is only a different kind of knowledge and has to be built into the decision-making process.

From this work we learn that the public decision "process" is as important as scientific "evidence," sometimes more so. Citizens react as much to *who* is talking as they do to what is being said. In this respect, they are responding to the possibilities of deception and manipulation often associated with hierarchical decision structures and with asymmetrical communicative relations. Citizens want to know that a decision is reached fairly without bias and deceit. Does the process reflect hidden interests? The answer to such mistrust requires a more open set of communicative relationships.

If the foregoing discussion suggests that citizens are not so hostile to technical data per se—that is, that they might well be inclined to accept data that is advanced and deliberated in an open and democratic discourse—such a conclusion appears to be just what new experiences in Canada are demonstrating. In particular, the siting of a hazardous waste treatment facility in the Canadian provinces of Alberta and Ontario have begun to cast a new ray of hope on the problem of NIMBY. Contrary to the traditional technocratic approaches, the case provides evidence that suggests the answer to be more, rather than less, democracy.

The most impressive experience comes from Alberta. Faced with the NIMBY syndrome, the regional government of Alberta has adopted an open and direct approach to the opposition (Rabe, 1991; 1992; Paehlke and Torgerson, 1991). Working together, government, industry, and local groups in Alberta devised a participatory process in which the conflictual issues of siting were transformed in such a way that all of the major stakeholders preferred negotiation to conflict, and through the process came to believe they could all reap the benefits of cooperation. Gone were the winners and losers that have typically framed the "zero-sum" politics of NIMBY and the results have been significant. The regional government there has sited, built, and operated the only successful major new waste facility in North America during the past decade that has not been held up or thwarted by a major NIMBY challenge.

Basic to the success in Alberta was the effort to build participation into the decision process from the beginning, commencing with a local plebiscite on the general acceptability of siting a facility in the area and the community's willingness to participate in the deliberative process. The regional government then supplied the local community with funds to hire its own experts and their consultants and subsequently organized extensive public meetings to discuss with community members and their consultants the specifics of the proposed plant and its consequences. Once the site was formally accepted, the government provided the community with additional monies to offset the inordinate burdens that were incurred by the local infrastructure and for paying the costs of ongoing expert consultations.

To maintain an active community involvement in the decision process, the local leadership committee in Alberta has used the money to organize regular seminars and meetings for the community residents regarding hazardous waste treatment. To provide facility managers with a steady source of information about community attitudes and ideas, the local committee also reviewed the plant's environmental monitoring reports. Consultants translated the reports from technical language into an easily understood format. The consultants, moreover, have assisted the committee in monitoring the facility's operations. Though the Canadian experience might not work everywhere, it has shown that a democratically inspired discourse can lead to a positive end for the most complex and fearful type of facility. The Canadian experience suggests that the likelihood of siting clean facilities requires long-term oversight arrangements that provide for significant community power and risk sharing (Mazmanian and Morell, 1993: 243).

## GREENING RISK ASSESSMENT: TOWARD A PARTICIPATORY APPROACH

If the local community is to monitor plant operations, the need for some adjustments to the technocratic model of expert advice giving might be anticipated. As already noted in the Canadian example, the operational reports are translated from a technical language into a format easily understood by the ordinary citizen and the community is provided with money to hire a consultant to help it grapple with the key issues in the reports. If, however, the community is to become truly involved in this deliberatory process, one might expect to see this process evolve as something more than an oversight function. And that is in fact just what has begun to happen.

Since the beginning of NIMBY and the community movement against the siting of toxic wastes, green-oriented scientists have begun to experiment with a form of "participatory research" designed to bring local residents more directly into the investigatory process, including the possibility of a form of community risk assessment (Chess and Sandman, 1989: 20). For instance, since the toxic waste crisis at Love Canal in upstate New York, one almost typically finds present in such struggles a citizen expert of some kind who assists the community in answering its own questions on its own terms (Levine, 1982). Such experts emerge to help the community "understand the significance of new developments, plot strategies, and even take on adversaries directly." Accounts of the Love Canal Homeowners Association's struggles with state and local officials emphasize the work of a cancer researcher who helped the community association "to reinterpret government data, develop the capacity to collect additional information, and interpret this information credibly inside and outside the neighborhood" (Edelstein, 1988).

A direct outcome of this Love Canal experience was the formation of a national organization designed to provide just such alternative expertise to other NIMBY groups across the country. The Citizens' Clearinghouse for Hazardous Wastes was started by Lois Gibbs the Love Canal homemaker who had organized the community and extracted major concessions from the State of New York and the federal government (Gibbs, 1982). With only a high-school education and no former experience in such matters, she went on to establish a major Washington-based organization to assist other communities across the country in struggles against toxic wastes. Among its various activities, the Citizens' Clearinghouse offers instruction and advice on how to deal with the technical dimensions of the hazardous waste problem, in particular the problem of incineration (Collette, 1987). Fundamental to such instruction is training in how to talk to experts, how to understand the expert's research findings, and in some cases how the community can derive its own calculations. But the Clearinghouse's function is only to facilitate. Its staff advisors have made a practice of waiting for such groups to find *them,* rather than directly attempting to organize community groups across the country.

Underlying such consultation is an emerging alteɪnative method for "participatory research." Evolving in the context of struggles against environmental hazards in both the community and workplace, participatory research is founded on the efforts of citizens both to broaden their access to the information produced by scientists and citizens, with a view to research that meets people's needs (Merrifield, 1989; Fals-Borda and Rahman, 1991).

Grounded in a critique of professional expertise, participatory research is put forward in an effort to gear expert practices to the requirements of democratic empowerment.[14] Rather than providing technical answers designed to bring political discussions to an end, the task is to assist citizens in their efforts to examine their *own* interests and to make their own decisions (Hirschhorn, 1979). Beyond merely providing analytical research and empirical data, the expert is conceptualized as a "facilitator" of public learning and empowerment.[15] As a facilitator, he or she becomes an expert in how people learn, clarify, and decide for themselves (Fischer, 1990). This includes coming to grips with the basic languages of public narrative argumentation, as well as knowledge about the kinds of environmental and intellectual conditions under which citizens can formulate their own ideas. It involves the creation of institutional and intellectual contexts that help people pose questions and examine technical analyses in their own ordinary everyday languages and decide which issues are important to them.

The practitioners of participatory research point to two important payoffs. One, the process identifies real and important dangers that hide behind the assumptions and generalities buried in the expert's calculations.[16] That is, it brings to the fore the very problems, especially problematic assumptions, that have been overlooked by standard policy analysts. And second, participation in decision making helps to build both credibility and acceptance of research findings (Dutton, 1984; Friedmann, 1987), the critical failure facing the contemporary approaches.

To conventionally trained physical and social scientists, the idea of participatory research often sounds outrageously unscientific. In response to this concern, participatory researchers can give at least two replies. First, the process is a methodology primarily designed for research problems characterized by a mix of technical and social problems. Scientists concerned with pure physics have little need to consult the ordinary citizen. Second, where the methodology is used, it is in most ways only the scientific methods made more time consuming and perhaps more expensive, at least in the short run (Fischer, 1993).

CONCLUDING OBSERVATIONS: BEYOND IDEOLOGICAL CLASH

The purpose here is not to choose between these techno-cratic and ecological ideologies per se. Rather, the point has been to demonstrate the way in which ideological commitments bear directly on otherwise pragmatic policy issues. Indeed, as was seen, they can at times be the decisive factors in the evaluation process. As we posed it in the previous chapter, the key question is: How does one move discourse beyond the gulf between such ideologies? For insight into this question, we outlined Habermas's theory of social learning in the preceding chapter.

The Habermasian theory would seem to bear directly on the ideological debate at hand: techno-industrial society confronts an environmental crisis that threatens the productive system at its foundations; the Green movement—as harbinger of the bad news—advocates a new set of ideological principles and a corresponding institutional order better able to deal with the crisis. The progress of the movement's struggle, however, remains difficult to assess. One thing is clear. The movement can take credit for having advanced the environmental issue to a top priority on the political agenda, international as well as national. Whereas the issue of technological risk to the environment was traditionally understood as a technical issue, it has been reconceptualized in political terms.

With regard to the green alternative itself, the primary question concerns its viability. Simply stated, is it realistic? Is its radical conception of environmental democracy workable, both as a solution to the ecological problem and as a political possibility (Goodin, 1992)? Some have argued that the solution requires just the opposite: less democracy and more authoritarianism (Ophuls, 1977; Heilbroner 1974).

What is more, we cannot altogether forego the possibility that the techno-managerial elites will be able to steer the system out of the crisis. The question here is whether or not the techno-industrial system can manage to adapt to or mitigate the crisis within the framework of its own institutions and values. Many say yes and point to a long history of creative adaptation on the part of industrial capitalism (Simon, 1984; Ostrom, 1990). Indeed, capitalist supporters typically argue that the environmental movement is little more than a disguised ideological attack on capitalism by people who don't understand how it works.[17] Rather than taking environmental arguments seriously on their own terms, industrial capitalists insist on opposing greens as a threat to the established American way of life.

In large part, the answer depends on the seriousness of the crisis. And it is here that science itself fuels the controversy. At the present time, there are distinguished scientists who argue both sides of the issue. Some say that it may already be too late to save the planet—at least without immediate and drastic action—while others see such assertions as unsupported by the available evidence. The problem, in this regard, is the fact that sufficient evidence to make a definitive prediction is not available. For this reason, the existing data lends itself to scientific interpretation, which opens the door for the ideologists. This, for instance, brings us back to the initial judgment: Do we live in the safest or the riskiest of times?

Given the contemporary ideological standoff, greens have argued that in the face of such uncertainty it is better to err on the side of safety. As the consequences of underestimating the severity of the problem can be extremely dire, the proper course for them is to err conservatively on the side of environmental protection. In fact, many techno-industrialists agree with such an assessment, but take grave exception to the ecological conception of such a strategy. To the degree that the ecological program will jeopardize economic growth, they argue, it undercuts the very possibility of generating the resources essential to an effective attack on the problem. Thus, even translated into more pragmatic terms, the argument only goes around again.

## READINGS

Robert Paehlke. 1989. *Environmentalism and the Future of Progressive Politics*. New Haven, CT: Yale University Press.

Jonathon Porritt. 1986. *Seeing Green*. Oxford: Blackwell.

Mary Douglas and Aaron Wildavsky. 1982. *Risk and Culture*. Berkeley: University of California Press.

Charles Piller. 1991. *The Fail-Safe Society: Community Defiance and the End of American Technological Optimism*. New York: Basic Books.

Daniel Mazmanian and David Morell. 1992. *Beyond Superfailure: America's Toxic Policy for the 1990s*. Boulder, CO: Westview.

Andrew Szasz. 1994. *Ecopopulism: Toxic Waste and the Movement for Environmental Justice*. Minneapolis: University of Minnesota Press.

Robert E. Goodin. 1992. *Green Political Theory*. London: Polity.

## DISCUSSION QUESTIONS

1. In what way does the resolution of NIMBY depend less on specific policies than on the normative assumptions underlying the policies? How does the case illustrate this point?
2. Some people say we live in the riskiest of times; others say we live in the safest of times. What kinds of evidence might be brought to bear on an evaluation of each of these positions?
3. Describe how risk-benefit analysis works. What does it mean to say that it is a "technocratic" methodology?

4. Conservatives and business leaders often maintain that further industrial progress is itself a precondition for environmental renewal. Only with greater wealth, according to this argument, can we garner the resources needed to clean up the environment. How would greens counter this argument? Discuss.

5. Whereas technocrats tend to see the need for more centralized governmental authority to deal successfully with the environmental challenge, greens call for decentralization and greater citizen participation. Which of these positions do you find most credible? Why?

6. This chapter has emphasized the green critique of techno-industrial society and focused on its alternative conception of the good society. How might the economic and political leaders of the industrial system reply to the green arguments put forth in this chapter? Be specific.

# Part Five
## CONCLUSION

# 10   Policy Deliberation as Political Methodology: Implications for Theory and Practice

The logic of policy deliberation as advanced here would have a range of impacts on the discipline of policy analysis. In addition to the multimethodological challenge which we have examined in the preceding chapters, the process also holds out important implications for transforming the institutional structures and practices of policy decision processes more generally. Most important are its potential democratizing influence on policy evaluation.

The idea of democratizing policy evaluation is not as unique as it might sound. Although policy analysis has primarily emerged as a technocratic discipline, the concern for democracy has always been present. Policy analysis was initially conceived to serve a system founded on liberal democratic values. Indeed, its founder, Harold Lasswell, attempted to set out nothing less than a "policy science of democracy." The logic of policy deliberation is advanced as an effort to help make good on that claim. In this closing chapter, we examine some of the larger normative and political issues which frame this effort. We begin with the central issue that has guided the discussion throughout the book, namely the task of developing a normative language suitable for a political-deliberative approach to the theory and practice of policy evaluation.

## POLITICS AND DISCOURSE: THE DISCURSIVE CONSTRUCTION OF SOCIETY

In recent years there has been a renewed interest in political discourse. In particular, two interrelated approaches have gained considerable influence, one descriptively concerned with political rhetoric and the discursive construction of society generally, the other prescriptively focused on the role of discourse in democratic practices. Both relate directly to the kinds of

---

**BOX 10.1**
**Discourse and the Constitution of Society**

"A discourse is a series of rules by which meaningful statements can be formed. As Foucault (1973) argues, society is constituted through the formation of a dominant discourse, or 'regime truth' within which society exists. A discourse enables some statements to be made, and excludes others from consideration. Certain types of reality are highlighted, and others are obscured. Consequently, it limits what constitutes a social world, and what types of practices can be pursued. The range of human activities is thus limited by the nature of the dominant discourse. This definition of social [reality] by the dominant discourse enables the consistent reproduction of stable patterns of human interaction, or in other words, enables the practical creation of a social order. It also excludes other types of practices from consideration. Hence the key to the realization of a stable social order is the ability to define what constitutes the common sense reality that applies to a field of practice."

Discourse analysis allows the social scientist "to view the strategies implicit in the creation of different discourses and shows the links between a particular world view [or ideology], how it is constructed, and how it can function to establish a group's political power. By examining their structures, we can determine the political practices that these discourses engender and exclude. Hence to study rhetoric and discourse is to study the process of how social order is created and maintained."

Source: Brulle and Dietz (1992), 4–5.

---

practical implications posed by the logic of policy evaluation. We first take up the emphasis on political rhetoric, as it attempts to outline a general theory or understanding of society based on language and discourse.

The rhetorical approach to discourse in society focuses on how the human community forms symbolic expression of worldviews or ideologies. Common or shared language is seen to create a horizon of understanding within which the world is constituted; it becomes a comprehensible phenomenon. Such understanding, derived through dialogue among participants, requires intersubjective agreement on the symbolic structures that organize human experience. Rhetorically constructed, the knowable world is a practical achievement of a social community over time (Box 10.1). Truth, in this view, is a matter of collective opinion gained through persuasive argumentation (Brown, 1983).

The creation of social knowledge and power are thus intimately linked. To act together, a human community must come to some agreement on what version of reality it will accept as both factually correct and normatively legitimate. Such rhetorical closure on the definition of reality establishes the foundation of the social order. This "stable definition" of the social world is said to provide basis for the dominant social discourse in the society. In the United States, for example, basic definitions and understandings about capitalism and democracy establish the contours of the dominant American discourse.

On one hand such discourses make the very thing we call society possible, but on the other they also permit certain social groups to dominate others. In this sense, the dominant discourse offers a definition of reality that facilitates the interests of some groups (e.g., capitalists) while relegating those of others to a subordinate status (e.g., workers). Other groups, to be sure, advance their own discourses, but these discourses are the challengers. In this respect, politics can most fundamentally be understood as a struggle over the basic operative definitions of social reality: what is good and bad; what works and what doesn't; whose opinion is most valuable; who should be permitted to participate, and so on (Berger and Luckmann, 1966; Schram, 1993).

Building on this conception of society, Habermas and his followers have sought to elucidate the intimate relationship between knowledge and interests. For Habermas, the political discourse of modern society—or any society—takes the form of "systematically distorted communication" (Habermas, 1973). By this he means that the dominant ruling groups seek to secure their power by controlling and manipulating the ideological assumptions that underlie the primary social discourses. Setting up barriers to discourses that challenge their own ideological consensus, the power elite restricts or refuses to admit certain types of factual propositions and value judgments into the public deliberative processes (Hajer, 1993). Politics becomes an arena for conflict over the concepts and definitions used in framing political judgments on social problems, public policies, and political leaders and enemies (Unger, 1976; Edelman, 1988; Sederberg, 1984).

## POLITICAL DISCOURSE: DEMOCRATIC DELIBERATION AND DISCOURSE ETHICS

In addition to this emphasis on the discursive construction of society, largely descriptive in nature, a second group of writers has focused more prescriptively on the role of discourse and deliberation in the rejuvenation or reconstruction of democratic society. In a focus that is compatible with the rhetorical view of society, these writers emphasize words and talk as the basic form of political action. Indeed, words are fundamental to all stages of the political process—electorates debate political issues, parties discuss competing candidates, legislators argue over the wording of laws, executives negotiate specific program requirements, and courts hear legal arguments. In short, democracy is nothing if it is not "government by discussion" (Majone,1989: 1).

Basic to this emphasis on discourse is a contemporary revival of democratic political theory, especially in its participatory forms. Even though the quality of democratic politics in the United States today leaves much to be desired, participatory democratic theory is very much alive and flourishing in scholarly debates. Fundamental to this renewal has been a recognition of the role of language and argumentation in the constitution of democratic politics itself (Barber, 1984). Today, language is understood to be much more than a medium of political discussion. Beyond merely reflecting our grasp of a given concept of political reality, it possesses the power to create that reality itself. Language has transformative power.[1]

An essential aspect of participatory democracy is the argument that democratic experiences transform individuals in democratic ways. Individuals who engage in such experiences are said to become more public spirited, tolerant, knowledgeable, and self-reflective than they would otherwise be. This assumption depends on viewing the self as socially and discursively constituted, a view that contrasts with the standard liberal-democratic view of the self as prepolitically constituted and narrowly self-interested.

Habermas has developed the self-transformative position by arguing that liberal democracy needs—but more and more lacks—"public spheres" in which political opinions and ideas can be discursively tested and debated. Beyond the reconciliation of conflicting political interests, according to Habermas, the goal of democracy must also be the development of institutions that foster discourse aimed at public will formation. It must, as such, identify and differentiate common and plural interests, as well as uncover newly emerging interests and concerns (Habermas, 1973: 108). As Warren (1992: 12) puts it, "Without the experience of argument and challenge within the democratic public spheres, individuals will have little sense for what relates them to, and distinguishes them from, others; and this deprives them of an essential condition of self-development" (Box 10.2). By elevating "one's wants, needs, and desires to the level of consciousness and by formulating them in speech, one increases one's sense of identity and autonomy—aside from any advantages that might accrue from the substantive outcomes of collective decisions." Democratic discourse thus does more than merely mediate individual and public will formation, as in the standard conception of liberal democracy; it produces it as well.

This emphasis on language and deliberation has led Dryzek (1990) to put forward the concept of "discursive design." For Dryzek, following Habermas, the task is to redesign political institutions in ways that facilitate authentic democratic exchanges between citizens and decision makers.[2] Decision-making structures are themselves viewed as normative epistemological arrangements, that is, they are based on specific theories of knowledge, ethics, and rationality. An important aspect of this project, has come to be called "discourse ethics."

Discourse ethics can be understood as the search for ethical principles to govern the design of deliberative institutions and processes. In this perspective, the development of political consensus takes the place of ethics' traditional concern for the pursuit of moral principles. Ethics, as such, is reframed

---

## BOX 10.2
## Democratic Theory and Self-Transformation

Mark Warren (1992: 11–13) has outlined four dimensions of the self-transformation thesis:

1. First, the interests and capabilities that define the self are determined not only by prepolitical factors but also by the constraints and possibilities of political institutions. The selves that often seem endemic to liberal democracies—selves characterized by selfishness, apathy, alienation, lack of knowledge, and prejudice—are reflections as much of limited means for meaningful political discourse and participation as of more general limits to the capacities of citizens for self-governance.
2. Second, transformations of the self are important for expansive democrats because they view democracy as justified not so much because it allows maximization of prepolitical wants or preferences as because it maximizes opportunities for self-governance. That standard liberal democrats view "preferences as given allows us to recognize democracy's contribution to the proper aggregation of wants through the counting of votes, but it obscures the contribution of democratic institutions to human development—their unique capacity to foster in people the ability intelligently and creatively to control their lives" (Bowles and Gintis, 1986: 123).
3. Democracy has an intrinsic, as well as an instrumental value. Although some values of democracy are means to nonpolitical values, others grow out of the democratic processes themselves. Participation completes individuals, in part by enabling them to discover and develop their public dimensions, in part by providing the kinds of interactions that develop capacities for autonomous judgment.
4. The self-transformation thesis includes a fourth argument as to why we should expect increased democracy to enhance governability rather than (as in the standard view) threaten the overload and breakdown of democratic processes. On the expansive view, the "demand overload" thesis overgeneralizes from contemporary liberal democracies, which lack institutional encouragements for transformational effects and rely almost exclusively on adversarial mechanisms that encourage conflict.

as a practice of discourse rather than a body of ethical knowledge per se (Ackerman, 1989). The focus of such ethics is how members of a community develop a sense of what their shared problems are, and how to determine what they have in common (Jennings, 1990: 18). The task of discourse ethics is to specify the properties that serve as prerequisites of a legitimate consensus, that is, how we should structure discourse and the interactions of speech agents so as to give their consensus moral force (Habermas, 1990). Such a rationalization of the communicative process, as Dryzek (1990a: 15) explains it, "obtains to the degree social interaction is free from domination (the exercise of power), strategizing by the actors involved, and (self-) deception." Moreover, "all actors should be equally and fully capable of making and questioning arguments" (that is, as Habermas puts it, "communicatively competent"). Once these conditions exist, "the only remaining authority is that of a good argument, which can be advanced on behalf of the veracity of empirical description, explanation, and understanding and, equally important, the validity of normative judgments."

Consensus produced through discourse (about empirical as well as normative judgments) can thus be rationally evaluated in terms of the discursive conditions under which it is produced. While, to be sure, the conditions of "ideal speech" are beyond reach—and may remain so—the standards of discourse ethics can be employed to determine the degree to which a given discourse approximates or deviates from ideal conditions, as well as for guiding the design and institutionalization of deliberative processes. Such a commitment to rational argumentation, according to Habermas, implies an ethical commitment to developing the material conditions of life in which an open communication system can exist (Habermas, 1991).

## POLITICAL DISCOURSE AND POLITICAL RATIONALITY

One of the more concrete and insightful approaches to such rational institutional design is that of Paul Diesing (1962). Diesing has sought to understand the task of designing institutions for political deliberation in terms of what he calls "political rationality," which is concerned with the rationality of the communicative structure itself. It refers to the rationality of the institutional structures within which all subsequent reasoning about goals and values takes place. A politically rational structure is one that integrates the normative as well as the empirical processes relevant to a policy deliberation.

What then does a "politically rational" decision structure look like? In institutional terms, a political decision-making structure can be defined as an orderly and more or less formal collection of human habits, expectations, and roles. According to Diesing, there are three essential elements characterizing such a decision-making structure. The first is a discussion relationship—that is, a relationship for talking and listening, asking and answering, and suggesting and accepting courses of action—that is more or less institutionalized, depending on the complexity of the society. The second element is a set of roles defining the participants in the discussion relationship and their manner of participation. The third is a set of beliefs and values generally held in common by the participating members—beliefs establishing the types of factual propositions that are admissible to the participants, and values determining acceptable goals and objectives.

Viewed in this way, the decision structure refers in essence to the set of sociocultural determinants of practical reason—determinants that organize both thought itself and the system of communication within which the particular habits of thought are applied to decision problems. The organizational relationships that underlie a decision-making structure are thus epistemological relationships in the practical world of affairs. The elements of the structure (the discussion relationship, the rules for defining who participates, and the belief and value systems that govern the admissibility of evidence) form a communication process that establishes and certifies practical social knowledge and goals.

Broadly conceived, the politically rational decision can be understood as a decision that preserves and/or improves the capacity of the political community to make future decisions. Political rationality, in this regard, is fundamentally concerned with the integrative character of political deliberation. Unlike the technical or instrumental decision, the integrative decision is never based solely on its contribution to goal achievement. First and foremost, it is based on its ability to secure normative acceptability or agreement on those objectives important to the various participants involved. In questions of efficient achievement of objectives "the best available proposal should be accepted regardless of who makes it or who opposes it." But in a political judgment, the emphasis turns to consensus formation: "Action should be designed to avoid complete identification with any proposal and any point of view," regardless of how popular or good. "The best available proposal should never be accepted just because it is best; it should be deferred, objected to, and discussed until all major opposition disappears." Although decisions based on compromise are generally less than acceptable in nonpolitical decisions, they can represent the essence of wisdom in political judgments. Only political decisions that have eliminated major opposition—regardless of efficacy—contribute to the preservation and improvement of decision structure integration.

Diesing (1967) has suggested four general criteria for judging the effects of a decision on the communicative structure: (1) the ability to reconcile or harmonize conflicting factors that blocked decision making; (2) the ability to increase toleration between various groups and their respective beliefs and values; (3) an ability to establish equilibrium among opposing forces in a destructive struggle with each other; and (4) an ability to reject, repress, or otherwise exclude the threatening factors from the decision problem.

But what would a theory of political rationality mean for policy evaluation? It could, in short, provide a theoretical foundation for the evaluation of the deliberative process itself—or, in the language of policy analysis, "process evaluation." That is, it could serve as a theory for guiding the evaluation of the openness and authenticity of the deliberative structures and processes in which evaluative discourse takes place. To be useful, however, such theoretical contributions must be transformed into particular practices and methodological techniques (Fischer, 1990). While such work is only in its emergent stages in policy analysis, a number of scholars have begun to devote themselves to developing rational communicative structures (Fischer and Forester, 1993).

## COMMUNICATIVE PROCESSES AND THE LOGIC OF POLICY DELIBERATION

An important effort to evaluate and develop deliberative processes for policy analysis has been that of C. West Churchman and his associates. According to Churchman (1971), policy analysis should be redesigned as an organized deliberation between competing normative worldviews. Like the work of Weiss (1977; 1990), his proposal emphasizes the more general goal of "enlightenment" rather than scientific decision making. Like that of Paris and Reynolds, his approach tests ideological propositions. Unlike other theorists however, Churchman's efforts focus much more on an operational level concerned with how such an inquiry might in fact be organized and introduced in practical decision contexts.

Churchman and his followers suggest that the procedure should take the form of a debate. The problem posed by the absence of appropriate evaluative criteria, they maintain, can be mitigated by designing rational procedures to govern a formal communication among the various points of view that bear on the decision-making process. The fact that normative-oriented decision makers and empirical policy analysts have fundamentally different approaches to problem solving need not lead to an irreconcilable standoff. Where the qualitative decision makers attempt to coordinate relevant interests around specific norms and goals, the quantitative analyst's task is to provide information about the probable success of various means to reach these goals. Instead of merely assuming the traditional scientific orientation, namely supplying empirical analysis, the policy analysts would take a further step and participate in preparing arguments for and against particular policy positions. In this scheme, policy analysts and decision makers would each take on the assignment of preparing briefs for and against particular policy positions.

Argumentation would start with the recognition that the participants do not have solid answers to the questions under discussion, or even a solid method of getting the answers. With this understanding, policy analysts and decision makers attempt to develop a meaningful synthesis of perspectives. Churchman maintains that by establishing an understanding drawn from their separate perspectives, decision makers and analysts can work out a functional synthesis through a "dialectical communication" governed by the rules and procedures of formal debate.

In the debate, each party confronts the other with counterproposals based on varying perceptions of the facts. The participants in the exchange organize the established data and fit them into the worldviews that underlie their own arguments.[3] Not only must the analysts employ the same data, the grounds or criteria for accepting or rejecting a proposal must be the same grounds for accepting or rejecting a counterproposal and must employ precisely the same data. Operating at the point where theory and science confront practice and ethics, each participant cites not only causal relationships, but also norms, values, and circumstances to support or justify a particular decision. Such practical arguments permit decision makers and analysts to explore and compare underlying assumptions. By illuminating the features of the situations that provide grounds for policy decisions, participants can also establish the potential connections between policy options and specific circumstances.

The formalized debate itself is seen as the most instructive part of the analytical process. The technique is designed to clarify the underlying goals and norms that give shape to competing worldviews, and enables qualitative judgment to be exercised in as unhampered a way as possible. The free exercise of normative judgment, released from the restrictions of the formal policy model, increases the chance of developing a synthesis of normative perspectives that can provide a legitimate and acceptable foundation for decision and action resting on the strongest possible argument. Even if analysts and decision makers cannot agree, the approach provides a procedure for probing the normative implications of recommendations and for indicating certain favored normative conclusions. At the minimum, the technique goes a considerable distance toward removing the ideological mask that often shields policy analysis from genuine objectivity.

Where the empiricist attempts to adapt qualitative data about norms and values to an empirical model through quantification, the communications model reverses the process by fitting the qualitative data into the normative worldview. In the latter case, pragmatic validity is tested, criticized, and interpreted by qualitative arguments based on value perspectives or worldviews. The focus of the interpretation process moves from the scientific audience to the practical world of the decision makers. In the transition, the final outcome of evaluative inquiry shifts from scientific demonstration and verification to the giving of reasons and the assessment of practical arguments; the accepted interpretation is the one that survives the widest range of criticisms and objections.

This communicative approach is an important step toward the development of a discursive methodology designed to facilitate complex dialectical normative exploration throughout the policy research process. Like any step forward, however, it brings the methodologist to the next set of hurdles. If the analysts and decision makers are supposed to integrate empirical and normative perspectives, what would be the methodological framework for doing that? The communications model itself encounters the fundamental fact-value problem: Are there grounds for mediating normative-based practical discourse? Practical debate brings the value dimensions of policy into sharper focus, but this is not to be confused with methodology per se. Given the long history of arguments in philosophy and the social sciences about value judgments, it is reasonable to surmise that the methodological success of the debate model ultimately rests on the elaboration of requirements that govern the integration of facts and values. Rational inquiry—whether scientific or normative—depends upon the availability of criteria for valid judgment (i.e., operational guidelines for permitting the formulation of more or less general propositions or conclusions that are not specifically included in the data but legitimately deduced, inferred, or extracted from them). It is to this challenge—the development of a practical framework that integrates both empirical and normative judgment—that the present work has been addressed. As illustrated in earlier work, the logic of policy deliberations can be brought to the service of a communicative model of policy analysis (Fischer, 1980).

Insofar as the participants in a communications or argumentation model of policy analysis are required to specify their normative arguments in advance, the four discourses of policy evaluation can serve as a framework of component parts designed for explicating a complete policy argument. Instead of supplying empirical information per se, the discourses indicate the types of data that require examination and direct attention to unperceived angles or forgotten dimensions that require exploration. They probe for empirical accuracy, logical clarity, and normative contradictions (Fischer, 1980); they serve to indicate the kinds of evidence needed to support, reject, or modify a policy proposal.

The answers to the questions of the four discourses constitute the "reasons" given for or against supporting a policy. "Good" reasons are those providing facts or circumstances that satisfy the logical and empirical requirements of the four-level deliberation. The validity of the answers obtained from such questions hinges on the persuasive force of the arguments advanced, rather than resting on proof per se. The persuasive argument aims first at establishing a way of viewing the problem. The policy analyst's job is to marshal the facts and values (objectives, goals, and ideals) in such a way as to stress or emphasize those dimensions of a social situation or system that favor a particular view. The validity of a policy argument thus depends upon its ability to withstand the widest possible range of objections and criticisms in an open, clear, and candid exchange among the relevant participants. The valid claim is the one that generates consensus under agreed-upon discursive procedures.

The development of such policy proposals must remain as much an art as a science. The process is a paper-and-pencil exercise involving conjecture and speculation, analogy and metaphor, and logical extrapolation from established causal relationships and facts. Unlike the scientist's analysis which is based on a closed, generalized model, the political analyst's proposal is open and contextual.[4] As Jennings (1987: 18) has put it, success "depends on the personal, intellectual characteristics of the analyst, his or her insight and creativity." It is in large part a rhetorical or persuasive medium. "Literary, figurative, and stylistic considerations and skills play a much more important role in this genre than in positivistic social analysis."

### POLICY EVALUATION AND THE POLITICAL COMMUNITY

Churchman's communicative model was largely designed for a managerial setting. But, as Churchman and Schainblatt (1969) and Mason and Mitroff (1981) have further illustrated, there is nothing to prohibit extending the model to a wider range of differing viewpoints drawn from the larger policy environment (Mitroff et al., 1983). We examine in this section the need to expand the political community of policy evaluation. Here the work of Deborah Stone (1988) is particularly insightful.

Traditional policy analysis, as we have seen, emerged as a discipline to guide the decision processes of a society governed by large-scale techno-managerial institutions. In sharp contrast, a vigorous democracy ultimately requires a more participatory set of institutions and methods, including those of policy evaluation. A deliberative model of evaluation would broaden the goal to include an assessment of the political needs and interests of the larger political community, rather than emphasizing the technical efficiency of the governing institutions as an end unto itself. In this alternative perspective, the political community is inhabited by citizens who "live in a web of interdependencies, loyalties, and associations [in] which they envision and fight for the public interest as well as their individual interests" (Stone, 1988: vii).

Unlike contemporary policy analysis, a politicized policy evaluation would not "take individual preference as 'given' . . . but would instead have to account for where people get their images of the world and how those images shape their preferences" (Stone, 1988). In contrast to mainstream economic approaches to policy evaluation, which provide no way of talking about how people fight over visions of the public interest or the nature of the community, a political conceptualization of policy evaluation emphasizes discourse as "a creative and valuable feature of social existence." It requires a discursive or

---

## BOX 10.3
## Political Knowledge: Community and Consensus

Political knowledge, according to Barber, is a communal and consensual product. Independent of abstract criteria, it is applied and practical and can be understood as a form of praxis (i.e., as theory for action). Always concerned with historically changing circumstances and evolving social consciousness, political knowledge is creative and willed—something *made* rather than something derived or represented. "The mutability that permits politics to adapt to history and to the evolving priorities that the expanding human consciousness discovers, as it moves from private to public modes of seeing and doing, also entails the mutability of the maxims and norms that govern that expanding consciousness." As he explains this:

The norms yielded by political judgment are provisional not because they are relative or, feeble—they may in fact be vigorous and inspire decisive action—but because they issue from a communal will that is itself provisional and subject to constant emendation. They are produced by an ongoing process of democratic talk, deliberation, judgment, and action, and they are legitimized solely by that process, which exhibits and refracts the political culture's changing circumstances and evolving communal purposes.

The status of such norms can be legitimate but always remains conditional depending upon further deliberative consideration.

The conditionality of political knowledge in a strong democracy embodies the openness and flexibility that must define a genuinely self-governing people. Since the objective is to find working maxims rather than fixed truths—scientific or otherwise—and shared consciousness rather than immutable principles, what is needed is a common language and a mode of common seeing that facilitates legitimate political judgments.

In designing political institutions, Barber argues that we are sculpting our knowledge. To found a constitution, for example, is to determine the shape and character of our political epistemology. Indeed, "in these tasks political judgment is our chief, perhaps only resource."

Source: Barber (1984), 170.

deliberative method that "understands analysis in and of politics as *strategically crafted argument,* designed to create paradoxes and to resolve them in a particular direction" (Stone, 1988: 4).

In this approach, ideas move to the center of policy evaluation. They are the medium of all political conflicts; they make possible the shared meanings which motivate people to action and weld individual striving into collective causes (Reich, 1988). Policy making is thus a constant struggle over the ideas that guide the ways people think and behave, the boundaries of political categories, and the criteria for classification—what Fischer and Forester (1987) have called the "politics of criteria." Basic to this approach must be the recognition that analytical concepts are themselves based on political claims and cannot be granted privileged status as universal truths.

The constituent ideas of policy and policy evaluation should be understood in terms of their transformational impacts on political community (Box 10.3). A policy idea is seen as an argument, or more accurately as a set of arguments, in favor of different ways of seeing the world. The process of reasoning is based on language, especially analogy and metaphor; it "involves trying to get others to see a situation as one thing rather than another" (Stone, 1988). The enduring values of politics serve as community aspirations, into which people read contradictory interpretations. Behind every policy issue lurks a contest over conflicting, though often equally plausible, interpretations of the same abstract goal. The various modes of defining problems in policy discourse are languages within which people offer and defend conflicting interpretations. Symbols and numbers, for example, are respectively about verbal and numerical languages, both of which examine the devices of symbolic representations within those languages (Stone, 1988).

## POLICY EVALUATION AS A COMMUNICATIVE ENTERPRISE

The discursive model is also amenable to more sophisticated concepts of knowledge and expertise, particularly those advanced by postpositivists (see Epilogue). Important, in this regard, is the idea that the goal of a discursive exchange between citizens and policy experts need not be the establishment of consensus on high-level, abstract normative or ideological principles. Indeed, many argue that the development of such rules or principles—for example, as Rawls has attempted to do—can only be a philosophical ideal with little immediate political or practical relevance. Against those who would like to believe that consensual positions about such rules and principles can be established, such critics point to the deep cleavages of contemporary social relations—of class, race, gender, and culture—which can only be resolved, some argue, through power struggles among conflicting forces. Accepting the relativity underlying political and policy argument, however, it is still possible for participants to learn from each other, change their ideas, adapt to each other, and act in the world together. For example, Healey (1993: 239) argues that while it is never possible to construct a stable, fully inclusionary consensus—and that our agreements are mainly temporary accommodations of different perceptions—our frames of reference can and do shift and evolve in response to discursive encounters. Policy analysis, in this view, does not necessarily need recourse to agreement on fundamental ideals or principles of the good society to offer useful guidance.

In this conception, the outcome of a policy evaluation is a course of action that we choose after deliberation. As Healey (1993: 238) writes, "knowledge for action, principles of action, and ways of knowing are actively constituted in the particularities of time and place." Such deliberative discourse can transcend the confines of scientific analysis by including both aesthetic experience and moral principles. Good or right actions are "those we can come to agree on, in particular times and places, across our diverse differences

---

## BOX 10.4
## Policy Evaluation as Counsel

Jennings (1987: 129) has sought to set out a hermeneutic or interpretive policy evaluation based on the concept of counsel. Designed as the application of practical reason informed by common sense, or what in the contemporary idiom we would call interpretive social science, the goal of counsel is threefold:

(1) to grasp the meaning or significance of contemporary problems as they are experienced, adapted to, and struggled against by the reasonable, purposive agents, who are members of the political community;

(2) to clarify the meaning of those problems so that strategically located political agents (public officials or policymakers) will be able to devise a set of efficacious and just solutions to them; and

(3) to guide the selection of one preferred policy from that set in light of a more general vision of the good of the community as a whole, as well as the more discreet interests of the policymakers themselves.

Fundamentally, "the counselor must construct an interpretation of present political and social reality that serves not only the intellectual goal of explaining or comprehending that reality, but also the practical goal of enabling constructive action to move the community from a flawed present toward an improved future." For policy evaluation as counsel, interpreting the world and changing it are two complementary enterprises. "Counsel presses interpretation into the service

in material conditions and wants, moral perspectives, and expressive cultures and inclinations." The fundamental goal of such policy analysis can be reformulated as discovering ways of "living together differently but respectfully" (Healey, 1993: 238).[5]

Especially important, in this view, is the need to bring together the roles of the analysts, citizens, and the decision makers. There is, for example, a tendency in Churchman's formulation to maintain the standard separation of functions between analysts and their clients: decision makers bring the normative data to the deliberation, and policy analysts take charge of the empirical chores. As critical studies of social epistemology make clear, a more sophisticated understanding of the nature of an open and democratic exchange must confront the need to bring these roles together in a mutual exploration. In accordance with postpositivist theory, the expert must establish a participatory relationship with the client (Hawkesworth, 1988; Schön, 1983; Kelly and Maynard-Moody, 1993).

---

of change. Not just any change, but change that is itself directed by the human moral values and possibilities that the practice of interpretation uncovers."

The Counsel Model holds that policy evaluation should strive for a special kind of objectivity, a post-positivist objectivity. "[I]n doing so it will seek to fashion an interpretation of what the public interest requires that can survive a collective process of rational assessment and deliberation." Analysis that survives an open and nondistorted process of collective deliberation can be said to be "objective" in the relevant sense. A consensus based on such deliberation is seen to have authentic normative force.

> No individual analyst's specific policy advice will achieve this fully and hence it will represent only one of several plausible perspectives on the public interest. But, though limited and essentially contestable in this way, each policy analysis or assessment will at least be a perspective on the public interest rather than a self-conscious articulation of some particularistic or group-specific interest.

Policy evaluation as counsel, according to Jennings (1993: 105), "recasts the relationship between policy analysts, policymakers, and citizens in the form of a conversation with many voices." Such an approach relies on a procedural route to just and rational policy choice. The process it envisions is one "of adjudicating among multiple perspectives on the public interest and fashioning policy on the basis of the complementary "fit" among these perspectives."

Source: Jennings (1987, 1993).

In methodological terms, what is needed is an approach capable of facilitating the kind of open discussion essential to a participatory context. The method would provide a format and a set of procedures for organizing the interactions between policy experts and the laypersons they seek to assist. Toward this end, writers such as deLeon (1992), Durning (1993), Laird (1993), and Fischer (1990; 1994) have called for a "participatory policy analysis."

A participatory policy analysis, as we saw in the previous chapter, would gear expert practices to the requirements of political empowerment. Rather than providing technical answers designed to bring political discussions to an end, the task would be to assist citizens in their efforts to examine their *own* interests and to make their own decisions (Hirschhorn, 1979; Maguire, 1987). The expert would be redefined as a "facilitator" of public learning and empowerment. Beyond merely providing data, the facilitator would seek to integrate process evaluation with the empirical requirements of technical evaluation. As such the facilitator would become an expert in how people learn, clarify, and decide for themselves (Fischer, 1990). This includes coming to grips with the basic languages of public normative argumentation, as well as knowledge about the minds of environmental and intellectual conditions with which citizens can formulate their own ideas. It involves the creation of institutional and intellectual conditions that help people pose questions and examine technical analysis in their own ordinary (or everyday) languages and decide which issues are important to them.

In this formulation, the role of participatory policy analyst is that of interpretive mediator between theoretical knowledge and competing normative arguments (see Epilogue). Policy analysts seek a mediated confrontation between the policy actors and the analytical frameworks of social science. Dryzek (1982) suggests that the exchange can be likened to a conversation in which the horizons of both citizens and social scientists are extended through a confrontation with each other. Similarly, Jennings has called for an interpretive approach which he identifies as the "counsel" model of policy analysis. The counsel model is based on a "post-positivist" concept of objectivity. Its goal would be to reshape the relationship of the analyst and the policymaker as that of a conversation with many voices, adjudicated by the procedural standards of a discourse ethics (Box 10.4). Seen this way, the role of the policy expert would not be so radically different from that of the citizen. The analyst would better be seen as a "specialized citizen" (Paris and Reynolds, 1983).

To be sure, a participatory methodology is not appropriate for all scientific problems. There is little need for the economist engaged in a statistical analysis of the national debt to consult the layman. On the other hand, it appears quite applicable to a range of *socio-technical* problems, especially a growing number of "wicked problems" (problems in which the ends as well as the means are uncertain). In some cases, the method even begins to appear necessary for successful problem solving (Fischer, 1994; Dunn, 1988). For those problems to which participatory research does apply, the method encounters numerous difficulties (Eldon, 1981). Most of the problems, however, are social and interpersonal rather than scientific per se: it takes a lot of time, political commitment, and interpersonal skills to build people into complex decision processes. On just what sort of political and moral grounding could such relationships be established and guided? It is here that discourse ethics can be helpful.

Finally, we need to address the feasibility of a genuine policy science of democracy. Clearly, it differs markedly from the standard conceptualization of the policymaking model which largely limits the citizen role to stating individual preferences. But is it realistic to expect citizens to become more deeply involved in the analytical and decision-making processes?

## THE PROSPECTS OF DELIBERATIVE DEMOCRACY

What evidence is there that the American political system is capable of more informed citizen participation, let alone the practice of participatory expertise? Indeed, a significant number of social scientists argue just the opposite: namely, that there is *too much* participation in the American system and that the result, especially in the contemporary age of complexity, is "deadlock." As we have already seen, this claim is basic to the technocratic conception of decision making; it is offered as a way around an otherwise "chaotic situation." Individuals, in this view, are basically self-interested and unable to deal rationally with the wider range of technical and public-regarding interests that must be taken into consideration.

Seen this way, the best one can hope for is a representative democracy, a system in which elected politicians serve as the delegates of a largely inactive public. The test of these delegates is to aggregate the interests and demands of their citizen constituents and to convert them into public policy. The political system is understood as a mechanism which brokers these invariably conflicting claims, the outcome of which are bargains and compromises. The result is a mass society governed by a relatively small number of political elites. Under the control of the elite, and directly at its service, is a cadre of enlightened experts capable of supplying the advice deemed essential to the running of a complex society.

We do not deny the validity of this conception of politics; it is a reasonably accurate description of how the existing system functions. The concern is instead directed at those who tend to treat the extant reality as an unalterable given. Not only does this view commit a normative fallacy—namely, the idea that the mere presence of a system can be used to justify its existence—it defies as well basic features of American politics. In both the more-or-less common understanding of American political norms and the actual workings of the political system, participation and deliberation are pervasive values. Citizens and politicians both appeal to motives that transcend narrowly construed pri-

vate interests; both appeal to rational argument in the name of the public interest. There is, of course, a good deal of cynicism, manipulation, and hypocrisy
in contemporary policy discourse. But this should not let us overlook the
power of persuasive argument. Paris and Reynolds have captured the significance of this tension in these words: "If the interest-focused understanding of
politics . . . were truly accepted as legitimate, one would expect it to be more
frankly acknowledged—and not just sometimes implicitly followed—in our
political life." The norm that rational argument and public-regarding motiva-
tions should guide policy decision making has in fact a demonstrable impact
on political action.

The need to attend to the language and practices of democracy does not,
however, offset the validity of the larger and more difficult question: Can participatory democracy *work* in a complex technological society? To what extent
is it possible for citizens to participate meaningfully in contemporary society?

It is clear that not everyone must—or even can—participate in all matters. In a complex technological society this is as impossible as it is undesirable. The more appropriate and pressing question for American democracy is
this: How can we *lessen* the substantial gap between elite decision-making
centers and the generally undifferentiated mass of citizens largely left out of
the process? Can we build participatory institutions that establish and mediate
procedural and discursive relationships between elite decision makers and the
public? Is it possible to design participatory political structures at the organizational and community levels of a complex techno-industrial society that can,
in turn, be authentically linked up with the top-level decision processes of a
representative government?[6] In short, is it possible to establish a participatory
community capable of engendering a political conversation between the rulers
and the ruled?

These questions are scarcely new. They have in fact generated a substantial literature from both ends of the political spectrum. With regard to expertise, those on the political left have tended to call for more democracy and
participation; for those on the political right the emphasis has mainly been on
the need for efficiency and skills, funneled through a system of representative
government. This work sides with the advocates of participation, without at
the same time rejecting the need for efficiency and expertise. Rather than
positing democracy and expertise as a choice of "either/or," we recognize the
possibility of an irreducible tension between them. The tension may never be
completely eliminated, but, we contend here, it can nonetheless be significantly mitigated by alternative methodologies and practices.

Although grounded in the ideals of democratic participation, this work
has attempted to remain practical. Focusing on the methodology of policy
evaluation, it has sought to point in the direction of the possible. In this respect, the position acknowledges the necessity of technical knowledge and ef-

ficiency. The fact that efficiency has often been misused to further the interests of particular groups over others does not vitiate its fundamental importance in the realms of organization and policy. Instead of rejecting technical knowledge as an ideological ploy in the struggle for control, as is often the case in the literature of the political left, the critical task is to restrict such instrumental knowledge to its proper role in the organization and evaluation of action.

But what is the proper role? No attempt is made here to say how much efficiency or participation should exist in a particular society or decision context. This we leave to the relevant participants to work out among themselves in the context of particular pragmatic experiences. It is a question that must in part be determined normatively and empirically within the social and technical structures of society and, in part, through the processes of democracy itself. Citizens, in fact, must decide their own relationships to democracy itself. Our principal concern is the need to open and extend the transformative processes that make such democratic determinations possible. The logic of policy deliberation is offered as a contribution toward that end.

We also acknowledge that a serious discussion concerned with expanding democratic practices must concede a basic political fact: Throughout the history of the idea, democracy has remained as much a vision as a reality. Indeed, in today's complex society, concepts such as "town hall democracy" have largely become utopian dreams. To say this, however, is not to overlook the functions of such concepts in the critically important realm of political discourse. The virtue of democratic theory is to be found in the legacy of the standards it has bequeathed. Although political theorists will continue to debate the proper application of such standards, they nonetheless provide valuable criteria against which political practices can be discussed and judged. The very purpose of democracy is to establish a framework for engaging in open discourse and, in turn, for judging its quality. As public ideology, democratic standards are essential to the processes of open and candid discussion of public affairs.

Some say that to worry about language and standards of judgment in the face of power is to fall into the trap of idealism. We argue that this need not be the case. Such a concern typically confuses political discourse with political power itself. Discourse has a subtle and complex relationship to power. While it is not power per se, political discourse produces and transmits power. It can serve as a tool of either domination or liberation. To use Foucault's words, discourse can "be a hindrance, a stumbling block, a point of restraint and a starting point for an opposing strategy." It produces and reinforces power, but it can also "render it fragile and make it possible to thwart it." The long history of democratic struggles is in very large part a story of the liberating functions of political discourse.

In the emerging "knowledge society," where policy experts move more and more to the center of the decision-making processes, the political role of discourse becomes increasingly evident. Policy experts—like experts in gen- eral—are committed to the art and science of their technical discourses. As Gouldner (1979) makes clear, it is a "culture of discourse" that defines and unites the technical intelligentsia itself. Thus, preoccupation with discourses— their standards, criteria, and rules of evidence—makes it difficult for technical experts to ignore competing discourses, including democratic discourse.[7] But democratic theorists who wish to engage technical experts in such discourse must also confront the challenge of technological society. No longer can they limit themselves to the tasks of theoretical critique. To effectively undermine the technocratic position, they must also show the ways in which democracy can be made compatible with technical complexity. Democratic theorists must take up what one writer has called "the nuts and bolts of democracy" (Sclove, 1987). At this level, democratic theorists must turn from their preoccupation with the history of ideas to the analysis of operant political theories that under- lie contemporary institutional practices. What we need is a democratic theory capable of moving from critique to social reconstruction.

Committed to democratic principles, a new breed of theorists must be knowledgeable in the intricacies of organizations, policy processes, and even in some cases technologies (Fischer, 1990). Nothing is more basic to the chal- lenge than the question of the relations of expert practices—such as policy evaluation—to democratic politics. Can we, in short, build a meaningful sys- tem of participatory decision processes in the age of expertise? While we can- not at present definitively answer the question, its importance should be clear. It's time to take up the challenge.

## READINGS

Frank Fischer and John Forester, eds. 1993. *The Argumentative Turn in Policy Analysis and Planning*. Durham, NC: Duke University Press.

Daniel Lerner and Harold Lasswell, eds. 1951. *The Policy Orientation*. Stanford, CA: Stanford University Press.

John Dryzek, 1990. *Discursive Democracy.* New York: Cambridge University Press.

Charles E. Lindblom and David K. Cohen. 1979. *Usable Knowledge,* New Haven, CT: Yale University Press.

Giandomenico Majone. 1989. *Evidence, Argument, and Persuasion in the Policy Process*. New Haven, CT: Yale University Press.

C. West Churchman. 1971. *The Design of Inquiry Systems*. New York: Basic Books.

# Epilogue: Policy Deliberation in Postpositivist Perspective

The epistemological foundations of the logic of policy deliberation are examined in this epilogue. The discussion seeks to show that the methodology broadly corresponds to the general requirements of a postpositivist mode of inquiry. It is offered for those with an interest in the deeper theoretical issues which underlie the logic of policy deliberation. Proceeding in two parts, the epilogue first outlines the methodological bases upon which the scheme is developed; it then more specifically examines the postpositivist underpinnings of the framework.

## COMPREHENSIVE RATIONALITY

The logic of policy deliberation is set forth as an effort to refound policy evaluation on a more comprehensive concept of rationality (Grauhan and Strubelt, 1971). In sharp contrast to the narrow technical/empirical conception of rationality that has largely shaped the discipline to date, the methodology presented here is designed to systematically integrate empirical and normative judgments in a unified framework. Toward this end, the framework constitutes a multimethodological approach that builds on three theoretical efforts designed to extend the concept of rationality: Jürgen Habermas's concept of comprehensive rationality, Stephen Toulmin's informal logic of practical arguments, and Paul Taylor's logic of evaluative discourse.

Despite postmodern critiques of Habermas's work, his contribution is taken to be the most important and useful clarification of the requirements of such a methodological reconstruction.[1] As Habermas has shown, a more comprehensive concept of rationality must be able to integrate the epistemological requirements of three primary modes of reason, the empirical-analytical mode associated with the scientific method, the hermeneutic-interpretive mode con-

227

cerned with historical and social contexts, and the process of societal critique based on critical reflection and the methods of social and political philosophy. Each of these modes of reason, as he demonstrates, generates a type of knowledge that is associated with the practices of specific social domains and the institutional practices connected with them (Habermas, 1971; McCarthy, 1978).[2] Furthermore, each of these three modes of discourse is shown to be linked to the structure of ordinary language and the process of practical argumentation (Fischer, 1990: 217–39).[3]

From a Habermasian perspective, then, empirical analysis, the interpretation of social meaning, and the political critique of society are the basic epistemological components of a comprehensively rational evaluation of social and political action. As such, a more comprehensive—multimethodological—concept of rationality not only incorporates but also transcends its empirical data by interpreting their meaning both in the specific context of action and a fundamental critique of society's normative assumptions, principles, and axioms. In these terms, a critical-comprehensive evaluation is one that explicates and assesses the full range of empirical and normative assumptions that contribute to a particular judgment, from manifest to latent, from concrete to abstract. The integration of the methods of each of these three modes of reasons is taken here to be a necessary requirement for the construction of a postpositivist concept of rationality.

While Habermas has supplied the epistemological basis for relating the empirical, interpretive, and critical-reflective modes of reason to one another, his work offers little by way of clarification as to how these cognitive orientations might be employed in an integrated framework at the practical level of policy evaluation.[4] Beyond the demonstration that all three modes of rationality are component parts of a comprehensive theory of rationality, the viability of the contribution for the formal practice of policy evaluation depends on the possibility of specifying the logical interconnections that integrate these cognitive strategies within the frame of an ongoing discourse. What is needed is a logical framework designed to clarify the structures and functions of the different propositions that constitute a comprehensive evaluation argument. As a metastructure, such a framework provides a logical basis for judging the soundness, strength, or conclusiveness of a policy argument. By clarifying the nature of an evaluation's propositions, it serves to guide an assessment of the relevance of the different types of objections that might be validly offered as criticisms in the various phases of a policy discourse (Fischer, 1990: 215–64).

## THE INFORMAL LOGIC OF PRACTICAL ARGUMENTS

The integration of these empirical and normative requirements into a more concrete cognitive framework is based on Toulmin's analysis of the structural form of the practical or "substantial" argument and

Taylor's logic of evaluative discourse. Working in the "ordinary-language" tradition of philosophical analysis, Toulmin's writings constitute a fundamental challenge to the positivist contention that normative argumentation is irrational. His "good reasons" approach is a seminal effort to clarify the nature of the "informal logic" that rationally governs practical deliberation.

Toulmin's work is addressed to the problems that arise from positivism's overreliance on the empirical-analytical mode of inference, the classical (deductive) syllogism in particular (Toulmin, 1958). Whereas positivists argue that explanations that fail to approximate the ideals of the formal syllogism are imperfect or incomplete, Toulmin has demonstrated the ways in which such a model rests on a limited conception of logic appropriate only to various stages of inquiry, both scientific and normative. As he explains, an argument in a particular "substantial" context that fails to fulfill the requirements of the formal syllogism need not be judged incomplete or irrational. Its rationality can be properly judged only by the rules of inquiry appropriate to its own context (or "knowledge domain" in Habermas's terms). In distinction to empirical statements about the factual nature of a situation or case, the primary function of the normative/practical statement is to advise, suggest, admonish, or protest.[5] Knowing what to do requires knowing something about the case, but knowledge of the case does not—in and of itself—tell us what to do. This latter question can only be pursued through the informal logic of practical discourse.

For Toulmin, the problem of establishing judgmental criteria for practical discourse is resolved by taking account of the diversity of explanations actually used in real world argumentation. Although formal deduction is one of the valid types of explanation, deductive inference and the meaning of concepts such as "valid" and "certain" do not necessarily have to be interpreted in terms of formal logic. Formal deduction is only one standard among many available for judging the infinite variety of substantial arguments.

The social context of a normative argument is the source of the variety of practical explanatory modes. For Toulmin, it is the pragmatic context in which a normative judgment is made that supplies the practical criteria capable of validating or "warranting" the giving of specific reasons. In contrast to positivism's search for context-invariant laws and universal standards, the completeness, validity, or cogency of an informal normative statement is seen to depend on standards that are pragmatic and context-bound.

Toulmin's emphasis on the diversity of explanatory modes is derived from his study of the ways in which normative judgments are made in "ordinary" or "everyday" language, as opposed to scientific language. A contribution to the ordinary-language approach to normative analysis, his informal logic is designed to reflect the way people *actually* deliberate about normative judgments and is thus grounded in empirical reality. That is, to the degree that the informal logic of ordinary-language discourse is accurately reconstructed, the scheme is more than simply Toulmin's conception of how we should talk about normative arguments; it seeks to represent the way people in fact make such arguments and is itself subject to empirical confirmation.

For present purposes, the importance of this approach lies in the fact that it escapes the positivist criticism concerning the inability to verify empirically the final validity of normative arguments. Although practical judgments may not be true or false in the scientific sense of the term, they can be powerful and persuasive or weak and unconvincing; choices can be better or worse. Important is the way practical statements are "warranted by reasons." Insofar as practical inquiry, like scientific inquiry, is seen to be supported by the giving of reasons, the focus can be shifted from the positivist's overly narrow concern with the verification of normative arguments to a more complex and varied process of giving evidence warranted by context-dependent reasons. By substituting the concept of "warranted by reasons" for verified truth, Toulmin has established the more tentative but nonetheless rational character of practical statements. They are warranted by certain evidence yet remain more subject to modification, correction, and rejection than verified statements.

Toulmin provides a six-element representation of the logical structure of a substantial argument. As a scheme for mapping out arguments, the elements D, W, and C parallel the model of the formal syllogism. The principal difference between the classical form and the substantial model is based on the introduction of Q, R, and B. Q and R express the tentative and contextual character of substantial arguments; Q expresses the degree of cogency or force attributed to a claim, while R specifies the contextual conditions under which the acceptability of the claim can be challenged. B reflects the demand for discursive redemption of the warrant. While in the classical syllogism the warrant (as a major premise) deductively establishes universal proof of the claim, in the substantial argument good reasons must be given to back a warrant. This opens the possibility of a second form of argument required to justify the use of the warrant (Toulmin, 1958).

**Figure E.1:** The Structure of a Substantial Argument

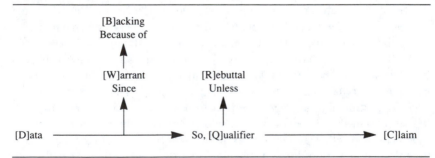

It is this second form of argument that differentiates a comprehensively rational methodology from the conventional approach in the social sciences. Where rationality in the positivist's evaluation of social action culminates with evidence concerning the technical efficiency or causal effectiveness of specific means to given ends, a comprehensive evaluation includes the justification of the warrant. But what does this form of argument look like? Beyond the justification of B, Toulmin has not schematically worked out this line of the model in sufficient detail. For this purpose the present work has turned to Taylor's (1961) logic of normative discourse, in particular as I have adapted it for policy evaluation (Fischer, 1980).

In earlier work, I have demonstrated the way in which Toulmin's model of practical argumentation can be extended by incorporating into it Taylor's logic of normative discourse (Fischer, 1980). Taylor's (1961) contribution, also following in the tradition of "informal logic," makes clear what it means to clarify and elaborate the nature of a full justification of the warrant (B).

Fundamentally, Taylor is concerned with two questions: What does it mean to evaluate something normatively? And how can such evaluations be justified? Toward this end, he focuses on the rules implicitly or explicitly followed in an attempt to judge a rule or standard to be good, to justify a goal as right, or to show that a decision to take an action ought to be made. In particular, he sketches out the way in which "good reasons" are given to fully justify a practical judgment. The result is a set of rules of reasoning for both determining what makes a reason *relevant* to a validity claim, and what makes a reason a *good* one in support of such claims.

Structured around four interrelated discourses of an evaluative deliberation, the logic extends from concrete empirical questions to abstract normative issues concerning the way of life. As already seen, these four phases and their respective questions interrelate two fundamental levels of evaluation, first- and second-order discourse. Each of the levels has specific queries that must be addressed in making a complete justification of a value judgment. For a reason to be considered a "good reason" it must meet all of the questions of the levels or phases of the probe.[6]

Adapted as a framework for the evaluation of public policy, the model tests the reasons given concerning a policy's technical efficiency, its relevance to the circumstances of the situation, its instrumental implications for the social system as a whole, and its relation to the ideological principles that justify the societal system (Fischer, 1980). In terms of Toulmin's model, this represents an extension of the justification of the warrant (figure E.2).

In this model, we understand a critical judgment to be one that has been pursued progressively through the four phases of evaluation.[7] The formal logic of an empirical assertion moves from D (data) to C (conclusion), mediated by

**Figure E.2:** The Logical Structure of a Comprehensive Evaluation

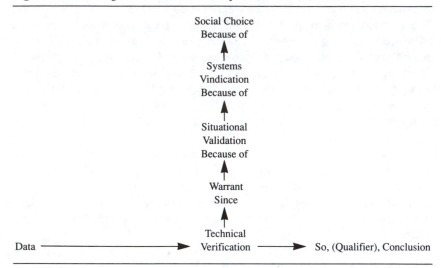

a warrant backed by normative and empirical assumptions. In normal discussion, these assumptions are called into question only during disputes. The task of a comprehensive-critical evaluation is to make explicit these assumptions through a progressive critique extending from validation to rational social choice (or from social choice to validation). It is here that we can understand Habermas's classical Aristotelian contention that in the last instance an empirical statement must be judged by its intentions for the good and true life. As reflected through the logical link of an empirical assertion to the level of rational social choice, a full delineation of the logic of an evaluative argument discloses its meaning and implications for the pursuit of a particular conception of the ideal society.

For policy evaluation, the ability to plug empirical data into normative policy deliberations is especially important. One way to illustrate this is to relate the metanormative framework to the naturalistic conception of ethical theory, which emphasizes the factual dimensions of normative discourse. Philosophical naturalists specify six types of factual knowledge that can influence value judgment: (1) knowledge of the consequences that flow from alternative actions; (2) knowledge of alternative means available; (3) knowledge of the established norms and values that bear on the decision; (4) the particular facts of the situation; (5) general causal conditions and laws relevant to the situation; (6) knowledge about the fundamental needs of humankind. Figure E. 3 shows that these six types of facts (numbered in the figure) can be located across the questions of policy deliberation (Fischer, 1983).

**Figure E.3:** The Place of Empirical Analysis in the Logic of Policy Deliberation

| Policy Deliberation | Empirical Analysis |
| --- | --- |
| Empirical outcomes | Empirical knowledge of consequences (1) |
| Unanticipated effects | Knowledge of consequences (1) |
| Alternative means | Knowledge of alternative means (2) |
| Relevance | Knowledge of established means (3) |
| Situational context | Particular facts of the situation (4) |
| System consequences | Causal conditions and laws (5) |
| Alternative social orders | Knowledge of fundamental needs (6) |

These types of data can also be organized in terms of four major competing methodological orientations in the social sciences: empirical/means-ends analysis; phenomenological social science; systems analysis; and political philosophy. They can as well be distributed across the four levels of evaluation. As the four methodological chapters make clear, these methods correspond respectively to program verification, situational validation, systems vindication, and social choice. It is thus possible to argue that all four methods are part of a comprehensive, multimethodological scheme. While each of these methods has traditionally challenged the others, the approach here permits us to see that the advocates of each method must settle for more modest epistemological claims. Each methodology has something essential to contribute, but ultimately is only a component part of the whole.

PRACTICAL DELIBERATION AND POSTPOSITIVISM

The second purpose of this epilogue is to sketch the postpositivist foundations of the logic of policy deliberation. We begin the discussion with this question: What is "postpositivism"?

Postpositivism can be understood as a radical elaboration of the more traditional fact-value critique long leveled against positivist social science. Fundamentally, postpositivist theory is built on two interrelated concerns. One focuses on rational deliberation in the realm of values. Postpositivists accept the concept of informal logic and the possibility of establishing a reasoned consensus through discourse, as just discussed. But they also go further. In analytical terms, postpositivists extend the fact-value critique from the realm of social action to the realm of science (Bernstein, 1976). They have, as such, shown the ways in which the activity of science is a normative product of the social world it seeks to explain—that is, how its activities are grounded in the normative assumptions and social meanings of that world (Kuhn, 1970). Revealing scientific research to involve far more than the passive reception and organization of sense data, such theorists demonstrate science's dependence on the particular constellation of presuppositions, both theoretical and practical, that prestructure empirical observations (Bernstein, 1983). Thus science, like all other forms of human knowledge, is grounded in and shaped by the normative assumptions and social meanings of the world it explores. It too is "theory-laden"; it gains access to the world only through "theory-directed research" (Brown, 1977).

Indeed, science is discovered to depend on normative theoretical assumptions in multiple and complex ways. All of the central concepts of science—perception, meaning, relevance, explanation, knowledge, and method—are now widely recognized to be theoretically constituted concepts. In Hawkesworth's (1988: 49) words, "theoretical presuppositions shape perception and determine what will be taken as a fact; they confer meaning on experience and control the demarcation of significant and trivial events; they afford criteria of relevance according to which facts can be organized, tests envisioned, and the acceptability of scientific conclusions assessed; they accredit particular models of explanation and strategies of understanding; and they sustain specific methodological techniques for gathering, classifying, and analyzing data." As such, normative theoretical suppositions set the terms of scientific debate and organize the elements of scientific activity. They often "do so at a tacit or preconscious level, and it is for this reason that they appear to hold such unquestionable authority."[8]

Most fundamentally, then, the positivist conception of knowledge is seen to be incompatible with the requirements of human cognition. It involves, moreover, "the realization that science is no more capable of achieving the Archimedian point or escaping human fallibility than is any other human endeavor." Indeed, it demands "acknowledgement of science as a human convention rooted in the practical judgments of a community of fallible scientists struggling to resolve theory-generated problems under specific historical conditions" (Hawkesworth, 1988: 52).

The alternative postpositivist image of scientific activity is to be sure far less encompassing and much more human than the one put forward by the traditional conception of science. In sharp contrast, it offers a conception of knowledge premised on the recognition that all human knowledge depends on theoretical assumptions whose congruence with nature cannot be established conclusively by reason or experience. Rooted in social traditions, these normative assumptions provide the conceptual lenses through which the world is viewed; they socially identify that which is taken to be natural, normal, and real from that which is understood to be unnatural, deviant, or utopian.

Generally operating at the tacit level of awareness, such suppositions structure preunderstandings and prejudgments in ways that make it difficult to isolate and illuminate the full range of assumptions that affect cognition at any given time. Moreover, any attempt to elucidate the presuppositions must operate within an hermeneutic (or interpretive) circle—that is, an effort to examine or challenge certain assumptions or expectations must itself occur within a frame of reference established by other presuppositions. Although certain suppositions must remain fixed if others are to be subjected to systematic critique, postpositivists seek to demonstrate that individuals are more than mere prisoners of their own framework of assumptions, experiences, and modes of discourse. They are in fact able to engage in reasoned critique of their normative assumptions and experiences, thus escaping the hopeless dead end of relativism to which positivists have traditionally relegated such thought.[9]

Any conceptualization of knowing must thus begin from the premise that the world is far richer in complexity and nuance than the scientific theories devised to grasp it. Theories can never be determined by facts alone; there can always be competing explanations of particular events. This, however, does not imply the relativist conclusion that all theoretical interpretations are equal; the fact that there can be no positivist appeal to neutral (theory-independent) facts to adjudicate between competing theoretical interpretations does not mean there is no rational way to make and warrant critical evaluative judgments concerning alternative views. Such a conclusion is merely the product of the positivist commitment to the empirical verification of social judgments. Only if one starts from the assumption that the sole test of the validity of a statement lies in its measured correspondence to an empirically "given" reality does it follow that in absence of the "given" no rational judgments can be made concerning the validity of particular claims.

For postpositivists, then, the task is to realign our understanding of social science to conform to the interpretive nature of human cognition itself. Once the positivist's myth of an empirically "given" social world is disregarded, postpositivists argue, it becomes possible to identify the existence of reasoned criteria for assessing the merits of alternative theoretical interpretations. Such criteria, the products of an informal logic, "are dependent on theoretical suppositions, but they are nonetheless empirically connected to the external world. That is, the process of cognition constitutes a confrontation between the preunderstandings brought to an event by an individual (subjective perceiver) and the stimuli in the external (physical or objective) world which instigate the process. Even though objects can be characterized in many different ways, the number of descriptions is nonetheless constrained by the external stimuli of the material world. Such stimuli serve to restrict the range of plausible descriptions without, at the same time dictating one absolute interpretation. In short, some descriptions can be shown to be better than others (Hawkesworth, 1988).

Postpositivism, as such, is fundamentally an interpretive or hermeneutic activity. Although there are numerous schools of hermeneutic thought (Bernstein, 1983; Bleicher, 1980), my own use of the term is similar to that advance by Dryzek (1982). In this view, hermeneutics is "defined as the evaluation of

existing conditions and the exploration of alternatives to them, in terms of criteria derived from an understanding of possible better conditions, through an
interchange between the frames of reference of analysts and actors." The social scientist should mediate a confrontation between specific social practices
and the intellectual frames of reference—both theoretical and everyday—
brought to bear on the situation. Such a dialectic exchange can be analogized,
according to Dryzek, to a "conversation in which the horizons of both participants [social scientists and citizens] are extended through a confrontation with
one another." Rather than the domination of social scientific empirical knowledge, as advocated by positivists, the goal is to develop a synthesis of both
kinds of knowledge.

Given this interpretive understanding of the nature of scientific activity,
a postpositivist/hermeneutic approach advances a "practical" conception of
reason as an alternative methodological framework to the traditional form of
scientific rationality. Practical reason is concerned with the processes of deliberation and the giving of "good reasons." Rather than advancing reasons as absolute "proof" of the validity of a theory, scientists are seen in reality to offer
them more as a form of evidentiary support for the credibility of particular
propositions or contentions. Emphasizing the processes of argumentation as
well as the cumulative weight of evidence, such practical assessments are too
rich and varied to be captured by the positivist reliance on the rules of induc-
tive or deductive logic. Instead of merely marshaling factual evidence, practical reasoning emphasizes such considerations as the organization of data, the
interpretive application of differing criteria of explanation, and the implications of alternative strategies of argumentation. Beyond a one-dimensional reliance on analytical logic, the creative processes of insight, interpretation, and
judgment are recognized to be central to the assessment of scientific arguments.

Finally, how does this postpositivist approach relate to postmodern theory (Shapiro, 1992; Dobuzinskis, 1992)? Postpositivism, as conceived here,
shares common ground with some postmodern writings and not with others.
It appreciates the fact "that reality is . . . socially constructed and discursively
constituted" and that "there is a politics to how we go about making sense of
the world and the ways in which we communicate those understandings to
others" (Schram, 1993: 250). It is also compatible with postmodernism's
stress on "perspectivism," namely that "we always understand things from a
partial (both in the sense of incomplete and biased) perspective." The approach further accepts the argument that there is no longer the possibility of
establishing a "grand narrative" under which all other valid perspectives can
be subsumed. But it departs from those postmodernists who see no chance of
establishing a common basis for valid discourse among or across perspectives. Anchored to practical reason and discourse ethics, the approach here

maintains the existence of reasoned evaluative discourse in the absence of established principles. Having drawn in part on Habermas's approach to practical discourse, the author is cautiously sympathetic to his attempt to ground normative discourse in the pragmatics of linguistic communication, a project that remains the subject of intense methodological and epistemological controversy. As developed in this book, however, the logic of policy deliberation in no way presumes a commitment to the Habermasian concept of the "ideal speech situation."

## POSTPOSITIVIST POLICY EVALUATION

How, then, does the logic of policy deliberation resonate with these epistemological considerations? The logic (or "metalogic"), as we have seen, is constructed around four different but interrelated discourses—deliberations about program outcomes, the circumstances to which the program objectives are applied, the instrumental impact of the larger policy goals on the societal system as a whole, and an evaluation of the normative principles and values underlying the societal order. Taken together (although in no prescribed order), these four deliberations are designed to supply a discursive framework capable of transcending the limits of the technical conception of rationality that underlies much of policy-oriented social science.

In the language of practical reason, the logic of policy deliberation as a whole situates empirical social science methodology within the structure of a more comprehensive conception of rationality or reason. Specifically, it outlines a practical methodological framework that not only includes but logically transcends empirical analysis (primarily program verification) by interpreting the meaning of its data in both the context of action (situational validation) and a larger investigation of the workings of society (societal vindication), including a critique of its social and political values (social choice). Structured to move inquiry from the most concrete level of empirical investigation up through the higher levels of abstract exploration of norms and values, the methodological framework facilitates the explication and assessment of the full range of empirical and normative assumptions that contribute to a particular judgment.

Inherent to such a methodological assignment are numerous pitfalls. Particularly problematic is the fact that any attempt to say what a methodology might look like requires the introduction of analytical distinctions that can appear "hard and fast." Breaking things down into component parts is always a liability in methodological theorizing and must be cautiously approached as a necessary transgression designed heuristically to assist in talking about things that otherwise cannot be easily discussed and clarified. There are, in this respect, no "requirements" or "rules" in the sense of a methodological calculus per se—that is, the point is not to "plug in" answers to specific questions, or to fulfill prespecified methodological requirements. Instead, it is to engage in an open and flexible exploration of the concerns raised in the various phases of the probe. The questions that organize each discourse must in no way be answered in any specific or formal way. They are designed to orient policy evaluation to an interrelated set of concerns as they arise. Within the framework of each discourse, the deliberation follows its own course in the pursuit of understanding and consensus. Toward this end, the questions serve as guidelines to facilitate a discursive inquiry. The methodological orientations accompanying each phase are tools capable of supporting the deliberative process, but need only be brought into play where deemed appropriate. For example, as noted earlier, it is in no way mandatory to carry out a cost-benefit analysis in the verification of a program outcome. Cost-benefit analysis is understood to be a methodological technique that addresses the empirical concerns of program verification, although only employed when the parties to the deliberation find it relevant to the specific concerns at hand. There are thus no set procedures that must be followed in every case. The objective is only to initiate and pursue dialogue and consensus in each of the four discourses. Short of consensus, the goal is clarification and mutual understanding.

Important to the scheme is a place for both empirical-analytic and normative knowledge, including their interdependencies in each of the four different discourses. Whereas interpretive approaches have often dismissed empirical analysis as "technocratic ideology," the logic of policy deliberation helps us to see that empirical research is in no way to be disregarded. Given the applied nature of policy science, it will remain central to the discipline. Empirical relationships exist between social entities and knowledge of them is an essential concern for effective social action. What cannot be accepted, however, is the "giveness" of the social meanings of the relationships that are measured. All empirical measurements are understood to be built upon constructed understandings of the social world and how it works. As there is nothing "natural" here, it is the task of interpretive methodologies to probe the social ground upon which an action or program is constructed and measured. In the logic of policy evaluation, that happens at two points: first, at the level of the action situation, where situational validation probes the normative construction of the problem-situation underlying the program and its objectives; second, at the level of the social system, where social choice evaluates the normative underpinnings of the societal system. That is to say, both first-order discourse (program verification and situational validation) and second-order discourse (social systems level vindication and social choice) are conceived of as interactions between empirical and interpretive moments in a broader process of understanding. In no case does the empirical stand alone. At the same time, the interpretive must always confront the empirical, a point that critical hermeneutics alone generally fails to grasp.

The task, as formulated here, is not to establish the superiority or independence of either the empirical or the interpretive, but rather to determine how they logically fit together in a more critical-comprehensive methodological framework. This is not to say, however, that the interpretive/hermeneutic role is narrowly circumscribed, as is technical rationality. All four discourses include both empirical and interpretive decisions, although the emphasis shifts in each phase of the logic. In this regard, two levels emphasize—but are not limited to—interpretive analysis: a phenomenologically oriented interpretive investigation at the level of situational validation and a political-philosophical investigation at the level of social choice. Correspondingly, two discourses emphasize—but are not limited to—questions of empirical investigation: empirical program evaluation (program verification) and social scientific systems-oriented research (societal-level vindication). Understood in this way, the scheme as a whole can be defined as hermeneutical; first and second-order evaluation are both fully grounded in interpretive analysis.

First- and second-order levels of discourse can further be interconnected through an alternative conception of practice defined as "participatory policy analysis" (Fischer, 1992, 1994; Cancian and Armstead, 1992). Participatory policy analysis is designed to facilitate the exchange between the everyday or commonsense perspectives of the social actors in the situational action context (first-order discourse) and the available theoretical knowledge (empirical and normative) about the larger social system in which the action context is situated, that is, knowledge about both existing societal conditions and alternative possibilities (second-order discourse). The task of participatory policy analysis, very much in the spirit of Dryzek's (1982) hermeneutic conception of policy analysis, is to mediate between the tacit social theories and program practices of the actors within the policy process, and the analytical frameworks of social science.

The logic of policy deliberation can be understood as an attempt to move beyond the epistemological critique of positivism. While critique remains the foundation of an emancipatory perspective, it is important to recognize that at some point endless critique without the substitution of an alternative, teachable, methodological framework serves only to perpetuate the marginalization of the postpositivist project. Indeed, insofar as methodology is the essence of modern empirical social science, any effort to expand the scope of a postpositivist approach within the mainstream of the discipline must engage the issues of methodological reconstruction. As I have argued elsewhere, the possibility of training a new generation of social scientists to reject positivism and technology altogether depends on the ability to provide alternative methodologies for science and decision making (Fischer, 1990).

What are the chances of developing and introducing such methods? At this point, all we can say with certainty is that the answer is not yet in. One thing is clear however. Unless the advocates of postpositivism and participatory policy analysis take up the challenge, they will continue to lose by default.

## READINGS

Bernstein, Richard J. 1983. *Beyond Objectivism and Relativism: Science, Hermeneutics, and Praxis.* Philadelphia: Univ. of Pennsylvania Press.

Bleicher, Joseph. 1980. *Contemporary Hermeneutics.* London: Routledge and Kegan Paul.

Dryzek, John. 1982. "Policy Analysis as a Hermeneutic Activity." *Policy Sciences,* 14: 309–29.

Frank Fischer. 1990. *Technocracy and the Politics of Expertise.* Newbury Park, CA: Sage.

Frank Fischer. 1980. *Politics, Values, and Public Policy: The Problem of Methodology.* Boulder, CO: Westview.

Hawkesworth, M. E. 1988. *Theoretical Issues in Policy Analysis.* Albany: State Univ. of New York Press.

# Glossary*

**Discourse:** An orderly, structured, and elaborated exchange of ideas in which both assertions and prospective tests of normative and empirical claims are deliberated.

**Empirical evaluation:** A form of evaluation that seeks to determine the degree to which a specific program or policy empirically fulfills or does not fulfill a particular standard or norm.

**Empirical statement:** A descriptive statement about what "is" the case in the "real world" rather than what "ought" to be the case. Empirical statements are typically expressed in numerical terms.

**Ethical-neutrality:** A methodological doctrine that seeks a strict separation between empirical and normative judgments. According to the doctrine, the advocacy of value judgments in the research process introduces subjective biases which contaminate the social scientist's perceptions of the phenomena under investigation. In the interest of "objectivity," social scientists are instructed to suspend or bracket their own value orientations in order to achieve ethical- or value-neutrality.

**Evaluation:** The process of assigning a value or worth to something. See *empirical evaluation* and *normative evaluation*.

**Epistemology:** A branch of philosophy concerned with the theory of knowledge, the forms that knowledge takes, and the problem of obtaining such knowledge.

* The definitions are designed only to clarify the meanings of the conceptual terms as they are used in this book.

**Hermeneutics:** The philosophical field of study concerned with the interpretive understanding of an event or a text. Hermeneutics' search for "meaning" is typically contrasted with positivist forms of explanation, such as "causal," "teleological," or "functional" explanations. In hermeneutics the subject matter of social inquiry, human action, is irreducibly distinctive from that of the natural or physical sciences. Explanations of social action must involve consideration of the historical and cultural contexts that shape social meaning. For this reason, social inquiry cannot be value-free in the manner prescribed by positivist methodology.

**Interpretive inquiry:** Social science approach to hermeneutic inquiry. Such inquiry employs research methods qualitatively different from those of the physical sciences. Whereas scientific explanation is aimed at relating events to deterministic theories and laws, interpretive inquiry attempts to "understand" or "make sense of" social phenomena in terms of the social actors' own motives, goals, and explanations. The social scientist must try to get inside the actors' realm of subjective experience and to reconstruct the actors' own reasons for their actions. Such qualitative research uses methods ranging from interviews to participatory observation. In the latter case, the researcher lives with the subjects and participates in their way of life in an effort to experience firsthand the nature and purposes of the action or actions under investigation.

**Methodology:** The systematic study of the methods and techniques used to gain knowledge. More concrete than epistemology, methodology seeks to explain the logic and procedures that govern the research process.

**Norm:** A rule or principle that serves as a criterion against which achievement or effectiveness can be judged. Typically, norms are logically derived from values. They are the more concrete, situation-bound specifications that link social action and values. Norms are shared cultural definitions of behavior which are typically learned through socialization.

**Normative evaluation:** A form of evaluation that focuses on the standard(s) or norm(s) employed as a criterion in an empirical program or policy. Normative evaluation seeks to determine the appropriateness of the application of a criterion in both the general and the specific contexts into which it is introduced.

**Normative ideal:** An abstract, high-level value (or set of values) which serves to orient action. Like distant points on the horizon, people strive toward but never finally reach their ideals. Policy goals are typically deduced from or related to normative ideals. A liberal education is an ideal, while schooling is a goal.

**Normative statement:** A prescription of specific rules or principles of conduct against which behavior "ought" to be judged and approved or disapproved. Typically contrasted with empirical statements.

**Policy analysis:** A discipline or field that is concerned with the evaluation of public policy. The term is often used interchangeably with "policy science" or "policy sciences."

**Policy evaluation:** The activity of policy analysis broadly conceived. Not to be confused with the more specific methodological techniques of "program evaluation" or "evaluation research," the term is used here to refer to the components of a larger, multimethodological evaluation.

**Policy goal:** A goal that is an attainable end or an "end-in-view." A policy goal is more concrete than an "ideal" but lacks the full specificity of an "objective."

**Positivism:** A term used to refer to the legacy of a philosophical movement called "logical positivism." Originally developed in reference to the natural and physical sciences, positivism advances a theory of knowledge based on the rigorous testing of empirical propositions. Positivist social science, founded on specific normative and empirical assumptions, employs deductive methods to construct and empirically test hypotheses. It seeks to define the epistemological and methodological foundations of verifiable causal explanations and general laws. To account for modifications that have occurred in positivist theory, the term "neopositivism" is often used.

**Postpositivism:** A contemporary school of social science that attempts to combine the discourse of social and political theory with the rigor of modern science. It calls for a marriage of scientific knowledge with interpretive and philosophical knowledge about norms and values.

**Principle:** A fundamental rule of right conduct; for example, the principle of racial equality.

**Program objective:** A specific concrete measure or measures systematically designed or deduced to mirror empirically (or "operationalize") a policy goal. Standing in for the goal, the objective is the specific criterion that is empirically measured.

**Qualitative research:** Social research that employs interpretive methods.

**Quantitative research:** Social research that employs empirical methods.

**Rationality:** The possessing or using of reason. Rationality typically refers to arriving at a judgment through the use of specific logics or methods of thought. Such methods of thought can refer to "technical" rationality, "political" rationality, "cultural" rationality, and so on.

**Rule:** An established guide or regulation for action, conduct, method, or arrangement.

**Standard:** A measure established as a criterion for comparison in judging capacity, content, extent, value, and/or quality.

**Values:** Abstract and generalized ideals to which individuals or groups feel strong commitments. Values are sources of standards and norms for judging specific goals and acts.

# Notes

## Chapter 1   Public Policy Analysis as Practical Deliberation

1. Consider a few examples: Thomas Dye (1984: 1): "Public policy is whatever governments choose to do or not to." Hugh Heclo (1972: 85): Public policy is "a course of action or inaction [which has to be perceived or identified] rather than specific decisions or actions." Harold Lasswell and Abraham Kaplan (1950: 71): Public policy is "a projected program of values and practices." Fred Frohock (1979: 11): Public policy "is, in its most general sense, the pattern of action that resolves conflicting claims or provides for cooperation." W. I. Jenkins (1978: 15): Public policy is "a set of interrelated decisions taken by a political actor or group of actors concerning the selection of goals and means of achieving them within a specific situation where these decisions should, in principle, be within the power of these actors to achieve."

2. According to deHaven-Smith (1988), public policy is often thought of as a social experiment, "as some sort of projectile aimed at a 'target' population," but is in fact "better conceived as a multifaceted effort to mitigate complicated social problems, the causes of which are subject to dispute." In this view, these disputes are typically left unresolved by traditional approaches to social and political research, as such research is generally both too narrowly focused and too weakly grounded in theoretical terms.

3. For instances of such skepticism about the usefulness of policy analysis see Alice Rivlin (1971: 59) and Charles Schultze (1968: 89).

4. See, for example, the journal *Knowledge: Creation, Diffusion, and Utilization,* established in 1980.

5. Alvin Gouldner (1970: 500) wrote that "In the context of the burgeoning Welfare-Warfare State . . . liberal ideologies serve . . . to increase the centralized control of an ever growing Federal Administrative Class and of the master institutions on behalf of which it operates. Liberal sociologists have thus become the technical cadres of national governance."

6. Beyond its more immediate methodological manifestations, the positivist theory of knowledge is today difficult to define precisely. One reason is that it has undergone numerous embellishments and perhaps is now in the social sciences more loosely identified as a form of "neopositivism." In addition, the term itself now functions as a

polemical epithet in addition to its designation for a distinct intellectual movement. For this reason, it is best understood to refer more generally to the heritage of logical positivism and its rationalistic mode of thought. According to McCarthy (1978), neopositivism refers to "a legacy of convictions and attitudes, problems and techniques, concepts and theories,—[that] pervades contemporary thought." Relying on empirical measurement and analytical precision, neopositivism constitutes in the social sciences a "logical, practical, problem-solving, instrumental, orderly and disciplined approach to objectives" (Bell, 1971: 10).

7. This position is called the "correspondence theory of truth." Empirical research in this tradition rests on several fundamental epistemological assumptions. Most important, social actors are held to encounter, through their social-psychological perceptions and experiences, an extant social life-world that is independent of their beliefs, attitudes, and values. It is a world that, from the social actor's position, is "out there." Knowledge about it can be derived independently of the actor's sense perceptions or emotional framework.

Such knowledge is organized in the form of propositional statements about empirical relationships (between two or more objective variables) that deductively explain and predict defined social phenomena. The objectivity of such knowledge is tested through controlled observation and the principles of formal logic, induction, and deduction. The truth of a hypothesis, measured as its validity and reliability, can be verified by evidence gathered from the objective world of facts by a neutral investigator (Kaplan, 1964; Bobrow and Dryzek, 1987).

8. Basic to neopositivism and its rationalistic worldview has been a fairly ambitious epistemological assumption: The empirical-analytical method is held by its staunchest defenders to be the only valid means of obtaining "true knowledge." Still, some say today that modern neopositivism will in time subordinate all other modes of thought to its principles. Rigorous adherence to the methodology is believed to pay off eventually in the discovery of valid empirical regularities, if not the "laws" of society. Such knowledge is not only seen to make possible the resolution of many economic and social problems, it is also said to facilitate the rational design of social systems in ways that enable us better to predict and manage, and in some cases even eliminate, the persistent conflicts and crises that now plague modern society. As such, neopositivism is founded on an unswerving belief in the power of the rational mind to direct societal change in constructive directions (Stanley, 1978; Bobrow and Dryzek, 1987).

9. Melvin Anshen and David Novick, cited by Aaron Wildavsky, "The Political Economy of Efficiency," in *Planning Programming Budgeting,* ed. by Fremont J. Lyden and Ernest G. Miller (Chicago: Markham, 1967), p. 394.

10. Fundamentally, the fact-value dichotomy is based on positivism's adherence to a meta-ethic theory known as "value noncognitivism" (Hawkesworth, 1988). According to this theory, human value judgments are essentially subjective responses to life conditions.

11. Undiscernible through direct empirical sensory perceptions, and therefore dependent on subjective assessments, value questions must be relegated to the province of philosophy and metaphysics. To the degree that social science has to be concerned with such judgments, it need only involve itself with the explication and elaboration of the internal consistency of normative statements and value judgments, including their

implications for thought and action. Approached as a matter of conceptual clarification, the task of normative evaluation is to sort out and separate the objective foundations of empirical referents from the normative ambiguities that plague scientific research. As such, the analysis of norms and values is viewed as a secondary analytical function subordinate to the larger empirical assignment.

To be sure, important aspects of value statements can be investigated scientifically. Statements about the conditions that lead to the adoption of specific values or value systems, as well as statements about the consequences of holding them, can be empirically assessed. But for positivists, the more fundamental point is the conviction that there is no way to scientifically establish the categorical truth of a value judgment.

12. Weber (1949), founded his position on a distinction between formal and substantive rationality. Formal rationality is the procedural rationality of the scientific method. The task of the researcher is to investigate those aspects of the social and political world that lend themselves to scientific procedures. Substantive rationality, in contrast, is identified with the realm of norms and values: questions of right and wrong, of good and bad, of what ought and ought not to be done.

13. Concerned with factual questions (i.e., questions concerning "What is the case?"), the focus of formal rationality is on the empirical premises of social research. In the case of more practically oriented applied research, such as policy analysis, the task is restricted to the determination of the optimal means-ends relationships that link policy goals to their programmatic outcomes (Weber, 1949: 49–112).

14. This position is also referred to as "decisionism" (Hawkesworth, 1988; Gunnell, 1968).

15. The term "level" captures the fact that the four phases of the evaluative framework move through increasingly abstract levels of evaluation. It is not used here to refer to more sophisticated questions concerning the nature of reason. The question of whether or not the logical form of normative reasoning is structured in a hierarchical fashion, as opposed, for example, to something more akin to a network, is not an issue to be engaged here.

16. Rational social choice is not to be confused here with the decisionistic rational choice theories that have proliferated in the social sciences in recent years.

## Chapter 2   Evaluating Program Outcomes: Empirical Logic and Methods

1. In the vocabulary of science the process of translating abstract terms (concepts) into empirical variables is called "operationalization" (Lin, 1976: 63).

2. The experimental method is the ideal method because it is the primary method capable of determining "causality." See Lin, 1976: 245–73.

3. To determine the original intent of legislative goals and objectives it is often necessary to consult the records of legislative deliberations preceding the passage of a law, to interview people knowledgeable about the program area, or to seek a legal interpretation from the courts.

CHAPTER 3    DEBATING THE HEAD START
PROGRAM

1. To measure cognitive abilities, Westinghouse relied mainly on the "Metropolitan Readiness Test," the "Stanford Achievement Test," and the "Illinois Test of Psycholinguistic Abilities."

2. To measure affective development, the research corporation developed a "Children's Self-Concept Index," a "Classroom Behavior Inventory," and a "Children's Attitudinal Range Indicator."

3. For the purpose of the analysis that follows, the discussion excludes the evaluation of emotional development, which received far less attention than reading scores in the public debate.

4. Among the criticisms were the following: (1) The study was based on an *ex post facto* design which was inherently faulty because it attempted to generate a control group by matching former Head Start children with non–Head Start children; (2) The study tested the children in the first, second, and third grades of elementary school after they had left Head Start; thus, its findings merely demonstrated that Head Start achievements did not persist after the children returned to poverty homes and ghetto schools; (3) The study failed to give adequate attention to variations among the Head Start programs; (4) The study was not representative, because many of the original randomly chosen centers had to be eliminated; (5) The test instruments used in the study for measuring cognitive and affective states in children were primitive. In particular, they were not developed for disadvantaged populations (Williams and Evans, 1972).

5. It is not actually the case that Westinghouse evaluators altogether ignored the role of socially relevant experiences. To supplement their experimental evaluation, Westinghouse had in fact made a qualitative investigation of the Head Start program, albeit a meager one. A limited number of interviews and surveys of Head Start officials and parents were conducted to assess administrative problems with the program and to gain some overall subjective impressions. The surveys of Head Start officials focused primarily on the quality of equipment and resources, suggestions for more effective interactions with children and parents, and such matters as the home learning environment, attitudes toward children, opinions about education, and the vocational and educational aspirations they had for their children. Based on this more qualitative research, the Westinghouse Report suggested that both administrators and parents were strongly supportive of the educational initiative. What is important, however, is the fact that the Westinghouse Learning Corporation—as well as elected officials, the media, and others—did not emphasize this qualitative assessment of the program.

6. In the 1980s a somewhat similar version of this argument was advanced by the Reagan administration, which in very large part was founded on a political reaction to the Great Society and its War on Poverty. As such, much of its critique concerned the economic and social impacts of the poverty program. While President Reagan and his advisors criticized the Great Society on numerous grounds, most important, at least for present purposes, was the argument that the War on Poverty actually *exacerbated* the problems of the poor, rather than reducing or mitigating them. Indeed, beyond unemployment the policy was seen as responsible for a host of other social pathologies as well, such as drugs, crime, broken families, prostitution, etc. The basis of this criticism

was the theory of "welfare dependency" developed by Gilder (1981) and expanded by Murray (1984). Like the theory of the culture of poverty, the theory of welfare dependency assumed the poor to have dysfunctional attitudes. But rather than attributing these to a lack of opportunity, welfare dependency theory attributed them to unearned income and in-kind transfers of the type employed by the War on Poverty. By providing poverty mothers with an income greater than what poverty fathers can earn in low-wage jobs in the labor market, it was argued, the government poverty programs weakened the male role in poor families, causing the breakup of such families, and thus created a class of single, separated, and divorced males whose cultural habits and attitudes dominate life in the ghettos (Gilder, 1981: 83, 94, 169–82).

7. Perhaps the best compendium of published and unpublished experimental research on Head Start is the U.S. Department of Health and Human Services 1985 report entitled *The Impact of Head Start on Children, Families and Communities*. After reviewing seventy-two of Head Start's effects on cognitive development, the report concludes that children showed significant gains in their reading and language skills as a result of participating in Head Start. Furthermore, an examination of seventeen studies on the socio-emotional impact of Head Start revealed that the program did improve the self-esteem and social behavior of children who completed the program. While many of these studies raised questions about the lasting effects of such cognitive and affective gains, one highly publicized study, the Perry Preschool Project, followed a sample of children for over twenty-two years and found that children who attended a preschool program were more prone to complete high school, to enter college, and to do better than average on functional competence exams.

8. There are several explanations for the differences between the new studies and the Westinghouse evaluation. One is that the positive results in the later studies are in part attributable to use of innovative curricula and the improvement of measurement indicators, as well as a number of administrative restrictions. Second, the experiments themselves were better. In response to the criticisms of the Westinghouse Report, many of the internal and external validity problems in the first evaluation were minimized in the subsequent research. In particular, the new studies utilized different measures of Head Start goals, such as the use of student school performance rather than IQ tests as the measure of cognitive development. Greater care was also taken to select equivalent random samples, to use pretest as well as posttest instruments, to examine program effects over a longer period of time, and to conduct experiments in different social settings. As a whole, the new empirical studies have demonstrated that the Westinghouse findings were in fact contaminated by methodological errors and that the program is actually effective in significant respects.

9. A significant amount of research elaborated and improved on the qualitative assessment of Head Start begun by Westinghouse. Drawing on the holistic techniques of anthropologists and interpretive sociologists, several evaluations validated the role of social relevance in the Head Start program by focusing on the meaning of Head Start for parents and communities. For example, interviews and observations of families and communities involved with Head Start showed the program met several tests of socially relevant experiences. In particular, it was found to bring many poor and underprivileged families into contact with community social services agencies.

10. George Bush speaking on CNN International News, Berlin, Germany, Jan. 21, 1992.

## CHAPTER 4    EVALUATING PROGRAM OBJECTIVES: MULTIPLE CRITERIA AND SITUATIONAL RELEVANCE

1. Of necessity, as Wildavsky (1979) explains, "problems are manmade. There are always multiple conceptions. . . . They are not uniquely determined." According to Elder and Cobb (1984), "To define a situation as a policy problem is to imply its solution and to delimit its solution possibilities. It is to presume not only that something can be done but that what should be done falls within the legitimate purview of governmental authority. All of these presumptions are subject to challenge and each constitutes a critical test upon which the success of a particular definition may hinge." As Gusfield (1981) puts it, "Without both a cognitive belief in alterability and a moral judgment of its character, a phenomenon is not at issue, not a problem. . . . The reality of a problem is often expanded or contracted in scope as cognitive or moral judgments shift."

2. Likewise, the communication across an organizational decision structure hinges on the definition of the situation and its problems. As Norton Long (1962: 141) explained, "to a considerable extent the holders of power in an organization hold their power because they are able to get their definitions of the situation accepted by others."

3. Taylor (1961: 96–97) provides the following illustration: "Suppose a new library building is being planned for a city. One of the architectural principles (standards) accepted by the city officials is that of functionalism—the best building is the one that most effectively serves the purposes for which it is to be used. According to this standard [or objective], good-making characteristics of a library would include such things as spaciousness of stacks and reading rooms, quietness, efficiently organized offices, easy availability of books, and so on. Let us suppose, furthermore, that the best library building as judged by the standard of functionalism would cost so much to build that the city would have to take funds allotted to another project (say, slum clearance) to pay for it. The choice becomes: fulfill the standard of functionalism and damage the slum clearance project, or fail to fulfill the standard and preserve the clearance project. An evaluation is then made of these two alternatives *according to a standard,* such as the welfare of the people of the city. An evaluation according to this standard might result in ranking the second alternative as better than the first. An exception would then be made to the standard of functionalism in architecture. If an architect were to present two plans for the library building, one of which was clearly better than the other according to the standard of functionalism, the better one would *not* be chosen. It would not be considered really better in the given circumstances. Hence an exception to a standard is justified on the basis of the circumstances in which the evaluation occurs. The standard of what is 'really better' is the standard of the public welfare."

4. Other critics, of course, more generally questioned the value of an American middle-class way of life. But this question shifts the debate to second-order discourse in the logic of policy evaluation, namely social choice. Such questions are reserved for the discussion in chapter 8.

5. Taylor (1961: 128–29) offers the following example: "Suppose an army has two rules: 'Always obey the commands of a superior officer,' and 'No one is to enter this building without a pass.' If an officer without a special pass commands the soldier on duty to let him enter the building, which rule ought the soldier obey? A well-run army unit will specify the relative precedence of such conflicting rules by means of a [higher]-order rule. After the statement of the rule requiring a special pass, there might be added the [higher]-order rule, 'Absolutely no personnel of any rank will be exempted from the requirement.' "

6. Richard Flathman (1966) has provided an interesting example of the logical-analytical process of bringing competing norms under higher-order principles designed to mediate conflict. He has labored to show how the concept of the "public interest" has emerged in the ordinary language of political argumentation to serve as a basis for justifying public policies. Employed as a higher-order principle, the principle of the public interest is essentially a logical test of a policy's generalizability.

7. Clifford Geertz (1973: 24) describes this interpretive process as "thick description," a concept he borrows from the philosopher Gilbert Ryle. This description is needed to gain "access to the cultural world in which our subjects live so that we can, in some extended sense of the term, converse with them."

8. Patricia Carini (1975), for example, advances a method called "documentation." Borrowing heavily from ethnomethodological techniques, documentation involves a "process of selecting and juxtaposing recorded observations and other records of phenomenal meaning in order to reveal reciprocities and therefore to approach the integrity of the phenomenon." Since the task is not to exhaust the singular meaning of an event but to reveal the multiplicity of meanings, and since it is through the observer's encounter with the event that these meanings emerge, no standard format for collecting observations would be appropriate for different settings and purposes.

## CHAPTER 5    CONTESTING THE TIMES SQUARE REDEVELOPMENT STUDY

1. By the early 1980s, twenty-three states and most communities had economic development agencies implementing urban renewal projects. Economically successful projects were implemented in San Diego, Boston, St. Louis, and Dallas (Frieden and Sagalyn, 1989). New York City's Jacob Javits Convention Center and Battery Park City were two projects that similarly demonstrated the ability of the public and private sectors to transpose deteriorated areas into clean, modern, urban focal points (Emickie, 1991).

2. Serving as the president of the Actors' Equity Association, actress Ellen Burstyn put it in these words: "Construction of the office towers proposed in the plan will pose a direct threat to legitimate Broadway theaters by artificially and rapidly inflating land values. Legitimate theaters will be demolished when they cannot compete economically in the real estate market and theater related uses will be priced out of the district" (UDC, 1984: 10–76).

3. The report further stated that: "On a regular basis, there are 24 uniformed police assigned to the two blocks daily, plus an undisclosed number of plainclothes po-

lice, and members of the Tactical Control unit, just to keep criminal activity down from its current high levels. The opinion of enforcement agencies in the area, based on experience (e.g., prostitution on Eighth Avenue) is that criminal activity in the project area will not decrease until the urban environment that supports it is changed" (UDC, 1984: 10–118).

4. The study continued to add that "by improving the business conditions in West Midtown and by broadening the appeal of Clinton as a residential neighborhood, the proposed project could eventually lead to an increase in rental rates and consequently to the displacement of some of the existing businesses in Clinton (UDC, 1984: 10–124).

5. Interview with Gretchen Dykstra, president of the Times Square Business Improvement District.

6. Interview with Susan Fainstein, urban planner and consultant to a Clinton neighborhood group.

## CHAPTER 6    EVALUATING POLICY GOALS: NORMATIVE ASSUMPTIONS AND SOCIETAL CONSEQUENCES

1. One of the most central questions in contemporary political theory concerns the empirical conceptualization of the social system itself. This point is vividly illustrated in contemporary debates between "modern" and "postmodern" social scientists.

2. The theory-testing model of policy research has origins in the work of Karl Popper (1966), who argued that everyday governmental activities can be conceptualized as "piecemeal social experiments."

3. According to Albinski (1986: 157), in all public policy processes there are three elements of particular importance: (1) the existing situation; (2) values, goals, and other normative elements; and (3) an action program designed to realize goals with the given situation as the starting point. A policy-oriented theory is expected to aid "policymakers by providing them with a frame in which their goals, possible means to achieving them, and the possible solutions to them as well as their limitations can be placed and related to each other."

## CHAPTER 7    REASSESSING DISABILITY POLICY GOALS: EQUAL RIGHTS VERSUS SOCIETAL COSTS

1. The rejuvenation of the rehabilitation program through a distinctively professional approach was largely the work of Mary Switzer. Having long worked in the health and rehabilitation bureaucracies, as well as having participated in the establishment of the Social Security program itself, Switzer championed a professional approach to social programs. By 1954 Switzer had managed to convince the Eisenhower administration to sponsor major new legislation that would put rehabilitation on a more professional basis. "The legislation initiated new types of federal grants to establish professional training programs in universities, to subsidize research on rehabilitation methods, and to enable counselors to attend the new programs at public expense" (Berkowitz, 1987: 171).

2. By 1965, professional training programs in universities had grown dramatically. About forty colleges and universities offered graduate degrees in rehabilitation counseling; by 1980 the number had grown to almost one hundred. By the mid-1980s universities were receiving more than $15 million in federal funds for rehabilitation research and the support of training centers (Rehabilitation Research Admin., 1982: 55; Berkowitz, 1987: 172).

3. It is difficult to find the kind of full-fledged macro cost-benefit analysis of disability policy that the Reagan administration called for (confirmed through personal correspondence with Dr. Murray Wiedenbaum, former Chairman of President Reagan's Council of Economic Advisors). The Job Accommodation Network ("A Service of the President's Committee on Employment of People with Disabilities") published a study that compared the benefits to the costs of hiring the handicapped (Job Accommodation Network, 1987). In contrast to many conservative arguments, it found that benefits compared favorably to costs.

4. One of the most aggressive stances has been taken by the bus industry. In the view of the industry's leaders, the Act's guarantee of "equal access to transportation" will mean that many Americans will ultimately be denied access to affordable intercity, charter and tour transportation. People in rural areas, they point out, will be hit especially hard. Airlines regularly serve only about 500 communities; passenger rail, about the same. Regularly scheduled private passenger bus service extends to some 10,000 communities. This means, according to the industry, that without access to buses some 9,500 communities would be totally isolated from intercity public transportation. Abandoned also would be hundreds of nonurban communities that are being encouraged by federal and state government to diversify their fragile economies by developing travel and tourism attractions, most of which are reachable only by road. Consider the comments of Wayne J. Smith, executive director of the United Bus Owners of America. In a piece published in the New York *Times* under the title "Bye, Bye, Bus Industry," Smith (1989) put the complaint this way: "We're concerned, first, that the vast majority of the association's nearly 1,000 private, predominately small businesses will be forced to fold in the wake of the bill's mandate that all new buses must be made 'fully accessible' to handicapped riders." Congress will now mandate the industry "to pay for the costly addition of wheelchair lifts and the redesign of all new buses (at costs ranging from $15,000 to $50,000)." But the legislators have "failed to renounce a 'worst case' interpretation." In addition to installing new equipment, "it expects the widening of onboard restrooms and aisles to accept wheelchairs. . . ." Such modifications "would cost at least a third of the revenue-producing seats in a business in which a 5 percent annual profit is cause for celebration."

Opponents contend that the debate on the bill has been entirely framed by handicapped proponents who insist that it is inappropriate to discuss cost in a "civil rights" issue. This means, as Smith puts it, "many Americans will stay at home—equally denied access to affordable . . . transportation."

CHAPTER 8    EVALUATING IDEOLOGICAL COMMITMENTS:
PUBLIC POLICY, SOCIAL VALUES, AND THE GOOD
SOCIETY

1. Jennings (1991) describes the bottom-up approach of the social and policy sciences in these words: "From the specific option of the choice situation to existing guidelines or maxims; from there to general rules; from there to more general covering principles; and from there to some basic assumptions contained in a moral theory, or, depending on the account one follows, to some process of reflexive equilibrium in order to reach some coherence among conflicting principles. Each step upward in the chain of reasoning is motivated by indeterminacy or conflict between inconsistent guidelines, rules, or conflict at the lower levels."

2. From Aristotle to Machiavelli politics was defined as the pursuit of the "good life."

3. An example of such a new class or group is the Calvinistic entrepreneurs of the sixteenth and seventeenth centuries who, in the throes of a collapsing feudal system, served to usher in the capitalist principles upon which modern economic and social organization are founded.

4. During the period of domestic crisis and epistemological debate in the 1960s, for example, political philosophy was an essential part of the radical spirit. The "New Left" of that period relied heavily on such works as Herbert Marcuse's *One-Dimensional Man* (1964), Eric Fromm's *The Sane Society* (1963), and Paul and Percival Goodman's *Communitas: Means of Livelihood and Ways of Life* (1960).

5. "[H]ow," as French (1983: 29) puts it, "does one find out if the reason one has for choosing to act in one way rather than another can be made a principle and hence universal? Surprisingly, in ordinary life we use a variety of unsophisticated versions of the procedure Kant had in mind. We may be asked, 'Would you want everyone doing *that?*' Or, we may be told to imagine what it would be like to be the 'other guy.' 'Would you like that to happen to you?' . . . [T]hese are unsophisticated versions of what Kant had in mind, but we should not confuse this theory with another deontological theory, golden rule ethics. Kant believed that we ought to test the principles (or maxims) upon which we act by making them universal to see if in their universal forms they remain coherent and rational."

6. Philosophers who emphasize the test of universalization, "among whom we may include those known as deontologists (from the Greek *deon,* duty), maintain that certain *features* of actions, not just their consequences, determine the moral standing of actions. It may be argued that an act has a special moral quality because it was required by God or by the rules of an important institution to which one has freely committed oneself or because one has promised another person to do it or because one stands in a particular relation to someone else" (French, 1983: 29).

7. The public interest, reflecting the generalization or universalization principle, "requires that political actors consider the impact of their actions and demands on the other members of society, reduce idiosyncratic demands, and seek constantly to find common grounds with other men." Citizens must recognize themselves as members of particular groups and social classes with both general and particular goals, through an appeal to higher (more general) principles in political discourse, they must attempt to

"subsume their interests under a larger precept or maxim and thereby begin to transform them into claims which can legitimately be pressed in the public forum" (Flathman, 1966: 41).

## CHAPTER 9   ENVIRONMENTAL POLICY AND RISK-BENEFIT ANALYSIS

1. Maurice Strong, for example, makes this argument in the film, "After the Warming," produced by the Public Broadcasting System. Strong was the organizer of the world environmental conference in Brazil in 1992.

Whether or not people like Strong exaggerate the situation, the statistics are always dramatic. For example, consider population growth. While the world's population only reached one billion by 1830, it is projected to reach six billion by the year 2000—a veritable population explosion. At the same time, the United Nations reports that between 13 and 17 million acres of cropland are being lost for agricultural production every year—i.e., at the exact time when production will need to be doubled again to feed the world's increased population. Add to this the fact that sixty percent of the planet's natural oil reserves have already been used; the fact that eighteen million acres of the world's tropical rain forest are being cut down each year; the fact that the build up of the greenhouse gas $CO_2$ is at current rates projected to double by the middle of the next century. And so on. One statistic sounds more foreboding than the next. Taken together, for many social ecologists such statistics portend the apocalypse.

2. This concern often reflects very concrete experiences, the nuclear power industry being the most important example (Rosenbaum, 1985: 227–34). What started out as one of the magnificent peacetime wonders of modern technology has been brought to a virtual standstill in the United States by the environmental movement and the assistance of such accidents as Three Mile Island and Chernobyl. In the United States, for example, construction of all new plants largely came to a halt by 1980.

3. Whereas in earlier periods people feared political turmoil resulting from imbalances in the distribution of goods, Beck argues that in contemporary society people are increasingly worried about the risks engendered by their own systems of production. Moreover, the growing awareness of risks among men and women also produces today a new and distinctive pattern of consciousness. The social class awareness of the earlier period, Beck maintains, is increasingly overlaid by the omnipresence of a risk awareness common to all. A nuclear accident, for example, recognizes no social boundaries; the same moribund consequences hit both the rich and the poor. No one, regardless of economic resources, can escape the risks of technological disasters. Ironically, as he maintains, these risks have in their consequences become "socially just."

4. But NIMBY is not a term designed to reflect just any opposition. As a theoretical construct, NIMBY is a phenomenon based on a conceptual attempt to describe a specific type of opposition. It is a reflection of a public attitude that seems to be almost self-contradictory—that people feel it is desirable to site a particular type of facility somewhere as long as it is not where they personally live (Dear, 1992).

5. Playing it safe, so the argument goes, actually tends to reduce opportunities to benefit from new entrepreneurial changes. Even further, risk taking is itself said to be a

fundamental source of safety. Like joggers who routinely risk heart attacks to improve overall health, societies must run short-term risks in order to expand future wealth and security (Wildavsky, 1988). What is more, the resulting expansion of wealth is said to make it possible for society to absorb the impact of greater disasters, thus directly increasing its overall level of safety. In short, risk raises issues fundamental to the future of Western industrial societies and has ushered in a deep-seated political struggle to shape the very way we think and talk about it.

6. William Ruckelshaus (1989: 54), head of the Environmental Protection Agency during this period, explained the turn to risk assessment in these words: "We are now in a troubled and emotional period for pollution control; many communities are gripped by something approaching panic, and the public discussion is dominated by personalities rather than substance. . . . I believe part of the solution to our stress lies with the idea that disciplined minds can grapple with ignorance and sometimes win: the ideas of science. . . . Somehow our democratic technological society must resolve the dissonance between science and the creation of public policy. Nowhere is this more troublesome than in the formal assessment of risk. . . ."

7. Consider, for example, the case of hazardous waste landfills. Without question, such landfills are a threat to their neighbors. But from the perspective of risk assessment this threat must in some way be balanced against the larger benefits to be derived from the chemical industry. The inclusion of the benefits will surely favor the chemical industry, as well as the industrial system generally. (The chemical industry, in fact, is basic to the modern system of production as a whole.) But the threat will almost never be attractive to the community neighboring on the disposal site. Such communities almost invariably turn to the environmental movement for assistance in presenting their interests and values in the larger public forums, and risk assessment is typically portrayed as a sophisticated technocratic tool designed to impede, if not altogether block, community interests and values.

8. Consider the role of new technologies. Basic to the history of techno-industrial society has been a fundamental commitment to the development and introduction of new technologies. As these are perceived as the source of most things good, little more than scant attention has traditionally been given to the possibility that they might cause harm. (In the best of circumstances, such considerations have typically only come after the fact.) Thus, for example, decades of haphazard use of industrial chemicals provide a background of expectations for today's deliberations on the safety of such chemicals. Indeed, pollution of the air, land, and water are not simply to be understood as policy failures in twentieth century America, but rather the norm. In this regard, risk assessment implicitly builds into the deliberation an acceptance of the technological and environmental practices long associated with high levels of techno-industrial production, most often the very practices that environmentalists struggle to reform. Those who seek to place moral and political limits upon such practices thus have to challenge the assumptions of risk assessments rather than their calculations per se.

9. Especially important for the ecological problem is liberalism's conception of nature. Under liberalism, following Locke, nature and the earth have been essentially conceptualized as God's gift to humankind; they provided for the "comfort and support of human life in this world." But in its natural state God's gift is seen to be virtually

worthless. It is man's task to create the conditions of earthly comfort by taming and subduing God's original gift, through "tilling, improving, planting, and cultivating." Only by mixing one's labors with the materials of nature, as the argument goes, can one create the conditions of happiness, if not merely survival, on earth. Indeed, it is just this mixture that comes to be the foundation of the concept of "private property," the concept most basic to the American political-economic system. "In short, Lockean philosophy led to a strong ideology of man's relationship to the earth, in which autonomous individuals seek comfort and enjoyment through hard work and material acquisitions." No belief can be said to be more fundamental to the American way of life (Leeson, 1979).

10. John Kemeny (1980), former chairperson of the presidential commission appointed to investigate the Three Mile Island nuclear disaster, offered this assessment to an audience at Massachusetts Institute of Technology: "I've heard many times that although democracy is an imperfect system, we somehow always muddle through. The message I want to give you, after long and hard reflection, is that . . . it is no longer possible to muddle through. The issues we deal with do not lend themselves to that kind of treatment. . . . Jeffersonian democracy cannot work in the [contemporary world]—the world has become too complex."

11. In the Western context, this view is manifested in a belief that the contemporary malaise—budgetary crises, inflation, pollution, poverty, energy shortages, educational decline, crime, environmental decay, and so on—is largely attributable to the way decision making is organized in democratically structured governments. Political systems governed by bargaining and compromise are seen to be out of place in the exacting world of technology.

12. As a leading official in the Bush administration put it, the term "environmentalism" is basically "a green mask" under which the different faces of an ideology hostile to the capitalist system can hide.

13. For such social ecologists (as "philosophical naturalists") there is no need, as in the case of liberalism, to base the argument for equality on intellectual abstractions. For ecologists, it is empirically observable in nature.

For some, the principles of nature are also linked to the femininity of nature and feminist values. There is, in this regard, a tendency to map onto nature the beneficial characteristics of the female personality. "Thus nature and women come to be tender, nurturing, caring, sensitive to place, and substantially defined by the (high) office of giving birth to life." Toker (1987: 85) puts it this way: "The values of nurturance, cooperation and sharing which are traditionally identified more closely with women than with men need to become the deepest underlying principles of our society." Many ecologists, in fact, claim feminism as a guiding star.

14. This effort to deprofessionalize science rests on a radical critique of the professions. Following the theorists of democratic empowerment, social ecologists argue that the professions have too often misappropriated their specialized knowledge to serve both their own interests and those of the power elite intent on maintaining dominance over the rest of society. Professional experts are portrayed as elite functionaries of the establishment. Their mandates, licenses, and authenticity are said to work toward a profoundly unjust distribution of social benefits and thus serve as mechanisms of social control, particularly the control of the have-nots, the poor, the dispossessed, ethnic

and racial minorities, women, and others by dominant elites. Complaints, moreover, do not only concern the interests of the minorities and the poor. Professionals have also suffered harsh criticisms from segments of the middle and upper classes as well. Here the complaints tend to have more to do with the overextension of technical strategies into social and cultural realms. Most typically, they concern the acceleration of a technocratic society in which many people prefer not to live. This is especially the case among relatively affluent groups more concerned with the quality of everyday life than the struggle for economic subsistence.

15. As Hirschhorn puts it: "In such settings the professional becomes a *facilitator* of group processes. He or she must design the setting for the group (where it takes place, how many members there are, the range of professionals that can be called upon) and then function as a consultant to it. . . . The emphasis is on establishing the institutional conditions within which clients can draw on their own individual and collective agencies to solve their problems. . . . The professional acts as a programmer, mobilizer of resources, and consultant to a self-exploration and learning process on the part of group members."

Perhaps the most influential theorist in this tradition has been Paulo Freire (1973). His work on "problematization" or "problem-posing," is basic to the development of participatory research. Problem-posing, according to Freire, must supersede the "magister dixit" behind which hide those who regard themselves as the "proprietors, administrators," or "bearers" of knowledge. Problematization, moreover, is the direct antithesis of technocratic problem solving. Whereas in the technocratic approach the expert establishes some distance from reality, analyzes the problem into component parts, devises means for resolving difficulties in the most efficient way, and then dictates the strategy or policy, problematizing seeks to help people codify into symbols an integrated picture or story of reality, which in the course of its development can generate a critical consciousness. In contrast to technocratic problem solving, which distorts the totality of human experience by reducing it to those dimensions that are amenable to treatment *as mere difficulties to be solved,* problematization seeks to generate a critical consciousness capable of empowering people to alter their own relations to both the physical and social worlds.

16. At the outset of a participatory risk assessment, for example, a wider range of stakeholders and societal interests must be built into the initial discussion of what the risk problem is. Once the fundamentally social nature of technological systems is recognized, definitional questions concerning what the technology actually is, what are its significant components and connections, and what are its boundaries and external contexts become critically important. These interests must again be brought into the process of identification and search for risks. In particular, workers familiar with the everyday operations of a plant have important experiential knowledge about how the socio-institutional structures and processes of the system actually function. Then there is the matter of assigning weights to risks and benefits. While this process appears highly technical in nature, it, too, is grounded in a large number of normative considerations. How, for example, are risks and benefits to be counted? If a benefit is intangible or not traded in markets, how should we establish price values for it, and so on? Finally, citizens and workers must have important inputs into the process of interpreting the meaning and uses of an analysis. Especially important in this respect is the relationship

of the findings to the specific situational circumstances to which they are to be applied. The production of generalized information about the risks of a technological system can never be more than guidelines that must be interpreted within the specific contexts to which they are applied.

For a case study that employs the four levels of policy evaluation presented in this book to identify and analyze the norms and value judgments that underlie a specific risk assessment, see Jerald Wamsley (1992).

17. It is interesting to note that a number of Marxists share this view of the environmental movement (e.g., Harvey, 1989).

## CHAPTER 10    POLICY DELIBERATION AS POLITICAL METHODOLOGY: IMPLICATIONS FOR THEORY AND PRACTICE

1. Political democracy in a "strong democracy" is creative rather than representational. "Creativity and the capacity to see anew, to see empathetically, become the special virtues of an effective political epistemology. For the challenge is to envision the human future and then to inspire a passion in others for that vision—often adapting it to their own vision." But such political judgment, or way of seeing, is not subjective, as "it arises out of social interaction and out of the imaginative effort by individuals to see in common. But neither is such judgment objective, for it makes no claim to be universal or to proceed from an independent order of things. It is a kind of 'we' thinking that compels individuals to reformulate their interests, purposes, norms, and plans in a mutualistic language of public goods" (Barber, 1984: 170–71).

2. Numerous writers have criticized the idea of designing institutions, given the fact that the word "designing" connotes the manipulation of conditions and thus all too problematically smacks of instrumental rationality, the very form of reason that critical theorists seek to displace. Dryzek (1990: 41), however, asks how warranted this fear of designing institutions is? As he puts it, "If one draws a parallel between the design of political institutions and architectural and engineering design, the critical theorists should indeed fear it. But the design of social and political practices can be *itself* a discursive process in which all the relevant subjects can participate. Any conjectures and proposals for model institutions can be offered for validation by these individuals."

3. Following a similar line of argument, Rivlin (1973: 25) has suggested that analysts and decision makers should state what their own positions are "and bring together all of the evidence that supports their side of the argument, leaving to the brief writers of the other side the job of picking apart the case that has been presented and detailing the counter evidence."

4. The ability to logically analyze policies advanced by others also provides insight into the construction of acceptable alternative policies. After organizing a policy argument into its component parts, an analyst may choose to try his or her hand at political consensus formation. Essentially, this involves an attempt to convert a static conception of a policy argument into a dynamic one that has persuasive power. Identifying possible areas of policy consensus and conflict, the analyst designs an alternative policy proposal that addresses the key issues of conflict. The test of the alternative pro-

posal is its ability to stand up to the criticism and objections of the political audiences it must convince or persuade, the breadth of its appeal, the number of views it can synthesize, and so on. In many cases, this means the political analyst must attempt dialectically to move the proposal beyond the narrow defense of a particular argument in order to present a more comprehensive picture of the political situation. Since a narrow argument can be defended only within a limited context of belief, the policy analyst must at times try to offer a new or reformulated view to replace the belief system that impedes the construction of consensus.

5. This line of argument is compatible with those strands of postmodern theory which leave space for collective activity in planning and policy development (Healey, 1993: 235).

6. Attempts to answer such questions all too often work from an overly restrictive distinction between the practices of representative and participatory democracy. Rather than positing the question as a choice between one or the other, it is just as reasonable—and surely more practical—to think of a truly representative system as one undergirded by an authentic system of participatory democracy. That is, a test of a representative system should be the quality of the participatory system which supports it. Such an integration not only avoids the traditional problem confronting radical participatory democracy—namely, how to aggregate a wide range of interests in the hope of arriving at effective decisions—but also the elitist bias that has come to plague representative systems of government cut off from the broad base of their citizenry.

7. Such a politics can take on particular significance in the university. Insofar as the professional schools of the university are primary locations for technocratic training, such strife is at times a major source of concern for those charged with furthering professional ideologies and their technocratic modes of governance.

## EPILOGUE

1. Postmodernists are correct in arguing that Habermas's effort to reconstruct the Enlightenment concept of reason leaves many questions unanswered. His categories, in fact, raise problematic questions at the level of society. Postmodernists have themselves yet to offer a systematic conceptualization of "post-Enlightenment" reason (Ross, 1988). But even if we await a new form of reason, as some postmodernists seem to suggest, it is nonetheless difficult to imagine how, at the level of organizational action, decision making and political strategy could proceed without the analytical categories of rational discourse and consensus formation. Habermas's effort to rescue normatively the concepts of rational action from positivist interpretations represents an unprecedented epistemological advance for those interested in the reconstruction of the organizational and policy sciences. In this respect, the issue appears to be more a matter of how to relate the concept of rational action to a more encompassing form of reason than one of discarding it altogether.

2. The empirical-analytic, interpretive/hermeneutic, and critical/reflective forms of knowledge relate respectively to the three most fundamental categories of a social order (work, communicative interaction, and political power).

3. For Habermas (1971), following Toulmin, practical or "substantial" argu-

ments are the "pragmatic unities" that situate ordinary language sentences in relation to the basic societal categories and their respective cognitive strategies.

4. Although Habermas does not explore this more practical level of the problem, he provides an important insight. The progress of knowledge, he maintains, takes place through explanations or justifications based on a nonpositivistic (nondeductive) "informal" logic.

5. Toulmin demonstrates this point with a reference to John Stuart Mill's defense of liberty. While, as Toulmin puts it, scientists speak of the "proof" of the law of gravity, political philosophers refer not to Mill's "proof" of liberty but rather his "magnificent defense" of it.

6. The use of the term "level" captures the fact that the evaluative framework moves through increasingly abstract evaluative discourses. It in no way refers to more sophisticated questions concerning the nature of reason. The question of whether or not the logical form of normative reasoning is structured in an hierarchical fashion—as opposed, for example, to something more akin to a network—is not an issue to be engaged here.

7. In figure 2, the arrows connecting verification to social choice point upward. This is because the discussion here focuses on the reconstruction of empirical policy analysis and thus begins at the bottom of the diagram with D and C. In general, however, the arrows move in either direction, up or down, depending on the particular issues in question.

8. This pervasive role of theoretical presuppositions on the organization and practice of science has profound implications for the positivist theory of truth. It challenges the conception of empirical "reality" upon which positivism's "correspondence" theory of truth rests, in particular the belief that facts are given, that empirical experience is by its nature funndamentally—or "ontologically"—distinct from the theoretical constructs which are advanced to explain it. Experience, in this alternative view, does not present itself labeled as "empirical," nor does it come self-certified as such. "What we call experience depends upon assumptions hidden beyond scrutiny which define it and which in turn it supports." Recognition "that 'fact' can be so designated only in terms of prior theoretical presuppositions implies that any quest for an unmediated reality is necessarily futile." This means that "the nature of perception and the role of presuppositions preclude direct access" to experience (Hawkesworth, 1988: 55).

9. Toward this end, postpositivism advances what has been called a "coherence theory of truth."

# References

Ackerman, Bruce. 1989. "Why Dialogue?" *Journal of Philosophy,* 86: 5–22.

Advisory Commission on Intergovernmental Relations. 1989. *Disability Rights Mandates: Federal and State Compliance with Employment Protections and Architectural Barrier Removal.* Washington, DC: ACIR.

Aharoni, Yair. 1981. *The No-Risk Society.* Chatham, NJ: Chatham House.

Albinski, Marian. 1986. "Policy-Oriented Theories." *Knowledge,* 8(1): 154–66.

Amy, Douglas, J. 1987. "Can Policy Analysis Be Ethical?" In *Confronting Values in Policy Analysis,* Frank Fischer and John Forester, eds. Newbury Park, CA: Sage.

Anderson, Charles. 1978. "The Logic of Public Problems: Evaluation in Comparative Policy Research." In *Comparing Public Policies,* Douglas E. Ashford, ed. Beverly Hills, CA: Sage.

––––––. 1979. "The Place of Principles in Policy Analysis." *American Political Science Review,* 73: 711–23.

Anderson, Martin. 1990. *Revolution: The Reagan Legacy.* Stanford, CA: Hoover Institution Press.

Andrews, Edmund L. 1991. "Advocates of Disabled File Complaint about the Empire State Building." *New York Times,* Jan. 28, B3.

Andrews, Richard. 1990a. "Risk Assessment: Regulation and Beyond." In *Environmental Policy in the 1990s,* Norman J. Vig and Michael Kraft, eds. Washington, DC: Congressional Quarterly Press.

––––––. 1990b. "Deregulation: The Failure at EPA." In *Environmental Policy in the 1980s: Reagan's New Agenda,* Norman Vig and Michael Kraft, eds. Washington, DC: Congressional Quarterly Press.

Argyris, Chris, et al. 1985. *Action Science.* Cambridge, MA: Harvard Univ. Press.

Asante, Molefi Kete. 1987. *The Afrocentric Idea.* Philadelphia, PA: Temple Univ. Press.

––––––. 1991. "Multiculturism: An Exchange." *American Scholar,* Spring, 299–311.

Bachrach, Peter, and Martin Baratz. 1963. "Decisions and Non-Decisions." *American Political Science Review,* 58: 632–42.

Bahro, Rudolf. 1986. *Building the Green Movement.* London: GMP.

Banfield, Edward C. 1970. *Unheavenly City: The Nature and Future of Our Urban Crisis.* Boston, MA: Little, Brown.

Banfield, Edward C. 1980. "Policy Science as Metaphysical Madness." In *Bureaucrats, Policy Analysis, Statesmen: Who Leads?* Robert A. Goldman, ed. Washington, DC: American Enterprise Institute for Public Policy Research.

Barber, Benjamin R. 1984. *Strong Democracy.* Berkeley: Univ. of California Press.

———. 1991. "The Reconstruction of Rights." *American Prospect,* 5 (Spring): 36–46.

Barnes, Barry. 1985. *About Science.* Oxford: Basil Blackwell.

Baxter, William F. 1986. "People or Penguins: The Case for Optimal Pollution." In *People, Penguins, and Plastic Trees,* Donald Van DeVeer and Christine Pierce, eds. Belmont, CA: Wadsworth.

Beardsley, Philip L. 1980. *Redefining Rigor: Ideology and Statistics in Political Inquiry.* Beverly Hills, CA: Sage.

Beatley, Timothy. 1989. "Environmental Ethics and Planning Theory." *Journal of Planning Literature,* 4 (1) (Winter): 1–32.

Beck, Ulrich. 1993. *The Risk Society.* Newbury Park, CA: Sage.

Bell, Daniel. 1971. "Technocracy and Politics." *Survey,* 16.

———. 1973. *The Coming of Post-Industrial Society.* New York: Basic Books.

Beneveniste, Guy. 1987. "Some Functions and Dysfunctions of Using Professional Elites in Public Policy." In *Research in Public Policy Analysis and Management,* vol. 4, Stuart Nagel, ed. Greenwich, CT: JAI Press.

Benhabib, Seyla. 1982. "The Methodological Illusions of Political Theory: The Case of Rawls and Habermas." *Neue hefte fur Philosophie,* 21: 47–74.

———. 1989-90. "In the Shadows of Aristotle and Hegel: Communicative Ethics and Current Controversies in Practical Philosophy." *Philosophical Form,* 21: 1–31.

Bennett, Douglas. 1986. "Democracy and Public Analysis." In *Research in Public Policy Analysis and Management,* Stuart Nagel, ed. vol. 3. Greenwich, CT: JAI Press.

Berger, Peter L., and Thomas Luckmann. 1966. *The Social Construction of Reality.* Garden City, NY: Doubleday.

Berkowitz, Edward D. 1987. *Disabled Policy: America's Programs for the Handicapped.* Cambridge: Cambridge Univ. Press.

———, and Kim McQuaid, 1992. *Creating the Welfare State: The Political Economy of Twentieth Century Reform,* rev. ed. Lawrence: Univ. Press of Kansas.

Bernstein, Richard J. 1976. *The Restructuring of Social and Political Theory.* New York: Harcourt Brace Jovanovich.

———. 1983. *Beyond Objectivism and Relativism: Science, Hermeneutics, and Praxis.* Philadelphia, PA: Univ. of Philadelphia Press.

Best, Joel, ed. 1989. *Images of Issues: Typifying Contemporary Social Problems.* New York: Aldine de Gruyter.

Bigler, Eric. 1987. "Give Us Jobs, Not Admiration." *Newsweek,* April 1987, 62.

Bingham, James R. 1985. "The 42nd Street Development Project: The City's Perspective." *City Almanac,* Summer, 9–12.

Bleicher, Jospeh. 1980. *Contemporary Hermeneutics*. London: Routledge and Kegan Paul.

Bloom, Allan. 1975. "Justice: John Rawls vs. the Tradition of Political Philosophy." *American Political Science Review*, 69 (June): 648–62.

Bobrow, Davis B., and John S. Dryzek. 1987. *Policy Anlaysis by Design*. Pittsburgh: Univ. of Pittsburgh Press.

Bonnen, J. T. 1969. "The Absence of Knowledge of Distributional Impacts." In *The Analysis and Evaluation of Public Expenditures*, Joint Economic Committee. Washington, DC: U.S. Government Printing Office.

Bookchin, Murray. 1982. *The Ecology of Freedom*. Palo Alto, CA: Cheshire.

Bowers, C. A. 1982. "The Reproduction of Technological Consciousness: Locating the Ideological Foundations of a Radical Pedagogy." *Teachers College Record*, 83 (4): 531.

Bowles, Samuel, and Herbert Gintis. 1976. *Schooling in Capitalist America*. New York: Basic Books.

———. 1986. *Democracy and Capitalism: Property, Community, and the Contradictions of Modern Social Thought*. New York: Basic Books.

Bozeman, Barry. 1979. *Public Management and Policy Analysis*. New York: St. Martin.

Brandon, William P. 1984. "Public Policy as the Continuation of Moral Philosophy by Other Means." *Policy Studies Review*, 4 (Aug.): 60–70.

Brilliant, Eleanor L. 1975. *The Urban Development Corporation*. Lexington, MA: Lexington Books.

Brown, Bernard. 1977. "Long-Term Gains from Early Intervention: An Overview of Current Research." Paper delivered at the annual meeting of the American Association for the Advancement of Science, Feb. 1977.

Brown, Harold. 1977. *Perception, Theory and Commitment: The New Philosophy of Science*. Chicago: Precedent Pub.

Brown, Phil. 1990. "Popular Epidemiology: Community Response to Toxic Waste-Induced Disease." In *The Sociology of Health and Illness in Critical Perspective*, Peter Conrad and Rochelle Kern, eds. New York: St. Martin.

———, and Edwin J. Mikkelsen. 1990. *No Safe Place: Toxic Waste, Leukemia, and Community Action*. Berkeley: Univ. of California Press.

Brown, Richard. 1983. "Theories of Rhetoric and the Rhetoric of Theory: Toward a Political Philosophy of Sociological Truth." *Social Research*, 50 (1): 126–57.

Brulle, Robert, and Thomas Dietz. 1992. "Greening Rhetoric: Beyond Anthropocentrism in Communicative Studies." Paper presented at the Conference on Academic Knowledge and Power, University of Maryland, College Park, Nov. 21.

Bruner, J. 1987. "Life as Narrative." *Social Research*, 54 (1): 11–32.

Brzezinski, Zbigniew. 1976. *Between Two Ages: America's Role in the Technetronic Era*. New York: Viking.

Burghardt, Steve, and Michael Fabricant. 1987. *Working under the Safety Net: Policy and Practice with the New American Poor*. Beverly Hills, CA: Sage.

Caldwell, Bruce. 1982. *Beyond Positivism*. London: Allen and Unwin.

Campbell, Donald T., and Julian C. Stanley. 1963. *Experimental and Quasi-Experimental Designs for Research*. Chicago: Rand McNally.

Cancian, Francesca, and Cathleen Armstead. 1992. "Participatory Research." *Encyclopedia of Sociology*, E. F. Borgatta and Maria L. Borgatta, eds. New York: Macmillan.

Caplan, Nathan, et al. 1975. *The Use of Social Science Knowledge in Policy Decisions at the National Level*. Ann Arbor: Institute for Social Research, University of Michigan.

Capra, Fritjof, and Charlene Spretnak. 1984. *Green Politics*. London: Hutchinson.

Carini, Patricia F. 1975. *Observation and Description: An Alternative Methodology for the Investigation of Human Phenomena*. Grand Forks: Univ. of North Dakota Press.

Carroll, William K. 1992. *Organizing Dissent: Contemporary Social Movements in Theory and Practice*. Toronto: Garamond Press.

Catton, William R, Jr., and Dunlap E. Riley. 1980. "A New Ecological Paradigm for Post-Exuberant Sociology." *American Behavioral Scientist*, 24 (1): 15–47.

Chess, Caron, and Peter M. Sandman. 1989. "Community Use of Quantitative Risk Assessment." *Science for the People*, Jan.-Feb.: 20.

Churchman, C. West. 1968. *The Systems Approach*. New York: Dell.

———. 1971. *The Design of Inquiry Systems*. New York: Basic Books.

———, and A. H. Schainblatt. 1969. "PPBS: How Can It Be Implemented?" *Public Administration Review*, 29 (March/April): 178–89.

Cohen, Joshua, and Joel Rogers. 1983. *On Democracy*. New York: Penguin.

Collette, Will. 1987. *How to Deal with a Proposed Facility*. Arlington, VA: Citizen's Clearinghouse for Hazardous Wastes.

Commoner, Barry. 1972. *The Closing Circle*. New York: Bantam.

Conn, George A. 1982. "New Concepts and Directions in Rehabilitation." *American Rehabilitation*, 7: 18–20.

Connolly, William. 1987. "Modern Authority and Ambiguity." In *Authority Revisited*, J. Roland Pennock and John W. Chapman, eds. New York: New York Univ. Press.

Coudroglou, Aliki, and Dennis L. Poole. 1984. *Disability, Work, and Social Policy: Models for Social Welfare*. New York: Springer.

Counts, Robert. 1978. *Independent Living: Rehabilitation for Severely Handicapped People*. Washington, DC: Urban Institute.

Covello, Vincent T. 1993. Risk Assessment Methods. New York: Plenum Press.

Crouch, E., and R. Wilson. 1982. *Risk/Benefit Analysis*. Cambridge, MA: Ballinger.

Daro, Deborah. 1988. *Confronting Child Abuse: Research for Effective Program Design*. New York: Free Press.

Davis, Charles E. 1993. *The Politics of Hazardous Waste*. Englewood Cliffs, NJ: Prentice-Hall.

Dear, Michael. 1992. "Understanding and Overcoming the NIMBY Syndrome." *Journal of the American Planning Association*, 58 (Summer): 288–300.

deHaven-Smith, Lance. 1988. *Philosophical Critique of Policy Analysis: Lindblom, Habermas, and the Great Society*. Gainesville: Univ. of Florida Press.

deLeon, Peter. 1989. *Advice and Consent: The Development of the Policy Sciences*. New York: Russell Sage Foundation.

————. 1992. "The Democratization of the Policy Sciences." *Public Administration Review,* 52 (March-April): 125–29.

DeLoach, Charlen P., Ronnie D. Wilkins, and Guy W. Walker. 1983. *Independent Living: Philosophy, Process, and Services.* Baltimore, MD: University Park Press.

DeParle, Jason. 1993a. "Social Investment Programs: Comparing the Past with the Promised Payoff." *New York Times,* March 2, A1.

————. 1993b. "Sharp Criticism for Head Start, Even by Friends." *New York Times,* March 19, A18.

Derthick, Martha. 1987. "The Plight of the Social Security Administration." In *Social Security after Fifty,* Edward D. Berkowitz, ed. Westport, CT: Greenwood.

Diesing, Paul. 1962. *Reason in Society: Five Types of Decisions in Their Social Contexts.* Urbana: Univ. of Illinois Press.

————. 1967. "Noneconomic Decision-Making." In *Organizational Decision-Making,* Marcus Alexis and Charles Wilson, eds. Englewood Cliffs, NJ: Prentice-Hall.

DiPerna, Paula. 1985. *Cluster Mystery: Epidemic and the Children of Woburn.* St. Louis, MO: Mosby.

"Disabled Find a Voice and Make Sure It Is Heard." 1990. *New York Times,* March 14.

"Disabled-Rights Bill Inspires Hope, Fear." 1990. *Wall Street Journal,* May 21, B1.

Dobson, Andrew. 1990. *Green Political Thought.* London: Unwin Hyman.

Dobuzinski, Laurent. 1992. "Modernist and Postmodern Metaphors of the Policy Process: Control and Stability vs. Chaos and Reflexive Understanding." *Policy Sciences,* 25: 355–80.

Dodd, Lawrence C. 1991. "Congress, the Presidency, and the American Experience: A Transformational Perspective." In *Divided Government,* James A. Thurber, ed. Washington, DC: Congressional Quarterly Press.

Doherty, Joe, Elspeth Graham, and Mo Malek, eds. 1992. *Postmodernism and the Social Sciences.* New York: St. Martin.

Dolbeare, Kenneth M., and Patricia Dolbeare. 1976. *American Ideologies.* New York: Random House.

Donovan, John C. 1967. *The Politics of Poverty.* New York: Pegasus.

————. 1970. *The Policy Makers.* New York: Pegasus.

Douglas, Mary, and Aaron Wildavsky. 1982. *Risk and Culture.* Berkeley: Univ. of California Press.

Dryzek, John S. 1982. "Policy Analysis as a Hermeneutic Activity." *Policy Sciences,* 14: 309–29.

————. 1987. *Rational Ecology: Environment and the Political Economy.* New York: Basel Blackwell.

————. 1990a. *Discursive Democracy.* Cambridge: Cambridge Univ. Press.

————. 1990b. "Designs for Environmental Discourse: The Greening of the Administrative State?" In *Managing Leviathan: Environmental Politics and the Administrative State,* Robert Paehlke and Douglas Torgerson, eds. Peterborough, Ontario: Broadway Press.

Dubnick, Melvin J., and Barbara A. Bardes. 1983. *Thinking about Public Policy: A Problem-Solving Approach.* New York: Wiley.

Dugger, Celia W. 1991. "Yes, New York City Plans Sidewalk Toilets." *New York Times,* June 27, B1.

Dunlap, David W. 1992. "Long Delay Likely in Rebuilding Plan for Times Square." *New York Times,* Aug. 3, 1.
_____. 1993. Choreographing Times Sq. into 21st Century. *New York Times,* Sept. 16, B1.
Dunn, William N. 1981. *Public Policy Analysis.* Englewood Cliffs, NJ: Prentice-Hall.
_____. 1988. "Methods of the Second Type: Coping with the Wilderness of Conventional Policy Analysis." *Policy Studies Review,* 9:720–37.
Durning, Dan. 1993. "Participatory Policy Analysis in a Georgia State Agency." *Journal of Policy Analysis and Management,* 12 (2): 297–322.
Dutton, Diana. 1984. "The Impact of Public Participation in Biomedical Policy: Evidence from Four Case Studies. In *Citizen Participation in Science Policy,* James C. Peterson, ed. Amherst: Univ. of Massachusetts Press.
Dworkin, Ronald. 1977. *Taking Rights Seriously.* Cambridge, MA: Harvard Univ. Press.
Dye, Thomas R. 1984. *Understanding Public Policy.* Englewood Cliffs, NJ: Prentice-Hall.

Edelman, Murray. 1988. *Constructing the Political Spectacle.* Chicago, IL: Univ. of Chicago Press.
Edelstein, Michael R. 1988. *Contaminated Communities.* Boulder, CO: Westview.
Elder, Charles D., and Roger W. Cobb. 1984. "Agenda-Building and the Politics of Aging." *Policy Studies Journal,* 13 (1): 115–29.
Eldon, Max. 1981. "Sharing the Research Work: Participatory Research and Its Role Demands." In *Human Inquiry,* Peter Reason and John Rowan, eds. New York: Wiley.
Elliot, Michael L. Poirier. 1984. "Improving Community Acceptance of Hazardous Waste Facilities Through Alternative Systems of Mitigating and Managing Risk." *Hazardous Waste,* 1: 397–410.
Emickie, William. 1991. "Housing New York: The Creation and Development of the Battery Park City Authority. In *Public Authorities and Public Policy: The Business of Government,* Jerry Mitchell, ed. New York: Greenwood.
Eulau, Heinz. 1977. *Technology and Civility.* Stanford, CA: Hoover Institution.

Fainstein, Susan. 1987. "The Politics of Criteria: Planning for the Redevleopment of Times Square." In *Confronting Values in Policy Analysis,* Frank Fischer and John Forester, eds. Newbury Park, CA: Sage.
_____. 1993. *The City Builders: Property, Politics and Planning in London and New York.* Cambridge, MA: Blackwell.
Falco, Maria J. 1973. *Truth and Meaning in Political Science.* Columbus, OH: Merrill.
Fals-Borda, Orlando, and Mohammad A. Rahman, eds. 1991. *Action and Knowledge: Breaking the Monopoly with Participatory Action-Research.* New York: Apex Press.
Fay, Brian. 1975. *Social Theory and Political Process.* New York: Holmes and Meier.
Fernandes, Walter, and Rajesh Tandon, eds. 1981. *Participatory Research and Evaluation: Experiments in Research as a Process in Asia.* New Delhi: Indian Social Institute.

Fischer, Frank. 1980. *Politics, Values, and Public Policy: The Problem of Methodology.* Boulder, CO: Westview.

———. 1982. "Science and Critique in Political Discourse: Elements of a Postpositivist Methodology." *New Political Science,* 3 (9/10) (Summer/Fall): 3–32.

———. 1985. "Critical Evaluation of Public Policy: A Methodological Case Study." In *Critical Theory and Public Life,* John Forester, ed. Cambridge, MA: MIT Press.

———. 1987. "Policy Expertise and the 'New Class': A Critique of the Neoconservative Thesis. In *Confronting Values in Policy Analysis: The Politics of Criteria,* Frank Fischer and John Forester, eds. Newbury Park, CA: Sage.

———. 1990. *Technocracy and the Politics of Expertise.* Newbury Park, CA: Sage.

———. 1991a. "American Think Tanks: Policy Elites and the Politicization of Expertise." *Governance,* 4 (3): 332–53.

———. 1991b. "Risk Assessment and Environmental Crisis: Toward an Integration of Science and Participation." *Industrial Crisis Quarterly,* 5: 113–32.

———. 1992. "Participatory Expertise: Toward the Democratization of Policy Science." In *Advances in Policy Studies since 1950,* W. Dunn and R. Kelly, eds. New Brunswick, NJ: Transaction.

———. 1993a. "Reconstructing Policy Analysis: A Postpositivist Perspective." *Policy Sciences,* 25: 333–39.

———. 1993b. "Citizen Participation and the Democratization of Policy Expertise: From Political Theory to Practical Cases." *Policy Sciences,* 26 (3): 165–87.

——— and John Forester. 1993. *The Argumentative Turn in Policy Analysis and Planning.* Durham, NC: Duke Univ. Press.

Fishkin, James. 1983. *Justice, Equal Opportunity and the Family.* New Haven, CT: Yale Univ. Press.

Fitz-Gibbon, Carol T., Lynn L. Morris and Elaine Lindheim. 1987. *How to Measure Performance and Use Tests.* Newbury Park, CA: Sage.

Flathman, Richard E. 1966. *The Public Interest: Essays on Normative Discourse in Politics.* New York: Wiley.

Fogleman, Valerie. 1990. *Guide to the National Environmental Policy Act: Interpretations, Applications, and Compliance.* New York: Quorum.

Forester, John. 1989. *Planning in the Face of Power.* Berkeley: Univ. of California Press.

Forrester, Jay. 1971. *Urban Dynamics.* Cambridge, MA: Wright-Allen Press.

Foucault, Michel. 1972. *Power/Knowledge.* New York: Pantheon.

———. 1973. *The Order of Things.* New York: Vintage Books.

Fowler, Floyd J. 1988. *Survey Research Methods.* Newbury Park, CA: Sage.

Fox, Martin. 1989. "Litigating Times Square: Eight Years and Counting." *New York Law Journal,* 201 (Feb. 27): 1, 3.

Freire, Paulo. 1973. *Education for Critical Consciousness.* New York: Seabury.

———. 1979. *Pedagogy of the Oppressed.* New York: Seabury.

French, Peter. 1983. *Ethics in Government.* Englewood Cliffs, NJ: Prentice-Hall.

Frieden, Bernard J., and Lynne R. Sagalyn. 1989. *Downtown, Inc.: How America Rebuilds Cities.* Cambridge, MA: MIT Press.

Friedman, Josh Alan. 1986. *Tales of Times Square.* New York: Delcorte.

Friedmann, John. 1987. *Planning in the Public Domain*. Princeton, NJ: Princeton Univ. Press.

Frohock, Fred. 1979. *Public Policy: Scope and Logic*. Englewood Cliffs, NJ: Prentice-Hall.

Fromm, Erich. 1963. *The Sane Society*. London: Routledge and Kegan Paul.

Galbraith, John Kenneth. 1967. *The New Industrial State*. Boston, MA: Houghton Mifflin.

Gans, Herbert J. 1968. *More Equality*. New York: Pantheon.

———. 1982. *The Urban Villagers*. New York: Free Press.

Gastil, Raymond D. 1977. *Social Humanities*. San Francisco, CA: Jossey-Bass.

Gaventa, John. 1980. *Power and Powerlessness: Quiescence and Rebellion in an Appalachian Valley*. Urbana: Univ. of Illinois Press.

———. 1988. "Participatory Research in North America." *Convergence*, 21: 19–29.

Geertz, Clifford. 1973. *The Interpretation of Cultures*. New York: Basic Books.

Geuss, Raymond. 1981. *The Idea of Critical Theory*. New York: Cambridge Univ. Press.

Gibbs, Lois Marie. 1982. *Love Canal: My Story*. Albany: State Univ. of New York Press.

Gilder, George. 1981. *Wealth and Poverty*. New York: Basic Books.

Ginsberg, Benjamin. 1982. *The Consequences of Consent: Elections, Citizen Control, and Popular Acquiescence*. New York: Addison-Wesley.

Goldstein, Jack L. 1985. "Development and the Threat to the Theater District." *City Almanac*, Summer, pp. 23–24.

Goodin, Robert E. 1992. *Green Political Theory*. London: Polity.

Goodman, Paul, and Percival Goodman. 1960. *Communitas*. New York: Vintage Books.

Goodman, Robert. 1971. *After the Planners*. New York: Simon and Schuster.

Goodson, Barbara Dillion, and Robert D. Hess. 1977. "The Effects of Parent Training Programs on Child Performance and Parent Behavior." Paper delivered at the annual meeting of the American Association for the Advancement of Science, Denver, Feb..

Gordon, Edmund W. 1972. "Guidance in the Urban Setting." In *Opening Opportunities for Disadvantaged Learners*, Harry Passow, ed., pp. 213–24. New York: Teachers College Press.

Gordon, Kermit. 1975. *Equality and Efficiency: The Big Trade-off*, Arthur M. Okun, ed. Washington, DC: Brookings Institution.

Gottlieb, Benjamin, and Andrew Farquharson. 1985. "Blueprint for a Curriculum on Social Support." *Social Policy*, Winter, 31–34.

Gouldner, Alvin. 1970. *The Coming Crisis of Western Sociology*. New York: Avon. .

———. 1979. *The Future of the Intellectuals and the Rise of the New Class*. New York: Oxford Univ. Press.

Graham, Elinor. 1965. "The Politics of Poverty." In *The Great Society Reader: The Failure of American Liberalism*, Marvin Gettleman and David Mermelstein, eds. New York: Vintage Books.

Gramlich, Edward M. 1990. *A Guide to Benefit-Cost Analysis*. Englewood Cliffs, NJ: Prentice-Hall.

Gratz, Roberta Brandes. 1989. *The Living City: How Urban Residents Are Revitalizing America's Neighborhoods and Downtown Shopping Districts by Thinking Small in Big Way*. New York: Touchstone.

Grauhan, Rolf-Richard, and Wendelin Strubelt. 1971. "Political Rationality Reconsidered: Notes on an Integrated Scheme for Policy Choice." *Policy Sciences*, 2: 270.

Green Program, The. 1991. Greens (USA).

Greenwalt, R. Kent. 1983. *Discrimination and Reverse Discrimination*, New York: Knopf.

Gross, Barry, ed. 1977. *Reverse Discrimination*. New York: Prometheus Books.

Gross, Bertram M., and Michael Springer, eds. 1970. "Political Intelligence for America's Future." *The Annals*, 388 (March).

Guba, Egon, and Yvonna S. Lincoln. 1981. *Effective Evaluation*. San Francisco, CA: Jossey-Bass.

―――. 1987. "The Countenances of Fourth-Generation Evaluation: Description, Judgment and Negotiation." In *The Politics of Program Evaluation*, Denis J. Palumbo, ed. Newbury Park, CA: Sage.

Gunnell, John G. 1968. "Social Science and Political Reality: The Problem of Explanation." *Social Research*, 35 (Spring): 187-200.

Gusfield, Joseph. 1981. *The Culture of Public Problems*. Chicago, IL: Univ. of Chicago Press.

Gutin, Joann. 1991. "At Our Peril: The False Promise of Risk Assessment." *Greenpeace*, 4 (March/April): 13–18.

Habermas, Jürgen. 1970. *Toward a Rational Society*. Boston, MA: Beacon Press.

―――. 1971. *Knowledge and Human Interest*. Boston, MA: Beacon Press.

―――. 1973. *Legitimation Crisis*. Boston, MA: Beacon Press.

―――. 1979. *Communication and the Evolution of Society*. Boston, MA: Beacon Press.

―――. 1990. *Moral Consciousness and Communicative Action*. Cambridge, MA: MIT Press.

Hahn, Harlan. 1987. "Advertising the Acceptably Employable Image: Disability and Capitalism." *Policy Studies Journal*, 15 (March): 552-65.

Hajer, Maarten. 1993. *The Politics of Environmental Discourse*. Oxford: Oxford Univ. Press.

Hardin, Garrett. 1968. "The Tragedy of the Commons." *Science*, 162: 1243–48.

Harmon, Michael M., and Richard Mayer. 1986. *Organization Theory for Public Administration*. Boston: Little, Brown.

Harrison, Bennett. 1974. *Urban Economic Development: Suburbanization, Minority Opportunity, and the Condition of the Central City*. Washington, DC: Urban Institute Press.

Harsanyi, John. 1975. "Can the Maximin Principle Serve as the Basis for Morality?" *American Political Science Review*, 69 (June): 594–606.

Hart, David K. 1974. "Social Equity, Justice, and the Equitable Administrator." *Public Administration Review*, 34 (Jan./Feb.): 3–17.

Harvey, David. 1989. *The Condition of Postmodernity: An Enquiry into the Origins of Cultural Change*. Oxford: Blackwell.

Haveman, Robert H., and Burton A. Weisbrod. 1975. "Defining Benefits of Public Programs: Some Guidelines for Policy Analysts." *Policy Analysis*, 1: 171.

Hawkesworth, M. E. 1988. *Theoretical Issues in Policy Analysis*. Albany, NY: State Univ. of New York Press.

————. 1992. "Epistemology and Policy Analysis." In *Advances in Policy Studies Since 1950*, William N. Dunn and Rita Mae Kelly, eds. New Brunswick, NJ: Transaction.

Healey, Patsy. 1993. "Planning Through Debate: The Communicative Turn in Planning Theory." In *The Argumentative Turn in Policy Analysis and Planning*, Frank Fischer and John Forester, eds. Durham, NC: Duke Univ. Press.

Heclo, Hugh. 1972. "Policy Analysis." *British Journal of Political Science*, 2 (Jan.): 85-112.

Heilbroner, Robert. 1974. *An Inquiry into the Human Prospect*. New York: Harper and Row.

Heineman, Robert A., William T. Bluhm, Steven A. Peterson, and Edward N. Kearny. 1990. *The World of the Policy Analyst: Rationality, Values, and Politics*. Chatham, NJ: Chatham House.

Hennessey, Timothy M., and Richard H. Feen. 1974. "Social Science as Social Philosophy: Edward C. Banfield and the 'New Realism' in Urban Politics." In *Varieties of Political Conservatism*, Matthew Holden, Jr., ed. Beverly Hills, CA: Sage.

Henry, Nicholas. 1975. *Public Administration and Public Affairs*. Englewood Cliffs, NJ: Prentice-Hall.

Hexter, J. H. 1971. *Doing History*. Bloomington Indiana Univ. Press.

Himmelfarb, Gertrude. 1987. *The New History and the Old*. Cambridge, MA: Belknap Press.

Hirschhorn, Larry. 1979. "Alternative Service and the Crisis of the Professions." In *Co-ops, Communes and Collectives: Experiments in Social Change in the 1960s and 1970s*, John Case and Rosemary C. R. Taylor, eds. New York: Pantheon: 153–93.

Hiskes, Ann L., and Richard Hiskes. 1986. *Science, Technology, and Policy Decisions*. Boulder, CO: Westview.

Hiss, Tony. 1990. *The Experience of Place*. New York: Knopf.

Hofferbert, Richard I. 1990. *The Reach and Grasp of Policy Analysis*. Tuscaloosa: Univ. of Alabama Press.

Hofmann, Jeanette. 1993. *Implizite Theorien in der Politik: Interpretationsprobleme Regionaler Technologiepolitik*. Opladen: Westdeutscher Verlag.

Holmes, Steven A. 1990. "Disabled People Say Home Care Is Needed to Use New Rights." *New York Times*, Oct. 14, p. 22.

————. 1991. "U.S. Rules Would Force Businesses to Make Alternatives for the Disabled." *New York Times*, Feb. 22, p. A14.

————. 1991. "U.S. Proposes Rules on Disabled in the Workplace." *New York Times*, March 12, p. A19.

Hoogstraten, Nicholas Van. 1991. *Lost Broadway Theaters*. New York: Princeton Architectural Press.

Hoppe, Rob, and Aat Peterse. 1993. *Handling Frozen Fire*. Boulder, CO: Westview.

Hughes, Robert. 1992. "The Fraying of America." *Time*, Feb. 3, pp. 44–49.

Huntington, Samuel. 1981. *American Politics: The Promise of Disharmony*. Cambridge, MA: Belknap Press.

Hyman, Eric, and Bruce Stiefel. 1988. *Combining Facts and Values in Environmental Impact Assessment*. Boulder, CO: Westview.


Ingram, Patricia. 1987. "Toward More Systematic Consideration of Policy Design." *Policy Studies Journal*, 9: 611–28.

International Center for the Disabled. 1986. *The ICD Survey of Disabled Americans: Bringing Disabled Americans into the Mainstream*. New York: Louis Harris.

———. 1987. *The ICD Survey II: Employing Disabled Americans*. New York: Louis Harris.


Jarvie, I. C. 1972. "The Logic of the Situation." In *Concepts and Society*. London: Routledge and Kegan Paul.

Jay, Martin. 1973. *The Dialectical Imagination*. Boston, MA: Little, Brown.

Jenkins, W. I. 1978. *Policy Analysis: A Political and Organizational Perspective*. New York: St. Martin.

Jennings, Bruce. 1987. "Policy Analysis: Science, Advocacy, or Counsel?" In *Research in Public Policy Analysis and Management*, vol. 4, S. S. Nagel, ed. Greenwich, CT: Jai Press.

———. 1990. Possibilities of Consensus: Toward Democratic Moral Discourse. Unpublished paper.

———. 1991. "Ethical Frameworks in Public Administration: Moral Reasoning Versus Moral Judgment." Paper presented at the annual meeting of the New York State Political Science Association, May.

Jernigan, Kenneth. 1979. "Blindness: Is the Public Against Us?" In *The Blind and Physically Handicapped in Competitive Employment: A Guide to Compliance*. Baltimore, MD: National Federation of the Blind.

Job Accommodation Network. 1987. *Job Accommodation Network Evaluation Report: Executive Summary*. Morgantown: West Virginia Univ.

Johnson, Kurt L. 1986. *Incentives and Disincentives in the Vocational Rehabilitation Process*. Washington, DC: Catholic Univ. of America.


Kamieniecki, Sheldon, Robert O'Brien, and Michael Clarke. 1986. "Political Philosophy, Pragmatic Politics, and Environmental Decision Making." In *Controversies in Environmental Policy*, Sheldon Kamieniecki, Robert O'Brien, and Michael Clarke, eds. Albany: State Univ. of New York Press.

Kahn, Mark E. 1986. "Environmental Democracy in the United States." In *Controversies in Environmental Policy*, Sheldon Kamieniecki, Robert O'Brien, and Michael Clarke, eds. Albany: State Univ. of New York Press.

Kaplan, Abraham. 1964. *The Conduct of Inquiry: Methodology for Behavioral Science*. Scranton, PA: Chandler.

Kassan, Yusuf, and Kemal Mustafa, eds. 1982. *Participatory Research: An Emerging Alternative in Social Science Research.* Nairobi: African Adult Education.

Katzman, Robert A. 1986. *Institutional Disability: The Saga of Transportation Policy for the Disabled,* Washington, DC: Brookings Institution.

Kelling, George L., et al. 1974. *The Kansas City Prevention Patrol Experiment.* Washington, DC: Police Foundation.

Kelly, Marisa, and Steven Maynard-Moody. 1993. "Policy Analysis in the Post-Positivist Era: Engaging Stakeholders in Evaluating the Economic Development Districts Program." *Public Administration Review,* 53 (2): 135–42.

Kelman, Steven. 1982. *Cost-Benefit Analysis and Environmental Regulation: Politics, Ethics, and Methods.* Washington, DC: Conservation Foundation.

Kemeny, John, "Saving American Democracy: The Lessons of Three Mile Island." *Technology Review,* 83 (7) (June-July) 10–17.

Kennedy, Paul M. 1993. *Preparing for the Twenty-First Century.* New York: Random House.

Kitshelt, Herbert. 1989. "Explaining Contemporary Social Movements: An Exploration in the Comparison of Theories." Paper delivered at the American Political Science Association meeting, Atlanta, GA, Aug.-Sept.

Kolata, Gina. 1991. "Saying Life Is Not Enough, the Disabled Demand Rights and Choices." *New York Times,* Jan. 31, p. B7.

Kornblum, William (Project Director, West 42nd Street Study). 1979. "The Bright Lights Zone." City University of New York Graduate School and University Center.

————, and Vernon Boggs. 1985. "Redevelopment and the Night Frontier." *City Almanac,* Summer, pp. 16–18.

Kotz, Nick. 1981. "Citizens as Experts." *Working Papers,* March-April, pp. 42–48.

Kuhn, Thomas. 1970. *The Structure of Scientific Revolutions.* Chicago, IL: Univ. of Chicago Press.


Laird, Frank. 1993. "Participatory Analysis, Democracy, and Technological Decision Making." *Science, Technology, and Human Values,* 18 (3): 341–61.

Lampman, Robert J. 1965. "Approaches to the Reduction of Poverty." *American Economic Review,* 55: 521–29.

Lasswell, Harold. 1951. "The Policy Orientation." In *The Policy Sciences: Recent Developments in Scope and Methods,* David Lerner and Harold Lasswell, eds. Stanford, CA: Stanford Univ. Press.

————, and Abraham Kaplan. 1950. *Power and Society.* New Haven, CT: Yale Univ. Press.

Leeson, Susan A. 1979. "Philosophical Implications of the Ecological Crisis: The Authoritarian Challenge to Liberalism." *Polity,* 11 (3) (Spring): 303–18.

Leiss, William. 1974. *The Domination of Nature.* Boston, MA: Beacon Press.

Lerner, Daniel, and Harold Lasswell, eds. 1951. *The Policy Sciences: Recent Developments in Scope and Methods.* Stanford, CT: Stanford Univ. Press.

Levine, Adeline. 1982. *Love Canal: Science, Politics, and People.* Boston, MA: Lexington.

Levitan, Sar A. 1969. *The Great Society's Poor Law: A New Approach to Poverty.* Baltimore, MD: Johns Hopkins Univ. Press.

Levy, John M. 1990. *Economic Development Programs for Counties and Towns.* New York: Praeger.

Lewis, Oscar. 1959. *Five Families: Mexican Case Studies in the Culture of Poverty.* New York: Basic Books.

Leys, Wayne A. R. 1962. *Ethics for Policy Decisions: The Art of Asking Deliberate Questions.* Englewood Cliffs, NJ: Prentice-Hall.

Liachowitz, Claire H. 1988. *Disability Policy as a Social Construct: Legislative Roots.* Philadelphia: Univ. of Pennsylvania Press.

Lin, Nan. 1976. *Foundations of Social Research.* New York: McGraw-Hill.

Lillienfeld, Abraham. 1980. *Foundations of Epidemiology.* New York: Oxford Univ. Press.

Lindblom, Charles E. 1968. *The Policy-Making Process.* Englewood Cliffs, NJ: Prentice-Hall.

_____. 1977. *Politics and Markets.* New York: Basic Books.

_____, and David K. Cohen. 1979. *Usable Knowledge: Social Science and Social Problem-Solving.* New Haven, CT: Yale Univ. Press.

Long, Norton. 1962. "Administrative Communication." In *Concepts and Issues in Administrative Behavior,* Sidney Mailick and Edward H. Van Ness, eds. Englewood Cliffs, NJ: Prentice-Hall.

Lopes, L. L. 1987. "The Rhetoric of Irrationality." Paper presented at the Colloquium on Mass Communications, Univ. of Wisconsin, Nov. 19.

Lowi, Theodore J. 1969. *The End of Liberalism.* New York: Norton.

McCarthy, Thomas. 1978. *The Critical Theory of Jürgen Habermas.* Cambridge, MA: MIT Press.

McClelland, David C. 1961. *The Achieving Society.* Princeton, NJ: Van Nostrand.

McCloud, Darlene. 1985. "Preserving the Core of the Big Apple." *City Almanac,* Summer, pp. 19–21.

McCollough, Thomas. 1991. *The Moral Imagination: Raising the Ethical Question.* Chatham, NJ: Chatham House.

McCoy, Charles A., and John Playford. 1967. *Apolitical Politics: A Critique of Behavioralism.* New York: Thomas Y. Crowell.

McHugh, Peter. 1968. *Defining the Situation: The Organization of Meaning in Social Interaction.* New York: Bobbs-Merrill.

MacIver, Robert M. 1942. *Social Causation.* Boston, MA: Ginn.

McLellan, David. 1986. *Ideology.* St. Paul: Univ. of Minnesota Press.

MacRae, Duncan, Jr. 1976. *The Social Function of Social Science.* New Haven, CT: Yale Univ. Press.

Majone, Giandomenico. 1989. *Evidence, Argument and Persuasion in the Policy Process.* New Haven, CT: Yale Univ. Press.

Manfred, Stanley. 1978. *The Technological Consciousness: Survival and Dignity in an Age of Expertise.* Chicago, IL: Univ. of Chicago Press.

Mangham, Ian L., and Michael A. Overington. 1983. "Dramatism and Theatrical Metaphor." In *Beyond Method: Strategies for Social Research,* Gareth Morgan, ed. Newbury Park, CA: Sage.

Maquire, Patricia. 1987. *Doing Participatory Research: A Feminist Approach.* Amherst, MA: Center for International Education.

Marcuse, Herbert. 1964. *One-Dimensional Man.* Boston, MA: Beacon.

Marris, Peter, and Martin Rein. 1967. *Dilemmas of Social Reform: Poverty and Community Action in the United States.* New York: Atherton.

Mashaw, Jerry L. 1983. *Bureaucratic Justice: Managing Social Security Disability Claims.* New Haven, CT: Yale Univ. Press.

Mason, Richard, and Ian Mitroff. 1981. *Challenging Strategic Planning Assumptions.* New York: Wiley.

Mazmanian, Daniel, and David Morell. 1992. *Beyond Superfailure: America's Toxics Policy for the 1900s.* Boulder, CO: Westview.

———. 1993. "The 'NIMBY' Syndrome: Facility Siting and the Failure of Democratic Discourse." In *Environmental Policy for the 1990s,* Michael Kraft and Norman Vig, eds. Washington, DC: Congressional Quarterly Press.

Merrifeld, Juliet. 1989. *Putting the Scientists in Their Place: Participatory Research in Environmental and Occupational Health.* New Market, TN: Highlander Center.

Merton, Robert, K. 1957. *Social Theory and Social Structure.* New York: Free Press.

Meyers, William R. 1981. *The Evaluation Enterprise.* San Francisco, CA: Jossey-Bass.

Miller, Eugene F. 1972. "Positivism, Historicism, and Political Inquiry." *American Political Science Review,* 66 (Sept.): 817.

Miller, Nathan. 1983. *F.D.R.: An Intimate History.* New York: Meridian.

Miller, Richard. 1976. "Rawls and Marxism." In *Reading Rawls,* Norman Daniels, ed. New York: Basic Books.

Mitchell, Joyce, and William Mitchell. 1986. "Policy Analysis: The Elementary Uses of Efficiency." In *Research in Public Policy Analysis and Management,* vol 3, Stuart Nagel, ed. Greenwich CT: Jai Press.

Mitroff, Ian I., Richard O. Mason, and Vincent P. Barabba. 1983. *The 1980 Census: Policymaking amid Turbulence.* Lexington, MA: Lexington Books.

Morgan, Richard E. 1986. *Disabling America: The "Rights" Industry in Our Time.* New York: Basic Books.

Moynihan, Daniel P., ed. 1968. *On Understanding Poverty.* New York: Basic Books.

Mueller, Dennis C. 1979. *Public Choice.* Cambridge: Cambridge Univ. Press.

Mumford, Lewis. 1970. *The Culture of Cities.* New York: Harcourt, Brace, Janovich.

Murray, Charles. 1984. *Losing Ground: American Social Policy, 1950–1980.* New York: Manhattan Institute for Policy Research.

Muschamp, Herbert. 1992. "Time to Reset the Clock in Times Square." *New York Times,* Nov. 1, p. 1.

———. 1993. "42nd Street Plan: Be Bold or Begone!" *New York Times,* Sept. 19, p. H33.

Nathan, Richard P. 1985. "Research Lessons from the Great Society." *Journal of Policy Analysis and Management,* 2 (3).

———. 1986. "Social Sciences and the Great Society." In *The Great Society and Its Legacy: Twenty Years of U.S. Public Policy,* Marshall Kaplan and Peggy Cuciti, eds. Durham, NC: Duke Univ. Press.

———. 1988. *Social Science in Government: Uses and Abuses.* New York: Basic Books.

National Council on the Handicapped. 1986. *Toward Independence: An Assessment of Federal Laws and Programs Affecting Persons with Disabilities—With Legislative Recommendations: A Report to the President.* Washington, DC: National Council on the Handicapped.

National Research Council. 1989. *Improving Risk Communication.* Washington, DC: National Academy Press.

New York State Urban Development Corporation. 1981. *42nd Street Redevelopment Project: A Discussion Document.*

———. 1984. *42nd Street Development Project: Final Environmental Impact Statement,* vols. 1 and 2.

———. 1990. *Annual Report.*

Noble, Charles. 1987. "Economic Theory in Practice: White House Oversight of OSHA Health Standards." In *Confronting Values in Policy Analysis: The Politics of Criteria,* Frank Fischer and John Forester, eds. Newbury Park, CA: Sage.


Oberman, Esco. 1965. *A History of Vocational Rehabilitation in America.* Minneapolis, MN: T. S. Denison.

Offe, Claus. 1984. *Contradictions of the Welfare State,* John Keane, ed. Cambridge, MA: MIT Press.

Oi, Walter Y. 1990. "Toward More Crippling Lawsuits and More Dependent Disabled." *Wall Street Journal,* Oct. 13, p. 1.

Okun, Arthur M. 1975. *Equality and Efficiency: The Big Tradeoff.* Washington, DC: Brookings Institution.

Oliver, Michael. 1990. *The Politics of Disablement: A Sociological Approach.* New York: St. Martin.

Ophuls, William. 1977. *Ecology and the Politics of Scarcity.* San Francisco, CA: Freeman.

Optner, Stanford L. 1973. *Systems Analysis.* Harmondsworth: Penguin.

O'Riordan, T. 1981. *Environmentalism.* London: Pion Ltd.

Ostrom, Elinor. 1990. *Governing the Commons: The Evolution of Institutions for Collective Action.* New York: Cambridge Univ. Press.

Ostrom, Vincent, and Elinor Ostrom. 1971. "Public Choice: A Different Approach to the Study of Public Administration." *Public Administration Review,* 31: 203–16.


Paehlke, Robert C. 1989. *Environmentalism and the Future of Progressive Politics.* New Haven, CT: Yale Univ. Press.

———. 1990. "Democracy and Environmentalism: Opening a Door to the Administrative State." In *Managing Leviathan: Environmental Politics and the Administrative State,* Robert Paehlke and Douglas Torgerson, eds. Peterborough, Ontario: Broadway Press, 1990.

————, and Douglas Torgerson, 1991. "Toxic Waste as Public Business." *Canadian Public Administration,* 35 (3) (Fall): 339–62.

Paris, David C., and James F. Reynolds. 1983. *The Logic of Policy Inquiry.* New York: Longman.

Participatory Research Network. 1982. *Participatory Research: An Introduction.* New Delhi: Society for Participatory Research in Asia.

Pateman, Carol. 1970. *Participation and Democratic Theory.* Cambridge: Cambridge Univ. Press.

Patton, Michael Quinn. 1975. *Alternative Evaluation Research Paradigm.* Grand Forks: Univ. of North Dakota Press.

————. 1987. *How to Use Qualitative Methods in Evaluation.* Newbury Park, CA: Sage.

Payne, James S. 1973. *Head Start: A Tragicomedy with Epilogue.* New York: Behavioral Pubns.

Percy, Stephen L. 1989. *Disability, Civil Rights, and Public Policy.* Tuscaloosa: Univ. of Alabama Press.

Piller, Charles. 1991. *The Fail-Safe Society: Community Defiance and the End of American Technological Optimism.* New York: Basic Books.

Piven, Frances Fox, and Richard A, Cloward. 1977. *Poor People's Movements.* New York: Pantheon.

————. 1993. *Regulating the Poor: The Functions of Public Welfare.* New York: Vintage Books.

Plough, Alonso, and Sheldon Krimsky. 1987. "The Emergence of Risk Communication Studies: Social and Political Context." *Science, Technology, and Human Values,* 12 (3-4) (Summer/Fall): 4–10.

Popper, Karl. 1963. *The Open Society and Its Enemies.* Princeton, NJ: Princeton Univ. Press.

————. 1972. *Objective Knowledge: An Evolutionary Approach.* Oxford: Clarendon Press.

————. 1976. "The Logic of the Social Sciences." In *The Postpositivist Dispute in German Sociology,* Theodor W. Adorno, et al., eds. New York: Harper and Row.

Porritt, Jonathon. 1986. *Seeing Green: The Politics of Ecology Explained.* Oxford: Basil Blackwell.

———— and David Winner. 1988. *The Coming of the Greens.* London: Fontana.

Portis, Edward B., and Michael B. Levy, eds. 1988. *Handbook of Political Theory and Policy Science.* New York: Greenwood Press.

Portney, Kent E. 1991. *Siting Hazardous Waste Treatment Facilities: The NIMBY Syndrome.* New York: Auburn House.

Pressman, Jeffrey, and Aaron Wildavsky. 1984. *Implementation.* Berkeley: Univ. of California Press.

Proctor, Richard N. 1991. *Value-free Science? Purity or Power in Modern Knowledge.* Cambridge, MA: Harvard Univ. Press.

Putt, Allen D., and J. Fred Springer. 1989. *Policy Research: Concepts, Methods, and Applications.* New York: Prentice-Hall.

Quade, E. S. 1991. *Analysis for Public Decisions.* New York: Elsevier.

Rabe, Barry G. 1991. "Beyond the NIMBY Syndrome in Hazardous Waste Facility Siting: The Albertan Breakthrough and the Prospects for Cooperation in Canada and the United States." *Governance*, 4 (April): 184–206.

———. 1992. "When Siting Works, Canada-Style." *Journal of Health Politics, Policy and Law*, 17: 119–42.

Raloff, J. 1984. "Woburn Survey Becomes a Model for Low-Cost Epidemiology." *Science News*, Feb. 18, p. 1.

Rasky, Susan F. 1989. "How the Disabled Sold Congress on a New Bill of Rights." *New York Times*, Sept. 17, p. E5.

Rawls, John, 1971. *A Theory of Justice*. Cambridge, MA: Belknap Press.

Reason, Peter, and John Rowan, eds. 1981. *Human Inquiry: A Sourcebook of New Paradigm Research*. New York: Wiley.

Regan, Edward V. 1988. *Government, Inc.: Creating Accountability for Economic Development Programs*. Washington, DC: Government Finance Research Center.

Rehabilitation Research Administration. 1982. *Annual Report*. Congressional Research Service (Jan. 27). Washington, DC: U.S. Government Printing Office.

Reich, Robert B., ed. 1988. "The Power of Public Ideas." Cambridge, MA: Harvard Univ. Press.

Rein, Martin. 1976. *Social Science and Public Policy*. New York: Penguin.

———, and Donald Schön. 1993. "Reframing Policy Discourse." In *The Argumentative Turn in Policy Analysis and Planning*, Frank Fischer and John Forester, eds. Durham, NC: Duke Univ. Press.

———, and Robert S. Weiss. 1969. "The Evaluation of Broad-Aim Programs: A Cautionary Note and a Moral." *The Annals*, 385 (Sept.): 139–40.

Rich, Richard, ed. 1979. *Translating Evaluation into Policy*. Beverly Hills, CA: Sage.

Ripley, Randall B. 1977. "Policy Research and the Clinical Relationship." Mershon Center Position Papers in the Policy Sciences, No. 1.

Rittel, Horst W. J., and Melvin Webber. 1973. "Dilemmas in a General Theory of Planning." *Policy Sciences*, 4 (2): 155–69.

Rivlin, Alice. 1971. *Systematic Thinking for Social Action*. Washington, DC: Brookings Institution.

———. 1973. "Forensic Social Science." *Perspectives on Inequality*, Harvard Educational Review Reprint Series, no. 8. Cambridge, MA: Harvard Univ. Press.

Robinson, William H., and Clay H. Wellborn, eds. 1991. *Knowledge, Power and the Congress*. Washington, DC: Congressional Quarterly Press.

Rochefort, David A. 1986. *American Social Welfare Policy: Dynamics of Formulation and Change*. Boulder, CO: Westview.

Rodgers, Harrell. 1979. "Head Start—Where Are the Headlines Now?" *Dissent*, Spring, p. 234.

Rosenbaum, Walter. 1985. *Environmental Policy and Politics*. Washington, DC: Congressional Quarterly Press.

Ross, Andrew, ed. 1988. *Universal Abandon? The Politics of Postmodernism*. Minneapolis: Univ. of Minnesota Press.

Roszak, Theodore. 1978. *Person/Planet: The Creative Disintegration of Industrial Society*. Garden City, NY: Anchor Books.

Ruckelshaus, William D. 1989. "Science, Risk, and Public Policy." In *Taking Sides: Clashing Views on Controversial Environmental Issues,* Theodore D. Goldfarb, ed. Guilford, CT: Dushkin.

Ryan, William. 1981. "The Art of Savage Discovery: How to Blame the Victim." In *Social Welfare and Society,* George T. Martin and Mayer N. Zald, eds. New York: Columbia Univ. Press.

Sabatier, Paul A. 1987. "Knowledge, Policy-Oriented Learning, and Policy Change: An Advocacy Coalition Framework." *Knowledge: Creation, Diffusion, Utilization,* 8 (4) (June): 649–92.

Sagen, Leonard A. 1987. *The Health of the Nations: True Causes of Sickness and Well-Being.* New York: Basic Books.

Sales, Amos, and Fred Harcleroad. 1986. "Emerging Professional Organizations and Interest Groups in Rehabilitation." In *Rehabilitation Administration and Supervision,* William G. Emener, Richard S. Luck, and Stanley J. Smits, eds. Baltimore, MD: University Park Press.

Saloma, John S., III. 1984. *Ominous Politics: The New Conservative Labyrinth.* New York: Hill and Wang.

Sandman, Peter D. 1986. "Getting to Maybe: Some Communications Aspects of Hazardous Waste Facility Siting." *Seton Hall Legislative Journal,* 9 (Spring): 437–65.

Sartori, Giovanni. 1969. "Politics, Ideology, and Belief Systems." *American Political Science Review,* 63 (June): 398–411.

Schlesinger, James. 1969. Testimony before the U.S. Senate, Subcommittee on National Security and International Operations. Planning-Programming-Budgeting Hearings, 91st Cong. 1st. Sess.

Schmacher, E. 1976. *Small Is Beautiful.* London: Sphere.

Schmid, A. Allen. 1989. *Benefit-Cost Analysis: A Political Economy Approach.* Boulder, CO: Westview.

Schneider, Anne L., and Helen Ingram. 1993. "Social Construction of Target Populations: Implications for Politics and Policy." *American Political Science Review,* 87 (2): 334–47.

Schön, Donald. 1983. *The Reflective Practitioner.* New York: Basic Books.

Schram, Sanford F. 1993. "Postmodern Policy: Discourse and Identity in Welfare Policy." *Policy Sciences,* 26: 249–70.

Schultze, Charles L. 1968. *The Politics and Economics of Public Spending.* Washington, DC: Brookings Institution.

Schumaker, Paul, John M. Bolland, and Richard C. Feiock. 1986. "Economic Development Policy and Community Conflict: A Comparative Issues Approach." In *Research in Urban Policy,* Terry N. Clark, ed. Greenwich, CT. JAI Press.

Schutz, Alfred. 1967. *The Phenomenology of the Social World.* Chicago, IL: Northwestern Univ. Press.

Schwarz, Michael, and Michael Thompson. 1990. *Divided We Stand: Redefining Politics, Technology and Social Choice.* New York: Harvester and Wheatsheaf.

Schwarz, Walter, and Dorothy Schwarz. 1987. *Breaking Through.* Bideford, England: Green Books.

Sclove, Richard. 1987. "Democratic Theory and Technological Design: The Nuts and Bolts of Democracy." Paper delivered at the American Political Science Association meeting, Sept.

Scotch, Richard K. 1984. *From Good Will to Civil Rights: Transforming Federal Disability Policy.* Philadelphia, PA: Temple Univ. Press.

Scott, Robert A., and Arnold R. Shore. 1979. *Why Sociology Does Not Apply: A Study of the Use of Sociology in Public Policy.* New York: Elsevier.

Scott, William G., and David K. Hart. 1973. "Administrative Crisis: The Neglect of Metaphysical Speculation." *Public Administration Review* 33 (Sept./Oct.): 415–22.

Scribman, David. 1990. "Unnatural Foes, Backpackers and the Disabled, Battle Over 'Upgrading' Access to Remote Pond." *Wall Street Journal,* July 26, p. A18.

Searle, John R. 1971. *The Campus War.* New York: World.

Sechrest, L. 1985. "Social Science and Social Policy: Will Our Numbers Ever Be Good Enough? In *Social Science and Social Policy,* R. L. Schotland and M. M. Mark, eds. Newbury Park, CA: Sage.

Sederberg, Peter C. 1984. *The Politics of Meaning: Power and Explanation in the Construction of Social Reality.* Tuscon: Univ. of Arizona Press.

Seidman, Steven, and David G. Wagner, eds. 1991. *Postmodernism and Social Theory.* Cambridge, MA: Basil Blackwell.

Shapiro, Michael J. 1992. *Reading the Postmodern Polity: Political Theory as Textual Practice.* Minneapolis: Univ. of Minnesota Press.

Sibley, Mulford Q. 1970. *Political Ideas and Ideologies.* New York: Harper and Row.

Simon, Julian Lincoln, ed. 1984. *The Resourceful Earth: A Response to Global 2000.* New York: Basil Blackwell.

Sjoberg, Gideon. 1975. "Politics, Ethics, and Evaluation Research." In *Handbook of Evaluation Research,* Marcia Guttentag and Elmer L. Struening, eds. Beverly Hills, CA: Sage.

Slovic, Paul, B. Fischoff, et al. 1980. "Facts and Fears: Understanding Perceived Risk." In *Social Risk Assessment: How Safe Is Safe Enough?* R. Schwing and W. A. Albers, eds. New York; Plenum.

Smith, M. S., and J. S. Bissell. 1970. "Report Analysis: The Impact of Head Start." *Harvard Educational Review* 40 (Winter): 51–105.

Smith, Wayne J. 1989. "Bye, Bye, Bus Industry." *New York Times,* Nov. 30, p. A31.

Spragens, Thomas A, Jr., 1976. *Understanding Political Theory.* New York: St. Martin.

Stanley, Manfred. 1978. *The Technocratic Consciousness: Survival and Dignity in an Age of Expertise.* Chicago, IL: Univ. of Chicago Press.

Starling, Grover. 1989. *Strategies for Policy Making.* Chicago, IL: Dorsey.

Starr, Chauncey. 1969. "Social Benefit versus Technological Risk." *Science,* 77 (165): 1232–38.

Sternberg, Ernest. 1989. "Incremental versus Methodological Policymaking in the Liberal State." *Administration and Society,* 21 (May): 54–77.

Stewart, David W. 1984. *Secondary Research: Information Sources and Methods.* Newbury Park, CA: Sage.

Stier, Jeffrey C. 1990. "Economy Efficiency of Forest Tree Improvement Programs in the North Central Region." *Evaluation Review,* 14 (June): 227–46.

Stokely, Edith, and Richard Zechhauser. 1978. *A Primer for Policy Analysis*. New York: Norton.

Stone, Deborah. 1988. *Policy Paradox and Political Reason*. Glenview, IL: Scott Foresman.

Strauss, Leo. 1959. *What Is Political Philosophy?* Glencoe, IL: Free Press.

Stull, Donald D., and Jean J. Schensul, eds. 1987. *Collaborative Research and Social Change*. Boulder, CO: Westview.

Sullivan, Oscar M., and Kenneth O. Snortum. 1926. *Disabled Persons: Their Education and Responsibility*. New York: Century.

Sullivan, William M. 1983. "Beyond Policy Science." In *Social Science as Moral Inquiry*, N. Haan, P. Rabinov, and W. M. Sullivan, eds. New York: Columbia Univ. Press.

Susman, Gerald I. 1983. "Action Research: A Sociotechnical Systems Perspective." In *Beyond Method*, Gareth Morgan, ed. Beverly Hills, CA: Sage.

Sylvia, Ronald D., Kenneth J. Meier, and Elizabeth M. Gunn. 1991. *Program Planning and Evaluation for the Public Manager*. Prospect Heights, IL: Waveland Press.


Taylor, Paul W. 1961. *Normative Discourse*. Englewood Cliffs, NJ: Prentice-Hall.

Taylor, Robert William. 1992. *Inventing Times Square: Commerce and Culture at the Crossroads*. New York: Russell Sage.

Theodorson, George A., and Achilles G. 1969. *Modern Dictionary of Sociology*. New York: Thomas Crowell.

Thompson, Dennis, and Amy Gutmann. 1984. *Ethics and Politics*. Chicago, IL: Nelson-Hall.

Thornton, Joe. 1991. "Risking Democracy." *Greenpeace*, March/April, pp. 14–17.

Tierney, John. 1991. "Some are Mourning the Street of Sleaze." *International Herald Tribune*, Jan. 16, p. 18.

Todorovich, Miro M. 1975. "Discrimination in Higher Education: A Debate on Faculty Employment." *Civil Rights Digest*, Spring, pp. 37–38.

Tokar, Brian. 1987. *The Green Alternative*. San Pedro: R. and E. Miles.

Tolchin, Susan J., and Martin Tolchin. 1985. *Dismantling America—The Rush to Deregulate*. New York: Oxford Univ. Press.

Tong, Rosemarie. 1987. "Ethics and the Policy Analyst: The Problem of Responsibility." In *Confronting Values in Policy Analysis*, Frank Fischer and John Forester, eds., pp. 192–211. Newbury Park, CA: Sage.

Torgerson, Douglas. 1986. "Between Knowledge and Politics: The Three Faces of Policy Analysis." *Policy Sciences*, 19: 33–59.

Toulmin, Stephen. 1958. *The Uses of Argument*. Cambridge: Cambridge Univ. Press.

Townsend, Davis. 1988. "The New Politics of Deafness." *New Republic*, Sept. 12, p. 22.

Tribe, Lawrence J. 1972. "Policy Science: Analysis or Ideology." *Philosophy and Public Affairs*, 2: 66–110.

Tribe, Lawrence J. 1974. "Ways Not to Think about Plastic Trees: New Foundations for Environmental Law." *Yale Law Review*, 83 (7): 1315–48.

Tullock, Gordon. 1979. "Public Choice in Practice." In *Collective Bargaining Decision Making Applications from Public Choice Theory*, Clifford Russell, ed. Baltimore, MD: Johns Hopkins Univ. Press for Resources for the Future.

Ulrich, Werner. 1983. *Critical Heuristics of Social Planning*. Bern: Haupt.

Unger, Roberto. 1976. *Knowledge and Politics*. New York: Free Press.

U. S. Dept. of Education, Office of Special Education and Rehabilitative Services. 1988. *Summary of Existing Legislation Relating to the Handicapped*. Washington, DC: U.S. Government Printing Office.

U. S. Dept. of Health and Human Services, Head Start Bureau. 1985. *Final Report: The Impact of Head Start on Children, Families and Communities* (#90-31193). Washington, DC: U.S. Government Printing Office.

U. S. Dept. of Labor, Office of Policy Planning and Research. 1965. *The Negro Family*, prepared by Daniel Patrick Moynihan. Washington, DC: U.S. Government Printing Office.

U. S. Office of Technology Assessment. 1983. *Technology and Handicapped People*. Washington, DC: U.S. Government Printing Office

Veatch, Robert M. 1975. "Ethical Principles in Medical Experimentation." In *Ethical and Legal Issues of Social Experimentation*, Alice M. Rivlin and P. Michael Timpane, eds. Washington, DC: Brookings Institution.

Vedlitz, Arnold. 1988. *Conservative Mythology and Public Policy in America*. New York: Praeger.

Voegelin, Eric. 1952. *The New Science of Politics*. Chicago, IL: Univ. of Chicago Press.

Walker, Brian. 1992. "Habermas and Pluralist Political Theory." *Philosophy and Social Criticism*, 18 (1): 81–102.

Wallerstein, Imanuel, and Paul Starr, eds. 1971. *The University Crisis Reader*. New York: Random House.

Walsh, David. 1972. "Sociology and the Social World." In *New Direction in Sociological Theory*, Paul Filmer et al., eds. Cambridge, MA: MIT Press.

Wamsley, Jerald S. 1992. Using Fischer's Policy Methodology to Separate and Evaluate Positive and Normative Issues in Risk Assessment. Master's thesis, University of North Carolina, Chapel Hill.

Warren, Mark. 1992. "Democratic Theory and Self-Transformation." *American Political Science Review*, 86 (1) (March): 8–23.

Wartenburg, Daniel. 1989. "Quantitative Risk Assessment." *Science for the People*. Jan./Feb. pp. 18–23.

Weaver, Carolyn L. 1991a. "Disabilities Act Cripples Through Ambiguities." *Wall Street Journal*, Jan. 31, p. A16.

———. 1991b. *Disability and Work: Incentives, Rights and Opportunities*. Washington, DC: American Enterprise Institute.

Weber, Max. 1949. *The Methodology of the Social Sciences*, Edward A. Shils and Henry A. Finch, eds. and trans. New York: Free Press.

Weimer, David L., and Aidan R. Vining. 1988. *Policy Analysis: Concepts and Practice*. Englewood Cliffs, NJ: Prentice-Hall.

Weiss, Carol H. 1972. *Evaluation Research*. Englewood Cliffs, NJ: Prentice-Hall.

———. 1977. "Research for Policy's Sake: The Enlightenment Function of Social Research." *Policy Analysis* 3 (Fall): 553–65.

———. 1990. "Policy Research: Data, Ideas, or Arguments? In *Social Sciences and Modern States: National Experiences and Theoretical Crossroads*, Peter Wagner et al., eds. Cambridge: Cambridge Univ. Press.

Weldon, T. D. 1953. *The Vocabulary Politics*. London: Penguin.

Wells, Gerald K., Laura A. Edwards, and David R. Ziskind. 1986. "Administrative Strategies in Rehabilitation: Retrenchment or Stability?" *American Rehabilitation*, 6: 19–22.

Westinghouse Learning Corp. 1969. *The Impact of Head Start: An Evaluation of the Effects of Head Start on Children's Cognitive and Affective Development*. Athens: Ohio Univ.

White, Stephen K. 1988. *The Recent Works of Jürgen Habermas: Reason, Justice and Modernity*. Cambridge: Cambridge Univ. Press.

Whyte, William F. 1989. "Advancing Scientific Knowledge Through Participatory Action Research." *Sociological Form*, 4: 367–86.

Whyte, William H. 1988. *City: Rediscovering the Center*. New York: Doubleday.

Wildavsky, Aaron. 1967. "The Political Economy of Efficiency." In *Planning Programming Budgeting*, Fremont J. Lyden and Ernest G. Miller, eds. Chicago, IL: Markham.

———. 1979. *Speaking Truth to Power*. Boston, MA: Little, Brown.

———. 1988. *Searching for Safety*. New Brunswick, NJ: Rutgers Univ. Press.

Williams, Walter, and John W. Evans. 1972. "The Politics of Evaluation: The Case of Head Start." In *Evaluating Social Programs*, Peter Rossi and Walter Williams, eds. New York: Seminar.

Winner, Langdon. 1986. *The Whale and the Reactor: A Search for Limits in an Age of High Technology*. Chicago: Univ. of Chicago Press.

Wolin, Sheldon S. 1969. "Political Theory as a Vocation." *American Political Science Review*, 63 (Dec.).

Woods, Diane E., Arnold Wolf, and David Brubaker, eds. 1983. *The Clinical Model in Rehabilitation and Alternatives*. New York: World Rehabilitation Fund.

Wright, George Nelson. 1980. *Total Rehabilitation*. Boston, MA: Little, Brown.

Wynne, Brian. 1987. *Risk Management and Hazardous Waste: Implementation and the Dialectics of Credibility*. Berlin: Springer.

Yin, Robert K. 1984. *Case Study Research*. Newbury Park, CA: Sage.

Zigler, Edward, and Jeanette Valentine. 1979. "Head Start—A Retrospective View: The Founders." In *Project Head Start*, Edward Zigler and Jeanette Valentine, eds. Ithaca, NY: Cornell Univ. Press.

Zigler, Edward, and Susan Muenchow. 1992. *Head Start: The Inside Story of America's Most Successful Educational Experiment*. New York: Basic Books.

Zimmerman, Dennis. 1989. "Federal Tax Incentives for Enterprise Zones: Analysis of Economic Effects and Rationales." *CRS Report to Congress*. Washington, DC: Congressional Research Service.

# Index

285